Uncle John's Bathroom Reader® Salutes the Armed Forces

Uncle John's Bathroom Reader® Salutes the Armed Forces

By the
Bathroom Readers'
Institute

Bathroom Readers' Press
Ashland, Oregon, and San Diego, California

For information, write The Bathroom Readers' Institute
P.O. Box 1117, Ashland, OR 97520 • (888) 488-4642
mail@bathroomreader.com • www.bathroomreader.com

Cover design by Michael Brunsfeld, San Rafael, CA
(*Brunsfeldo@comcast.net*)

ISBN 13: 978-1-59223-980-1
ISBN 10: 1-59223-980-3

Library of Congress Cataloging-in-Publication Data

Uncle John's bathroom reader salutes the Armed Forces /
[Bathroom Readers' Institute].
p. cm.
ISBN 978-1-59223-980-1 (pbk.)
1. United States—Armed Forces—Miscellanea. 2. United States—
History, Military—Miscellanea. I. Bathroom Readers' Institute
(Ashland, Or.) II.
Title: Bathroom reader salutes the Armed Forces.
UA23.U447 2009
355.00973—dc22

2008051410

First printing

09 10 11 12 13 5 4 3 2 1

THANK YOU!

The Bathroom Readers' Institute thanks the following people whose hard work, advice, and assistance made this book possible.

Gordon Javna

JoAnn Padgett

Stephanie Spadaccini

Dan Mansfield

Amy Miller

Melinda Allman

Julia Papps

Michael Brunsfeld

Bonnie Vandewater

Brian Boone

John Dollison

Monica Maestas

Lisa Meyers

Amy Ly

Ginna Stanley

Sydney Stanley

Cynthia Francisco

Kait Fairchild

(Mr.) Mustard Press

Ginger Winters

Jennifer Frederick

Rod Parayno

Sean Erb

David Culley

Steven Edwards

Thom Little

Mark Molitor

Brian Lahlum

David Calder

Karen Malchow

Jay Newman

Steven Style Group

Publishers Group West

Porter the Wonder Dog

TOP GUN SCHOLARS

The Bathroom Readers' Institute thanks the following writers who contributed selections to this book along with heroic enthusiasm and encouragement.

Amy Briggs
C. Mark Brinkley
Brian Boone
Myles Callum
Leslie Elman
Sharon Freed
Diane Harrington
Chet Hearn
John Hogan
Heidi Krumenauer
Carl Lavo
Andrew Lubin
Dan Mansfield
Lea Markson
Scott McGaugh
Art Montague
Ken Padgett
William Dylan Powell
Susan Shaphren
Stephanie Spadaccini
Sue Steiner
Alan Tesseaux
Bonnie Vandewater
Jodi Webb
Adele Woodyard
Fred Wright

* * *

Gen. Patton: I don't know why, but the image of a bullet coming straight for my nose was more horrifying than anything else.

Gen. Bradley: Well, I can understand that, George. It's such a handsome nose.

—***Patton*, 1970**

CONTENTS

AT SEA

FLYBOYS

TOUGH GUYS

BATTLE STATIONS

COASTING TO SUCCESS

INTRODUCTION

LOYAL READER, WE SALUTE YOU

The history of the United States armed forces is *America's* history. It's the story of colonists who won freedom from the British and the fight to end slavery. It's found in the trenches of World War I and in the Allied stand at the Battle of the Bulge, and in Seoul, Saigon, and Baghdad. Since the first minutemen grabbed their rifles and called themselves Americans, the men and women who've served in the five branches of the armed forces have shaped our language, our literature, our music, our movies, our fashion . . . in fact, our entire culture.

Choosing topics among a history and tradition that large wasn't easy. But we love a challenge. Our goal: to inform and entertain you, our readers. So we pulled on our camo fatigues and tracked down some of the most exciting and little-known stories to come out of the U.S. military's 200-year history. In these pages, you'll read about . . .

- Picasso's contribution to camouflage
- The Army's Camel Corps
- Why the Pentagon has twice the number of bathrooms it needs
- The original tough guys, whose motto was "You have to go out, but you don't have to come back"
- The Air Force's $1 billion plane
- Lincoln the soldier, before he became president
- Where to scuba dive on an aircraft carrier
- Bing Bong, America's top flying ace
- What happens when a Navy man crosses the equator for the first time
- Why midshipmen at the U.S. Naval Academy try to scale a 21-foot obelisk greased with 200 pounds of lard

There is no shortage of heroes or brave deeds in the armed forces. Military service fosters a brotherhood among comrades in arms, and war engenders man's most selfless behavior—the giving of your life for another. We also share more serious but no less engrossing tales of . . .

- George Washington's secret navy
- How Mathew Brady photographed the Civil War
- The little boats that helped the Allies win World War II
- The real Private Ryan
- The only enemy that defeated Admiral "Bull" Halsey—typhoons
- Top 10 admirals and generals (and movies for all five service branches)
- Great ships, from Old Ironsides to the USS *Ronald Reagan* to the USS *Midway*
- The courageous actions of the five most recent recipients of the Medal of Honor

We're sure you'll learn something here that you didn't know. But more than that, we hope this book adds to your appreciation for the sacrifice and service of our men and women in uniform.

One final salute: This book was inspired by and is dedicated to former Staff Sergeant Joseph A. Fisher, the father of our colleague JoAnn Padgett. Sergeant Fisher flew 70 missions as a turret gunner in an A-20 Havoc light bomber for the U.S. Army Air Corps during World War II, and received 14 Air Medals and the Distinguished Flying Cross.

—Uncle John and the BRI Staff

THE CUTTING EDGE OF COMBAT

Ask a Marine to name his most trusted companion and he just might tell you it's his KA-BAR fighting knife. It's a weapon, a tool, a symbol of honor—and even though the Army, Navy, and Coast Guard might use it too, the KA-BAR fighting knife will always be most closely identified with the United States Marine Corps.

RIGHT TO THE POINT

On December 9, 1942, almost a year to the day after the United States officially entered World War II, the Union Cutlery Company of Olean, New York, approached the U.S. Marine Corps with a design for a "fighting knife" that it hoped the Corps would adopt for its troops. The knife was designed as part of the company's KA-BAR line, so named because one devoted backwoodsman client claimed he'd used such a knife to kill a bear—or as he had written in a letter to the company, "k a bar."

Union Cutlery was earnest in its desire to assist in the U.S. war effort, but the company probably did not have any inkling of just how perfect its timing was. Early experiences with jungle combat in the Pacific had made it clear that the Marines needed a reliable fighting and utility knife for their ground forces, many of whom had joined the fray carrying weapons of their own selection because a standard-issue knife had not been determined. After the Battle of Guadalcanal in August 1942, the Marines were closer to formulating a list of the characteristics that they required in a fighting and utility knife. Conditions in the Pacific campaign were unlike any they had faced before, and the knife had to be up to the challenge. Union Cutlery was eager to provide the Corps with precisely what they wanted.

Colonel John M. Davis and Major Howard E. America, of the Plans and Policies and Quartermaster Department respectively, worked with Union Cutlery to refine its proposed design, devising a tough, reliable knife that could serve countless purposes in the field. Certainly it was a weapon viable for attack or defense, but it could also be a tool for everything from digging trenches to pound-

Actor Gene Hackman lied about his age to get into the Marines at age 16 in 1946.

ing tent stakes to opening ration cans and chopping food for cooking. World War II Marines found dozens of uses for it—and today's Marines still do.

IT SLICES, IT DICES, IT SAVES LIVES

The Marine-issue KA-BAR knife—designated 1219C2—is 11⅞ inches long and has a 7-inch blade made of high-carbon steel that is hardened and tempered to resist breakage and to retain sharpness. Its leather handle is formed from 22 slotted cowhide disks compressed to form a shockproof, moisture-resistant surface. The elliptical hand guard that separates the handle from the blade is sometimes curved slightly downward to protect the hand. The pommel, or butt cap, at the end of the handle is made from solid steel attached to the handle with a steel pin. Although the design has been altered slightly over the years, the KA-BAR remains true to its original conception. If it ain't broke, there's no need to fix it.

Besides the Marines, the Army, Navy, and Coast Guard, the KA-BAR was also standard issue for the Navy's Underwater Demolition Teams (UDTs) in World War II. Those brave frogmen—known with admiration as "naked warriors"—were generally issued not much more than swim trunks, canvas sneakers, face masks, and KA-BAR knives, then sent into the waters of the Pacific to do reconnaissance, clear enemy mines and obstacles, and set charges. Their KA-BAR knives proved to be useful tools and valuable companions.

In a 2008 newspaper interview, one World War II veteran recounted his experience working with a UDT setting charges at Peleliu Island on September 15, 1944, when, suddenly, he found himself engaged in hand-to-hand combat with a Japanese soldier. With nothing but his KA-BAR to protect him, he drew the knife and did what he had to do. "I still have the KA-BAR that saved my life," the vet told the newspaper reporter. He added, "I treasure that knife."

STILL SHARP

Even when the UDTs evolved into the elite group known as the Navy SEALs, with all the high-tech equipment available to them, the KA-BAR was still their knife of choice.

More than a million KA-BAR knives were produced during World War II, by Union Cutlery and by other firms who came on

Fearless in battle, Revolutionary War Gen. Anthony Wayne was called "Mad Anthony"...

as subcontractors to meet the immediate demand. (True KA-BAR knives—stamped with the KA-BAR mark on their tangs, or ricassos, just above the hand guard—remain the most prized.) KA-BAR knives were still being issued to SEAL trainees during the Vietnam War. Even though the frogmen knew the knives were "leftovers" from World War II, they soon discovered that the good old knives were still the best knives and they kept the KA-BAR legacy alive.

In the same way, the sons and grandsons of the first Marines to carry KA-BAR knives are entering battle today bearing the same knives their forefathers did. One Marine who deployed to Kuwait in 2003 carrying the KA-BAR his father had used in Vietnam from 1968 to 1972 said, "I'd go ballistic if this knife got lost."

Today KA-BAR knives have taken on a symbolic significance in the Marine Corps—they're often given as presentation pieces to outstanding personnel, celebrities, or dignitaries, and numerous special-edition commemorative versions have been made especially for collectors. Yet the reliable, all-purpose KA-BAR has not outlived its usefulness.

In February 2008, 20 Marines with the 5th Air Naval Gunfire Liaison Company, 3rd Marine Expeditionary Force, embarked on a basic jungle survival course equipped only with a poncho, canteen, canteen cup, plastic bags, a piece of flint and, of course, a KA-BAR, which they used for everything from building a shelter to cutting firewood to kindling the fire (with the help of a flint to strike the spark). Sure, you can ask a Marine to give up his KA-BAR, but that probably won't happen anytime soon.

* * *

PLAYING AT WAR

The game of Battleship is thought to have been created by British POWs in Germany during World War I. It was first marketed to the public in 1931 as "Salvo."

The board game we call Risk was the brainchild of French film director Albert Lamorisse, who won an Oscar and a Palme d'Or for his film *The Red Balloon*. Lamorisse called his game (originally released in 1957) La Conquête du Monde—The Conquest of the World.

...The Erie (Pennsylvania) Brewing Co. sells a pale ale, Mad Anthony's, named after him.

A SOLDIER'S LIFE

It can be a hard-knock life, and soldiers deserve a lot of respect.

"There is nothing more exhilarating than to be shot at without result."

—Winston Churchill

"There are no atheists in the foxholes."

—William T. Cummings

"Good soldiers never pass up a chance to eat or sleep. They never know how much they'll be called on to do before the next chance."

—Lois McMaster Bujold

"As every combat veteran knows, war is primarily sheer boredom punctuated by moments of stark terror."

—Harry G. Summers Jr.

"Older men declare war, but it is the youth that must fight and die."

—Herbert Hoover

"Valor, glory, firmness, skill, generosity, steadiness in battle and ability to rule—these constitute the duty of a soldier."

—The *Bhagavad Gita*

"I am a soldier, I fight where I'm told, and I win where I fight."

—General George S. Patton

"In war, there are no unwounded soldiers."

—Jose Narosky

"The first virtue in a soldier is endurance of fatigue; courage is only the second virtue."

—Napoléon Bonaparte

"In the final choice, a soldier's pack is not so heavy as a prisoner's chains."

—Dwight D. Eisenhower

"A coward dies a thousand deaths . . . a soldier dies but once."

—Tupac Shakur

"'Tis the soldier's life to have their balmy slumbers waked with strife."

—William Shakespeare

"I always considered statesmen to be more expendable than soldiers."

—Harry S. Truman

The Confederate warship *Virginia* was made from part of the captured Union warship *Merrimack*.

SITUATION: COMEDY

Sure, you remember M*A*S*H, *but how about some of these other TV sitcoms that depicted military life?*

SGT. BILKO

For the first year and a half of the show's 1955 to 1959 run, it was titled *You'll Never Get Rich*. For the rest of its life, it was technically titled *The Phil Silvers Show* after its star, but in reruns was retitled *Sgt. Bilko*. Silvers portrayed Sergeant Ernie Bilko, a con man on a peacetime Army base (Fort Baxter in Kansas) constantly involved in get-rich-quick schemes or ploys to extort money out of (or with the assistance of) his troops. Bilko's commanding officer, Colonel Hall (Paul Ford), always foiled the plots, with Bilko evading punishment (until the last episode, when he winds up in jail). *Sgt. Bilko* was canceled in 1959 when it got too expensive to produce, owing to the large (more than a dozen) cast of characters in the vast military base setting. Until recently, it was one of the most widely rerun series, appearing frequently on local channels throughout the 1970s, in prime time on BBC in the 1980s, and on Nick at Nite in the 1990s. Fun fact: the Hanna-Barbera cartoon *Top Cat* was an animated kiddie version of *Sgt. Bilko* (with a scheming cat instead of a scheming military man).

MCHALE'S NAVY

In 1962 Ernest Borgnine first played Lieutenant Commander Quinton McHale in "Seven Against the Sea," a dramatic World War II story in the anthology series *Fred Astaire's Premiere Theatre*. The episode was a ratings and critical hit and plans got underway to base a show around McHale. After deciding against continuing as either a drama or a military action series (the style in TV at the time), producers decided to make it a comedy, loosely influenced by the Henry Fonda World War II movie *Mister Roberts*. *McHale's Navy* (1962–66) was a broad slapstick comedy in which McHale oversaw a squadron of losers, gamblers, buffoons, and bumblers in and around the *PT-73*, stationed in the South Pacific during World War II, and who just wanted to cut loose and have fun.

The timing was impeccable—rising political star John F.

Qualified members of the armed forces can receive up to about $73,000 in tuition benefits.

Kennedy was becoming well-known for his heroic wartime service as the captain of a PT boat. The series also starred Tim Conway as Ensign Charles Parker, a bumbler assigned to restore order to a crew of more bumblers. The show was so popular it spawned two theatrical movies during its original run: *McHale's Navy* (1964) and the strangely titled *McHale's Navy Joins the Air Force* (1965).

NO TIME FOR SERGEANTS

In 1954 Mac Hyman published the comic novel *No Time for Sergeants*. The plot: a dim yokel named Will Stockdale gets drafted into the Air Force during World War II, butts heads with his commanding officer, and is assigned the job of P.L.O., or permanent latrine orderly. Hyman loosely based it on his own life—he was from a small town in Georgia and served as a navigator in the Army Air Forces. *No Time for Sergeants* was made into a hit Broadway play that ran for two years, launching the career of Andy Griffith. Next it was made into a 1958 movie with Griffith and then into a TV show in 1964 starring Sammy Jackson as Will. Critics didn't like how the show toned down the gruff, darkly comic, and realistic portrayals of Army life. (For example, Will's job in the show was permanent kitchen police). It died after a year; its competition in its time slot was, ironically, *The Andy Griffith Show.*

GOMER PYLE, USMC

This show (1964–69) has a premise very similar to *No Time for Sergeants:* a yokel joins the Marines, butts heads with his commanding officer, and gets assigned a lot of grunt work at which he constantly messes up. The show was a spinoff of *The Andy Griffith Show*, and it ran for five years. In *Gomer Pyle, USMC*, Gomer (Jim Nabors) signs up for a five-year stint as a private in the Marines. He never pleases his constantly angry commander, Sergeant Carter (Frank Sutton). And while the show aired at the peak of the Vietnam War, that ongoing conflict was never mentioned; the troops always stayed at California's Camp Henderson. The sitcom is also responsible for four enduring catchphrases: Shazam! (Nabors), Goooollly! (Nabors), Surprise, surprise, surprise! (Nabors), and Pyulllll! (Sutton)

For more military sitcoms, see page 217.

CITIZEN SOLDIERS

America's first soldiers forced the British army to retreat, galvanized their countrymen into taking up arms, and launched a revolution—all in one day.

YOU SAY YOU WANT A REVOLUTION?

When Massachusetts colonists held a shootout with British regulars in Lexington and then Concord, it wasn't exactly a formal affair. There weren't any famous generals present. There hadn't been any declaration of war, and it was months before the Continental Army was established with George Washington as commander in chief. The Revolution's first shots were fired by common citizen-soldiers.

They've been described as disorganized rabble and peaceful, embattled farmers. But it's a myth that a band of untrained yokels grabbed their hunting rifles and took potshots at the British army to protect their liberty. Many of those farmers were also soldiers in the Massachusetts Militia, an organization that had been defending the local population for more than 100 years. And some were minutemen, the best part-time soldiering force of their day.

The early colonists were vulnerable to attacks from Native Americans, from the French (when France was at war with Britain), and from social unrest. In Massachusetts, all males between the ages of 16 and 60 were required to keep a serviceable firearm and serve in the local militia. Training was mandatory—and so was the fighting. The militias had no central authority or commanding general; each town controlled its own.

JUST GIVE THEM A MINUTE

The minutemen gave the militias an extra fighting edge. Minutemen were young volunteers—usually under 25—strong, reliable, and with superior fighting skills. They were expected to keep their arms and equipment nearby so that if an alarm was spread, they'd be ready to march at a minute's notice—hence the nickname.

When hostilities between Massachusetts and Britain heated up, militias started training more often. They sent out spies and developed an alarm system to alert the command in case of emergency.

Many Civil War doctors were apprentices who had never been to medical school.

ARMED AND DANGEROUS

The British Parliament had been trying to collect more money in taxes from the colonies. Nowhere was resistance to "taxation without representation" stronger than in Massachusetts. After some rebel Bostonians dumped 342 chests of tea into Boston Harbor to protest a tea tax, Parliament closed the port, brought in more soldiers, and made the commander of the British troops, General Thomas Gage, the governor of Massachusetts. But Britain's hold over Massachusetts couldn't be complete until it disarmed the local militias who answered to the colonial assembly—not Parliament or King George.

DISPERSE, YE REBELS

On the evening of April 18, 1775, Gage sent 700 soldiers to Concord, Massachusetts, with orders to find and destroy the gunpowder and weapons that had been hidden there for the militia. The troops were under the command of Lieutenant Colonel Francis Smith. The mission, Gage warned, must be kept secret so that the provincials wouldn't have time to mount a resistance.

Militia leaders knew that there were plans to raid Concord; their spy system was already in operation. At about midnight, Paul Revere saw the Redcoats being ferried across Boston Harbor, and he hung lanterns in the steeple of Boston's North Church (a prearranged signal to other rebels) before riding off with two friends to spread the news. By the time the British troops were on their 20-mile march to Concord, sounds of signal guns firing, ringing church bells, and bonfire blazes on the hills were warning the entire countryside of the coming raid.

At dawn on April 19, about 400 British troops arrived at Lexington. Blocking their advance were 77 minutemen led by Captain John Parker. There had been confrontations like this before, but both sides had avoided violence. Now Parker instructed his soldiers, "Stand your ground; don't fire unless fired upon, but if they mean to have a war, let it begin here." Smith's second in command, Major John Pitcairn, took a different tack and ordered, "Disperse, ye rebels! Disperse!"

History is confused as to what happened next. A shot rang out, but no one knows which side fired or if the shot came from a hidden bystander. Either way, it provoked the Redcoats to shoot. The

***Grunt*, military slang for an infantryman, dates from the Vietnam era.**

minutemen broke for the surrounding woods. British officers tried to stop the shooting, but by the time they did, eight Americans lay dead—and word went out that the British were shooting to kill.

DID YOU HEAR THAT?

The British arrived in Concord, but most of the munitions had already been moved. Smith ordered his troops to guard town crossings, including 200 stationed at the North Bridge. While the British searched the town, minutemen were combining forces and local militias were gathering by the thousands. As a brigade of about 400 minutemen (and some militia) advanced on the bridge, the British fired warning shots. But the minutemen kept coming. When the British fired on them, the minutemen fired back. Never in all their confrontations had Redcoats been killed or wounded by Americans—until that day. Years later, Ralph Waldo Emerson wrote about the battle as the "shot heard 'round the world."

A NEW KIND OF WARFARE

Smith ordered a retreat. Hungry and tired, the Redcoats were chased back to Boston by more than 5,000 trained provincial soldiers. They used tactics learned from battles with Native Americans, shooting from behind trees, stone walls, and barns. With no line of enemy to aim at, the British hardly knew where to shoot. The British retreated to Lexington with Americans hard on their heels. But the chase wasn't over; the militia hammered the British all the way to Boston, where the Americans took over the hills surrounding the city and held Gage and his army under siege.

The British lost about 19 officers and 250 men; American casualties were fewer than 90. The colonies were euphoric. The success at Concord spurred the Continental Congress to declare war. Men, trained and untrained, took up arms; about 16,000 Americans surrounded Boston by the time General Washington took command. The new Continental Army eventually absorbed the militia. And the minutemen were disbanded—but they'll always be America's first elite rapid-deployment force.

* * *

"The security of every society must always depend, more or less, upon the martial spirit of the great body of the people."

—**Adam Smith**

In 1782 Deborah Sampson, disguised as a man, fought in the Continental Army.

THE START OF *SEMPER FI*

On Philadelphia's Front Street a historical marker labels the spot where Tun Tavern once stood and cites it as the "traditional birthplace of the United States Marine Corps." Countless Marines have toasted the memory of Tun Tavern, and the Marine Corps endorses the story. But is it true?

A SAILOR WENT TO SEA

The United States Marine Corps was born as the Continental Marines on November 10, 1775, during the Second Continental Congress in Philadelphia, where the Founding Fathers were meeting to prepare for their break with England. And where else to find seamen than in Philadelphia, one of the busiest ports in the American colonies?

It was left to Samuel Nicholas, the first commandant of the Marine Corps, to find a few (actually more than a few) good men. Nicholas could march up and down the wharves of the Delaware River with a placard reading "Seamen Wanted," or he could set up shop in one of the many taverns that lined the streets near the waterfront. He chose the latter and that very day walked to the corner of Water Street and Tun Alley, where Tun Tavern was located. ("Tun" wasn't the proprietor's name; it's an Old English word meaning "cask" or "barrel of beer.")

A TUN OF FUN

Nicholas didn't pick Tun Tavern by chance. It had been the original headquarters for organizations such as the first American Masonic lodge as well as the St. Andrew's Society and the St. George's Society, for aid to Scottish and English immigrants, respectively. George Washington, Thomas Jefferson, Benjamin Franklin, and other Founding Fathers met at the tavern and its restaurant—Peggy Mullan's Red Hot Beef Steak Club—to discuss business and draft resolutions for the First and Second Continental Congresses. In 1756 it was a recruiting center for the Pennsylvania Militia when they were raising forces to fight Indians.

The tavern's owner, Robert Mullan, served as chief Marine recruiter and raised two battalions in less than a month. He must

During the 1865 climax of the battle of Five Forks, where was Maj. Gen. George Pickett?...

have been a natural salesman—or maybe it was the free-flowing beer. No matter what his secret was, for more than 200 years and wherever they're stationed, Marines gather on November 10 to toast the birthday of the Corps and the place where it all began: Tun Tavern. Sadly, Marines can't visit the original Tun Tavern; it was demolished in 1781.

DON'T BLAME THE MESSENGER

Uncle John hesitates to incur the wrath of even one leatherneck, but is forced to report that recent research has uncovered a series of conflicting dates and facts that make it unlikely that Tun Tavern played this key role in launching the Marine Corps, at least according to the National Park Service. (Blame them!) Here's what historians and other nosy people have found:

• Robert Mullan sold Tun Tavern in 1773, several years before he supposedly began recruiting Marines there. Washington's diaries back up this fact when he writes of dining at Mullan's new restaurant on the Schuylkill River in 1775.

• Recruitment posters mentioning the Tun Tavern (supposedly dating from the 18th century) posted online could not be authenticated by either the person who posted them or by the curator of the Marine Corps Museum in Quantico, Virginia.

• Other historians say that Samuel Nicholas did the recruiting in a tavern called the Conestoga Wagon at Fourth and Market streets. The earliest mention these historians can find of Tun Tavern as the Marines' birthplace comes from the 1920s.

TRADITIONS DIE HARD

Okay, so it doesn't look good for all those Tun-toting Marines out there, but take heart. The National Park Service isn't ruling out Tun Tavern completely. It certainly was in the right area to attract rugged seamen; there just isn't any supporting documentation.

The USMC will no doubt continue to toast Tun Tavern every November 10. In the meantime, disappointed and/or confused Marines can always quench their thirst for possible authenticity at the "Tun Tavern–themed restaurant" at the National Museum of the Marine Corps in Quantico. Cheers and *Semper Fi*!

...He was at a shad bake a few miles away. Shad was a delicacy he couldn't resist.

WASHINGTON'S NAVY

To the British, they were pirates. To the colonists, they were patriots. To George Washington, they were essential.

CAN WE GET A LITTLE HELP HERE?

In April 1775, colonial militiamen surrounded Boston, putting the British garrison and thousands of Redcoats under siege. In July, George Washington was appointed commander in chief of these rebel militias who became the Continental Army. As the Redcoats and the Continentals squared off, Washington found himself facing a disciplined, well-equipped enemy. His own forces were plagued with shortages of food, equipment, and even shoes.

Worst of all was the lack of guns and gunpowder. King George had stopped any importation of ammunition into the American colonies in 1774, and the Continental Army had only enough powder for about nine shots per soldier. It was no way to launch a war. General Washington saw British merchant ships in Boston Harbor unloading supplies for the British troops. If he could capture those British supply ships, he could starve the British out of Boston and gain supplies for his destitute army. All he needed was a navy.

THE FIRST NATIONAL FLEET

The Continental Congress hadn't even proposed a navy, since some members felt that it would jeopardize any chance of patching things up with King George. Still, Washington knew there were thousands of local sailors who would attack British ships—especially if they were paid for their efforts as privateers. Privateers could earn as much as $1,000 on a single voyage, which was more than a hundred times the average monthly pay.

Both privateers and pirates captured ships, imprisoned crews, and stole the cargoes. The difference was that privateers worked with the permission of their government, and they (supposedly) only seized ships that belonged to an enemy. Washington disapproved of privateering, but he decided he had no choice. Without asking for permission from Congress, he formed America's first armed national fleet.

Sixty-three American pilots were shot down during the Persian Gulf War.

RASCALLY PRIVATEERS

As a farmer and a frontier soldier, Washington knew very little about boats. A member of his guard, Colonel John Glover, was the owner of a fleet of fishing vessels, so Glover found, leased, and armed schooners for the general. The boats were manned with sailors from the army who, as privateers, were offered a third of the value of any prizes captured.

On September 5, 1775, the *Hannah* sailed from Beverly, Massachusetts, under the command of Captain Nicholas Broughton. She was the first American armed ship sent to battle and carried four cannons—which could be fired only when "absolutely necessary" because of the gunpowder shortage. Washington ordered Broughton to seize only ships bound for the British garrison. But Captain Broughton had much lower standards; he seized one ship because its captain was "too polite" and therefore must be up to no good. None of Broughton's captures turned out to be enemy ships. One vessel even belonged to a Continental congressman (though it was piloted by a British crew who had captured it for their own use). *Hannah*'s crew was offered a bonus for the ship's recapture, but they mutinied because they still wanted a third of the cargo. Washington put down the mutiny, but soon afterward, Broughton ran the ship aground while being chased by a British warship and the *Hannah* had to be abandoned. Captain Broughton's failures were only the beginning of Washington's disappointment in what he later called "rascally privateers."

KIDNAPPING CANADIANS

In October 1775, the Continental Congress finally authorized a navy, but Washington still relied on his little fleet. Hearing that British ships were bringing weapons to Quebec, he sent two ships after them. Colonel Glover talked Washington into giving Captain Broughton another chance, and Broughton became the acting commodore of the *Hancock*. Captain Selman in the *Franklin* was the second in command. Washington was hoping to make Canada an ally, so he gave Broughton and Selman strict instructions: "Canadian vessels not in the British military service are not to be seized." Broughton and Selman, never good at following orders, seized Canadian ships anyway—and immediately began pilfering their cargo.

Rudyard Kipling wrote several propaganda books for Britain during World War I.

On November 17 (following up a false rumor about Canadians being recruited to fight Americans), Broughton and Selman raided Prince Edward Island. They attacked Charlottetown, kidnapping a judge and the governor. They looted the governor's mansion and office, then headed home with everything from the governor's official seal and household silver to 40 tons of butter. Washington apologized to Canada's kidnapped officials as he freed them and returned their property. He summoned Selman and Broughton to his office and gave them a heated lecture before he gave them the boot. He later wrote, "The plague, trouble and vexation I have had with all the armed vessels is inexpressible."

THE TIDE TURNS

Meanwhile, four other armed vessels had joined Washington's squadron. By early November, the *Warren*, *Lee*, *Harrison*, and *Washington* patrolled near Boston, and the situation slowly improved. The *Harrison* took the first legitimate prizes, capturing two British ships that brought in firewood and plenty of food—including 15 hogs. As the fleet captured cargoes that were meant for the British, they brought the Continental Army everything from turnips to Spanish coins. The biggest prize was captured by Captain John Manley of the *Lee*. On November 29, a British brig called the *Nancy* mistook the *Lee* for a pilot ship and asked for assistance. Manley was careful to have his men hide their weapons as he promised to guide the *Nancy* into Boston Harbor. Instead, his men jumped aboard with cutlasses and pistols and took their prize.

The *Nancy* carried over 2,000 muskets and bayonets, 31 tons of musket shot, thousands of cannonballs of various sizes, and a 3,000-pound mortar. The delighted Washington became the general of an army with actual weaponry. News of the *Nancy*'s capture made headlines in the colonial newspapers, and Captain Manley became the Revolution's first naval hero. Songs like "Brave Manley" were sung in his honor and taverns were named after him.

THE IMPORTANCE OF A NAVY

Washington had been looking for weapons on land as well as at sea, and had captured British cannons at Fort Ticonderoga. By March 5, 1776, he had established those cannons on the heights above Boston Harbor, and the British had to flee to New York.

The first known naval mine was invented in 1776 by American David Bushnell.

Washington followed them, leaving his fleet behind. The ships continued to make captures until they fell into disrepair, and the little squad was completely disbanded by late 1777. By that time, 11,000 American privateers were harassing British vessels, and the Continental Army had no more need of small schooners.

During its short lifetime, Washington's fleet helped his army survive through a time of dire need. They'd captured men from the British Royal Navy and supplies from the British army. They also helped drive up shipping prices, causing so much pain to Britain's economy that many of its citizens stopped supporting the war.

Most important, the "rascally privateers" taught the commander in chief about the importance of a navy, a lesson he never forgot. When Washington finally had access to France's navy, he deftly used its formidable power to cut off supplies to General Charles Cornwallis, forcing him to surrender at Yorktown in 1781—giving Americans victory in the Revolutionary War.

* * *

STANDARD BEARER

George Washington is credited with helping to popularize this expression's modern-day usage when he called on delegates of the 1787 Constitutional Convention in Philadelphia "to raise a standard to which the wise and honest can repair." In politics a standard bearer is the leader of a political party or movement. Although it remains a popular phrase in present-day politics, its origins are military.

A standard is a banner or flag that is carried on a long pole. In the military it is used to identify and rally the troops. The word "standard" comes from the French *étendard*, meaning banner. A standard bearer is a soldier or civilian who "bears" or carries the standard. This can be an occasional duty, which is also often viewed as an honor as in a parade, or a permanent job when a soldier is tasked with carrying the flag on the battlefield.

Eighty-eight percent of military jobs have direct civilian counterparts.

BELOW THE BELT

American sailors were recognized far and wide for their flared-leg bell-bottomed pants. Where did the idea for bell-bottoms come from? Therein lies the mystery.

NOW WEAR THIS!

No one is really sure why or how bell-bottoms became regulation wear for sailors in the U.S. Navy. The first ones debuted in 1817, when knee-length, gathered breeches were going out of style. Among the theories for the new pants:

- Once the knee-length noose of the former pantaloons was loosened, it just made sense to keep the shape going wider.
- The U.S. Navy copied the British Royal Navy (except for the fact they didn't start wearing bell-bottoms until the mid-1800s).
- Bolts of Melton wool, the fabric used for the pants, always measured 54 inches wide; the style wasted as little fabric as possible.
- Since sailors rarely wore shoes back then, the wide shape was an effort to help protect their feet.
- The design was created to set sailors apart from civilians.

MOST LIKELY SCENARIO

The most common belief is that the wider shape was created for practicality and safety's sake. The billowing bottoms let sailors roll the pants above the knee while washing down decks, thus keeping them clean and dry. And if you've ever tried to remove your pants while wearing your shoes, you know it isn't easy. Bell-bottoms made it easier to strip off the 20 to 30 pounds of soaked wool fabric in case a sailor went overboard. (Many sailors also swore you could tie the legs together to form a life preserver, but you'd need to blow a lot of air in them for buoyancy!)

DANCEY PANTS

When asked why so many of his war pictures involved the Navy instead of other military branches, dancer and movie star Gene Kelly said, "One of the first things that any dancer looks for when he is planning a big number is an eye-catching costume . . . For that, the Navy uniform can't be beat. Another, and even more important reason . . . is the comfort of the uniform."

FLARE TODAY, GONE TOMORROW

In their earliest days, the pants were actually just extremely wide-legged. In 1894 they were trimmed to fit a little more snugly above the knee and a little more loosely (by one inch) between the knee and cuff. For nearly a century, the shape stayed basically the same, although cotton denim replaced the wool. In 1973 they were traded for a straight-leg polyester suit-and-tie combo. That created so much extra fabric to pack and store, and grumbling from the men, that the Navy deep-sixed the suit by 1980.

GOING STRAIGHT

At the start of the 21st century, the Navy sliced the curve off the enlisted man's working pants yet again, going with a straight-leg, polyester-cotton blend. At least one recruit loved the change: "The bell-bottoms got caught in everything and got dirty. They got salt rings in winter and were tight in the upper legs."

BATTENING DOWN THE HATCH

Then there's the question of the buttons that add to the distinction of a sailor's pants. For decades, older sailors told incoming seamen that the 13 buttons on the front of the bell-bottoms represented the 13 original colonies. The myth was so commonplace, it actually had to be excised from Navy history texts.

Sailors originally used a drawstring to hold up their pants, but they threw away their drawstrings in 1864 when a new version of bell-bottoms was designed with seven buttons across the top holding the crotch flap. With a nod toward comfort in more tropical climates, the Navy elongated the flap (also called a "broadfall") in 1897, and two buttons were added to each side, making a total of 11. But as Navy men grew broader—possibly thanks to improvements in nutrition—the flap needed to grow longer. So in 1905 more buttons were added, creating those 13 buttons. Why buttons instead of zippers? Because buttons are much easier to replace on the fly, and early zippers may have corroded in the salty weather.

...during the world's first heavier-than-air flight on December 17, 1903.

THE U.S. COAST GUARD: THE EARLY YEARS

"You have to go out, you don't have to come back." For a time, it was the motto of the Coast Guard. But it's still the principle that guides the men and women of the USCG.

ALL AT SEA

From 1790, when the Continental Navy was disbanded, to 1798, when the United States Navy was created, the Revenue Cutter Service—the precursor of the Coast Guard—provided the only armed American presence on the sea. Organized by Secretary of the Treasury Alexander Hamilton, its job was to enforce trade laws, collect tariffs, and catch smugglers. The service existed without a formal name for 73 years, but was commonly referred to in official correspondence as the "Revenue Marine" or the "Revenue Service." Congress finally adopted the name "Revenue Cutter Service" in 1863.

JOIN THE NAVY AND SEE THE WAR

In 1797, when France began harassing American merchant shipping, President John Adams enlisted the cutters for coastal defense and commercial protection. When the U.S. Navy was mobilized, Adams placed 10 cutters at the disposal of Benjamin Stoddert, the first secretary of the Navy. Stoddert brought eight cutters into the Navy but only used three because the other five were too small for combat duty. Those he commissioned served with the Navy throughout the Quasi-War with France (1798–1801), together taking 15 armed French vessels, assisting in the capture of 5 others, and recovering at least 10 ships from their French captors. At the end of the war on February 3, 1801, the Navy sold the seven cutters it hadn't used as part of the general reduction of the naval establishment.

THE *AMISTAD* AFFAIR

Hamilton started using his Revenue Marine in 1794 to intercept ships illegally importing slaves into the country. Maritime courts auctioned off the captured ships and freed the would-be slaves.

U.S. military bases exist in 20 foreign countries.

Between 1794 and 1865, revenue cutters captured more than 500 slave ships—the most famous among them the *Amistad*.

In 1839, after the schooner *Amistad* had been taken over by its slave population, the USRC (United States Revenue Cutter) *Washington*, patrolling off the coast of Long Island, intercepted the slave-schooner and escorted the ship into New Haven, Connecticut. After a famous trial, the Supreme Court ruled for the Africans and the United States arranged for them to be returned home.

THE WAR OF 1812

In October 1798, President John Adams established the tradition of placing the Revenue Marine under the Navy during time of war. Not all cutters met Navy standards, but several saw action. When Congress declared war on Great Britain on June 18, 1812, the USRC *Jefferson* made the conflict's first capture by bringing the British brig *Patriot* into port.

But not every contest ended without bloodshed. On June 12, 1813, during a rainy and foggy night, 50 British sailors from the frigate HMS *Narcissus* used boats with muffled oars to approach the USRC *Surveyor* at anchor at the mouth of the York River in the Chesapeake Bay. Captain Samuel Travis's 15-man crew tried to repel the boats, first with 12-pounder carronades, then with muskets. When the British came aboard, a desperate hand-to-hand fight ensued until Travis surrendered when he realized that further resistance would only result in more bloodshed. Five cutter men were wounded, seven British were wounded, and three men were killed. The lieutenant who led the British boarding party paid tribute to the men of the *Surveyor* for their "gallant and desperate attempt" to defend the cutter and the "determined manner in which the deck was disputed inch by inch."

Several similar encounters took place during that war. The cutter men fought with the same tenacity as sailors in the U.S. Navy, and in the years ahead continued to do so with the same dogged determination and bravery.

A HUMANE SOCIETY FOR HUMANS

Britain's Royal Humane Society was originally founded in 1774 as the Society for the Recovery of Persons Apparently Drowned, with the mission of resuscitating people who had drowned. Resuscita-

Camel meat: Military slang for any unappetizing mess-hall entrée.

tion practices—a.k.a. "first aid"—were established in 1786 and adopted by the Massachusetts Humane Society (again, for people, not pets). The efforts of the society rapidly expanded from "first aid" to the more dangerous work of saving the lives of shipwrecked sailors and passengers. The work was physically hard and could be treacherous. The original lifesavers were unpaid—like volunteer firefighters—and worked from shanties about 10 months out of the year because of the harsh weather conditions along the Atlantic shore during the winter.

Congress started appropriating funds for boats and weaponry with the signing of the Newell Act in 1848, which created the United States Life-Saving Service. New Jersey representative William A. Newell had sponsored the bill, requesting funds for a lifesaving service along the shore south of New York Harbor. The Massachusetts Humane Society received funds that same year and more stations were built between 1848 and 1854.

Storms like the Great Carolina Hurricane of 1854 highlighted the poor condition of the equipment in the lifesaving stations, the poor training of the crews, and the need for more stations. Additional funds were appropriated by Congress, including funds to employ a full-time keeper at each station and two superintendents.

LET'S GET ORGANIZED

All the same, most of the stations were mismanaged until, in 1871, Sumner I. Kimball became the Treasury Department's chief of the Revenue Marine, and an inspection tour of every lifesaving station revealed that many were in disrepair and some in fact "ruined."

With an appropriation of $200,000 to operate the stations and employ full-time crews, Kimball instituted six-man lifeboat crews at all locations, built new stations, established lifesaving procedures, provided refuge shelters, and instituted regulations and performance standards for crews.

In 1878 the Treasury Department formally established the Life-Saving Service as a separate entity. By 1881 the lifesaving division had grown to 189 stations—139 on the Atlantic coast, seven on the Pacific coast, five on the Gulf coast, 37 on the Great Lakes, and one at the falls of the Ohio River. The Life-Saving Service would remain a separate division of the Treasury Department until 1915, when it merged with the Revenue Cutter Service into the U.S. Coast Guard.

MAKING IT OFFICIAL

President Woodrow Wilson signed into law the Act to Create the Coast Guard on January 28, 1915. The legislation effectively combined the Revenue Cutter Service with the Lifesaving Service to form the U.S. Coast Guard. By the 1890s, scores of partially submerged (old ships unfit for service) and abandoned derelicts began piling up in harbors, creating a maritime hazard. The government detailed the Coast Guard to blow up or ram the worthless vessels and save the others by towing them to a shipyard for salvage.

RUNNING WITH RUMRUNNERS

By 1920, now officially members of the U.S. Coast Guard, many of the same men began operating World War I four-stack destroyers to enforce Prohibition, that very unpopular 18th Amendment banning alcohol.

The rumrunners would anchor their large ships just beyond the three-mile limit, which became known as "Rum Row." From there, small, quick boats that could easily outmaneuver the Coast Guard would dash ashore with the goods. Most of the activity was off the coast of New York and New Jersey, but rumrunners kept the Coast Guard busy on the Great Lakes, in the Gulf of Mexico, and on the West Coast, too. The government extended the limit to 12 miles in 1924, which took its toll on the business, but still it thrived. The Coast Guard relied on its usual hard work and reconnaissance to do their bit, but quite often had to let a rumrunner escape to take care of its primary responsibilities: a sinking vessel or other emergency at sea.

The 21st Amendment, passed on December 5, 1933, ended the rumrunning business. The Coast Guard emerged from Prohibition a bigger and more effective service.

JOIN THE CLUB

The U.S. Lighthouse Service—another of Alexander Hamilton's projects—had been in operation since 1789. In 1939 Congress moved it out of the Department of Commerce, giving lighthouse men the choice of joining the Coast Guard in a military capacity or remaining as civilian employees. About half the men chose to keep their civilian status and the other half enlisted.

In 1942 another department, the Navigation and Steamboat

Among the five beaches used as D-day landing sites, Omaha Beach had the most casualties.

Inspection Service that had been established in 1852, also became part of the Coast Guard. Over the years too many steamboats had blown up, killing passengers because of sloppy maintenance, and the agency had come into existence to perform hydrostatic testing on boilers and create inspection standards to safeguard the public.

When in 1934 the Coast Guard rewrote its regulations to include all the technological changes made in the previous 150 years—including the use of the first seaplanes—they retained the motto of the Lifesaving Service: "You have to go out, but you don't have to come back." In fact, many of them, in the fulfillment of their duties, never did come back.

For more about the Coast Guard, turn to page 336.

*   *   *

THE LIGHTHOUSE JOKE

The following has received a lot of airplay on the Internet as a real incident. It is very funny, but it never happened. It is simply an old joke that resurfaces from time to time.

Here is the story, compliments of the U.S. Navy Web site:

Believe it or not . . . this is the transcript of an actual radio conversation between a U.S. Navy ship and Canadian authorities off the coast of Newfoundland in October 1995. The Radio conversation was released by the chief of naval operations on Oct. 10, 1995.

U.S. Ship: Please divert your course 0.5 degrees to the south to avoid a collision.

Canadian reply: Recommend you divert your course 15 degrees to the south to avoid a collision.

U.S. Ship: This is the captain of a U.S. Navy ship. I say again, divert your course.

Canadian reply: No. I say again, you divert YOUR course!

U.S. Ship: THIS IS THE AIRCRAFT CARRIER USS *CORAL SEA*. WE ARE A LARGE WARSHIP OF THE US NAVY. DIVERT YOUR COURSE NOW!!

Canadian reply: This is a lighthouse. Your call.

ENGINEERS DO IT BY DESIGN

The U.S. Army Corps of Engineers has been active in every American war since the Revolution.

FROM THE FIRST

Colonel Richard Gridley started it all. An American military engineer during the French and Indian War, Gridley was awarded a commission in the British army. But when the break with England came, he stood with the colonies. As chief engineer in the New England Provincial Army, he laid out the defenses on Breed's Hill (and was in fact wounded at the Battle of Bunker Hill). In July 1775, when the Continental Congress organized an army, Gridley was appointed General George Washington's first chief engineer.

AT THE CORPS OF IT ALL

The engineers were mustered out at the end of the war, but in 1794 Congress created a Corps of Artillerists and Engineers, then separated the two corps in 1802. The Corps of Engineers' immediate mandate was to establish the U.S. Military Academy at West Point. (In fact, the majority of West Point's superintendents have come from the Corps of Engineers and sometimes simultaneously were chiefs of the corps.) At about the same time, Congress started lobbying to have the corps assume civil as well as military engineering responsibilities.

DOING DOUBLE DUTY

The corps proved up to the task. Corps engineers secured pure water for the White House in 1824, built the Washington Aqueduct, and laid the first sanitary sewer in Washington, D.C. Later they replicated their water and waste systems in San Francisco, Philadelphia, Havana, and Manila, saving countless lives from typhoid, cholera, and other diseases. Along with the Corps of Topographical Engineers, they helped to map much of the American West.

...the French company Renault made the tanks used by the U.S. at the Battle of Saint-Mihiel.

On the military side, in the years prior to the War of 1812, the corps designed and supervised fortifications on the Atlantic, Pacific, and Gulf coasts. They built lighthouses, developed jetties and piers for harbors, and mapped navigation channels. During the Mexican-American War, a corps engineer successfully led the siege of Monterey, which enabled American forces to sweep through Mexico.

CIVIL WAR ENGINEERING

The Civil War placed new demands on the corps. They built railways, roads, bridges, and fortifications. In 1864 they directed construction of a 2,170-foot pontoon bridge across the James River, longer than any built before World War II. And when low water levels in the Red River near Shreveport, Louisiana, stranded 10 Union warships and 12 transports, the corps constructed dams and a sluiceway to concentrate water flow high enough to float the ships over rapids. It took 3,000 men to carry out the work, but not one ship was lost.

PEACETIME PROJECTS

After the war, there was still plenty for the corps to do. Construction of the Washington Monument had begun in 1848 by a private organization, but funds had run out in 1856 at the 152-foot level. Congress authorized funding in 1876 and the corps completed construction in 1884.

From 1879 on, the corps was an integral part of the work of the Mississippi River Commission, constructing levees, floodways, reservoirs, and tributary basin improvements to stabilize water flow.

EVERY DAM ONE

In 1890 the corps was also given authority of all dam construction, and later on, the authority for preservation of wetlands. The corps was at the forefront of hydroelectric power development in the United States, starting with three notable projects: the Passamaquoddy Tidal Power Project in Maine, the Bonneville Dam on the Columbia River, and the Fort Peck Dam on the Missouri River. The Columbia River and Snake River projects, completed by the corps in 1975, produced 27 percent of the United States' hydroelectric power.

Seoul, South Korea's capital city, changed hands four times during the Korean War.

IF YOU BUILD IT, THEY WILL COME

Before World War II, the Army's Quartermaster Department constructed most Army facilities, but in November 1940, the War Department selected the corps to build facilities for the Army Air Corps. Thirteen months later, they were given responsibility for all construction for the Army's war effort.

Back on the home front, the corps took on a historic project. Between a Thursday night in July 1944 and the following Monday, corps engineer Lieutenant Colonel Hugh Casey and civilian architect George Bergstrom designed the Pentagon, a structure of four million square feet. On Tuesday, the design was approved by the president and presented to Congress. Sixteen months later, the War Department moved in with its 33,000 workers—and took 16 months to complete a job that would have normally taken four years. (*See "How the Pentagon Got Its Shape" on page 130.*)

AND THAT'S NO JOKE

When 17-year-old Brooklyn-born Melvin Kaminsky enlisted in the Army in 1944, he soon found himself in Europe as a demolition engineer. It was a dangerous job: deactivating land mines, sometimes while under fire. Melvin made it through the war, and later became famous as the comedy genius Mel Brooks. Talking about his wartime experience, Brooks said, with tongue firmly in cheek, "I was a combat engineer. Isn't that ridiculous? The two things I hate most in the world are combat and engineering."

THEY SPECIALIZE IN EVERYTHING

In more recent years, the corps constructed the launch sites of the 13 Atlas ICBM squadrons across the United States and also designed and supervised construction of the Apollo, Saturn, and space shuttle vehicle assembly building—at the time the world's largest building by volume.

Today, the U.S. Army Corps of Engineers is at work in more than 90 countries, runs 609 dams, operates 24 percent of the U.S. hydropower capacity (3 percent of the total U.S. electric capacity), maintains 12,000 miles of commercial inland navigation channels, and supervises 926 coast, Great Lakes, and inland harbors.

A GENERAL SCANDAL

General Benedict Arnold tried to surrender West Point to the British. But we found someone much worse: General James Wilkinson—history's forgotten villain.

AMERICA'S TOP SCOUNDREL

James Wilkinson was the son of a well-to-do Maryland planter. When the Revolutionary War began, he put aside his medical studies and went to fight the British. Educated and charming, Wilkinson shot up the ranks of the Continental Army. By the end of 1776, he was a lieutenant colonel and an aide-de-camp to the powerful General Horatio Gates, his first mentor—and one of his first victims.

As commanding general at the 1777 Battle of Saratoga, Gates led the Continental Army to its first great triumph—the surrender of an entire British division of 9,000 men. When Gates sent Wilkinson to carry dispatches of the victory to Congress, Wilkinson exaggerated about his own role in the Saratoga victory, and Congress made him a brigadier general.

Knowing Gates would love to replace Washington as commander in chief, Wilkinson cooked up a plan to make it happen. Wilkinson found a letter from Major General Thomas Conway among Gates's correspondence saying that Gates's Saratoga victory had saved Americans from the mistakes of the "weak general," Washington. Wilkinson spread Conway's opinions among his influential friends, but the plot backfired. A furious Washington got news of the letter—and the scheme to replace him. Gates had to apologize to Washington and Congress; Wilkinson, now fallen from grace, resigned from the Army in 1778. But as he would do many times, the disgraced brigadier general bounced back into another good position and more bad behavior.

In 1779 a newly married Wilkinson won the job of clothier general in charge of supplying uniforms for the Continental Army. Complaints soon arose: Wilkinson was hardly ever at work, and there were irregularities in his accounts. Suspicions grew that he manipulated supply contracts for his own profit, and in 1781, under accusations of corruption, Wilkinson resigned from the Army (again). He moved to Pennsylvania, and then to Kentucky in 1784.

The Korean War was the first in which helicopters were used extensively in warfare...

SPANISH AGENT 13

Wilkinson's status as a former general made him a big shot in local politics. Kentucky was trying for statehood, but Spain worried that American growth there might threaten their colonies in Louisiana, Texas, Florida, and Mexico. To discourage settlers, Spain wouldn't let Kentuckians use the port of New Orleans when they shipped their goods down the Mississippi River. Kentucky's troubles inspired another of Wilkinson's schemes. History called it the "Spanish Conspiracy."

Wilkinson proposed a plan to Louisiana's Spanish governor, Esteban Rodriguez Miro: he would incite Kentucky to rebel and become a sovereign entity allied to Spain. As "Spanish Agent 13," Wilkinson received an annual salary and had a monopoly on all Kentucky trade that went into New Orleans. The rebellion never got off the ground. Kentucky eventually became the 15th state, and in 1791, a disappointed Wilkinson returned to the military. Spain dropped Wilkinson's monopoly on trade—but he was still their Agent 13.

A GENERAL TRAITOR

Wilkinson reentered the military with the rank of lieutenant colonel. He impressed his superiors, and by 1792 he was once again a brigadier general. He also impressed his Spanish paymasters by alerting them to an attack on New Orleans led by American General George Rogers Clark. For that bit of treason, Wilkinson billed Spain $8,640. Needless to say, Clark's attack failed.

Meanwhile, indifference to the well-being of his men led to the deaths of many of his soldiers from illness. He was accused of taking kickbacks from corrupt suppliers who gave the troops rotten food and inferior supplies. Secretary of War Henry Knox accused Wilkinson of "conduct tarnishing the military reputation of our country." But Knox had retired by 1796, and when General Anthony Wayne died, Wilkinson succeeded him as the commanding general, the nation's highest-ranking officer.

In a strange turn of history, President Thomas Jefferson, who wanted to curb Spain's power in America, sent Wilkinson to help take possession of the Louisiana Purchase and made him one of the commissioners in the new territory. The general repaid Jefferson by giving Spain reports on how to protect their colonies from a grow-

...but mostly in medevac and cargo delivery rather than combat. That came later, in Vietnam.

ing United States. Wilkinson could have done more damage if he hadn't entered into the most infamous conspiracy in U.S. history.

When Jefferson's vice president, Aaron Burr, was forced out of office after he killed Alexander Hamilton in an 1804 duel, he turned for help to an old buddy, General Wilkinson, who had command of all the U.S. troops in the Mississippi River Valley. Wilkinson suggested that Burr should raise an army to take over New Orleans, from where they could conquer more Spanish lands and create a private empire. Word got out that Burr was raising money for an army, and Wilkinson exposed the plot, calling Burr a traitorous schemer and portraying himself as innocent. The president believed every word. Burr stood trial for treason in 1807. Wilkinson testified against his friend, but Burr was acquitted because—as with so many of Wilkinson's schemes—nothing happened. Many suspected that Wilkinson was the real mastermind. Once Jefferson left office, Congress investigated Wilkinson twice, and in 1811 President James Madison had him court-martialed, not only for conspiring with Burr but also for suspected dealings with Spain. Wilkinson was acquitted for lack of evidence. Proof that he was a spy came to light only years after his death.

MAKING CUSTER LOOK GOOD

Cronyism kept Wilkinson in the Army as a major general. During the War of 1812, he led 7,000 troops up the St. Lawrence River. In November 1813, 100 miles from Montreal, they were attacked by a smaller force of about 800–1,000 British soldiers and Indians. Ill and taking so much opium that his men thought he was drunk, Wilkinson gave uncoordinated orders that left his army exposed to fire, demoralized, and forced to take on heavy casualties. He retreated; partly as a result, British troops recrossed the border, occupied Detroit, and burned Buffalo, New York, to the ground. Wilkinson invaded Canada again in March 1814, hoping a quick victory might make up for the previous fiasco. With 4,000 troops he bombarded Lacolle Mills, an outpost defended by a few hundred soldiers. The Americans dragged cannons over marshy fields, but the guns had little impact on the stone fort. Wilkinson kept his gunners in the field and vulnerable when nearby British reinforcements and two Canadian forces arrived. In spite of a big advantage in numbers, Wilkinson retreated. He was finally removed from command—and this time, there was no coming back.

Liberty cabbage: an American euphemism for sauerkraut during World War I.

GUERRILLA WARFARE, PART I

The beginnings of Army Special Forces in America.

About 2,000 years ago, the great Chinese military strategist Sun Tzu argued in his book *The Art of War* that the way to defeat a more powerful enemy is to employ your strength to exploit his weaknesses. Guerrilla warfare is one way to do that. *Guerrilla*—Spanish for "little war"—describes a method of fighting an enemy by employing small groups of irregulars within areas controlled by the enemy. Guerrilla units attack the enemy's communications and supply lines and other small or isolated enemy units.

Chinese Communist leader Mao Zedong described tactics he successfully used against the Japanese during World War II in *On Guerrilla War*: "The enemy advances, we retreat; the enemy camps, we harass; the enemy tires, we attack; the enemy retreats, we pursue."

U.S. ARMY SPECIAL FORCES

The Special Forces are elite units that engage in unconventional (i.e., guerrilla) warfare. Today, the U.S. Army relies heavily on elite units like the Rangers, Green Berets, and Delta Force to accomplish missions requiring smaller, more highly skilled and specialized units than found in the military in general. But guerrilla units have been around for a long time.

The European wars of centuries ago were fought by assembling large formations and meeting the enemy on open ground—tactics that were unsuitable for America's limited manpower and vast wilderness. The history of U.S. Special Forces begins with the French and Indian War (1754–63), in which France and England were fighting for control of North America. The objective was to harass the enemy till he decided to leave an area. Small, independent units were much more effective in pursuit of this goal.

ROGERS' RANGERS

The first and most famous of these British units was known as Rogers' Rangers after their commander, Major Robert Rogers. The

Rangers wore distinctive green outfits and practiced tactics called "Rogers' Rules of Ranging," which many in the British regular army considered unsporting, if not downright cowardly because they included sound advice such as, "If you are obliged to receive the enemy's fire, fall, or squat down, till it is over; then rise and discharge at them." Major Rogers hired men solely on merit and shocked regular commanders with his use of Native Americans and freed slaves.

Rogers' Rangers roamed the countryside between the New England states and Detroit, Michigan, attacking French army supply convoys and small units. They also sacked and burned French colonial homes and farms. These tactics were effective in forcing the French and their allies to abandon the countryside and concentrate their forces in Quebec City and Montreal (in eastern Canada), and in Detroit. The British and their colonial allies then concentrated their forces to lay siege to each city in turn until it fell and they could move on to the next. By the time Detroit fell, the British had control over all of North America.

THE SWAMP FOX

The greatest guerrilla fighter in the American Revolution was General Francis Marion. He formed Marion's Brigade in 1780, with 150 tattered and penniless patriots. None received pay, food, or even ammunition from the Continental Army. But they still managed to terrorize the British in South Carolina and Georgia with a series of hit-and-run raids in the face of overwhelming odds. Marion and his men would strike swiftly and then vanish into the swamps. His tactics were so effective that he was nicknamed the "Swamp Fox" by one very frustrated British general.

Later in the war, Marion and his men combined with larger, regular army forces to attack and defeat the British in South Carolina's big cities. In 1781 Marion rescued an American unit that was surrounded by British forces at Parker's Ferry, South Carolina, and received the thanks of Congress for his efforts. His victories eventually drove British forces out of South Carolina entirely.

Turn to page 75 for Part II.

The oldest U.S. nuclear submarine still in service: the USS *Los Angeles*, built in 1974.

OLD SOLDIERS

At the age of 105, Hiram Cronk, the last living soldier of the War of 1812, confessed the secret of his long life: "For many years Duffy's Pure Malt Whiskey has been my only medicine." Like Cronk, these three other veterans of American wars got a chance to tell their stories before they faded away.

REVOLUTIONARY WAR

Lemuel Cook (1759–1866): The last verifiable veteran of the American Revolution, Lemuel Cook claimed to be 17 when he left his Connecticut home to enlist as a private in the 2nd Light Dragoons in 1775. Like many boys eager to fight the Redcoats, he probably lied about his age and may have been closer to 13. The first time he "smelt gun powder" was in 1776, at Valentine's Hill in Westchester, New York, where his regiment engaged a troop of British soldiers on horseback. He served throughout the war, and witnessed Charles Cornwallis's men giving up their guns on October 19, 1781, when the British finally surrendered.

Cook's memories of General George Washington said a lot about Washington's ability to inspire loyalty. Two years into what Cook called "a hard war," he met the general at White Plains, New York. Cook was in the stables caring for his mount when Washington walked through. He asked Cook's name, admired his bay horse, and encouraged the boy to continue to take good care of it. Young Cook was awed at the height and stature of the great man and touched by his personal attention. Cook said, "I'll never forget though, all the things that must have been pressing on him, and he took time for a kind word."

It was at least two years before Cook saw Washington again. To Cook's shock, Washington called out to him by name. The general complimented him on how well the bay looked, and said that he had a similar horse at Mount Vernon. He'd grown a lot during the war, so he was sure that Washington had recognized the horse rather than him, but the fact that the general remembered his name still amazed and pleased him to the end of his life. Cook kept his discharge papers, signed by General Washington, all his life.

Fleet Admiral Chester W. Nimitz was the leading U.S. Navy authority on submarines.

A Last American Rebel

As a veteran, Cook was granted 100 acres in what was then the wilderness of Clinton, New York, where he farmed to a ripe old age. He and wife Hannah had 10 children. He lived long enough to see the Civil War, and as one who'd fought to establish the nation, he also noted that it was "a rebellion that must be put down."

CIVIL WAR GRAY

William "Josh" Bush (1845–1952): A Georgian from Wilkinson County, Josh was barely 16 years old when he enlisted in the Confederate army as a private in the Ramah Guards, Company B, of the 14th Regiment. He pretended he was older to get accepted. He liked to joke, "I told a lie to get into the war, and I'd have told another to get out." But then he would add seriously, "I fought to the end and I wouldn't have it any other way." His Georgia Militia fought in the Battle of Atlanta when his fellow Confederates under Lieutenant General John Bell Hood were badly outnumbered. Though they held on to the city for some weeks, their final retreat was particularly bitter because of Major General William Tecumseh Sherman's burning of Atlanta. When the war ended in 1865, Private Bush surrendered at Stephen's Station in Georgia.

The Last Georgia Confederate

After the war, Bush was one of more than 300,000 Confederate veterans in his state. He became active in the Confederate Veterans Association and, in recognition of his work, was eventually named honorary "General Bush." The wounds of the Civil War were slow to heal, and the burning of Atlanta remained a source of anger to many Southerners, but Bush helped symbolize understanding between soldiers on both sides of the war.

In the 1890s, when drought turned the Midwest into a dustbowl, reducing many to starvation, Georgia sent food and helped 2,700 displaced Union veterans resettle in Fitzgerald, Georgia. Former Confederates like Josh Bush marched alongside Union veterans in parades and made them feel at home.

As the last Georgia Confederate, Bush was Fitzgerald's most famous citizen. He posed for pictures, signed autographs, and received piles of fan mail. On Memorial Day, while his "friendly enemy" Henry Brunner (a Union veteran) was alive, the two pals

Bugs Bunny was inducted into the Marine Corps, complete with dog tags...

visited a local cemetery together. Bush laid flowers on Union graves and Brunner put them on Confederate graves. After Brunner died, Bush went alone to lay flowers for both the Blue and the Gray.

CIVIL WAR BLUE

Albert Woolson (1847–1956): Albert was living in Antwerp, New York, in 1861 when his father left his job as a circus bandmaster to join Lincoln's army. By 1862 Albert and his mom moved to Windom, Minnesota, to be near the hospital where his father eventually died from wounds received at the Battle of Shiloh. In 1864 Albert enlisted with Company C of the First Minnesota Volunteer Heavy Artillery and marched with them to Fort Oglethorpe in Tennessee. Albert's real ambition was to replace Company C's drummer boy. He later admitted that he got the other boy's job "by knocking his block off."

Because it worked behind the front lines, Company C didn't see any real action in the Civil War. As drummer boy, Albert played slow, muffled drums to accompany fallen soldiers to the grave. In an interview given 88 years after the war, he still remembered those funeral processions. "We went along with a burying detail. Going out, we played proper sad music, but coming back we kinda hit it up. Once a woman came onto the road and asked what kind of music that was to bury somebody, I told her that we had taken care of the dead and that now we were cheering up the living."

The Last Union Man

Woolson married and took up the trade of carpentry, though he never stopped "cheering up the living." He played in a drum corps with a friend from the Minnesota Infantry, and in his later years, he entertained Duluth schoolchildren. For much of his long life, Woolson was a member of the Grand Army of the Republic (GAR), an organization of Union veterans who worked for better pensions, health care, and jobs for former servicemen. When he became the last of the 490,000 soldiers who served in the GAR, he deeded its records to the Library of Congress and its official seal to the Smithsonian Institution. Woolson's death came just before he could be presented with a Congressional gold medal, but a statue honoring him—the last member of the Grand Old Army—stands in Zeigler's Grove at Gettysburg National Park.

...He was officially "discharged" at the end of World War II as a master sergeant.

CLIMBING HIGH

"Sir, the Air Force can deliver anything."
—Major General Curtis E. LeMay, USFAF

"I made my first solo, my first landing, and my first crack-up—all the same day."

—Major General Benjamin D. Foulois, U.S. Army Air Corps

"Our capacity to rapidly project power over long distances has been a godsend to our allies, and has struck fear in the hearts of our adversaries."

—Secretary of the Air Force F. Whitten Peters

"We Americans had developed the best system of air fighting that the world had ever seen."

—Brigadier General William Mitchell

"If you're in a fair fight, you didn't plan it properly."

—Nick Lappos, Chief R&D Pilot, Sikorsky Aircraft

"Know and use all the capabilities in your airplane. If you don't, sooner or later, some guy who does use them all will kick your ass."

—Dave "Preacher" Pace

"It got more exciting with each war. I mean the planes were going faster than hell when I was flying a Mustang, but by the time I got to Nam, it scared the piss out of a lot of guys just to fly the damn jets at full speed. Let alone do it in combat."

—Brigadier General Robin Olds, USAF

"To become an ace, a fighter must have extraordinary eyesight, strength, and agility, a huntsman's eye, coolness in a pinch, calculated recklessness, a full measure of courage—and occasional luck!"

—General Jimmy Doolittle

"To be a good fighter pilot, there is one prime requisite—think fast, and act faster."

—Major John T. Godfrey

"He who has the height controls the battle. He who has the sun achieves surprise. He who gets in close shoots them down."

—Anonymous

The Soviet MiG-15 dominated the skies in the early part of the Korean War.

THAT'S THE POINT

With very few exceptions, the tune that West Point's long gray line of cadets and graduates march to is the motto Duty, Honor, Country.

TAKING THE HIGH GROUND

The United States Military Academy sits on some of the choicest real estate on the East Coast, 50 miles north of Manhattan. Its name was a natural, sitting as it does on a point on the west side of the Hudson River. When George Washington first saw it, he wasn't admiring the view—he described it as the most important strategic position in all of America. Not only could he and his army see for miles around, they could also easily blockade the river to unwanted—that is, British—traffic. Washington claimed it as his headquarters in 1778, making it the longest continually occupied military post in the United States.

EARLY AMERICAN HISTORY

President Thomas Jefferson, after assuring himself that the school would reflect the makeup of a democratic society, signed the papers that established West Point as the United States Military Academy in 1802. The curriculum, devoted to the art and science of warfare, was heavy on engineering. Before West Point, America relied on foreign engineers like Polish military hero Tadeusz Kosciuszko, who designed the fortifications in 1778. The academy was the only engineering school in America until Rensselaer Polytechnic Institute was founded in 1824. In its early days, some cadets were as young as 10, while some were well into their 30s, and the length of study could last from six months to six years. The school became more like a modern-day college as the country got closer to sending its graduates off to war.

The Mexican-American War (1846–48) was the first chance for West Point grads to distinguish themselves in battle. When the Civil War broke out in 1861, more than 400 West Point alumni fought as general officers on either side, with the advantage going to the North, which had almost twice as many West Point officers as the South. In fact, West Point graduates commanded either or both sides in every major battle—60 in all.

The class of 1891 graduated early to fill the Army's officer ranks for the Spanish-American War, as did the class of 1901 for the Philippine-American War. The 1900 student body stood at 481 cadets, but in 1916 it swelled to 1,332 in anticipation of America's joining the war in Europe. By the end of World War I, the only cadets left at West Point were the freshmen. Four of the five World War II five-star generals were West Point alumni, and nearly 500 graduates gave their lives in that war.

JOINING THE "LONG GRAY LINE"

Cadets come from every U.S. state and territory—Congress insists on it—but getting in isn't easy. A cadet must be between the ages of 17 and 22, a U.S. citizen, unmarried, and must not be pregnant or obligated to provide support to a dependent. Applicants must be nominated by an "authorized source"—usually a congressperson—to be considered. Good grades and SAT scores are a must, as is passing the school's Candidate Fitness Assessment and a physical.

Once admitted, cadets have to follow the cadet honor code: "A cadet will not lie, cheat, or steal, or tolerate those who do." Any cadet accused of a violation and found guilty by a jury of peers can be sentenced to repeating an academic year or expulsion.

The first-year (freshman) class is officially called the "fourth class," and so on up to the seniors, or the "first class." Fourth-class cadets are also known as "plebes," third class are "yearlings" or "yuks," second-class cadets are "cows," and the first class are "firsties." Females were admitted in 1976 and currently represent 17 percent of all cadets—the same percentage as in the U.S. Army.

WHAT'S YOUR MAJOR?

The academy offers a typical four-year academic program with 31 majors; the most popular are foreign languages, management information systems, history, economics, and mechanical engineering. Military and leadership education is included in academic instruction. Physical training is intense: Swordsmanship is no longer a required course, but applied gymnastics and swimming are. Cadets must pass the Army Physical Fitness Test twice a year. Regardless of major, all cadets graduate with a bachelor of science degree (because of the engineering requirements) and as second lieutenants. Post-grad assignments are determined by class rank—calculated by performance in the following areas: academic (55 percent), military leadership (30 percent), and physical fitness and

"Sky Dragons" is the nickname of the U.S. 18th Airborne Corps.

athletics (15 percent). The academy is generally ranked as the best college in the United States among public institutions, followed closely by the U.S. Naval Academy. Four years of tuition (estimated at $225,000) for the approximately 4,000 cadets is paid for by your tax dollars. Cadet-graduates repay that debt by serving at least five years of active duty and three years in the reserves after graduation for a total of eight years..

A QUICK CAMPUS TOUR

The academy's 16,000-acre campus is loaded with Americana: fort ruins, monuments, and buildings in every popular style since the Revolutionary War. Of special significance are Trophy Point's Battle Monument (designed by architect Stanford White) and erected to honor the Civil War dead; the 1910 neo-Gothic Cadet Chapel; military statues; and a cemetery that's the final resting place of many alumni from the Revolutionary War to today.

WHO'S WHO OF THE ACADEMY

Among its nearly 65,000 graduates are two American presidents—Ulysses S. Grant and Dwight D. Eisenhower—and one Confederate States of America president, Jefferson Davis. It produced a notorious traitor—Benedict Arnold—and the architect of one of America's most famous defeats—George Armstrong Custer, who graduated last in his class (1861).

Since then, West Point has graduated famous generals like John J. Pershing, Matthew Ridgway, Henry H. "Hap" Arnold, Omar Bradley, Douglas MacArthur, George S. Patton, William Westmoreland, Alexander Haig, Norman Schwarzkopf, and David Petraeus—and scads of other fine officers you've never heard of. The academy also produced 18 NASA astronauts, including Buzz Aldrin and Michael Collins of *Apollo 11*.

West Point has some noteworthy dropouts too. Edgar Allan Poe (1834) was discharged for gross neglect of duty and disobedience and was the first well-known American to make a living as a writer. James McNeill Whistler (1855) painted *Arrangement in Grey and Black: The Artist's Mother* (*Whistler's Mother*). Timothy Leary (1943) became a 1960s counterculture symbol and a vocal proponent of LSD. Richard Hatch (1986) the first winner of the *Survivor* series was sentenced to four years in prison in 2006 for tax evasion.

Ships' bells are so important that maritime law requires all ships to carry a working bell.

UNCLE SAM NEEDS YOU! PART I

Conscription—drafting men to serve as soldiers—dates back at least 2,500 years to the ancient Greeks and Romans. Toward the end of the second century BC, however, the Greeks and Romans turned to professional soldiers who were more battle-ready than ordinary citizens. Our armed forces have followed suit.

THE AMERICAN REVOLUTION

When the American colonies decided to revolt against British rule, militias organized themselves at the state and local levels; America's new government had the power to establish the Continental Army, but not the power to draft men into its ranks. It fell upon the states do it, often by means of incentives: land, clothes, and sometimes even slaves. In 1777 the Continental Congress told the states they had to provide 75,000 men to the federal forces; in turn, the states established quotas for each town. These townsmen could join the army, pay a fee, or recruit a substitute (often a young apprentice forced to serve on his master's behalf).

Young men joined the Continental Army with thoughts of adventure, but desertion was commonplace once they encountered the harsh reality of military life. Many of them abandoned their units before their one- or three-year commitments were up. The Continental Army never came close to reaching its Congress-imposed goal; at its largest, it had 35,000 men supplemented by tens of thousands more who belonged to the local militias. Despite the shortfall in numbers, Congress didn't consider a national draft as a way to increase its armed forces—a move like that would contradict the newly declared inalienable rights of every man to life, liberty, and the pursuit of happiness.

THE CIVIL WAR

America was engaged in wars and skirmishes on various fronts for much of the 1800s, but conscription wasn't applied on the national level until the Civil War. The Confederate states were the first to enact the draft, in 1862. Conscription was met with considerable resistance because it was viewed as being nearly on par with slavery. Soldiers were initially drafted for just one year's service, then offered bounties and furloughs to reenlist for three more years.

In March 1863, Congress passed a conscription act to fill the ranks of the Union army. But only 2 percent of the Union soldiers were actual conscripts; another 6 percent were paid substitutes. The majority, the enlistees, had been offered cash rewards to enlist. The threat of conscription was an encouragement to join the army as a volunteer—at the time, draftees were often viewed as derelicts or cowards.

NORTH VS. SOUTH

Wealthy Northerners could pay $300 or hire a substitute to take their place in the army. In the North, many viewed the conflict with the South as "the rich man's war and the poor man's fight." Escalating turmoil among the poor and new immigrants led to draft riots in New York City in July 1863, the first large-scale public protest to a draft in the United States.

In the South, the Confederate Conscription Act of 1862 exempted men who owned and operated agricultural and industrial businesses, a version of the draft that some historians consider the first modern form of conscription because it tried to distribute men where they were needed, both on the front lines and the home front. But it wasn't until World War I that a more organized and relatively fairer system would be used for military conscription.

WORLD WAR I

Congress passed the Selective Service Act in 1917. It required all men between 21 and 30 to register for the draft and be examined for physical and mental fitness. More than 9 million men registered in the first month, but only 687,000 were immediately inducted. A second conscription law a year later expanded the pool to include men from ages 18 to 45.

By the end of World War I in November 1918, more than 2.8 million men had been inducted into the U.S. military; another 2 million soldiers were volunteers. The ratio of conscripts to volunteers is in stark contrast to the Civil War, where more than 90 percent of the soldiers on both sides were volunteers. One

The Aztec Club was founded in 1847 by officers who fought in the Mexican-American War...

explanation for the disparity is that during World War I many Americans were opposed to intervention in Europe, whereas the Civil War was a national conflict.

ACCEPT NO SUBSTITUTES

The 1917 Selective Service Act made allowances for industrial and agricultural production. Exemptions were also given to clergymen, government officials, and some hardship cases. And, for the first time, conscientious objectors were excused from combat service and reassigned to supporting roles within the military. A wider range of social classes was now represented in the armed forces because this time no bounties were paid and no substitutes were allowed. After the war, most draftees were discharged. The United States maintained an all-volunteer military over the next two decades. Men were no longer required to register for the draft—after all, World War I was billed as "the War to End All Wars," and few thought a massive buildup of the armed forces would be needed again.

WORLD WAR II

The major war developing in Europe throughout the late 1930s led Congress to establish the first peacetime draft law in U.S. history—the 1940 Selective Training and Service Act, which provided for the annual induction of 900,000 men, aged 21 to 36, into the military. But shortly after the Japanese bombing of Pearl Harbor in December 1941, the act was revised and the draft age was lowered to 18 in order to expand the armed forces quickly. By the war's end in 1945, more than 45 million American men had registered for the draft; of these, 10 million were inducted into the military. From just 2 percent in the Civil War to almost 60 percent in World War I, conscripts now made up about 66 percent of the total manpower of the U.S. armed forces.

As in World War I, provisions were made for industrial and agricultural workers, exemptions were given for clergymen, and conscientious objectors were recognized. Draftees also had the right to reclaim their civilian jobs after the war. A lottery system, which was designed to be more equitable, was instituted in 1942.

Even with a fairer, more organized system in place, there was opposition to the draft, and to the war in general. More than 25,000 conscientious objectors served the military in noncombat

...Members included Ulysses S. Grant, Robert E. Lee, and Joseph Hooker.

roles; another 6,000 were imprisoned for their opposition to the war or their refusal to serve in any capacity. Draft dodgers were common, with nearly 375,000 being investigated and 16,000 imprisoned. As the government increasingly relied on the draft to meet its military needs, opposition to it became more widespread, more public, and less of a social stigma.

After the Selective Training and Service Act expired in 1947, a new act was passed by Congress in 1948. It required all men aged 19 to 26 to register for the draft; those selected would serve for 21 months. However, the enlistment of a large number of volunteers in the years following World War II allowed the Army to declare a draft hiatus in 1949. A total of just 30,000 men were inducted under the new Selective Service Act in 1948 and 1949, out of more than 9 million who were registered for the draft. But with another international conflict on the horizon in Southeast Asia, the Selective Service Act, which was set to expire in June 1950, was extended for another year until a new draft law was crafted.

See page 202 for the rest of the story.

* * *

PRESIDENTS WHO SERVED

- 16 Army Veterans: George Washington, James Monroe, Andrew Jackson, William Henry Harrison, John Tyler, Zachary Taylor, Franklin Pierce, Ulysses S. Grant, Rutherford B. Hayes, James Garfield, Benjamin Harrison, William McKinley, Theodore Roosevelt, Harry S. Truman, Dwight D. Eisenhower, and Ronald Reagan
- 6 Navy Veterans: John F. Kennedy, Lyndon B. Johnson, Richard Nixon, Gerald Ford, Jimmy Carter, and George H. W. Bush
- 1 Air Force Veteran: George W. Bush, through his time in the Texas Air National Guard
- No presidents have been members of the Coast Guard or Marine Corps.

Former British Officer Becomes President

One of our presidents enlisted in a foreign army, but he had a good excuse—there was no U.S. Army at the time. George Washington became a lieutenant colonel in the British army and fought the French and Native Americans from 1754 to 1759.

The Treaty of Ghent (Belgium) was the peace treaty that ended the War of 1812.

YOU'RE IN THE ARMY NOW

If you were a male under the age of 40 in 1942, you had to carry a Selective Service card. Then the local draft board would send you a letter of induction beginning with the word "Greetings" and going on to indicate the date and time you were to report to your local draft board for transportation to the induction center.

THE INDUCTION CENTER

Inductions weren't a lot of fun. They took place in a single day, often beginning in the predawn darkness. For the average civilian, it would be his first exposure to the Army's long-standing practice of having soldiers "hurry up and wait." First, men filed into a long assembly line for a physical examination, with about 25 men passing through the process per hour. They came into the examination area naked except for their briefs and an identifying number marked on the back of their hands. A few hours later, they emerged from the end of the building, either accepted or rejected.

The strange, intimidating atmosphere accelerated heartbeats and contributed to dysfunctional behavior—some men couldn't urinate into a cup; others did so on the floor. Most inductees found it discomforting to answer such personal questions as "Do you like girls?" as posed by one of the Army's inquisitive psychiatrists. Most men tried to affirm their manhood, and those with ailments tried to conceal them. To check for mental infirmities, a psychiatrist might ask, "Why does the sun rise in the morning and set at night?" Even people of normal intelligence struggled for the right answer. General Lewis B. Hershey, who presided over the Selective Service System, noted that psychiatric screenings "were not very effective" and that most rejections were "by guess and by God."

LET'S GET PHYSICAL

The percentage of the population who tried to avoid service used various techniques like doping themselves up with aspirin to elevate their heartbeat or ingesting substances to increase their blood pressure. Someone always dropped out of line and fainted—some real and some fake—but doctors ignored the theatrics and a body

H. G. Wells was the first to use the term "atomic bomb," in *The World Set Free* (1914).

of gruff sergeants kept the line moving. Unless a man was hopelessly obese, crippled, or afflicted with epilepsy, venereal disease, or flat feet, he would be fingerprinted and checked against FBI files.

Those who passed the screenings were interviewed briefly and asked what branch of service they preferred. Most men requested the Army Air Forces. Few chose the infantry, which was dangerous, unglamorous, and where, in the end, almost everyone went.

IN OR OUT?

The new draftees signed their induction papers and received a serial number with instructions to memorize it. After waiting for others to complete the ritual, the officer in charge assembled the men, ordered them to raise their right hand, and administered the Selective Service's oath of allegiance. The inductees received a two-week furlough and were sent home to settle their personal affairs with the reminder, "You're in the Army now."

Those who failed the physical exam went home with their new classifications—and occasionally with regrets or mixed emotions. Some of the "misdiagnosed" promptly enlisted in another branch of the service to avoid the taint of being rejected by the Army. Of more than 15 million men examined at induction centers, 1,846,000 were rejected for neuropsychiatric reasons. The Army eventually discharged more than 300,000 later for the same reason.

DO YOU QUALIFY?

Then and now, to qualify for service in the armed forces of the United States, you must meet certain medical standards as established by the Department of Defense:

1. Free of contagious diseases that would likely endanger the health of other personnel.

2. Free of medical conditions or physical defects that would require excessive time lost from duty for necessary treatment or hospitalization or would likely result in separation from the Army for medical unfitness.

3. Medically capable of satisfactorily completing required training.

4. Medically adaptable to the military environment without the necessity of geographical area limitations.

5. Medically capable of performing duties without aggravation of existing physical defects or medical conditions.

The Korean War was the first armed conflict of the Cold War.

TRIPOLI TO MONTEZUMA

In case you've ever wondered what the "shores of" the capital of Libya and the "halls of" the last king of the Aztecs are doing in the "Marines' Hymn."

BORN IN WASHINGTON

Following the 1783 peace treaty with Great Britain, the Continental Congress sold off all the Navy's ships. Upshot: the new country had no navy and, to protect its commercial interests in the Mediterranean, had to pay tribute to the Barbary pirates who operated along the North African coast. Three of the Barbary areas—Morocco, Tunis, and Tripoli—kept their demands within reason, but the pasha of Algiers raised his fees to levels that threatened the fledgling American trade and traders. In response, Congress established the United States Navy in 1794 and an independent United States Marine Corps in 1798.

THE FIRST BARBARY WAR

In May 1801 the pasha of Tripoli, Yussif Karamanli, decided that the United States wasn't paying him enough, and declared war. America responded by sending Navy ships to blockade the port city. They were joined by a captured enemy vessel commanded by Lieutenant Stephen Decatur Jr. A daring night raid into Tripoli's harbor in early 1804 made Decatur a national hero; a raid months later on an enemy gunboat earned him a promotion to captain. Despite Decatur's heroics, the naval campaign was dragging on too long to suit President Thomas Jefferson. He looked for another way to end the war.

THE SHORES OF TRIPOLI

Enter William Eaton and Lieutenant Presley O'Bannon. Eaton, a former U.S. consul in Tunis, was friendly with Pasha Karamanli's exiled brother Hamet, who would serve as the new pasha of Tripoli if Eaton could overthrow his brother. An army of about 400 Arab, Greek, and Christian mercenaries, led by O'Bannon and his seven Marines, marched west 600 miles from Alexandria, Egypt, to Tripoli. After seven weeks, they arrived at the border city of Derna.

While three ships of the Navy's Mediterranean Squadron bombarded Derna by sea, the Arab mercenaries attacked from the south, and O'Bannon, his seven Marines, and the Christian mercenaries attacked from the east. The bombardment silenced Derna's artillery and O'Bannon's men charged the city. In 30 minutes, O'Bannon and Eaton controlled Derna, and within the month Pasha Yussif Karamanli signed a peace treaty with the United States. The elegant Mamluk sword Hamet gave O'Bannon as a thanks-anyway gesture was adopted by the Marine Corps in 1826 as standard issue.

THE MEXICAN-AMERICAN WAR

By 1845 President James Polk's expansionist policies had led to a war with Mexico. After expelling the Mexican army from California, Navy seamen and Marines attacked Mexico's Pacific coastal cities of Cabo San Lucas, Guaymas, and Manzanillo. Soon the Navy had even captured Mazatlán, Mexico's second-largest seaport. But despite the capture of Monterrey, the Mexican government refused to sign a treaty. It was on to Veracruz.

THE HALLS OF MONTEZUMA

By September 1847 the American forces had fought their way to Chapultepec Castle outside Mexico City. The home of the Mexican military academy, the stone-walled castle sat atop a 200-foot-high volcanic hill and was defended by approximately 800 soldiers, including some 100 military academy cadets.

While American artillery bombarded the castle, the Marines advanced, but were halted by cannon fire 250 yards from the castle and took cover in a ditch. Other Marine and Army units flanked the castle and broke through its defenses. As the defenders turned to face them, the Marines rose, scaled the walls, and joined the melee. The Mexican troops had no choice but to surrender.

The next morning, a joint Marine and Army company attacked the Mexican capital. Closing on the San Cosmé Gate, they took heavy fire from entrenched artillery and infantry firing from the rooftops. As the Army troops returned fire from behind the walls of a garden, the leathernecks charged the gate and became the first to raise an American flag over the castle.

The triumphant Marines returned to Washington, where they were presented with a flag featuring an eagle and an anchor, inscribed with their new motto, "From the Halls of Montezuma to the shores of Tripoli."

Napalm was first used in warfare in 1944 near St.-Lô, France.

AN IRON CONSTITUTION

The USS Constitution *is America's most victorious ship, having gone to battle for her country at least 32 times with no defeats. She is still afloat as the world's oldest commissioned warship.*

A NAVY IS BORN

After the Revolutionary War, America wondered if it needed to maintain a navy as it struggled with the costs of running a country. The United States planned to stay neutral, but the world wouldn't cooperate. So in 1794, to protect Americans at sea, Congress ordered six warships that would become the country's original navy. The USS *Constitution*—named by George Washington—was one. She was built in a Boston shipyard and cost over $300,000—about a tenth of the entire national budget.

For that, American taxpayers got a powerful, three-masted warship that was 204 feet long. Although she was called a 44-gun ship (the guns were actually portable cannons), she could carry up to 56. Made to sail relatively fast if she needed to escape danger, the *Constitution* had a frame of live oak from Georgia, one of the most durable types of wood in the world. Her hull was paneled on two sides with white oak and was up to 25 inches thick at the waterline. Copper bolts and breast hooks were supplied by Paul Revere.

BATTLE-TESTED

In 1798 French privateers were commandeering many American ships and the United States had entered an unofficial war with France. The *Constitution*, with a crew of 450, was sent on patrol—first along America's East Coast, then to the West Indies. From 1798 to 1801, she protected American ships. When peace evolved between the United States and France (in part due to the efforts of the new U.S. Navy), the *Constitution* was called home.

Meanwhile, tensions were worsening in North Africa. Pirates from Tripoli regularly stopped American ships in the Mediterranean. The pirates gave American captains a choice of paying tribute or surrendering their ship, cargo, and sometimes even the crew. In 1803 President Thomas Jefferson sent the *Constitution* to the Barbary Coast. With a fleet of American ships, the *Constitution* captured pirate ships and led daring attacks on the harbor of Tripoli until the pirates were defeated in 1805.

Aboard the *Constitution*, a treaty was signed that gave American ships the right to sail the Mediterranean without paying blackmail to Tripoli. It was a big victory, as American citizens were now protected at sea, at least from the French and the Barbary pirates. However, Great Britain was still boarding American ships and impressing American sailors into the Royal Navy. About 10,000 Americans wound up in the Royal Navy by the time the War of 1812 began. With the world's most powerful navy, Britain planned to make short work of the U.S. fleet. Early on, it seemed that the *Constitution* would be one of the Royal Navy's prizes.

In July 1812, under the command of Captain Isaac Hull, the *Constitution* was on her way to New York to join a squadron of five ships. Instead, she met a fleet of five British warships. Outnumbered, Hull tried to escape, but there was barely a breeze to sail his ship. For 36 hours Hull and his crew kept the *Constitution* out of reach of British guns. The crew pulled the ship with rowboats, and when that wasn't fast enough, they tossed the ship's anchor ahead of the ship, pulled her close to the anchor, then reeled the anchor in and threw it out again. They took advantage of every breeze until a rainstorm hid them from view and allowed them to escape.

OLD IRONSIDES

Having lived to fight another day, the *Constitution* did just that. On August 19, 1812, she went after the British warship HMS *Guerriere*. Hull maneuvered the *Constitution* to fire at her enemy from close range. The two heavily gunned ships dueled in a fierce battle, and in 20 minutes, the *Guerriere*'s masts were toppled and she became an unseaworthy hulk. Meanwhile, the heavy American ship hadn't sustained much damage. During the battle, as British cannonballs bounced off her thick wooden hull, an unknown sailor shouted, "Huzzah, her sides are made of iron!" giving the *Constitution* her new nickname, "Old Ironsides."

Old Ironsides came home to a hero's welcome. The victory gave the country a needed morale boost at a time when the war was going badly. Britain was shocked that the Royal Navy could lose. The *London Times* predicted trouble because the Americans were "likely to be rendered insolent and confident." Maybe the

During the 19th century, naval mines were called torpedoes. When Adm. David Farragut cried...

Times had a point because in 1813, after another fierce battle that lasted four hours, the *Constitution* sank the British warship HMS *Java*. From then on, Royal Navy ships patrolled in pairs to better protect themselves from heavily armed American warships. But in December 1814, the *Constitution* forced the British warships HMS *Cyane* and HMS *Levant* to surrender.

POETRY IN MOTION

After the war, the *Constitution* remained a proud symbol to many Americans. Unfortunately, their unsinkable ship came close to destruction at the hands of the U.S. Navy.

In 1830 Oliver Wendell Holmes read an angry editorial in the *Boston Advertiser* about the Navy's plan to scrap the *Constitution*, which had suffered years of neglect. Holmes dashed off "Old Ironsides," a three-stanza protest poem. Published in the *Advertiser*, the poem was picked up by newspapers across the country. Soon the warship was a cause célèbre and children were reciting verses from Holmes's poem.

The Navy reversed its decision and the *Constitution* was refurbished in 1831. For the next 24 years, she served as a flagship for various Navy squadrons and as a diplomatic ship for goodwill tours all over the world. In 1853 she was patrolling the African coast when she caught her last prize, an American schooner smuggling slaves to the United States, which had been illegal since 1807.

A PENNY SAVED IS A SHIP SAVED

Two years later, Old Ironsides retired from active service. Used next as a teaching ship at the Naval Academy, she was smuggled to Rhode Island before she could be attacked by Confederates during the Civil War. After the war, she remained a teaching ship, and from 1879 to 1881, on her last active duty for the Navy, she sailed between the West Indies and Nova Scotia as a training ship for naval apprentices.

In 1937 American schoolchildren raised $148,000, mostly in pennies, to help keep the aging *Constitution* afloat. In 1997 a new generation of children sent in their pennies to buy sails for the newly refurbished *Constitution* so she could sail under her own power for the first time in 116 years celebrate her 200th birthday. She is now on exhibit at the Charlestown Navy Yard in Boston.

..."Damn the torpedoes! Full speed ahead!" he was referring to mines in Mobile Bay, Alabama.

PROFILES IN COURAGE

Hundreds of thousands of soldiers have served in Iraq and Afghanistan since 9/11. They have demonstrated coolness under fire and a commitment to their fellow troops while enduring combat conditions that ranged from –30°F in an Afghan winter to 125°F in an Iraqi summer. To date, only five have been awarded the Medal of Honor: a Marine, two Army soldiers, and two Navy SEALs. Here are their stories.

SERGEANT FIRST CLASS PAUL SMITH, U.S. ARMY, IRAQ

Baghdad Airport, April 4, 2003

The 11th Engineering Battalion had been ordered to restart the electrical power and water, fix the runways, and find a compound to hold prisoners. When an American armored personnel carrier (APC) rammed through the gate, a company of Republican Guard troops inside began shooting at the engineers with rocket-propelled grenades and small arms. Three soldiers in the APC were wounded. Several Iraqis raced up a tower in the compound and began firing down at the shocked and demoralized engineers, and wounded several more.

Sergeant Smith reacted quickly. Throwing a grenade at the Iraqis, he bought a few moments in which to drag his wounded soldiers to safety. He then climbed into the APC, drove it out into the middle of the compound, and began firing its .50-caliber machine gun at the attacking Iraqis. Smith held off the Iraqis until he was killed, but his quick actions and bravery enabled his fellow soldiers to flee the compound safely.

Smith's Medal of Honor was awarded posthumously on April 4, 2005, two years after he was killed.

CORPORAL JASON L. DUNHAM, U.S. MARINE CORPS, IRAQ

Karabilah, April 14, 2004

Jason Dunham was a squad leader in Kilo Company, 3rd Battalion, 7th Marine Regiment, who elected to extend his enlistment so that he could stay with his squad throughout its tour in Iraq. On April 14, 2004, Dunham was in the town of Karabilah, leading a convoy on a reconnaissance mission when radio reports came in that a roadside bomb had exploded nearby. Sunni insurgents had ambushed their battalion commander's convoy, and Dunham was ordered to provide fire support. He ordered his squad out of their vehicles and led one of his fire teams on foot several blocks south of the ambushed convoy. He led his team a few blocks south of the immediate ambush site and ordered his squad to block seven vehicles attempting to leave.

Dunham began inspecting the vehicles one by one. Suddenly the driver of a Toyota Land Cruiser burst out of the car door and grabbed Dunham by the neck. As Dunham fought the enemy hand-to-hand, two Marines saw their squad leader struggling and moved in to help him. Dunham noticed that the enemy fighter had a grenade in his hand, and ordered his Marines to move back as he wrestled the insurgent to the ground. As the fighting continued, Dunham screamed a warning to his Marines: "No, no, no—watch his hand!" Without hesitating, Dunham took off his Kevlar helmet, covered the grenade with it, and threw himself on top to smother the blast.

The two Marines were wounded in the explosion, and as the insurgent stood up, he was immediately killed by Marine small-arms fire. "By giving his own life, Corporal Dunham saved the lives of two of his men and showed the world what it means to be a Marine," President George W. Bush said later.

The hard-molded mesh of Dunham's helmet was scattered all around the site of the explosion, but Dunham survived the blast, although he was unconscious with a metal shard the size of a button wedged in his head. He never regained consciousness, and died eight days later, at the age of 22, in the National Naval Medical Center in Bethesda, Maryland.

He was awarded his Medal of Honor on January 11, 2007.

For more of the stories, see page 182.

* * *

"Bravery is the capacity to perform properly even when scared half to death."

—Omar Bradley

Army: Largest U.S. military service, with about 76,000 officers and 400,000 enlisted.

JEFFERSON DAVIS'S CAMEL CORPS

Camel Corps were used by the Allies in the Middle East in World War I and in Africa in World War II, but some enterprising Americans, with the help of Jefferson Davis, had already attempted to deploy them in the United States in the 19th century.

THE CAMEL CAPER

Second Lieutenant George H. Crosman wrote to the War Department in 1836 to suggest the use of camels as pack animals during Florida's Seminole Wars. Running camels through swamps and jungles didn't strike the War Department as a good idea, but Crosman didn't give up. Ten years later, during the Mexican War, he mentioned his idea to fellow officer Henry C. Wayne, who agreed that camels might be an asset because Mexico's terrain closely resembled Africa's deserts. But nothing came of it until Jefferson Davis became secretary of war in 1852. Wayne, now a major, made an official recommendation that a Camel Corps be established in the Southwest because the punishing climate had taken a terrible toll on horses and mules. Davis sent his opinion of the scheme to Congress: "For military purposes, and for reconnaissances, it is believed the dromedary would supply a want now seriously felt in our service." Three years later, Congress appropriated $30,000 for the project, and Davis dispatched Wayne to the Near East to buy 31 camels.

On April 12, 1855, Navy Lieutenant David D. Porter received orders to outfit the ship USS *Supply* with special stables for Major Wayne's camels. Porter virtually rebuilt the ship, adding a double row of stables, 20 portholes for ventilation, a hatch and tackles for lowering the animals into the hold, and a special scow for ferrying the camels to and from the shore. The scow could also be lifted from the water by manually operated cranes and set on the deck.

A LONG STRANGE TRIP

Porter sailed for Italy on June 12 and met Wayne a month later at La Spezia, Italy, near the farm of the grand duke of Tuscany, where

Not just a TV series: NCIS is the U.S. Navy's primary law-enforcement agency.

camels had been bred and used for 200 years. From there, Porter and Wayne sailed across the Mediterranean and stopped at Tunis to buy one camel so they could study the animal's habits before reaching Turkey, where all 30 camels were to be bought. The bey (ruler) of Tunis was in a charitable mood, and donated two more, one healthy and the other with a mysterious itch. During the voyage to Turkey, Porter did all he could to cure the ailing camel, but failed. While stopping at Constantinople to begin the search for camels, Porter sold the two unhealthiest dromedaries to a butcher.

The expedition suffered an immediate setback when Wayne and Porter learned that the British had taken all the better camels for use in the Crimean War. After wasting a month in Turkey, they crossed the Mediterranean and traveled up the Nile River to Cairo, Egypt, only to learn that the Egyptian viceroy had issued a general edict preventing the further exportation of camels. With help from the American consul, Porter haggled and eventually obtained two males and two females. Wayne insisted on finding a source for 20 more, so Porter sailed back to Turkey and entered Smyrna. At a local camel market, Wayne purchased 21 animals, all of which appeared to be healthy. Porter hired five locals to manage the penned herd during the voyage to their new, if temporary, home in Texas.

HOMEWARD BOUND

Porter made sure the camels were fed, watered, and brushed daily. For his part, Wayne had wanted as many camels as possible, so most of the females selected were with foal, and the handlers bred the others soon after they came on board. On the voyage home, a series of storms caused six premature births. Four calves died, three by the mother's refusal to nurse and one by being crushed during the ship's lurching. With the help of the five drivers, Porter transferred 33 camels, including newborns, from the ship to pens at Indianola, Texas. Upon landing and feeling solid ground under their hooves, the temperamental camels screamed, reared, kicked apart the pens, and finally settled down after Wayne's soldiers lassoed them.

THE U.S. ARMY CAMEL CORPS

Officially activated by the arrival of animals on April 29, 1856, the men of the U.S. Army Camel Corps set about preparing for active operations. Major Wayne took charge of his pet project and, after giving the herd several weeks to adapt to the climate and a new diet, moved the animals to permanent quarters at Camp Verde, 60 miles west of San Antonio. Although Wayne had originally informed Davis that the camels were wanted for "scientific purposes," he actually wanted them to solve his quartermaster problems in the Southwest. Through the 1848 Treaty of Guadalupe Hidalgo, Mexico had ceded present-day Arizona, California, Nevada, Utah, most of New Mexico, and parts of Wyoming and Colorado to the United States, but the area was still occupied by a few disaffected Mexicans and many angry American Indians.

Long ago, Wayne had decided that transporting supplies by camel was more efficient and less costly than using horses and mules, and he intended to prove it. His reasoning had merit. Camels were well suited to hot, arid regions and could carry loads four times greater than mules over longer distances with less food and water. The problem was that soldiers found the displaced creatures disagreeable. The camels bit, spit, and emitted a putrid odor that wouldn't wash away. Horses and mules bolted in their presence, which added to the soldiers' workload. And the camels' stubbornness and aggressiveness added to their unpopularity.

Two of the men who'd come to America with the camels taught the soldiers how to pack them. One, Hadji Ali, offered superior knowledge and management skills. Without him, the entire project might have ended disastrously even before the animals reached Texas.

CALIFORNIA, HERE WE COME

In June 1857, Lieutenant Edward Fitzgerald Beale departed from El Paso, Texas, on a mission to locate sites for Army posts, relay stations, and mail routes through the Southwest and into California. He took along 25 camels, a column of packed mules, 44 men, and Hadji Ali as chief camel driver. Each camel carried 600 to 800 pounds of supplies and traveled up to 30 miles a day. Months later, Beale returned to Texas and wrote a report praising them: "The harder the test they are put to, the more fully they seem to justify all that can be said of them. They pack water for days under a hot sun and never get a drop; they pack heavy bur-

Alfred Preis, the architect who designed the USS *Arizona* Memorial in Pearl Harbor...

dens of corn and oats for months and never get grain; and on the bitter greasewood and other worthless shrub, not only subsist, but keep fat." Beale neglected to mention that the camels didn't like the West's rocky soil and that horses and mules were afraid of them.

ANOTHER PACK OF CAMELS?

Jefferson Davis was so taken with the Camel Corps that he sent Lieutenant Porter back to Turkey for another load of animals while Major Wayne remained in Texas to run the operation. When Porter returned in 1857, the new secretary of war, John Floyd, urged Congress to purchase another thousand camels. But President James Buchanan and Congress were too preoccupied with the deterioration of relations between the North and the South to pay any attention to the proposal.

Lieutenant Beale tried to keep the Camel Corps active at the outset of the Civil War, but in November 1863 he finally shut it down. Beale let part of the herd live out their lives on his Texas ranch, but most were eventually released to the desert.

HADJI ALI'S DEPARTURE

Hadji Ali kept a few camels and started a freighting business between the Colorado River and some mining camps. Because rocks hurt the camels' feet, he tried wrapping their hooves in burlap. Later he made special shoes for their split toes, but the shoes didn't work that well. When his business failed, he released his camels in the desert near Gila Bend, Arizona.

Ali moved to Quartzsite, Arizona, and every so often would hear from a wandering American Indian that a great ugly beast with a horrible odor had swept through a campsite and disappeared into the night. The sightings pleased Ali because he knew his camels survived out in the hills. He died on December 16, 1902, and in the small community of Quartzsite, the Camel Corps is still remembered at Ali's grave. It's marked by a stone pyramid with an inscribed bronze plate recounting the history of the Camel Corps, and topped with a bronze camel facing into the desert.

...was detained in an internment camp during the war.

TOP 10 ADMIRALS, PART I

Prior to the Civil War, there were no admirals. The highest Navy rating was commodore, the equivalent of a rear admiral. Since World War II, there has never been an admiral exposed to serious combat with an enemy fleet.

1. JOHN PAUL JONES (1747–92)

The inscription on Jones's tomb at Annapolis reads, "He gave our navy its earliest traditions of heroism and victory." So people are often surprised to learn that he was born in Scotland. Jones went to sea at the age of 12 as a cabin boy. In 1766, after completing a seven-year apprenticeship, he became chief mate on a Jamaican slaver, but he was disgusted by the slave trade and obtained command of a merchantman instead. During a voyage to Tobago, he flogged a sailor, who later died. Imprisoned for murder and released on bail, Jones returned to Tobago to clear his name and unintentionally killed another sailor, whereupon he fled to Virginia and changed his surname to Jones.

The American Revolution

In 1775 Jones fitted out the 20-gun *Alfred*, the first ship purchased by the Continental Navy. Commissioned senior lieutenant, he sailed with Commodore Esek Hopkins's squadron and in March 1776 participated in the capture of New Providence in the Bahamas. Jones earned distinction battling the HMS *Glasgow* and became captain of the 12-gun *Providence*, which he used to capture 16 British ships. Jones continued to raid British shipping until June 1777, when he took command of the 18-gun sloop of war *Ranger*.

When Jones sailed the *Ranger* to France in 1778, he received the first salute to the Continental flag as he entered Quiberon Bay. He then sailed into the Irish Sea, raided two forts at Whitehaven, England, and after a second raid on St. Mary's Island in Galway Firth, he captured the 20-gun HMS *Drake* in a battle off Ireland's coast in April 1778. On May 8 he sailed into Brest, France, with seven prizes, marking the beginning of his international notoriety.

France, intending to go to war with England, hailed Jones as a hero, and put him in charge of an Anglo-French squadron comprised of two Continental ships—the 42-gun *Bon Homme Richard*

James K. Polk was the U.S. president during the Mexican-American War.

and the 36-gun *Alliance*—and two French ships, the 32-gun *Pallas* and the 12-gun *Vengeance*. Jones encountered a British merchant fleet escorted by the 50-gun HMS *Serapis* in the North Sea. In a fierce three-hour moonlit battle on September 23, 1779, and with his ship battered and taking on water, Jones demonstrated superior seamanship, maneuvered into a raking position, and forced the surrender of the *Serapis*. Two days later, when the *Bon Homme Richard* sank, Jones sailed back to France in the *Serapis*.

What Made Him Great

Jones returned to America with the greatest naval combat record of the war and received the Congressional Gold Medal. His remains were returned from France in 1905 and are enshrined at the Naval Academy at Annapolis.

2. STEPHEN DECATUR (1779–1820)

As a young man, Decatur worked at the Philadelphia shipbuilding firm of Gurney and Smith during the construction of the 44-gun frigate *United States*. He left the University of Pennsylvania in 1798 to join the Navy as a midshipman on the *United States*.

The Barbary Wars

Decatur served in Commodore Richard Dale's squadron during the First Barbary War (1801–5). Commanding the 12-gun schooner *Enterprise*, in 1803 he captured the Tripolitan ketch *Mastico* and on the night of February 16, 1804, used it to creep into Tripoli's fortified harbor and destroy the captured U.S. frigate *Philadelphia*. Admiral Lord Nelson described Decatur's action as "the most bold and daring act of the age." Decatur was just getting warmed up. On August 3, 1804, during the bombing of Tripoli, he boarded and captured an enemy gunboat. Presented a sword of honor by Congress, he became the Navy's youngest captain at the age of 25.

The War of 1812

At the outbreak of the War of 1812, Decatur took command of the 44-gun *United States*. He put to sea as part of Commodore John Rodgers's squadron and on October 25, 1812, captured the British frigate *Macedonian*. Decatur sent the prize to New York to be added to the fleet. Named commodore and given a squadron to defend

Veterans of Foreign Wars (VFW), the largest group of combat vets, has 1.6 million members.

New York harbor, in January 1815 he tried to sail the 44-gun frigate *President* through the British blockade. Surrounded by enemy ships, Decatur agreed to surrender. A month later, the war ended and Decatur returned to New York.

Another Barbary War

In May 1815, Decatur returned to the Mediterranean with 10 ships and quickly captured two large Algerian warships. He dictated his peace terms with the dey of Algeria "at the mouths of cannon," secured the release of American sailors, and returned to the United States to serve on the Board of Naval Commissioners. "Our Country! In her intercourse with foreign nations, may she always be right; but [I drink to] our country, right or wrong!" was Stephen Decatur's toast to America in November 1815.

What Made Him Great

Decatur had the temperament of a warrior and proved it by the way he fought. He lost his life on March 22, 1820, in a duel with Commodore James Barron. A fearless and resourceful commodore, Decatur had already become one of America's greatest admirals.

3. MATTHEW CALBRAITH PERRY (1794–1858)

The foremost naval officer of his time, Matthew Perry did more for America than fight. A Rhode Islander, Perry joined the U.S. Navy as a midshipman in 1809, served four years at sea, and in 1813 received his commission as lieutenant.

A Man of Many Talents

During the War of 1812, Perry served under Stephen Decatur on the USS *United States* and in 1815 sailed with him during the war with Algeria, where he first became involved in diplomatic missions. In 1822 he helped colonize Monrovia, the capital of Liberia, and in 1825–26, while commanding the 74-gun USS *South Carolina*, he worked on establishing the first treaty with Turkey. Perry returned to America, where he fostered the development of the Navy's first steam-powered ships. Promoted to commodore in June 1841, he also helped establish the Naval Academy in 1845.

At the outset of the Mexican-American War in 1846, Perry led raids along the east coast of Mexico and on March 21, 1847,

Operation Blue Bat: name of the 1958 operation when the U.S. intervened in Lebanon.

assumed command of the Home Squadron. He bombarded Veracruz on March 22–23, opening the way for Winfield Scott's amphibious landing. He then supported the general by assaulting ports along the Gulf of Mexico.

In 1852 Perry volunteered for a mission into the Pacific to open trade with Japan. Using the steam frigate USS *Mississippi* as his flagship, he assembled a four-ship squadron and on July 8 entered Tokyo Bay. The Japanese, who traditionally shunned contact with the outside world, were as much impressed by Perry's courtesy as by his heavily armed steamships. Perry presented a letter from President Millard Fillmore and promised to return for an answer. In February 1854, Perry reentered Tokyo Bay with eight ships, concluded the Treaty of Kanagawa, and the United States became the first Western nation to open relations with Japan.

What Made Him Great

Always a stern but energetic and visionary commander, Perry became the "father of the steam navy." A skilled diplomat, he masterfully succeeded at everything he did. Historian Samuel Eliot Morison called him the foremost naval officer of his time.

4. DAVID GLASGOW FARRAGUT (1801–70)

Farragut lost his mother in 1808 and became the foster son of Commodore David Porter. At age nine, he served as a midshipman on Porter's 32-gun frigate *Essex*; the crew called him "Mr. Farragut." After cruising in the South Pacific and surviving a battle with the HMS *Phoebe* during the War of 1812, Farragut became a lieutenant in 1825 and joined Porter's campaign against Caribbean pirates. Farragut never fought in the Mexican War. Instead, the Navy put him in command of the USS *Decatur* and in 1854 ordered him to California to establish the Mare Island Navy Yard.

The Civil War

With the outbreak of the Civil War, Secretary of the Navy Gideon Welles gave Farragut command of the West Gulf Blockading Squadron with orders to attack New Orleans. After much difficulty getting his heavy oceangoing ships over the sandbar of the Mississippi River, Farragut's squadron broke the chain barrier between Forts Jackson and St. Philip, endured 15 minutes of heavy crossfire, destroyed the Confederates' defense fleet, and on April 25 captured New Orleans. Farragut then led his ships upriver and on June 28 ran Vicksburg's batteries. Eighteen days later, he became the Navy's first rear admiral. Returning downriver, Farragut blockaded the Red River and aided Major General Nathaniel Banks's capture of Port Hudson.

During the summer of 1864, Farragut obtained approval from Welles to capture Mobile Bay. Confederate defenses consisted of Fort Morgan and Fort Gaines at the entrance to the bay and Fort Powell inside the bay. Between Morgan and Gaines lay a field of submerged contact mines called torpedoes. Admiral Franklin Buchanan commanded a small Confederate squadron, the centerpiece being the powerful CSS *Tennessee*, a heavily armed, impregnable ironclad. Welles barred Farragut from entering the bay without ironclad monitors, which he sent in July.

At dawn on August 5, Farragut steamed toward Mobile Bay with 14 wooden ships and four ironclad monitors. The lead monitor, *Tecumseh*, struck a torpedo and sank. The *Brooklyn*, steaming in front Farragut's flagship *Hartford*, stopped for fear of striking a torpedo and stalled the entire squadron under the guns of Fort Morgan. Farragut, standing in the tops, hollered to the deck, "Damn the torpedoes! Full speed ahead!" and led the squadron through the minefield and into Mobile Bay. In a two-hour battle, Farragut aggressively forced the surrender of the *Tennessee* and later assisted in the capture of the forts.

What Made Him Great

Farragut was the outstanding naval officer of the Civil War. A brilliant tactician, audacious in battle, and loved by his men, on July 25, 1866, Farragut became the Navy's first full admiral.

5. DAVID DIXON PORTER (1813–91)

The Civil War created 104 major generals but only seven rear admirals. Next to Farragut, Porter was the best, and in an unusual way, both came from the same family. Being the third of Captain David Porter's 10 children, David Dixon's large family included a foster brother, 12-year-old David Farragut, already a Navy midshipman. David Dixon joined the Navy in 1829, served in the Mediterranean, and while attached to the Coast Survey in 1841 became a lieutenant. During the Mexican-American War, he served in Commodore Matthew C. Perry's squadron, took part in the assault on Veracruz, and distinguished himself during the Tabasco campaign in June 1847. Like Farragut, peacetime service bored him, so in 1849 he took a furlough and for six years commanded packet steamers. He rejoined the Navy as a first lieutenant and made two trips to the Mediterranean to obtain camels for the Army. Posted afterward to another boring assignment, Porter thought of resigning, but the Civil War changed his mind.

The Civil War

When Secretary of the Navy Gideon Welles put Farragut in command of the New Orleans expedition, he sent Porter along with a flotilla of mortar schooners. The mortar squadron bombarded Forts Jackson and St. Philip and opened the way for Farragut's ships to run upriver. After Farragut captured New Orleans, Porter negotiated the surrender of the forts.

Following Farragut's squadron to Vicksburg, Porter remained upriver and eventually accumulated a squadron of 80 gunboats and mortar schooners. Commanding this force with superb skill, Porter became acting rear admiral of the Mississippi Squadron over the heads of every senior officer but Farragut. Nobody worked harder with General Ulysses S. Grant than Porter in forcing Vicksburg's surrender on July 4, 1863.

In late 1864, after Farragut became too ill to lead the Fort Fisher expedition, Welles put Porter in charge of the North Atlantic Blockading Squadron. Porter complained as soon as he learned General Benjamin F. Butler, perhaps the Union army's most incompetent political general, was to lead the assault. As Porter predicted, Butler failed. Grant replaced Butler, and Porter's second effort resulted in the capture of Fort Fisher.

What Made Him Great

Bold, energetic, and resourceful, Porter was, by all accounts, one of America's great fighting admirals. He let nothing stand in his way. After the death of Farragut in 1870, Porter became the second full admiral in the U.S. Navy.

For more top admirals, turn to page 119.

LINCOLN GOES TO WAR

He may have been a great president, but he was only a so-so soldier.

THE BRITISH BAND

In 1832 Illinois governor John Reynolds needed volunteers to repel an incursion by Sauk chief Black Hawk and his "British Band," a group of American Indian tribes that had supported the British in the War of 1812. The Sauk were joined by the Fox, Kickapoo, Ho-Chunk, and Potowatomi; the entire band consisted of about 500 warriors and 1,000 women, children, and old men. They were fighting for land in northwestern Illinois that had belonged to the Sauk before a series of treaties pushed them west.

Abraham Lincoln was 23 when he joined the Sangamon County militia on April 16, 1832, as a private. The general store in New Salem where he'd been working had closed and Lincoln—who was also running for the state legislature—hoped a war record would help him get more votes. His friends elected him company captain, and the unit became "Captain Abraham Lincoln's Company of the [Fourth] Regiment of the Brigade of Mounted Volunteers commanded by Brigadier General Samuel Whiteside." The Mounted Volunteers had no horses, however; they walked instead.

None of the volunteers had any experience fighting Indians, but state law compelled every able-bodied man between the ages of 18 and 45 to drill twice a year or pay a $1 fine. Nobody had a dollar to waste, so everybody drilled.

IN COMMAND OF CALAMITIES

Captain Lincoln had no experience giving orders, and he never became adept at using firearms. His first official order, to an independent-minded volunteer, drew the response "Go to hell." As an officer, Lincoln carried a pistol and a sword instead of a flintlock rifle. When he accidentally fired the gun in camp, violating rules issued by Whiteside, he had to serve a day under arrest.

One day, some hungry men from the company raided officers' supplies, stole whiskey, and went to bed drunk. When Lincoln's men appeared intoxicated at the morning roll call, General Whiteside, whose whiskey they had swiped, court-martialed Lincoln. He was found guilty of dereliction of duty and spent the next two days walking through camp carrying a wooden sword as punishment.

COMPANY HALT!

A week later, Colonel (and future president) Zachary Taylor arrived and assumed command of the regiment. In a prophetic speech he told 1,600 volunteers, including the Sangamon County men, that as Illinois citizens, among them "would probably be congressmen [who would] go to Washington" someday.

Perhaps in an effort to impress Taylor, Lincoln began drilling two platoons. One day, as the file marched toward a gate, he forgot the command that would change the men from a file to an endwise column of twos. As the file headed into the fence, Lincoln blurted, "This company is dismissed for two minutes, when it will fall in again on the other side of the gate."

Episodes like this didn't go unnoticed by Reynolds, who received regular reports on the conduct of his militia and, on occasion, visited the camps. Already embarrassed by the lack of discipline in Whiteside's command, the governor disbanded the so-called Mounted Volunteers.

PRIVATES HAVE MORE FUN

Because Lincoln still needed a job, and because of his belief that a war record might aid his political career, he and several friends reenlisted for 30 days in General Robert Anderson's brigade as privates. Anderson assigned Lincoln to Captain Elijah Iles's company of Independent Rangers, which carried messages and reported on Black Hawk's movements. Because the volunteers had no camp duties and drew rations as they pleased, Lincoln found being a private more to his liking than assuming the duties of a captain.

SECRET AGENT MAN

On June 16, Lincoln reenlisted for yet another 30 days and joined Captain Jacob M. Early's Independent Spy Corps. A Methodist minister from Springfield, Illinois, Early had once been a private under former Captain Lincoln and later under Captain Iles. The closest Lincoln came to fighting with the Indians occurred on June 25 at Kellogg's Grove on the upper Rock River. He arrived too late to participate in the battle, but came in time to bury five men who had been scalped. The company pursued Black Hawk into the Michigan Territory (present-day Wisconsin), which Lincoln recalled as the hardest march of his life. When provisions gave out on July 10, three weeks before the last battle, Early disbanded the company and sent the volunteers home. Someone stole Lincoln's horse, so he walked with friends as far as Peoria in central Illinois, bought a canoe, paddled down the Illinois River to the town of Havana, and walked the rest of the way back to New Salem.

FRIGHT IN THE NIGHT

By all accounts, Lincoln survived the campaign without ever seeing one of Black Hawk's warriors or participating in any fights, but he came close in one other action. While camping with his company beside the Fox River, an alarm startled them. Drums and fifes sounded, horses ran wildly through the camp, muskets were fired, and battle lines formed around the camp. Everyone clutched his gun, and no one slept that night, but nothing of note happened.

ABE GOES POSTAL

Lincoln's war record failed to launch his political career as a Whig, at least in 1832, when he won his hometown vote but lost his bid for the state legislature. He wasn't discouraged; six weeks later, he filled a local post as clerk for the September election in New Salem. Before the year ended, a political patron persuaded President Andrew Jackson to name Lincoln postmaster of New Salem.

UP THE POLITICAL LADDER

In a small way, the Black Hawk War gave Lincoln a boost in the polls. What he actually did mattered less than the fact that he had served: he'd marched in the mud, slept in the rain, and discharged his weapon—even if it was by accident. In 1834 he was elected to the state legislature and served four two-year terms. Licensed to practice law in 1836, he remained politically active and in 1847 served a term in the U.S. House of Representatives. As a member of the new Republican Party, Lincoln lost a close Senate race to Democrat Stephen A. Douglas in 1858, but it was enough to elevate him onto the national stage: in 1860, he became the 16th president of the United States.

...The U.S. Air Force's F-100 broke the sound barrier on May 25, 1953—its maiden flight.

IT'S A DOG TAG'S LIFE

The history of military identification tags.

Only 58 percent of the soldiers killed in action during the American Civil War were positively identified. Soldiers had a legitimate concern that if they were killed, their families would never know what happened to them—other than that they were missing in action. Each soldier started writing his name on a piece of paper or a handkerchief and pinning it to his clothing before going into battle. Some soldiers went to the trouble of carving small wooden disks with their names on them, then drilling a hole in the disk and hanging the disk from their necks with a piece of string. Others made their own ID tags by grinding off one side of a coin and then etching their name on it. Voilà! The first ID tags—but not yet called "dog tags."

IF YOU MAKE IT, THEY WILL BUY

Eventually, retail merchants started producing and selling metal disks to soldiers. During the Civil War, *Harper's Weekly* magazine advertised "soldier's pins" made of silver or gold and etched with the soldier's name and unit. Dogs wore similar identification tags, so it wasn't long before soldiers began referring to their ID tags as "dog tags."

STANDARD ISSUE

By the 1890s, the U.S. Army and Navy were experimenting with metal identification tags for recruits. ID tags were first officially issued to U.S. Army troops in 1906. During World War I, each French soldier wore a bracelet with a metal disk called a *plaque d'identité* that was engraved with the soldier's name, rank, and formation. When America entered the war in 1917, all soldiers were issued two aluminum tags that were stamped by hand with their name, rank, serial number, unit, and religion. The tags were suspended from their necks by cord or tape.

HEARST IS THE WORST

In the 1930s, when the government was considering ways to assign Social Security numbers, someone whose name is lost to history suggested that the numbers be stamped on a metal plate and worn like a dog tag by civilians. The idea was quickly shot down by the powers that be. But that didn't stop Franklin D. Roosevelt's adversary, William Randolph Hearst, from claiming during the very heated 1936 election campaign that the Roosevelt administration was planning to require everyone to wear dog tags.

THE GREATEST DOG TAGS

World War II dog tags were rectangular with rounded ends and a notch at one end (now stamped by machine). It was rumored that the notch was put in the tag so that the tag could be placed in a dead soldier's mouth to hold it open so that gases would escape and the body wouldn't become bloated. The truth was a lot less gruesome. The stamping machine required a notch to hold the blank tag in place while it was being stamped.

The tags were first made of brass and later of a corrosion-resistant alloy of nickel and copper. By the end of the war, all tags were made of stainless steel. They were suspended from the neck by a rope, a beaded chain, or a stainless-steel wire with a plastic cover.

THOROUGHLY MODERN DOG TAGS

During the Vietnam War, new stamping machines were used, and the notch was eliminated. Soldiers started taping their tags together so that they wouldn't make any noise and give away their position. By the end of the war, rubber covers were issued to keep the tags silent. A soldier often put one tag in his boot, in case his body was dismembered and normal means of identification were impossible.

IRAQI ARMY ISSUE

American-style dog tags are a worldwide phenomenon, thanks to the post–World War II export of blanks and stamping machines by the United States. In fact, during the two Persian Gulf wars, Iraqi soldiers wore dog tags that were identical to their American counterparts—except that the printing was in Arabic.

...Divided along the 38th parallel, North and South Korea are technically still at war.

HIGH-TECH DOG TAGS FOR HUMANS

The soldier of the future will wear dog tags that hold a microchip containing his or her medical and dental records, and which will be called a "personal information carrier." The U.S. Marines have developed their own version, called the Tactical Medical Coordination System, which can pinpoint the location of a wounded soldier using the Global Positioning System.

* * *

WORLD WAR I HERO STUBBY

Stubby, a bull terrier mix, volunteered for service by showing up at the 102nd Infantry Yale University training camp. Private J. Robert Conroy smuggled Stubby aboard when they shipped out to France. The stowaway soldier captured a spy on the battlefield by securely holding onto the German's posterior with his teeth! General John J. Pershing gave Stubby a gold Humane Society medal. President Woodrow Wilson shook hands with the canine hero.

* * *

WORLD WAR II DOG HEROES

Shortly after the attack on Pearl Harbor, "Dogs for Defense" partnered with the American Kennel Club to encourage patriotic Americans to donate dogs for military service. Dogs were initially trained as sentries, but their duties expanded to include serving on patrol, acting as messengers, and detecting land mines. (Canines sniff out land mines more often and more accurately than modern equipment!) In 1942 the Army assumed responsibility for the procurement and training of dogs when the demand for these valuable assets had grown too large for the civilian groups to manage.

"Crush" was the World War II Allied code name for the United States of America.

THE AGE OF WAR

Young, inexperienced soldiers are often eager to fight and show their bravery in combat. Veterans and elders have a different perspective.

"Old soldiers never die, just young ones."

—Unknown

"Older men declare war. But it is youth that must fight and die."

—Herbert Hoover

"Old soldiers never die: they just fade away."

—General Douglas MacArthur

"If you think old soldiers just fade away, just try to get into your old uniform."

—Jackie Gleason

"There is many a boy here today who looks on war as all glory, but boys, it is all hell."

—Gen. William T. Sherman, August 11, 1880

"I don't think old men ought to promote wars for young men to fight. I don't like warlike men."

—Walter Lippmann

"It is well that war is so terrible; otherwise, we would grow too fond of it."

—General Robert E. Lee

"The object of war is not to die for your country but to make the other bastard die for his."

—General George S. Patton

"The time not to become a father is eighteen years before a war."

—E. B. White

"In peace, the sons bury their fathers, but in war, the fathers bury their sons."

—Croesus

"No young man believes he shall ever die."

—William Hazlitt

"And like the old soldier in that ballad, I now close my military career and just fade away, an old soldier who tried to do his duty as God gave him the sight to see that duty."

—Douglas MacArthur

You can be fined up to $100,000 for making or selling a fake Medal of Honor.

GASBAGS GO TO WAR

No, we're not talking about generals giving bombastic speeches. We're talking about hot-air balloons and the daredevils who developed and flew them.

UP, UP, AND AWAY

Leonardo da Vinci conceived the idea of mechanical flight around 1500, and for the next three centuries men killed themselves trying to conquer the skies with various contraptions. The first to succeed and live to tell the tale were Frenchmen Jean-François Pilâtre de Rozier and Marquis d'Arlondes who, on November 21, 1783, stepped into a basket, filled an enormous gasbag with hydrogen, traveled 15 miles by air, and became the world's first successful balloonists.

Benjamin Franklin, in Paris on a diplomatic mission at the time, was fascinated by the event. Always ahead of his time, Franklin advised George Washington that balloons should be developed for military reconnaissance. Eight years later, when Jean-Pierre Blanchard visited the United States following a successful flight across the English Channel, Washington watched him lift off from Philadelphia and sail over the Delaware River before landing safely in New Jersey. Although Washington recognized the military potential of ballooning, Congress refused to appropriate funds.

DOWN AND OUT

Ballooning didn't take off again for more than 50 years. During the 1840 Seminole War, Colonel John H. Sherburne's requisition for several $900 balloons to aid in locating hostile Indians was rejected by the War Department. Six years later, John Wise's offer of several balloons to reconnoiter and bomb enemy positions during the Mexican War was ignored by the Army. Wise continued to develop the balloon's capabilities, and on July 1, 1859, established a world record by sailing 809 miles across the skies from St. Louis to New York in 19 hours and 40 minutes.

Civilians continued to develop the science of early aeronautics, but the Army ignored the technology until the Civil War. One week after the Battle of Fort Sumter, James Allen headed to Washington with two balloons and offered his services to the Army. Brigadier General Irvin McDowell, the recently appointed Army commander, was interested: he detailed Allen to perform reconnaissance of a Confederate outpost near Centreville, Virginia. Allen's portable gas generator failed and the balloon never left the ground. Next, he inflated his balloons at a gas plant outside Washington, where one promptly burst. Several days before McDowell's July 1861 Bull Run campaign, Allen carted the other one to Virginia for reconnaissance, where it was impaled by a telephone pole, thus ending Allen's war effort—but not ballooning's.

WHAT ELSE COULD GO WRONG?

Lieutenant Henry L. Abbot of the Corps of Engineers recognized the potential of aerial reconnaissance and encouraged the creation of a balloon corps. He contacted 53-year-old John Wise, whose offer of the use of balloons during the Mexican War had been ignored.

Major Albert J. Myer, the Army's signal officer, enlisted Wise in the Signal Corps and took charge of the project. Wise delivered the balloon on July 16, 1861, just in time for the first battle of Bull Run. Myer insisted the balloon be inflated at Alexandria and attached to a wagon driven by a team of horses, but overly anxious to reach the battlefield, the major pushed too hard. The balloon scuffed against roadside trees, the casing ripped, and the Union fought the first battle of Bull Run without aerial reconnaissance.

Wise repaired the balloon, and on July 25 made an ascent over Arlington, Virginia. Enemy gunfire punctured the casing, which slowly withered and fell in a heap of torn cloth and tangled cordage near the former home of Confederate General Robert E. Lee. Recognizing the advantages of transporting the balloons when flat and not inflating them until needed, Wise asked the Army to purchase a transportable hydrogen generator. The major receiving the request refused it, and Wise resigned in exasperation.

SUCCESS AT LAST

The use of balloons during the Civil War might have ended there were it not for another balloonist named John LaMountain. After being ignored by the War Department, he offered his services to Major General Benjamin F. Butler. The general enjoyed upstaging the War Department and invited LaMountain to his headquarters at Fort Monroe, Virginia. The balloonist made six ascents between June 25 and August 10, 1861, filing detailed reports of enemy activity following each reconnaissance. More innovative than Allen or Wise, LaMountain attached his balloon to the armed transport vessel *Fanny* and ascended to 2,000 feet, higher than any other balloonist had gone before. A few days later, this time from land, he lifted to 3,500 feet, spotted a Confederate force of 5,000 troops, and made sketches for General Butler from aloft.

But LaMountain's good fortune was short-lived. General Butler was delighted with LaMountain's performance, so he sent him to Washington to obtain a larger balloon. There, because of a bureaucratic mix-up in communications, LaMountain was reassigned to Major General George B. McClellan's Army of the Potomac, where he encountered balloonist Thaddeus S. C. Lowe, his biggest rival in the business of ballooning.

THE LOWE-DOWN

Lowe was only 29 years old, but was already quite the experienced balloonist. He'd once planned to sail across the Atlantic in a competition with LaMountain, but the Civil War had intervened. Lowe went to Washington on June 18, 1861, to demonstrate the usefulness of balloons by soaring overhead and telegraphing messages to the ground (a practice that was still in use during World War I). The next day he made an ascent from the grounds of the White House as Abraham Lincoln and his cabinet watched. The exhibition impressed the president, who personally escorted Lowe to General-in-Chief Winfield Scott's office so that the balloonist could be commissioned by the Army. Scott agreed, but reluctantly, and Lowe became the civilian chief of aeronautics, a job that earned him the same pay as a colonel. Lowe built a 25,000-cubic-foot balloon named the *Union* and on August 29 made his first ascent outside Washington. A month later he performed a new airborne first by directing the Union's artillery fire at Confederate targets near Manassas, Virginia.

Tanks were first used in 1916 at the Battle of Flers-Courcelette on the Somme.

When McClellan moved the Army of the Potomac to Virginia's peninsula during spring 1862, Lowe joined the campaign with a pair of balloons and two portable gas generators. He added photographic reconnaissance to his aerial observations, which launched a new dimension to tactical flight. McClellan rewarded Lowe's effort with an $8,600 appropriation to build more airships.

MY BALLOON'S BIGGER THAN YOUR BALLOON

During the Peninsula Campaign, Lowe and LaMountain each tried to diminish the accomplishments of the other. In an effort to inspire cooperation, McClellan added LaMountain to the payroll at the same daily pay rate that Lowe was getting. LaMountain proved to be the better balloonist. He developed a system using lower wind currents to fly over the enemy's position and upper wind currents as high as 18,000 feet to fly back. Confederate weapons didn't have the range to bring down LaMountain's balloon, which forced gun crews to use camouflage.

The rivalry between LaMountain and Lowe continued to fester because the latter had all the balloons. When LaMountain went to Washington to requisition one of Lowe's balloons, he made the mistake of denouncing his superior and McClellan dismissed him for insubordination. Lowe could be outspoken as well. He later ran afoul of Major General Joseph Hooker during the Chancellorsville Campaign in May 1863, so Hooker reduced Lowe's pay. The balloonist, who by then had completed 3,000 ascents, resigned in disgust.

AHEAD OF THEIR TIME

Allen, Wise, LaMountain, and Lowe pioneered military flight by ascending in what most Army officers derisively called "gasbags." Their efforts marked the beginning of flight in America's wars 40 years before Wilbur and Orville Wright succeeded in getting the first heavier-than-air contraption—the *Wright Flyer*—off the ground for 59 seconds on December 17, 1903. The airplane would render balloons obsolete, although the gasbags were still up, up, and away and performing reconnaissance throughout World War I.

The U.S. Civil Air Patrol has 52 wings and 1,500 units in eight geographic regions.

THE SENECA SOLDIER

When Lee surrendered his forces to Grant on April 8, 1865, Ely S. Parker—the only Native American in the room—was on hand to observe the historic moment.

THE MAKING OF ELY PARKER

The man who would become Ely S. Parker was given the Seneca name Hasanoanda at his birth in 1828. An Iroquois of the Seneca tribe, he spent his childhood on the Tonawanda Reservation in western New York. His mother enrolled him at a nearby Baptist mission school so he could receive a mainstream American education, and he adopted the first name of the school's minister and took the name Ely Samuel Parker. An exceptional student, he continued his education at Yates Academy in 1842, the only Native American student in a class of 119. Because of his exposure to white culture and his ability to speak fluent English, Parker could communicate with people inside and outside his tribe, a skill that would serve him well throughout his life. Lewis Henry Morgan, an attorney with a passion for Iroquois culture, became his mentor and helped him get into the elite Cayuga Academy in Aurora, New York, where Parker honed his debating skills. He would need them for what was ahead.

FAILURES AND SUCCESSES

The 1838 and 1842 Treaties of Buffalo Creek threatened to remove Parker's people from the ancient Tonawanda lands and relocate them to Kansas. Because of his language skills, Parker was appointed by his elders as translator, interpreter, and scribe. He helped them file state and federal appeals to keep their lands in New York and traveled to Washington, D.C., in 1846 to lobby for his people. When his efforts proved unsuccessful, Parker returned to New York to study law. But after three years of schooling, he wasn't allowed to take the bar exam because he wasn't an American citizen. So, with another assist from Lewis Morgan, Parker entered Rensselaer Polytechnic Institute to study engineering. He landed a job as a civil engineer working on the expansion of the Erie Canal in 1850, building his reputation in the field.

In World War I, the German army was the best equipped among all the powers.

HAIL TO THE CHIEF

His reputation was growing among the Seneca, too. In 1851, because of his earlier work in Washington trying to protect Seneca lands, Ely Parker was named one of the 50 sachems, the council of chiefs of the five Iroquois nations. He continued to work to protect their lands in New York and finally succeeded in 1857: a treaty was drawn up that allowed the Tonawanda Senecas to buy back more than 7,000 acres of their land using the monies set aside for their relocation to Kansas. Parker's efforts gave his people a permanent home, one that still exists today.

FRIENDLY AND FAMOUS

As Parker's reputation as a civil engineer continued to grow, he was sent to Galena, Illinois, to supervise construction of a federal customhouse (which still stands today as a landmark). It was there that he struck up a friendship with an ex-Army officer who had given up on a military career. The friend's name? Ulysses S. Grant.

After graduating from West Point, Grant fought in the Mexican-American War (1846–48) and served in various military posts before his mysterious resignation in 1854. He tried his hand at farming, and then worked as a bill collector prior to returning to Galena in 1860 to work as a clerk in his father's store, which is where Ely Parker met him. The two became lifelong friends.

YOU GO YOUR WAY . . .

In April 1861, after President Lincoln's call for 75,000 volunteers, Grant took an appointment in Springfield, Illinois, to train new recruits. When he asked for a field command, the Illinois governor promoted him to colonel and put him in charge of the 21st Illinois Infantry. Grant's successes on the Western fronts and a string of victories in important battles brought him fame and acclaim. He rose through the ranks to become general-in-chief of all Union forces in 1864.

I'LL GO MINE

Parker's path took a different turn. He returned to New York and offered his services as an army engineer but was turned down by the governor—Indians were not wanted in the New York Volun-

U.S. Navy enlisted personnel do not use the term "rank"...

teers. He tried to raise a volunteer regiment of Iroquois soldiers for the Union, but the War Department refused their services. Parker appealed to fellow New Yorker William Seward, the secretary of state. Seward allegedly told Parker that the war was a white man's affair and to "go back to his farm." Seeing no other options, Parker did return to his farm and spent two years there trying to find a way to fight for the Union.

GENERAL DELIVERY

The solution came in 1863, when an old Galena friend, John E. Smith, helped Parker finally obtain a commission. Smith had risen to the rank of brigadier general, so all it took was a letter to the War Department. Parker was made assistant adjutant general of volunteers, with the rank of captain. In July, Captain Parker traveled to Vicksburg, Mississippi, to serve in the Union army alongside his friend Grant. He joined Grant's staff as military secretary.

Grant came to rely heavily on his old friend for his skills as an engineer and as a writer. After the Union victory at Chattanooga, Grant asked Parker to draft a congratulatory letter to his soldiers because Parker was "good at that sort of thing." Even at the pivotal moment at Appomattox Court House, Parker played an important role: all of the surrender documents are in his handwriting. He transcribed the articles of surrender because, as another Union officer admitted, his handwriting was the best.

When Robert E. Lee first arrived at Appomattox Court House, Grant introduced Parker to Lee as one of his staff. Lee seemed taken aback because of Parker's darker skin, then apologized. As Lee shook Parker's hand, he said, "I am glad to see one real American here," to which Parker replied, "Sir, we are all Americans."

UNHAPPY ENDING

After the war, Parker followed Grant to Washington. Grant was best man at Parker's 1867 wedding to a white socialite—a marriage that alienated some Senecas. In 1869 Grant appointed him commissioner of Indian affairs, in which capacity he served until 1871. He moved to Fairfield, Connecticut, and became a successful businessman but lost his fortune five years later. His last job was as a desk clerk for the New York City Police Department.

...The correct term is "rate." Only officers have ranks.

GUERRILLA WARFARE, PART II

The Civil War (for Part I, turn to page 29).

The hit-and-run tactics of guerrilla warfare were further refined with the use of cavalry units during the Civil War. Men on horseback with revolvers and repeating rifles could surprise and outgun much larger infantry forces who were mostly armed with muskets. Then, they could withdraw quickly and disappear into the wilderness.

MOSBY'S RAIDERS

Colonel John S. Mosby led a band of Confederate soldiers behind Union lines in northern Virginia. Because of his ability to hit the North's supply lines and then disappear into the countryside, he was given the nickname "the Gray Ghost." He so dominated the area militarily that it became known as "Mosby's Confederacy."

In 1863 he and 29 of his men captured Union general Edwin H. Stoughton at the Fairfax Court House. Legend has it that the general was roused from his bed with a slap on the rear end. On another occasion, Mosby nearly captured the train on which Union general Ulysses S. Grant was traveling.

Mosby and his men were paroled at the end of the Civil War. He supported his former adversary, Ulysses S. Grant, when Grant ran for the presidency in 1868 because Mosby believed that Grant was the best man to restore the South and heal the country. Because of Mosby's distinguished war record, he was encouraged by Southern leaders to run for public office, but he declined. Later, President Rutherford B. Hayes named him the consul to Hong Kong and he served in that post with distinction. Mosby practiced law in San Francisco after his return to private life.

QUANTRILL'S RAIDERS

William C. Quantrill led a band of pro-slavery raiders in Kansas and Missouri before the Civil War. After the war started, he and

The Civil War's Battle of Perryville was the largest battle fought in the state of Kentucky.

his men were sworn into the Confederate army, and he was given the rank of captain.

In 1863 Quantrill led his 300-plus followers in a violent attack on Lawrence, Kansas, burning the major buildings and killing or executing between 150 and 200 men and boys in the town. Later that year, Quantrill and his men disguised themselves in Union blue to launch an attack on the Union's outpost at Baxter Springs, Kansas.

Quantrill's brutal tactics earned him a reputation as a cruel and vicious leader. The Northern generals were determined to stop him, and in 1865, in an ambush by Union guerrillas near Taylorsville, Kentucky, Quantrill was shot. He died a month later, at the age of 27.

JESSIE'S SCOUTS

Union General John C. Frémont organized a special-ops group called "Jessie's Scouts," named after his wife. They often wore Confederate uniforms and operated in western Virginia and the Shenandoah Valley, where they conducted raids on communications and supply lines and carried out assassinations.

IT AIN'T OVER TILL IT'S OVER

At the end of the Civil War, Confederate president Jefferson Davis and other Southern leaders wanted to continue the fight as a guerrilla war, but most of the Confederate generals opposed them, including Robert E. Lee, who considered that course of action to be dishonorable.

Many of the men who had fought with Mosby and Quantrill were unwilling or unable to return to civilian life. They became some of the era's most notorious outlaws—men like Jesse and Frank James, Cole Younger and his brothers, and the Dalton gang.

Turn to page 176 for Part III.

* * *

"War loses a great deal of its romance after a soldier has seen his first battle."

—John Singleton Mosby, 1887

A Marine Corps slogan: "When it absolutely, positively has to be destroyed overnight."

MEDICAL MARVELS

Many cornerstones of civilian health care can be traced back to American battlefields. Even George Washington got into the act.

REVOLUTIONARY TACTICS

George Washington contracted smallpox in his younger days, so he knew how debilitating it could be. His army was the first ever to be inoculated against smallpox. Some historians say that the decision was among the most critical factors in winning the Revolutionary War.

SAVING LIVES THE NEW-FASHIONED WAY

In the Civil War, a Union surgeon, Jonathan Letterman, was horrified by the thousands of wounded men abandoned on the battlefields in the early days of the war. After he was appointed medical director of the Army of the Potomac, Letterman developed two innovations. One was the aid station in battle, coupled with field hospitals and larger hospitals to the rear. His other innovation was the ambulance system. In two short years, Letterman's horse-drawn ambulance corps became so proficient that more than 14,000 wounded Union soldiers at Gettysburg—plus nearly 7,000 wounded Confederate soldiers who had been abandoned—were evacuated in only 24 hours. Where would civilian health care be today without the ambulance?

THE SPANISH-AMERICAN WAR

The Spanish-American War lasted only one year. During that time, fewer than 400 U.S. soldiers died of battlefield wounds, but more than 2,000 contracted yellow fever. Major General William Shafter said that disease was "a thousand times harder to stand up against than the missiles of the enemy." Yellow fever, a severe viral illness that often proved fatal, can cause bleeding from body openings such as eyes, nose, anus, as well as bloody vomit. Its name derives from the yellow tinge the victim's body takes on as the liver fails and yellow bile is released. Mortality rates approached 85 percent of those afflicted.

In 1900 the U.S. surgeon general appointed the U.S. Army yel-

The 1954 film *The Bridges at Toko-Ri*, starring William Holden, was about the Korean War.

low fever commission, led by Dr. Walter Reed (after whom the military hospital is named) to try to get a handle on this devastating disease. Reed devised an ingenious experiment whereby he separated soldiers into two groups. The first slept on the soiled clothes and bedding of yellow fever sufferers in a room screened to prevent mosquitoes; the second group was scrupulously kept away from anyone who was sick, but was exposed to the mosquitoes. No one in the first group got sick, but the second group had many casualties—proving conclusively that the mosquito is the vector in spreading the disease. Once the mosquito was identified as the cause of the sickness, actions were taken to control mosquito populations. Although yellow fever remains incurable, there hasn't been a major outbreak since. It has been said that the Panama Canal could not have been built if yellow fever had not come under control.

BAND OF BLOOD BROTHERS

At the start of World War I, blood transfusions were performed by sewing a forearm artery of the donor to the vein of the wounded—with no matching of blood types. The process was often fatal, but by the end of the war, military surgeons proved the viability of the blood bank system. All they needed was the technology to store blood safely for long periods of time. That arrived in World War II. By the time the Allies invaded Normandy, the military and Red Cross had developed such a comprehensive system that there was a reserve blood supply for every soldier and sailor who participated in the invasion. By the end of the war, military surgeons returned 1.3 million plasma units to civilian authorities and the blood bank was here to stay.

WHAT'S NEXT

More than 40 million Americans have served in uniform and more than 95 percent have returned home to their families, thanks to the valor of corpsmen and medics as well as advances in military medicine. Today, military researchers are working on vaccinations against pain, blood components that can be stored for two years, robotic surgery, and even injecting magnetic nanoparticles that mass at a wound site to promote clotting. From smallpox vaccines to battlefield emergency rooms, military medicine is one of the unsung heroes of service in uniform.

"Ping jockey" is submarine slang for a sonar operator.

MATHEW BRADY BY THE NUMBERS

Before the American Civil War, images of soldiers and battles were mainly pen-and-ink drawings sketched by war correspondents. All that changed with the development of the camera—and the images captured by the war's best-known photographer, Mathew Brady.

0

Photographs Brady took of Lee's surrender to Grant. He didn't get the news until after the surrender had happened. When he arrived at Appomattox, he could only photograph the outside of the building and the empty room inside; soldiers hunting for souvenirs had stripped the room of everything from pillow cushions to inkwells.

1

Number of photographs taken of an actual battle. The forgettable photo, taken at Sharpsburg, shows a man looking down on a smoky field. To the far right and far left you can make out horses facing the unseen battle. Technology didn't allow for action shots, so Brady's battlefield photos were limited to the aftermath of combat—gripping scenes of the carnage of war.

2

Photographic wagons complete with traveling darkrooms that Brady took to the battlefield. Because they looked so odd, soldiers nicknamed them "whatsit" wagons, as in "What is it?"

2

Countries, France and Britain, that wanted to buy Brady's Civil War photos, which he called "War Views." Brady didn't want to sell them to a foreign nation. The United States wasn't interested! The New York Historical Society wanted to but didn't have the money.

3

Minutes a subject had to pose motionless; otherwise, they'd appear as a ghostly, transparent image—or not at all.

$5

Bill that has Brady's portrait of Abraham Lincoln—a man famous for his dislike of having his photograph taken. One of eight photos Brady took when Lincoln visited his studio in February 1864, it was chosen by Lincoln's son Robert for the $5 bill because it was "the best likeness of my father."

6

The number of visiting card-sized photographs that soldiers could get for $1.50 when they came to Brady's studios in New York City or Washington, D.C. These studio portraits, known as *cartes des vistes*, funded Brady's project to record the war.

38

Brady's age when the Civil War started and he decided to become the historical photographer of the war.

1844

Year that Brady opened his first studio at the corner of Broadway and Fulton Street in New York City. Before the war, the rich and famous all came to be photographed by "Brady of Broadway."

5,000

Number of photographers active during the Civil War.

8,000

Images in Brady's "War Views." When the U.S. government declined to purchase them, Brady put them in storage. In 1871, when he couldn't pay the $2,840 storage bill, the photos became the property of the storage company and were finally purchased by the government at auction. Four years later, the government awarded $25,000 to the destitute Brady for all rights to the photos.

$100,000

What Brady estimated his "War Views" were worth. Coincidentally, this was the same amount as the debt he'd accrued after spending four years taking the photographs.

WAR AND PEACE

No, not a condensation of Tolstoy's massive work, but some reflections on two of life's greatest challenges.

"There never was a good war or a bad peace."

—**Benjamin Franklin**

"The mere absence of war is not peace."

—**President John F. Kennedy**

"Blessed are the peacemakers: for they shall be called the children of God."

—**Matthew 5:9**

"War is the unfolding of miscalculations."

—**Barbara Tuchman**

"The wages of war is debt."

—***Wall Street Journal***

"Peace has its victories no less than war, but it doesn't have as many monuments to unveil."

—**Frank McKinney Hubbard**

"They said this mystery never shall cease; the priest promotes war, and the soldier peace."

—**William Blake**

"It is always easy to begin a war, but very difficult to stop one, since its beginning and end are not under the control of the same man."

—**Sallust, 86–34 BC**

"You can't say civilization don't advance . . . in every war they kill you a new way."

—**Will Rogers**

"War is a series of catastrophes that results in a victory."

—**Georges Clemenceau**

"A professional soldier understands that war means killing people . . . war means families left without fathers and mothers. All you have to do is hold your first dying soldier in your arms, and have that terribly futile feeling that his life is flowing out and you can't do anything about it. Then you understand the horror of war. any soldier worth his salt should be antiwar. And still, there are things worth fighting for."

—**H. Norman Schwarzkopf**

Operation Killer: A successful UN action in Korea to force the enemy back.

SOLDIER'S NEWSPAPER

What's black, white, and red-white-and-blue all over? Stars and Stripes, *the newspaper that publishes an edition wherever American troops are deployed. It operates from within—and is partially subsidized by—the Department of Defense, but it's an independent newspaper—free of control and censorship by the military.*

NO NEWS IS BAD NEWS

Stars and Stripes dates to the Civil War, when some Union men in Illinois found an abandoned newspaper office and decided to produce a newspaper for their regiments. On November 9, 1861, an institution was born, although it got off to a slow start—only four one-page issues were produced during the Civil War. After that, *Stars and Stripes* had an on-again, off-again publication history, resuming for World Wars I and II; it has been published continuously since 1942 in Europe and 1945 in the Pacific.

VOLUME TWO

For much of World War I, the city of Paris was only about 75 miles from the closest combat line, but it still managed to maintain a relatively normal existence. Doughboys serving with the American Expeditionary Force (AEF) could read English-language papers like London's *Daily Mail*, the *Chicago Tribune*, and the *Paris Herald*. Then someone convinced General John J. Pershing that the doughboys needed their own newspaper, and the first issue of the new *Stars and Stripes*—produced by an all-military staff—was published on February 8, 1918. Pershing would later note, "I do not believe that any one factor could have done more to sustain the morale of the American Expeditionary Forces than the *Stars and Stripes*." The full-sized weekly ran for 71 issues until June 13, 1919, with a top circulation of 522,000.

THE STARS OF *STARS AND STRIPES*

The *Stars and Stripes* of World War I was aglow with literary lights. From December 1917 to April 1919, Private Harold Ross functioned as probably the lowest-paid managing editor in the history of journalism. After the war, Ross went on to found the *New Yorker* magazine.

Backbiter, Balsa, and Verb: World War II code names for Midway Island.

Also on staff was First Lieutenant Henry Grantland Rice of the AEF's 115th Field Artillery. After the war, Rice wrote a syndicated sports column called "Sportlight," and in his day he was widely regarded as the "dean of American sportswriters."

THE RETURN OF *STARS AND STRIPES*

The *Stars and Stripes* of World War II was founded by Mark Martin, an infantry lieutenant and former Des Moines newspaperman. It started as a weekly for Americans stationed in Northern Ireland in early 1942, and eventually became almost a daily (no Sunday edition) of eight pages on Monday and four pages the other five days. General Dwight D. Eisenhower championed the newspaper's absolute freedom of the press (except for military secrets).

Like the World War I version, World War II's *Stars and Stripes* was also written by enlisted men; the officers generally worked on the business side of the paper. Anyone could afford it: The World War I edition had sold for a mere 50 centimes (about half a penny), World War II soldiers could read all about it for one English penny or one franc (100 centimes), and those at the front received theirs for free. The World War I version had run lots of ads, but the World War II version contained no ads.

OF CHEESECAKE AND HOUSEKEEPING

Known as the soldier's "hometown newspaper," *Stars and Stripes* resembled the newspapers coming out of small towns all across the United States. The front page was reserved for big news, mostly war news. During World War II: the invasion of Sicily, the death of Mussolini, Churchill's visit to the White House, and labor strikes on the home front. News stories on the inside pages were mostly "local"—about that issue's "hometown": the London issue might run a story by a journalist who'd visited the London underground during a bombing raid; the Continental issue might have an interview with a soldier who narrowly avoided being captured by the Germans outside of Rome.

Of course, there was sports news—like how the Yankees, minus Sergeant Joe DiMaggio, were doing against the Cardinals in the 1943 World Series. The entertainment news consisted of interviews with performers who'd enlisted or were arriving with a USO tour. So-called housekeeping stories weren't teaching housewives

Mexican-American War victory of 1848: the U.S. won Texas, California, Nevada, Utah...

how to make a great pot roast; they told soldiers how to make a "homey" dugout, avoid trench foot, or make their C-rations a little more edible. The papers occasionally ran an advice column—how to find a new GI raincoat or where to buy your mom a postcard in Algiers. Readers contributed, too, writing poetry and letters to the editor. Among the most popular sections were the editorial cartoons, comic strips, and guest columnists like Ernie Pyle.

But in one way, *Stars and Stripes* wasn't *exactly* like a hometown newspaper. No week was complete without a "cheesecake" photo sent in by a budding actress, singer, or model—or her agent. Before this, cheesecake shots had been seen as, well . . . cheesy, but suddenly they were part of the "war effort" and perfectly acceptable. They were relatively tame compared to today's standards—all the pinup girls were fully clothed except for the very occasional bathing-suit shot, and bathing suits in those days covered all the interesting spots.

MORE STARS OF *STARS AND STRIPES*

The World War II version of the newspaper had its superstars, too. Andy Rooney of *60 Minutes* fame began his newspaper career in 1942 at *Stars and Stripes* in London, reporting firsthand on notable events and people. He was one of six correspondents who flew on the first American bombing raid over Germany, in February 1943. Later, he was one of the first American journalists to visit the German concentration camps as the war wound down, and one of the first to write about them.

Bill Mauldin drew his popular *Willie and Joe* cartoons, and after the war continued his career as an editorial cartoonist with the *St. Louis Post-Dispatch* and the *Chicago Sun-Times*, eventually winning two Pulitzer Prizes. (See page 126.) Peter Viereck was published in the "Pup Tent Poets" column, which accepted contributions from all of its military readers. Viereck won the Pulitzer Prize in 1949 for his first poetry collection, *Terror and Decorum*. Edsel Ford was also a frequent contributor to "Pup Tent Poets," so frequent that a reader wrote, "I am getting bored with the works of Edsel Ford." Bil Keane, the cartoonist best known for his long-running newspaper comic strip *The Family Circus*, created the "At Ease with the Japanese" cartoons when he was stationed in Tokyo for the Pacific edition of *Stars and Stripes*.

...plus parts of present-day Colorado, New Mexico, Arizona, and Wyoming.

STARS AND STRIPES ON THE MOVE

A war fought on so many fronts in so many countries required several editions of *Stars and Stripes*. The London edition was followed by the Mediterranean edition in November 1942 (headquartered in Algiers, Casablanca, Oran, and Tunis). The Italian edition began in Palermo and moved north with the Army to Naples, Rome, Livorno, and Milan. The French edition had begun soon after D-day. A mid-Pacific edition served Honolulu, New Caledonia, Australia, the Aleutians, Chongqing, and the China-Burma-India theater. After the war, the Continental edition was based in Heidelberg, Germany; the Pacific edition in Tokyo, Japan.

Every move brought the same challenges: printing plant, supplies, employees, and circulation. Scouting crews would search for unused printing plants. In Paris they used the offices of the *Paris Herald*, which had been closed since the German invasion. At other times they moved into plants the retreating German army had used to produce Nazi propaganda flyers. Conditions were rarely ideal. Typesetters in Cherbourg, France, wore raincoats on cloudy days because their bombed-out plant had no roof. Broken machinery was fixed with rubber bands, hairpins, or baling wire. Often they were working with only a day or two worth of supplies or had to produce a short run because of lack of supplies.

SPECIAL DELIVERY

Getting the paper out began at 2:00 a.m. with a pickup at the plant by trucks that delivered papers to airplanes, trains, trucks, and jeeps. Wally Newfield, the *Stars and Stripes* circulation manager in France, "liberated" a donkey from the German forces, and actually delivered the papers to the front himself. A civilian photographer snapped a shot of him astride the donkey and the photo ran in his own paper with the caption: "Circulation Man Gets His Ass Up to the Front."

Their city desks, or main headquarters, were in "safe zones," but the news wasn't. Reporters flew with the troops in cargo planes and bombers, jumped with paratroopers, entered with invasion forces, and often lived for weeks at a time on the front lines. Reporters were taken prisoner, wounded, and killed. Sometimes even the city desks weren't that safe. Several headquarters were bombed frequently; at one point the French city of Strasbourg had

Actual MASH units are larger than the units shown in the M*A*S*H movie and TV series.

only two Allies in town—*Stars and Stripes* reporters Ed Clark and Vic Dallaire. They had just set up shop when the occupying GIs were pulled out to support troops under attack in the Ardennes. Unwilling to leave their new shop, the men remained behind, hoping the Germans wouldn't return. They even put out a two-page paper—using their rudimentary knowledge of high-school German and French—that they sold to the locals to raise money for food. It was the only trilingual edition of *Stars and Stripes* ever published.

TODAY'S *STARS AND STRIPES*

The paper now has a full-time civilian staff. Layout is done in Washington, D.C., then transmitted by satellite to printing facilities all over the world. There are five daily editions—Mideast, Europe, Japan, Korea, and Okinawa—and one weekly from the United Kingdom. The paper is available in over 48 countries at bases, posts, ships, embassies, and by home delivery in England, Germany, Guam, Italy, Japan, and Korea.

- On any given day, the average (print) daily newspaper readership of *Stars and Stripes* exceeds 365,000.
- *Stars and Stripes* prints approximately 31.5 million papers annually, still provided free to military personnel in combat zones.
- An electronic version is viewed approximately 4,000 times a day.

Per a Department of Defense directive, the paper is "editorially independent of interference from outside its own editorial chain-of-command" and dedicated to providing the news to military personnel without censorship, management, or unequal treatment.

A few of the people who worked at *Stars and Stripes* since WWII:

- Shel Silverstein, the multitalented writer of children's books (*The Giving Tree*), worked as a cartoonist and published a collection of his Army cartoons called *Grab Your Socks!* in 1956.
- Louis Rukeyser, stock market reporter and host of public television's *Wall $treet Week*, edited the "B-Bag" column, soldiers' letters to the editor.
- Steve Kroft of *60 Minutes* started out as a reporter for the Armed Forces Network covering his division's participation in the invasion of Cambodia. When the division was redeployed, he was reassigned to *Stars and Stripes* as a correspondent and photographer.

Uncle Sam's Canoe Club: Military slang for the U.S. Navy or Naval Academy.

AN ACT OF HONOR

War has no shortage of heroes.

RAFAEL PERALTA: 1979–2004

Rafael was born in Mexico City, Mexico. After his family moved to San Diego, "Rafa," as he was known, attended Morse High School. It was while at Morse that Rafa decided he wanted to join the Marines. He applied for a green card, and the day he received it, he enlisted in the Marines. After graduating from training in 2000, Peralta was assigned to the 3rd Marines Regiment on Oahu, Hawaii. He became a U.S. citizen while in uniform.

But 2003 brought tragedy to Peralta's personal life. The night before his wedding, his fiancée's mother died, so the wedding was postponed. When his fiancée traveled to Mexico to bury her mother, she was killed in a highway accident. Despite his grief, Peralta remained enthusiastic about serving his adopted country as a Marine. On the walls of his bedroom hung a photo from boot camp graduation, a copy of the Declaration of Independence, and a copy of the Bill of Rights.

ABOVE AND BEYOND

In 2004 Sergeant Rafael Peralta, a platoon scout, was assigned to Company A, 1st Battalion, 3rd Regiment in Iraq. On November 8, 2004, he was one of the 15,000 American troops who became part of Operation Phantom Fury in the urban center of Fallujah.

Squads of Marines—who worked in what were called "stacks" of six men each—had the dangerous job of searching homes and buildings to find hidden groups of armed insurgents. Sergeant Peralta had a reputation for extreme devotion to the Corps, taking its motto, *Semper Fidelis* (always faithful), to heart. He was well known for helping fellow Marines in any way he could, so on November 15, no one on the platoon's assault team was surprised when Peralta offered to help them with their dangerous search—even though he didn't have to.

The men went through three empty buildings. When they entered a fourth house, they were ambushed by insurgents hiding

General Colin L. Powell, former U.S. secretary of state, was a U.S. Army Ranger.

in a back room. Peralta, one of the first at the door to that room, was caught in the cross fire. Taking a friendly fire wound to the face, Peralta had dropped to the floor when an insurgent tossed a grenade toward the Marines. What happened in the next seconds has been verified by every American at the scene, including Lance Corporal T. J. Kaemmerer, a Marine correspondent. Kaemmerer wrote that Peralta in "his last fleeting moments of consciousness reached out and pulled the grenade into his body."

By tucking the grenade under him, Peralta smothered the force of the grenade blast. The 25-year-old sergeant had ensured his own death but saved the lives of his comrades. "He saved half my fire team," Corporal Brannon Dyer told the *Army Times*.

RECOGNITION

In 2006 the Marine Corps and Navy Department recommended that Peralta receive the Medal of Honor. However, in September 2008, Secretary of Defense Robert Gates ordered that Peralta would instead receive the service's second-highest award, the Navy Cross. Extensive reviews by forensic pathologists revealed that there might be doubt over whether Peralta's head wound, with its accompanying brain damage, would have allowed him to consciously decide to cover his body with the grenade. Even a slight doubt forces the Pentagon to change the award of a Medal of Honor to the Navy Cross.

The decision sparked intense controversy, and other investigators went on record that Peralta intentionally covered the grenade. Reserve Marine Lieutenant Colonel Scott Marconda, who investigated the incident in 2004 as a major and judge advocate, told *USA Today*, "There's no way that grenade got under the center of mass of his body without him putting it there. I'm not a cheerleader. It is what it is."

Delegates from California and Hawaii continue to press for a Medal of Honor, and Peralta's companions from Fallujah still insist that his actions are the reason they're alive today. Controversies aside, Peralta's undoubted faithfulness to his comrades has already made him a legendary hero among Marines. Peralta's story is told in *An Act of Honor*, a documentary produced by the History Channel.

At its high point in the 1940s, the USO had more than 3,000 clubs.

NORTH TO ALASKA

In 1897–98 everyone's attention was focused on the Klondike gold rush. As a result, they missed the drama of one of the most daring and dangerous rescue missions in history.

BEFORE THE COAST GUARD

In the 19th century, the Revenue Cutter Service, forerunner to the U.S. Coast Guard, was the only civil authority along the Alaskan coast. Besides policing the large whaling and seal-hunting fleets that worked the territorial waters every summer, the Revenue Cutter delivered mail and supplies to remote communities and on occasion provided the only medical services.

IT'S GONNA BE A LONG WINTER

In the fall of 1897, eight whaling ships crewed by 265 men were trapped in the ice near Point Barrow, Alaska's northernmost port. They knew they'd be stuck there until July and they only had enough supplies to last until February. When the ships failed to return to their home port of San Francisco, President William McKinley authorized a relief effort. The mission fell to the Revenue Cutter Service.

The cutter *Bear*, an Arctic veteran, was assigned the mission. When the U.S. Navy purchased her in 1884, the *Bear* had already been working in the Arctic waters as a seal-hunting vessel for 10 years. Her first and only mission for the Navy had been the successful 1884 rescue of seven survivors of an ill-fated expedition in northern Greenland. Afterward, the ship was passed on to the Revenue Cutter Service to patrol the Bering Sea off the Alaskan coast. For the task ahead, the *Bear* was hands down the only logical choice; with its six-inch-thick oak hull sheathed in steel plate, the ship could handle the frozen sea—and its veteran sailors could handle the ship.

THE WAY NORTH

Early in the mission, the *Bear* had to struggle through storm-driven seas and grinding mush ice in the Bering Sea, when it was not even close to Point Barrow. Finally, it had to berth at Port

Vancouver—1,500 miles short of the stranded whalers and 700 miles short of the port the captain had hoped to reach before the ice became impassable. Supplies would have to be hauled overland on trails that were more a system of landmarks than paths and which were known only to local Inuit. These trails would be snowbound and, along the coast, obstructed by ice that could be heaped as high as a three-story building by constant, often gale-force winds. Blizzards could be expected and temperatures far below zero were a certainty, as was immediate frostbite if the trekkers weren't careful. Adding to these hazards was the fact that the expedition would be traveling part of the way in darkness 22 to 24 hours a day. The odds against success were astronomical.

AN ARCTIC LEGEND UNFOLDS

The gold rush had put sled dogs at a premium. Recognizing the impossibility of achieving a 1,500-mile trek while hauling enough relief supplies to sustain 265 people for four months, to say nothing of transporting them across uncharted territory, the men of the *Bear* came up with a novel plan: a herd of reindeer would be rounded up and driven to Point Barrow in the style of a Texas cattle drive. The sleds accompanying the drive would be carrying 1,700 pounds of additional supplies, including food for the four sailors who would make the trip and for 40 sled dogs, plus mail, tobacco, and winter clothing for the whalers.

The Cutter Service contingent was made up of Lieutenants David Jarvis and Ellsworth Bertholf, Dr. S. J. Coll, and an enlisted man, F. Kolchoff. On December 16, 1897, they set out with Inuit guides on the first leg, a 700-mile march to where they hoped to round up some reindeer.

Reindeer weren't native to Alaska, but they thrived in the Arctic climate and could be domesticated. Several herds had been established in the early 1890s by a Presbyterian missionary who brought them from Siberia and introduced them in an effort to support the precarious Inuit economy. Reindeer milk is nourishing and the meat is similar in texture and taste to caribou, an Inuit staple. In addition, the hides can be used for clothing, shelter, and footwear. It turned out that the Inuit hadn't been interested in becoming herders, but fortunately some small herds remained.

From the beginning of the trek, temperatures hovered at -30°F.

The United States Marine Band is nicknamed "The President's Own."

Heavy snow sometimes held the party to 10 miles a day, but by late January they had located two reindeer herds and enlisted experienced herders. In the first week of February, the party set out with 448 reindeer and 18 sleds loaded with supplies. After two months and 800 miles of some of the worst terrain and weather conditions in North America, they reached the stranded whalers.

SHORT ON GRATITUDE—AND TEMPERS, TOO

Their arrival was timely. Three whalers had died and numerous others were showing the first signs of scurvy. Early in their ordeal, the whalers had been forced to dig up Inuit graves in search of warm winter clothing. They did have one short-lived stroke of luck. One of the stranded whaling ships had drifted close enough for the whalers to begin off-loading its 80 tons of coal. That was the good news. The bad news was that most of the coal was lost when a seaman accidentally set the ship on fire.

When they arrived, the rescuers quickly discovered that food, clothing, and comfort weren't enough. They were obliged to impose an activity regimen on the whalers to put a lid on widespread "cabin fever"—short tempers, constant disruptive bickering, and depression. The seamen had spent months in extremely overcrowded ramshackle cabins with little food or fuel. Outdoor temperatures were always well below zero and the constant Arctic night could weigh heavily on people used to sunlight. The whalers had also lost their season's income and, unable to get home in time to sign on for the 1898 season, would lose that potential income as well. The men from the *Bear* found themselves rescuing some very unhappy campers. They took charge until the July thaw allowed a successful evacuation.

Later in his career, Lieutenant Jarvis became captain of the *Bear*. As for the reindeer, several died during the trek and more than 200 were eaten, but with spring calving, the net loss to the herd was barely a dozen. Some of their descendants may still roam the Alaskan barrens today. The *Bear* would serve the United States for many years after the rescue, including three Antarctic expeditions and patrol work during the two World Wars. In 1963, after being outfitted as a floating restaurant/museum, the *Bear*—nearly 90 years old—sank in a gale while being towed from Halifax to Philadelphia.

A fleet at sea is the equivalent of an army on land.

"REMEMBER THE *MAINE*!"

The event that triggered the shortest, most popular, and most influential foreign war in America's history, at least until the end of the 20th century.

COURTESY CALL

The 300-foot battleship USS *Maine*, under the command of Captain Charles Sigsbee, had arrived in Havana harbor on January 20, 1898, on a "courtesy" visit. In actuality, the ship was there at the request of Cuba's U.S. consul, General Fitzhugh Lee, as a tacit indicator of U.S. support for Cubans rebelling against their Spanish colonial masters. There was plenty of popular support for the other side, too, so part of Lee's concern was to protect American citizens and business interests, which generated more than $100 million a year in revenue from Cuba's sugar and tobacco industries.

On the night of February 15, the *Maine* was on full alert, riding at anchor but under steam. At around 10:00 p.m. an explosion shook the ship and it listed to port. Within minutes of the explosion, the ship and the 260 U.S. servicemen aboard her sank to the bottom of Havana harbor. Spanish officials immediately mobilized a rescue effort and threw open hospitals for the injured.

THE BLAME GAME

Several inquiries have been held to determine the cause of the explosion. The immediate U.S. military investigation blamed the explosion on sabotage, with the most likely cause being a mine planted by the Spanish. A simultaneous Spanish inquiry suggested that the cause was due entirely to internal combustion and not to any external causes.

Years later, well-respected U.S. Navy Admiral Hyman Rickover's 1976 investigation said the cause was probably an internal explosion caused by a fire in a coal bunker adjacent to the ship's four powder magazines. A 1999 National Geographic Society investigation of the wreck didn't reach a conclusion, but it kept alive the possibility that an external explosion could have caused internal chain-reaction explosions of the ship's powder magazines.

Three separate villains were suggested over the years:

• Spaniards protecting vested interests in Cuba;

• Rebels attempting to draw the U.S. into military support of their cause; and

• American expansionists attempting to spur military intervention.

A fourth theory relegated the explosion to a simple accident that happened at the wrong time and the wrong place.

RUN-UP TO WAR

The United States used the *Maine*'s sinking to justify a declaration of war against Spain, but in reality, a series of events combined with the explosion led to the declaration.

Spain's government was torn by factionalism and its military was weak, particularly its navy. Years of civil war has loosened Spain's grip on its few remaining colonies. In Cuba, rebels virtually controlled the countryside and Spain resorted to civilian internment camps to maintain a fragile control. By 1898 these policies had resulted in the deaths of more than 100,000 Cubans.

For years a Cuban rebel operation based in New York City had been conducting a successful anti-Spanish propaganda campaign in the American media. As a result, many viewed the rebels as freedom fighters and the Spaniards as oppressors. In addition, the New York–based rebels funneled arms and other supplies to Cuban fighters, often with the complicity of Americans.

DOVES AND HAWKS

Grover Cleveland's administration, followed by William McKinley's, repeatedly tried to negotiate a Spanish withdrawal from Cuba, even to the point of offering to purchase the country from Spain. But the Spanish were unreceptive. Then there was the strong political faction in the United States anxious to expand American influence in the Caribbean; they considered military intervention not only valid but also heroic and destined.

The sinking of the *Maine* galvanized support for the interventionists, and extinguished any hope for a peaceful solution.

THE WAR IS ON

Americans demanded retribution. Public opinion was fueled by inflammatory newspaper editorials and self-righteous saber rattling by Congressional hawks. The cry "Remember the *Maine*, to hell with Spain!" was on everyone's lips. On April 25, 1898, President McKinley and Congress declared war. Almost immediately, Congress appropriated $50 million to build up the U.S. military. The media had done its job: the first call for 125,000 volunteers in April was oversubscribed, so the number was increased to 200,000 to accommodate everyone who wanted to fight.

MEANWHILE, ON THE OTHER SIDE OF THE WORLD

When war was declared, Admiral George Dewey's Asiatic Squadron was already on standby, stationed at Hong Kong on orders of the assistant secretary of the Navy, the hawkish Theodore Roosevelt. (The U.S. Naval War College had been planning for war with Spain for four years. In 1896 attacks against the Spanish Pacific fleet were incorporated into the plans, but with no intention of occupying the Philippines.) As soon as war was declared, Roosevelt dispatched Dewey's squadron to attack the Spanish fleet anchored in Manila Bay in the Philippines.

On May 1, six days later, Dewey's squadron crept through Manila Bay's perimeter defenses and laid waste to the decrepit wood-hulled Spanish ships caught at anchor with minimal onshore protection. The fleet was destroyed with no loss of life and only nine wounded on the American side.

The capture of Guam followed a few days later. American ships arrived and fired two salvos. The Spanish governor of Guam, unaware that war had been declared, sent an envoy to the ships to apologize for not returning a welcoming salvo and to explain it was because he had no ammunition. The governor and his 60 Spanish troops surrendered peacefully, if somewhat embarrassedly.

CARIBBEAN CONQUEST

The Cuban campaign began in June, when U.S. troops captured Guantanamo Bay and landed just east of Santiago. Most troops were happy to disembark, and not just to get into battle. Shipboard quarters had been seriously cramped. The soldiers' discomfort was exacerbated by poor food—a common characteristic of U.S. infantry life since the Revolution—and hot, humid weather, worsened by heavy uniforms ill suited to Cuba's subtropics. By the time

...He went on to become governor-general of India, then lord lieutenant of Ireland.

many soldiers touched land, they were seriously ill. Despite their physical debilitation, on July 1, U.S. troops—led by Brigadier General Jacob Kent, and assisted by 5,000 rebels—assaulted San Juan Hill overlooking Santiago. And Theodore Roosevelt, who had left his post as assistant secretary of the Navy to join the action, led his Rough Riders and other troops up Kettle Hill. Among these troops were the veteran African American Ninth and Tenth cavalries—the Buffalo Soldiers—who had seen service along the Midwest frontier. It was the Tenth that actually captured San Juan Hill, greeting Roosevelt when he finally arrived.

IT'S A ROUT

Roosevelt would build the romanticized warrior image of himself that propelled him into the presidency based on that day's action. While his troops were on foot, he rode horseback, open to enemy fire, urging on his troops by example as so many Civil War leaders had done. He did have the advantage that Spanish soldiers turned and fled early in the assault and, indeed, the only Spanish soldier Roosevelt shot (according to him) was shot in the back. The heights above Santiago were captured and, by July 16, Roosevelt's superior officer negotiated the city's surrender. The stage was set on July 3, when Spain's Atlantic fleet unsuccessfully tried to break a U.S. Navy blockade of Santiago harbor to maintain a supply line to the Atlantic. Shortly after that, Puerto Rico was surrendered with only token resistance. Spain's last colonial foothold in the Western Hemisphere was gone.

Unfortunately for American occupation forces in Cuba, the yellow fever season had started and the disease would be a far more formidable enemy than the Spaniards. Of 3,000 U.S. military fatalities in Cuba, 2,700 died of infection, mostly yellow fever.

MOPPING UP THE PACIFIC

In the Pacific theater, six weeks after Dewey's easy victory in Manila Bay, 15,000 U.S. troops finally arrived to secure the city of Manila and the Philippines. Spain and the United States signed a peace treaty on December 10, 1898. Cuba was to be an independent country under the protection of the United States; Guam and Puerto Rico became U.S. property; and the United States was permitted to purchase the Philippines for $20 million.

In World War I, a "dixie" was an Army cooking pot.

FROM DUNES TO BOOMS

What do flimsy, underpowered biplanes and supersonic F/A-18 Hornets have in common? San Diego.

DESERTED ISLAND

At the beginning of the 20th century, the peninsula of Coronado was just a windswept collection of sand dunes in the middle of San Diego Bay. As yet undeveloped by a city struggling for an identity, it was the perfect site for a new, untested concept: naval aviation.

A few years after the Wright brothers' first successful flight in 1903, the U.S. Navy sent its first aviator candidate, Lieutenant T. G. Ellyson, to a private flying school on the island. It was a seasonal school, used during San Diego's balmy winter months when Annapolis, Maryland, was too cold for training aspiring Navy aviators.

ACCIDENTAL BIRTH

One fateful day, as he taxied in front of thousands of spectators during a demonstration, Ellyson accidentally gave his biplane too much power and it jumped 15 feet into the sky. Startled, Ellyson managed to land it (mangling a wing) to the delight of all those present. At that moment, naval aviation was born.

Ellyson became the Navy's first accredited aviator a few months later in what was later designated the "Birthplace of Naval Aviation." Back then, in 1912, the flying school was a primitive collection of three planes, three pilots, three tents, and several mechanics.

TAKEOFFS AND LANDINGS

One thousand pilots were trained for World War I on the island. Early milestones included the first seaplane flight, and later the first air-to-air refueling and the first use of a radio in an airplane. When the Navy assigned its first aircraft carrier, a converted collier (cargo ship) called the USS *Langley*, to San Diego, daring young aviators had no idea of the dangers they faced.

In 1925 future World War II admiral John Dale Price, then just a lieutenant, made the first night landing on a carrier there. Another pilot was the first to be catapulted off a carrier (the *Langley*) in a wheeled aircraft the same year. Both were remarkable achievements given the technology of the day.

The next five U.S. Navy aircraft carriers all found a homeport in San Diego: the USS *Lexington*, *Saratoga*, *Ranger*, *Yorktown*, and *Enterprise*. The city became America's "Navy Town" and ultimately the largest naval ship base in the world.

HEY, ISN'T THAT TOM CRUISE?

As technology developed and conflicts around the world persisted, San Diego became famous for another reason. In 1969 American pilots were dying in the skies over North Vietnam. The Navy needed a school featuring the best pilots and expert instructors. TOPGUN (the popular name for the U.S. Navy Fighter Weapons School) was established at Naval Air Station Miramar, a few miles north of downtown San Diego. The nine original instructors devised a sophisticated training program, now based in Nevada, which remains the best in the world.

THAT ISN'T THUNDER YOU HEAR

Today, a few hundred yards from where Ellyson first lurched into the air a century ago, the Navy's newest aircraft carrier, the USS *Ronald Reagan*, is berthed, its massive flight deck ready to launch F/A-18 Hornets in a matter of seconds. From its uncertain beginnings, naval aviation evolved from fragile biplanes to the most advanced aircraft in the skies. Just imagine what another 100 years will bring.

*   *   *

USS *RONALD REAGAN*
Nickname: The Gipper (what else?)
Motto: "Peace Through Strength"

USS *MIDWAY*
Namesake: The Battle of Midway
Motto: *Successum Merere Conemur* ("Endeavor to Deserve Success")

IN THE TRENCHES

The use of trenches to conceal military forces predates 1914 by a long time, and in fact, they were called "trenches" from about 1500 on. But their use in World War I, where they far exceeded any prior deployment, gave our language a number of lasting terms.

IN THE TRENCHES. During the war being *in the trenches* meant being in action. The same thing today is meant by the term, that is, actively working at something. Thus, "He spent years in the trenches before they made him president of the company."

DIGGING IN. After the trenches were dug, soldiers on both sides lived in them for months on end, with neither side advancing or retreating measurably. From this, *digging in* acquired the meaning of standing firm in one's position or views.

FOXHOLE. In addition to very long trenches, soldiers occasionally used a small slit trench that housed one or a few men. Although it was used much more rarely, the name given it, *foxhole*, survived. It was to play a much larger role in subsequent wars.

TRENCH COAT. The trenches were frequently, if not always, wet. Consequently, the officers wore long waterproof coats, or *trench coats*, a noun later applied to and still used for similar civilian raincoats.

TRENCH MOUTH. The long months in the trenches took a terrible toll on a soldier's health. One condition that afflicted many of them was *trench mouth* (formerly called Vincent's disease), characterized by painful, bleeding gums and bad breath. It was caused by poor oral hygiene and nutrition, heavy smoking, and stress—all conditions endemic in the trenches. Today trench mouth is readily treated with dental care and antibiotics.

SHELL SHOCK. In addition to physical ailments, soldiers frequently suffered from nervous conditions. One was an acute stress

Ninety-one percent of Vietnam veterans say they are glad they served.

syndrome resulting from exposure to constant shelling by the enemy and therefore called *shell shock*. It was thought to be caused by both the noise of the artillery and the constant fear it engendered. Today this term is still loosely used to describe the aftereffects of any traumatic experience, as in, "That series of lousy boyfriends gave her a bad case of shell shock."

SCREAMING MEEMIES. A similar expression is *screaming meemies*, a term that was coined for German artillery shells that emitted an exceptionally high-pitched whine before exploding. The term was later used to describe a state of extreme nervousness, bordering on hysteria.

OVER THE TOP. When ordered to advance, the soldiers climbed over the parapet of front-line trenches to attack the enemy's front line. The "top" referred both to the trench's top and to the open no-man's-land between them and the enemy. After the war, the term survived, assisted by Arthur Guy Empey's use of the term as the title for his popular World War I account. In civilian use it was extended to mean taking the final plunge and doing something dangerous or notable.

NO-MAN'S-LAND. Although *no-man's-land* dates from the 1300s, when it meant the waste ground between two kingdoms, it didn't take on its military meaning until World War I, when it was applied to the territory between the thousands of miles of Allied and German trenches. This area, a virtually stationary battle line for three years, was covered with barbed wire and pitted with shell holes made by the artillery of both sides. Since then, this term also has been used loosely to describe an indefinite situation where one is neither here nor there.

TRIPWIRE. Troops who advanced close to the German line often had to cut through a wire that had been strung to set off a trap or an alarm. The soldiers called it a *tripwire*, because it was meant literally to trip them up. Later the term was used to signify anything that might trip someone up, as in a *New York Times* headline on October 7, 1997, "Looking for Tripwires, Ickes Heads to the Witness Stand." (The term today is also employed for a small military force used as a first line of defense.)

Women comprise about 22 percent of entering plebes at the U.S. Naval Academy.

TOP 10 GENERALS, PART I

Presenting, in our humble opinion, our leading leaders of men and women at war.

1. GEORGE WASHINGTON (1732–99)

Born in Westmoreland County, Virginia, Washington grew up under the guardianship of his eldest brother. After a spotty education, he became a surveyor and eventually inherited his brother's prosperous estate, Mount Vernon.

He joined the Virginia militia in 1752, advanced to major, fought during the French and Indian War (1754–60), and made it to the rank of honorary brigadier general. Washington didn't return to the battlefield until July 1775, after being appointed general by the Continental Congress. At Cambridge, outside Boston, he took command of the disintegrating Continental Army.

The American Revolutionary War—Washington energetically and skillfully revitalized the militias at Cambridge and organized them into Continental Army regiments. Using cannons borrowed from the colonies, he occupied Dorchester Heights and brilliantly forced Sir William Howe's British army to evacuate Boston and retire by sea to New York City. Washington tried to drive the British from New York but failed, partly due to his own inexperience and partly due to untrained troops and clumsy subordinates. His masterful withdrawal from Long Island and Harlem Heights into New Jersey and Pennsylvania during the autumn of 1776 saved the army from extinction.

General Howe captured most of New Jersey and made the mistake of believing Washington's army was militarily impotent. On the night of December 25–26, 1776, Washington's forces crossed the Delaware River in boats, drove Howe's Hessians out of Trenton, and on January 3, 1777, he routed three British regiments at Princeton. During the summer of 1777, Washington learned that General John Burgoyne planned to invade the Hudson Valley from Canada. Though soon hard-pressed defending Philadelphia, the national capital, he sent many of his best troops upriver and, in October, defeated the British at Saratoga. Having weakened his

"U-boat" is an abbreviation of the German *Unterseeboot*—an "undersea boat," or submarine.

forces defending Philadelphia, Washington abandoned the defense of the city on September 26, forcing the Continental Congress to move west to York. Not everything went well for Washington, but he managed to contain one British force in the north while sending forces south to fight another British force under General Charles Cornwallis at Yorktown. The strategy worked, and on October 19, 1781, Cornwallis surrendered.

What Made Him Great?

Washington's unorthodox military education kept him from becoming an orthodox 18th-century general, which led to his boldness. The Continental Army never numbered more than 35,000 men, and Washington never had more than a third of it under his personal command, yet he managed to subdue, with help from the French fleet, Great Britain's professional army. Underrated by modern standards, Washington was a brilliant strategist and self-taught tactician. He also became a gifted statesman. He believed in civilian government and the rule of law, spurning attempts by his officers to make him a military dictator.

2. WINFIELD SCOTT (1786–1866)

Known as "Old Fuss and Feathers," Scott was born outside Petersburg, Virginia, and studied law until 1807, when he enlisted in a cavalry troop. At 6'5" and 250 pounds, Scott could cripple a horse—and did—so he transferred to the light artillery as a captain. Suspended briefly in 1810 for making inappropriate remarks to his superior, Scott rejoined the Army as a lieutenant colonel when the War of 1812 broke out, and led more troops into more battles in that war than any other officer. He suffered two wounds at Lundy's Lane on June 25, 1814, but 10 days later won an important victory at Chippawa, Ontario. Raised to the rank of major general for distinguished service, Scott became a national hero.

For the next 30 years, except for two trips to Europe to study military developments, Scott fought Seminole Indians in the South and Plains Indians in the West. In 1845–46, when General Zachary Taylor's battles with General Santa Anna's army in northern Mexico were inconclusive, Scott recommended to President James K. Polk an amphibious landing at Veracruz as the fastest way to conquer Mexico City. Scott planned the massive operation, and

The great Shawnee leader Tecumseh was killed in battle during the War of 1812.

on March 9, 1847, landed near Veracruz and 18 days later captured the city. On April 8 he began the march inland, routed Santa Anna's larger army on April 18 at Cerro Gordo, and occupied Puebla on May 15. He paused to collect supplies, resumed his advance on Mexico City on August 7, and after fighting decisive battles at Contreras, Churubusco, Molino del Rey, and Chapultepec, captured the Mexican capital on September 14. He served as military governor there until April 22, 1848, when he returned to Washington.

Promoted brevet lieutenant general in February 1855, Scott became the highest-ranking officer in the Army since George Washington. As general-in-chief of the Army, he tried to prevent the American Civil War by counseling presidents James Buchanan and Abraham Lincoln. He sadly became what his nickname implied, "Old Fuss and Feathers," a man obsessed with strict adherence to Army red tape with the out-of-date habit of adorning his military headwear with feathers. Though physically infirm, his mind was still sharp, but he could no longer take the field and, on November 1, 1861, resigned.

What Made Him Great?

Scott left a remarkable record as a strategist, a diplomat, and a brave and skillful tactician. His Anaconda Plan for strangling the South by keeping it from its sources of supply during the Civil War was first sneered at by Union generals, but was later adopted by Lincoln, and turned out to be the overriding strategy that eventually won the war.

3. ROBERT E. LEE (1807–70)

The greatest Confederate general of the Civil War, Lee graduated from West Point in 1829, second in a class of 46, and joined the engineers. A Virginian by birth, Lee claimed that he fought for his home state more than for the Confederacy.

The Mexican War—During the Mexican War, Lee served with distinction as a member of General Scott's staff at Veracruz in March 1847, and at Cerro Gordo the following month. His eye for reconnaissance and tactical improvisations led to Scott's victories at Churubusco, Chapultepec, and eventually to the surrender of

Mexico City. Lee worked a desk job from 1852 to 1855 as superintendent at West Point, after which he became colonel of the 2nd U.S. Cavalry and served in the Southwest until shortly before the outbreak of the Civil War. Lee was offered but rejected a top command in the Union army and resigned when Virginia seceded. On June 1, 1862, he replaced wounded General Joseph E. Johnston and took command of the Army of Northern Virginia.

The Civil War—Lee became one of those rare generals who thought strategically, broadly designed his tactics, and took chances. He understood the generals of the North better than those generals understood themselves. He came up with the strategy for Major General Thomas J. "Stonewall" Jackson's Shenandoah Valley Campaign during the spring of 1862, making Jackson the most celebrated officer in the Confederacy—until he was later eclipsed by Lee. In late June, Lee's smaller force bluffed Major General George B. McClellan's army into withdrawing, and two months later Lee outmaneuvered Major General John Pope and defeated the Army of Virginia at the Second Battle of Bull Run on August 29–30. On September 17, with a force half the size of McClellan's Army of the Potomac, Lee repulsed the Federals in a drawn battle at Antietam. After President Lincoln replaced McClellan with Major General Ambrose Burnside, Lee bloodied the massive Union army on December 13 at Fredericksburg.

Lee's aggressive instincts were never more evident than at Chancellorsville. He ignored the maxims of warfare, divided his much smaller force, and on May 2–4, 1863, decimated the right flank of the Army of the Potomac with a surprise attack. But his greatest mistake occurred on July 1–3 at Gettysburg, when he was overly aggressive at a time when he should have fought defensively. He admitted the error and withdrew into Virginia.

By 1864 many of Lee's best officers had been killed and there were no more soldiers to replace those who'd been lost in battle. Forced to fight defensively, Lee held off Grant's offensive in the Battle of the Wilderness on May 5–6, at Spotsylvania on May 8–12, and repulsed the Union assault at Cold Harbor on June 3. Those battles cost Grant a third of his men, but Lee couldn't withstand the pressure and withdrew to Petersburg's trenches. It took Grant eight months to flush Lee out of Petersburg and force his surrender on April 9, 1865, at Appomattox Court House.

George M. Cohan's "Over There" was the leading American marching song of World War I.

What Made Him Great?

Lee's men adored him. In victory and defeat, they witnessed his great strength of character, his high sense of duty, and his humility and selflessness. Even Northerners accepted Lee as the greatest general of the Civil War.

4. ULYSSES S. GRANT (1822–85)

Born Hiram Ulysses at Point Pleasant, Ohio, the future general grew up on his father's farm. In 1839 he entered West Point and found himself listed by his middle name and his mother's maiden name. On that day he became Ulysses Simpson Grant, which in later years became "U.S." Grant and "Unconditional Surrender" Grant. In 1843 he graduated 21st in a class of 39 and became a second lieutenant in the 4th Infantry.

The Mexican-American War—During the Mexican-American War, Grant distinguished himself while serving under General Zachary Taylor in Texas and later under General Winfield Scott in Mexico, where he received two brevets (commissions of higher rank) for gallantry. Grant enjoyed fighting, but he found no pleasure in the peacetime army. In July 1854, he resigned as captain from a dismal post in Oregon and returned to his family in Missouri, where for six years he tried without much success to scratch out a living on the family farm.

The Civil War—Grant reemerged in June 1861 as colonel of the 21st Illinois Infantry. Promoted to brigadier general in August, Grant ran his own campaigns and on February 6, 1862, seized Fort Henry on the Tennessee River and 10 days later demanded the "unconditional surrender" of Fort Donelson. In April, after first being surprised by a Confederate attack at Shiloh, he repulsed the enemy. Privately, he feuded with Major General Henry W. Halleck and was accused of drunkenness, but redeemed himself on July 4, 1863, by capturing Vicksburg. When men like Halleck questioned Grant's ability, Lincoln countered with a brisk rejoinder, replying, "I can't lose him. He fights."

After Vicksburg, Grant's stature as a fighting general bloomed. When Major General William S. Rosecrans's army was bottled up at Chattanooga, Grant took charge, broke the siege, and drove the

Confederates into Georgia. Lincoln rewarded Grant with a promotion to lieutenant general and made him general-in-chief of the armies. Instead of establishing an office in Washington, Grant took the field with the struggling Army of the Potomac. With characteristic doggedness, he drove General Robert E. Lee's Army of Northern Virginia to its final defeat at Appomattox on April 9, 1865.

What Made Him Great?

Though the point is still argued, Grant was an effective strategist. He made mistakes and learned from them. His drive and resolution made him a first-class general. Grant's postwar popularity earned him the presidency in 1869, but he was a warrior, never a good businessman or a politician. In fact, his hapless presidency was marked by the corruption of unworthy appointees he trusted.

5. JOHN J. PERSHING (1860–1948)

Pershing grew up on a farm in Laclede, Missouri, and displayed a high level of intelligence as a child. He taught school for four years before getting an appointment to West Point in 1882.

The Indian Wars—Commissioned a second lieutenant in the 6th Cavalry Regiment in June 1886, he served in the West during the Indian wars. In 1895 he commanded the famous African American Buffalo Soldiers, which is where he got the nickname "Black Jack."

The Spanish- and Philippine-American Wars—During the Spanish-American War, he served with the 10th Cavalry at San Juan Hill, and he also commanded troops in the Philippine-American War from 1899 to 1901. He went wherever he could find action and eventually returned to San Francisco in 1914 to take command of the 8th Infantry Brigade.

The Mexican War—When the Mexican civil war of 1914 spread across the border, Pershing led a 4,800-man brigade and for 10 months unsuccessfully pursued Pancho Villa's forces into Mexico, an experience that prepared him for his next move—and a big one.

World War I—In 1917, after a short interview, President Woodrow Wilson decided that Pershing would command the American Expeditionary Force (AEF) in Europe. Pershing arrived in France on June 23 to begin a massive buildup of U.S. forces. When France demanded that American units fight under French field commanders, Pershing refused. He preserved the AEF as an independent fighting force and directed three major offensives in 1918: Aisne-Marne from July 25 to August 2, Saint-Mihiel from September 12 to 19, and the final Meuse-Argonne offensive on September 26 to November 11.

Pershing didn't use the same tactics employed by the French, which, after four years of war, had failed to dislodge the enemy. Trench warfare created enormous casualties. Taking a page from Robert E. Lee's playbook, Pershing operated on the flanks of the enemy. He was also the first to use air power to soften up fortified positions by bombing instead of relying entirely on artillery. While the French and British thought the war could be won by 1919 or 1920, Pershing said the AEF would end the war in 1918—and they did.

His appointment as General of the Armies of the United States in July 1919 made him the first and only general to receive the rank in his own lifetime. He avoided politics and served for two years as chief of staff, retiring in 1924. He is seldom remembered because the AEF didn't contribute to major European campaigns until 1918.

What Made Him Great?

Like Lee and Grant, Pershing took the field with his men and was recognized for his personal bravery. A strict disciplinarian, he was also cold, distant, and demanding, which many of his subordinates disliked—but he was also fair, just, and tenacious, virtues that his detractors overlooked. Had any other general been sent to France to command the AEF, American units would probably have been propelled into the French army to fight poorly conducted battles under generals using ineffective tactics.

Turn to page 169 for Part II.

U.S. Navy SEAL classes lose up to 80% of trainees to injury or voluntary dropout.

ANOTHER PERSPECTIVE

Among the best-known quotes on war is William Tecumseh Sherman's observation that "War is hell." Here are some other opinions.

"I know not with what weapons World War III will be fought, but World War IV will be fought with sticks and stones."

—Albert Einstein

"I propose getting rid of conventional armaments and replacing them with reasonably priced hydrogen bombs that would be distributed equally throughout the world."

—Idi Amin

"The world will never have lasting peace so long as men reserve for war the finest human qualities."

—John Foster Dulles

"Every vice was once a virtue, and may become respectable again, just as hatred becomes respectable in wartime."

—Will Durant

"Men should stop fighting among themselves and start fighting insects."

—Luther Burbank

"I'd like to see the government get out of war altogether and leave the whole field to private industry."

—Joseph Heller

"To be prepared for war is one of the most effectual means of preserving peace."

—George Washington

"War hath no fury like a noncombatant."

—Charles Edward Montague

"A doctor could make a million dollars if he could figure out a way to bring a boy into the world without a trigger finger."

—Arthur Miller

"Either war is obsolete, or men are."

—R. Buckminster Fuller

"I have already given two cousins to the war, and I stand reddy [ready] to sacfifiss [sacrifice] my wife's brothr ruther'n no see the reblyin krusht."

—Artemus Ward

The oldest U.S. Coast Guard Life-Saving station still in service is at Sandy Hook, NJ.

CHANGE IS GONNA COME

In 1989 General Colin Powell was named Chairman of the Joint Chiefs of Staff, becoming the first African American to hold the highest military position in the United States. Not too long before that, the idea of a black soldier rising so high in the ranks would have been unthinkable.

A LONG HISTORY OF SERVICE

Before the United States was formed, black soldiers were serving in state militias. The pre-Revolution militias were loosely organized, with few rules beyond the requirement that enlistees be able to fire a gun. But as the 18th century progressed, enlistment became more exclusive; black men were among the first to be barred. Some could still serve, but only without arms, and some could serve only if they were freemen rather than slaves.

When the American Revolution began, escaped slaves flocked to the British side to fight against their oppressive masters, thinking this would offer them the best chance for freedom. In fact, the British accepted slaves belonging to the enemy Patriots, but returned the slaves of Loyalists to their owners. An estimated 5,000 black men also served in the Continental Army, and the U.S. armed forces reached a level of racial integration that it wouldn't see again for nearly two centuries.

THE CIVIL WAR AND GLORY DAYS

The abolishment of slavery was one of the main issues that led to the Civil War, but black men at first weren't allowed to fight for the Union side, creating resentment among some in the North. A 1792 federal law barred black men from bearing arms, so even freemen who wanted to serve the Union were turned away. But two years after the war began, the Union formed the U.S. Colored Troops (USCT), all-black volunteer units led by white officers. USCT soldiers served with distinction in dozens of minor battles, but were used sparingly in major battles.

A notable exception was the 54th Massachusetts, which attacked Fort Wagner, South Carolina, in July 1863—the subject of the 1989 film *Glory*. Although the attack was unsuccessful, it raised the status of black soldiers among white leaders, many of whom had previously considered blacks to be poor fighters. It also spurred further enlistment in the USCT, swelling its ranks to nearly 180,000 men by the end of the Civil War—about 10 percent of the Union army's strength. In the Confederacy, slaves weren't considered for army service until the end of the war, but by then it was too late. And who knows how hard they would have fought?

After the Civil War—and despite their accomplishments—black soldiers who fought for the Union weren't granted the same treatment, training, and pay as white soldiers. They remained in all-black units led by white officers, and were given the least-desirable assignments. Few black soldiers became officers—and since the regulations stipulated that the black units be led by white officers, there was little reason to promote black soldiers. The trend continued throughout the late 1800s and early 1900s. Black units fought in the Spanish-American War, the Philippine Insurrection, and other conflicts, garnering Medals of Honor and the respect of white troops—but hardly any new rights.

THE WORLD WARS

Have you ever watched a World War II movie and noticed that all the American soldiers are white men? That's because the official policy of the U.S. armed forces, done in the name of efficiency, was to assign black soldiers to segregated units. Military leaders were hesitant to integrate troops at virtually any level, so entire divisions had to be formed and given separate training facilities, housing, and assignments. The military establishment believed that the intermingling of black and white troops would lead to unrest and violence, resulting in a less-effective fighting force.

Most black units were limited to support roles; few actually saw combat. A black man who entered the U.S. Army during either of the World Wars would most likely serve in the Quartermaster Corps (logistics and supplies) or the Engineer Corps (construction and other manual labor). Those entering the U.S. Navy were almost sure to be assigned to the nonwhite Steward's Branch, where they would work as cooks, janitors, porters, and in other noncombat duties.

The few black units that were dispatched to combat assign-

Unofficial motto of Army Ranger trainees: "With the tab, or on a slab." It means...

ments often earned low ratings, which was no surprise considering that they tended to be undertrained and served under white officers who viewed their own assignments as punishment. There were several exceptions, including the 761st Tank Battalion, which served in Europe attached to the 26th Infantry Division. The 761st arrived at Normandy in October 1944 and fought the Germans in the Battle of the Bulge, earning praise from General George S. Patton, who nevertheless said that he had "no faith in the inherent fighting ability" of black troops.

TIMES ARE A-CHANGING

Finally acknowledging that it hadn't used black troops in the most efficient manner possible during World War II, the U.S. Army formed a committee to investigate and address the issue. This committee, known as the Gillem Board and headed by Lieutenant General Alvan C. Gillem Jr., worked quickly to suggest how to increase the efficient utilization of black servicemen in the U.S. Army. Among its chief recommendations:

- Use a quota of approximately 10 percent black troops to match the percentage in the general population;
- Offer more specialty positions to qualified black troops;
- Promote black officers under the same standards as white officers; and
- Allow black troops to serve alongside white troops, while still segregated at the smaller platoon and company levels.

The result wasn't complete integration, but a step in that direction. Military leaders didn't believe in sudden change, and quite a few were reluctant to set a precedent on an issue that was only just gaining steam in American society.

When the board's recommendations were put into practice, however, there was little change. Black units were now segregated up to the battalion level, with one black battalion being assigned to each division. The practice of not giving a black officer command of white troops remained in place. The U.S. Army—as well as the Navy and Army Air Forces—continued to cite the poor performance of black combat units in World War II and concerns about social harmony to justify their old practices. Black units were still assigned to menial tasks, received inadequate training, and were segregated in nearly all activities. Qualified individuals were often denied promotions, and

...the trainee will win his Ranger Tab (a shoulder insignia) or die trying.

the military establishment remained firm in its belief that black men were simply not suited to being good soldiers.

A NEW ORDER

Executive Order 9981, signed by President Harry S. Truman on July 26, 1948, called for "equal treatment and opportunity" (not specifically "integration") for all black servicemen. With the advent of the Cold War, Truman saw a pressing need to make the best use of all enlisted men, and he saw EO9981 as one means to accomplish this goal. It's also worth noting that the order was given in an election year, at a time when black voters were becoming restless with the Truman administration's stance on civil rights. The order got many civil rights advocates off Truman's back (including the outspoken Asa Philip Randolph, who had called for widespread civil disobedience), but in the end it did little to ease segregation and discrimination in the armed forces. For one thing, there was no time frame for compliance. From the commanders' viewpoint, all-white units were more effective in combat than integrated units; the fact that black soldiers were not trained adequately wasn't factored into the argument.

THE TURNING POINT

When war broke out in Korea in June 1950, the service branches were still largely segregated. By using the Selective Service Act to draft men into the military, the U.S. Army doubled in size in just five months, and this growth included a disproportionate number of black troops due to the earlier elimination of the quota system in April 1950. Among first-time enlistees in the U.S. Army that year, 25 percent were black, far above the previous quota level of 10 percent. Many of these troops were sent to the Eighth Army in the Far East without specific assignments, because the Army's all-black units were already overstrength—some by as much as 50 percent. With losses mounting on the battlefield and a large number of black soldiers waiting to be deployed, the Eighth Army's commanders came up with the most practical solution: they assigned black troops to white units for the sake of expediency.

NO BIG DEAL

By May 1951, around 60 percent of the companies in the Eighth

The U.S. Navy has six active numbered fleets, from Second through Seventh.

Army were at least partially integrated without any specific directives from Washington. The sociology experts employed by the U.S. Army who had predicted that such intermingling would be destructive were proven wrong. White companies readily accepted black soldiers who were willing and able to fight, which was all that mattered to the troops. The racial tensions that many believed would lead to military inefficiency never materialized. As one white serviceman said, "An American is an American." Seeing the improved efficiency that integration had brought to his forces, General Matthew Ridgway formally requested authority to integrate the Eighth Army on May 14, 1951. His request was approved. In the end, the Korean experience finally taught the U.S. military establishment that race played no role whatsoever in determining a soldier's worth on the battlefield.

AMERICANS ALL

The complete integration of the U.S. armed forces worldwide took place progressively over the next few years (more slowly in the South, where local Jim Crow laws were still in effect). By 1954 the last all-black unit, based in Europe, was deactivated. The U.S. Army tried to downplay the integration of its troops at the time because it didn't want to take a lead role in the civil rights debate that was only just heating up in civilian life. Complete integration didn't mean the end of racism and discrimination, but the U.S. armed forces can take pride in knowing that it set a fine example for showing how individuals can look beyond the color of a person's skin to see what's truly inside: an American.

* * *

FIGHTING THE SYSTEM

During the Vietnam War, when the Army could induct any draftee except for some married men, one Army recruiting office fought back by posting this sign in the window: "Better two years than life."

In Vietnam, a "Mad Minute" was a brief, intense exchange of automatic-weapons fire.

TOP MARINE CORPS FLICKS

Hollywood has done its part to cement the role of the U.S. Marines as an almost indestructible fighting force—always willing, always able, and always faithful.

TELL IT TO THE MARINES (1926)

In this silent movie that was the first to be produced with the full cooperation of the U.S. Marine Corps, Lon Chaney stars as Sergeant Frank O'Hara, who leads his leathernecks on a tour of the Philippines. William Haines plays Private "Skeet" Burns, an undisciplined recruit looking for a good time and loose women rather than devoting himself to the rigors of the Marine Corps. General Smedley D. Butler served as a technical consultant for the film, and the scenes at sea were shot aboard the battleship USS *California*. Lon Chaney was named an honorary Marine for his performance—the first actor to be given that distinction.

GUNG HO! (1943)

Based on the actual events surrounding the August 1942 raid of Makin Island (now called Butaritari Island) in the Pacific, the film's plot follows a mishmash group of Marine Corps volunteers as they prepare for and execute their daring mission. Lieutenant Colonel Thorwald (Randolph Scott) worked with Chinese guerrillas prior to the outset of World War II, and now attempts to use the Chinese concept of *gung ho*, or "work together," to get all of his Marines on the same page. Although the film has many violent scenes, it provides an example of how Marine Corps soldiers are trained to put the success of a mission above all else.

PRIDE OF THE MARINES (1945)

This well-received film recounts the experiences of U.S. Marine Corps Sergeant Al Schmid (John Garfield), a hero of the 1942–43 Battle of Guadalcanal. Schmid had been manning a machine gun against the Japanese for several hours when a grenade exploded nearby, blinding him. Even without his sight, Schmid managed to continue firing his machine gun with the help of an injured comrade who served as his "eyes." Although the battle scenes take up only a small portion of the film's length, the portrayal of Schmid as a relentless hero helped give the Marine Corps a public identity as a force that never quit under any circumstance. *Pride of the Marines* was nominated for one Academy Award, for Best Screenplay.

SANDS OF IWO JIMA (1949)

John Wayne stars as grizzled Marine Sergeant John Stryker, whose training methods are universally despised by his troops until the bullets begin to fly. By the time the men get to the small island known as Iwo Jima, where the Japanese forces are dug in and waiting, the reasons for Stryker's relentlessness become clear. Arguably the most well-known movie to feature the Marine Corps, *Sands of Iwo Jima* was nominated for four Academy Awards, including a Best Actor nod for the Duke.

HEARTBREAK RIDGE (1986)

This film stars Clint Eastwood as quick-tempered and battle-hardened Gunnery Sergeant Thomas Highway, whose years in the military have left his life in disarray as he nears the end of his career. Assigned to whip a recon platoon into shape, "Gunny" finds himself doing what he does best—leading Marines in combat during the 1983 U.S. invasion of Grenada. Though many questioned the accuracy of the events portrayed in the film, Eastwood's solid performance has kept it on the fan list more than 20 years later. *Heartbreak Ridge* was nominated for one Academy Award, for Best Sound.

FULL METAL JACKET (1987)

Stanley Kubrick's vulgar and gritty film about Marines preparing for war and deploying to Vietnam is still a classic. The film catapulted actor R. Lee Ermey to stardom for his role as loud and unforgiving Gunnery Sergeant Hartman, whose harsh physical and psychological treatment of recruits have become legendary. The Marine Corps wasn't so impressed, however. The service offered no support for the making of the film, which was shot on location in England. *Full Metal Jacket* received an Oscar nomination for Best Writing, and Ermey received a Golden Globe nomination for Best Supporting Actor.

...The names are all words in the phonetic alphabet used by most U.S. armed forces.

BORN ON THE FOURTH OF JULY (1989)

Tom Cruise stars as real-life Vietnam vet Ron Kovic, whose traumatic experiences in the war have left him paralyzed and struggling with his place in the world. In the end, he becomes an outspoken critic of the conflict and the treatment of returning veterans. Directed by Oliver Stone (himself a Vietnam veteran), whose 1986 film *Platoon* earned an Oscar, the film was nominated for eight Academy Awards—including Best Picture and a Best Actor for Cruise—and took home the awards for Best Director and Best Film Editing.

A FEW GOOD MEN (1992)

"You can't handle the truth!" Colonel Nathan Jessup screams during the famous courtroom scene in this military legal drama that centers on the trial of two Marines charged with killing one of their own in a hazing incident gone bad. Jack Nicholson plays Jessup, a salty Marine officer who is believed to have ordered the attack, while Tom Cruise stars as Lieutenant Daniel Kaffee, the inexperienced Navy lawyer assigned to defend the Marines. The film was nominated for four Academy Awards, including Best Picture and a Best Supporting Actor for Nicholson.

FLAGS OF OUR FATHERS AND *LETTERS FROM IWO JIMA* (2006)

When taken together, this pair of films from director Clint Eastwood show one of the bloodiest battles of World War II from all angles. In *Flags of Our Fathers*, Eastwood explores the history surrounding the Pulitzer Prize–winning photograph of the American flag being raised on Mount Suribachi and the men who became national icons for planting it. In *Letters from Iwo Jima*, Eastwood attacks the subject again, but this time from the perspective of the Japanese fighters who took heavy losses as they attempted to defend the small island. *Flags of Our Fathers* was nominated for two Academy Awards and won for Sound Editing, while *Letters from Iwo Jima* was nominated for four Academy Awards, including Best Picture and Best Director, but did not take home any Oscars.

Hang out the laundry: Military slang for dropping paratroopers from a plane.

THE NAVY'S SONG

The U.S. Navy's unofficial song, "Anchors Aweigh," had less to do with serving on the seven seas than as a fight song to be sung at the annual Army-Navy football game in 1906. However, the tune has evolved lyrically into more than a football call to arms.

MARCHING WITH "ZIMMY"

Though "Anchors Aweigh" came into being in 1906, it was the culmination of a tradition that began with the selection of Navy Lieutenant Charles A. Zimmermann in 1887 as bandmaster at the Naval Academy. "Zimmy" was a graduate of the prestigious Peabody Conservatory in Baltimore. He became a beloved figure in 1892 when he began composing a march for every graduating class. To return the honor, the midshipmen presented him with a gold medal each year.

In November 1906, midshipman Alfred Hart Miles approached the bandmaster to request a new march. He wanted a fight song to inspire the Navy football team in its upcoming contest with Army in early December. So for the month of November, Zimmerman and Miles sat together at the Naval Academy Chapel organ as the bandmaster worked out the tune and Miles wrote the lyrics. Their song—"Anchors Aweigh"—was played by the Navy band as the entire midshipman brigade sang the lyrics. It helped inspire Navy to a 10–0 victory, their first win against Army in six years. Afterward, the song was dedicated to the Naval Academy's class of 1907. It was so popular that it was adopted as the unofficial song of the U.S. Navy.

Despite the tune's popularity, the Navy did not adopt it as its official song because the lyrics were so specific to the academy. In an attempt to change that, famed Hollywood lyricist George D. Lottman (who wrote the score for *An Officer and a Gentleman*) rewrote the first two verses to make it more acceptable.

With the inclusion of female students at the Academy since 1976, perhaps "Anchors Aweigh" will need yet another update before long. "Anchors Aweigh, my boys and girls" might be the future refrain.

IT FITS YOU TO A "T"

A brief history of the most popular shirt in the world.

YOU BE THE JUDGE

T-shirts have been around so long that nobody knows for sure where they originated or how they got their name. One theory: They were first worn by longshoremen who unloaded tea from merchant ships in Annapolis, Maryland, during the 17th century. They became known as "tea shirts" and eventually "T-shirts."

Another theory: They were invented by the British royal family for use by sailors in the Royal Navy. According to that version, "the monarchy ordered sailors to sew sleeves on their undershirts to spare royalty the unseemly experience of witnessing an armada of armpits. Ergo, the shirt shaped like the letter T."

UNDERSHIRTS ARE SUNK

T-shirts were part of American life as early as 1913, when the U.S. Navy added crewnecked cotton undershirts to its uniform. But they were generally limited to military use. To most American men, the only real undershirt was the sleeveless variety with totally exposed armpits, or what would be called a tank top today.

These, however, were dealt a serious blow in 1934 by actor Clark Gable. In the Oscar-winning film *It Happened One Night*, Gable took off his shirt . . . and wasn't wearing anything underneath. "Hardly a young man from coast to coast would be caught wearing one after that." Jim Murray wrote in the *Los Angeles Times*. "It almost wrecked an industry, put people out of work."

By then, the T-shirt's transition from underwear to outerwear was already underway, and in the early 1930s some stores began selling shirts with university insignias on them. But they were still primarily considered undershirts. In 1938 Sears, Roebuck and Company added the "gob-style" short-sleeved undershirts (U.S. Navy sailors were known as "gobs") to its catalog. Price:

24 cents apiece. They sold poorly—it was still too soon after the Gable fiasco.

T-SHIRT FASHION

It wasn't until World War II that T-shirts really began to take hold in American culture. Each branch of the military issued millions of "Skivvies" in its own color, and in the Pacific islands it was so hot that they were virtually the only shirts that most soldiers wore. When the fighting boys returned home from the war, they brought their taste for T-shirts with them.

"For a while," according to J. D. Reed in *Smithsonian* magazine, "the T-shirt suggested the kind of crew-cut cleanliness and neatness indigenous to the new, postwar suburbs." Then in 1951, the movies struck again: Marlon Brando electrified audiences by wearing a skin-tight T-shirt in Tennessee Williams's *A Streetcar Named Desire*. The actor's rippling muscles "gave the garment a sexual *je ne sais quoi* from which America has never recovered," wrote one critic. "Elvis Presley cheered it on, sneering in a T-shirt and leather jacket. And James Dean perpetuated the attitude-with-a-T look in *Rebel Without a Cause* in 1955."

By the end of the 1950s, the T-shirt was no longer just a piece of underwear—it was a fashion statement. Today the American T-shirt industry sells over a billion T-shirts a year. The average American owns 25 of them.

* * *

WORD ORIGIN

A term that came from the British rifle range during this period was *washout*. If a shot landed completely wide of the target, it was called a washout because on old iron targets the space they landed on was covered with some kind of paint, or "wash." At first, washout simply meant a bad shot, but it was soon broadened to mean any kind of failure, and it's still used that way.

TOP 10 ADMIRALS, PART II

We continue our salute to America's best admirals. For Part I, go to page 55.

6. GEORGE DEWEY (1837–1917)

Born in a cottage at Montpelier, Vermont, Dewey studied at Norwich University before graduating from the Naval Academy in 1858. During operations against New Orleans in April 1862 he served under Admiral Farragut aboard the steam sloop U.S.S. *Mississippi*. He admitted to learning more about tactics from Farragut than from any other navy admiral. Later he served under Admiral Porter during the two bombardments of Fort Fisher and rose in rank to lieutenant commander. During the next 30 years Dewey served in various commands, but his particular interest was in the development of armored cruisers and battleships. Promoted to commodore in February 1896, Dewey requested sea duty and in February 1897 took command of the Asiatic squadron.

The Spanish-American War

Dewey was a man of action who deplored peacetime duties. Dewey also understood that a man at sea during times of war could make opportunities for himself. In December 1897, after hoisting his commodore's pennant on the cruiser *Olympia*, he began training his men for combat. Dewey anticipated war with Spain and, contrary to doubtful naval friends, he predicted war in the Philippines.

Dewey's ships were scattered along the Asiatic coast, but by the end of March he had them fueled with coal, repainted battleship gray, and waiting for orders at Hong Kong. On April 25, 1898, orders arrived: "War has commenced between the United States and Spain. Proceed at once to the Philippine islands."

On April 30 Dewey reached the entrance to Manila Bay. Inside a Spanish fleet as imposing as the American squadron waited. The fight would be the first between modern ships using modern ordnance. Under cover of darkness on May 1, Dewey led the Asiatic squadron into the bay and past Spanish shore batteries. Off Cavite Navy Yard lay Rear Admiral Patricio Montojo y Parasón's Spanish

The Desert Hawk, a small unmanned surveillance plane, weighs just seven pounds.

Fleet. Dewey began circling off Cavite, and at 5:40 a.m. turned to his flag captain, and said, "You may fire when you are ready, Gridley." The *Olympia* opened fire, following up with two combined 3,700-pound broadsides. Dewey continued to circle, sinking three Spanish ships and disabling five small cruisers and gunboats. In an action that inflicted 371 casualties on the Spanish navy, Dewey did not lose a man.

What Made Him Great

A brilliant tactician and outstanding leader, Dewey became the first and only "Admiral of the Navy." He brought the navy into the 20th century and his contributions were considered so valuable that the government exempted him from mandatory retirement because of age. Dewey continued to serve as president of the Navy General Board until his death in 1917.

7. CHESTER WILLIAM NIMITZ (1885–1966)

Nimitz graduated from the U.S. Naval Academy in 1905 seventh in a class of 114. He spent the next 26 years working with submarines and expanding his education. In 1933 he moved to cruisers, and after promotion to rear admiral in 1938, he led a cruiser division and then a battleship division. Nimitz never commanded an aircraft carrier division, which became America's most effective weapon in the Pacific.

World War II

On December 31, 1941, following the Japanese attack on Pearl Harbor, Admiral Nimitz settled into Honolulu, Hawaii, as commander in chief of the Pacific Fleet. In March 1942 the Joint Chiefs of Staff added all naval, sea, and air forces in the entire Pacific Ocean area to his responsibilities. Aided by Pearl Harbor code-breakers, Nimitz stopped a Japanese assault on Port Moresby, New Guinea, which on May 7-8, 1942, in the Coral Sea was the first carrier battle of the war. A month later he sent the only three carriers in the Pacific to Midway and on June 2-6 repulsed four Japanese assault groups. Learning four Japanese carriers had been sunk, Nimitz informed Washington, "Pearl Harbor has now been partially avenged."

Nimitz pressed forward in the Pacific, beginning with the

The *Turtle*, invented by David Bushnell in 1775, was America's first functioning submarine.

amphibious assault by the 1st Marine Division on Guadalcanal on August 7, 1942. As more men and ships became available he expanded operations in the Solomon Islands and provided naval support for General Douglas MacArthur's New Guinea operations.

In 1943 Nimitz began a major offensive in the Central Pacific called "the island-hopping campaign." Starting in the Caroline Islands at Tarawa Atoll in November 1943, he then moved against the Marshall Islands and the Marianas in 1944. He left tactical control with commanders he could trust, putting Admiral William Halsey in the South Pacific and Admiral Raymond Spruance in the Central Pacific, with Rear Admiral Richmond Kelly Turner in charge of amphibious operations. In October 1944 Nimitz joined forces with General MacArthur for operations in the Philippines. Promoted to the new five-star rank of fleet admiral on December 5, 1944, Nimitz then formulated strategy for assaulting Iwo Jima and Okinawa.

What Made Him Great

Nimitz devised the strategy for winning the War in the Pacific and implemented it with the best officers and airmen in the Navy. After the official surrender of Japan in Tokyo Bay on September 2, 1945, Nimitz became Chief of Naval Operations on December 15. "They fought together as brothers in arms; they died together and now they sleep side by side...To them, we have a solemn obligation...to ensure that their sacrifice will help make this a better and safer world in which to live."—Admiral Nimitz at the official surrender of Japan on September 2, 1945, in Tokyo Bay.

8. WILLIAM FREDERICK "BULL" HALSEY. JR. (1882–1959)

Halsey graduated from the Naval Academy in 1904 43rd in a class of 62. During World War I he commanded destroyers out of Queenstown, Ireland, and afterwards graduated from both the army and the navy war colleges. At the age of fifty-two he became a pilot, headed the Pensacola Naval Air Station in 1937, and his promotion to rear admiral in March 1938 led to his career as a carrier commander. He was at sea with the carriers *Enterprise* and *Yorktown* when Japan struck Pearl Harbor on December 7, 1941.

Actor Robert Duvall grew up in a military family and served in the Army from 1953 to 1954.

World War II

Halsey struck back as fast as he could. During the next few months he raided Japanese-held islands in the Central Pacific and escorted Colonel Jimmy Doolittle's B-25 bombers across the Pacific for the first raid on Japan. In October 1942, after recovering from illness, he took command of naval forces in the South Pacific, prevented Japan from recapturing Guadalcanal, and provided naval and air support for a June-November 1943 campaign to capture the Solomon Islands. In 1944 Admiral Nimitz brought Halsey from the South Pacific and put him in charge of the Third Fleet in the western Pacific.

Assuming operational command in August, Halsey launched heavy air strikes on Japanese bases in the Philippines. He supported General MacArthur's landings on Leyte in October, but got lured away from the beachhead and went chasing after Admiral Jisaburo Ozawa's carriers. He sank four carriers off northeastern Luzon, but exposed MacArthur's forces to an attack from Japan's powerful Central Force off Samar. Criticized for abandoning MacArthur, who was never in trouble, Halsey continued to support operations in the Philippines when struck by a powerful typhoon that sank three destroyer escorts. (For the complete story see page 328.) After a sweep through the South China Sea, he turned the Third Fleet over to Admiral Spruance for the Okinawa campaign.

When kamikaze attacks at Okinawa began frustrating Spruance, Halsey resumed command of the fleet, destroyed Japanese air bases, ended the suicide attacks, and began air operations against the Japanese home islands. Although beset by another typhoon and another loss, Halsey remained in command of the Third Fleet until after the surrender of Japan.

What Made Him Great

Always colorful, aggressive, and outspoken, Halsey believed in taking calculated risks. He will always be among the great admirals, despite his patent impetuosity. The only enemies he couldn't defeat were typhoons. Promoted to a five-star fleet admiral in December 1945, Halsey remained on special duty until he retired in April 1947.

9. RAYMOND AMES SPRUANCE (1886–1969)

Spruance graduated from the Naval Academy in 1906 and spent

the next 15 years on battleships, cruisers, and destroyers. A quiet, unassuming, and brilliant organizer, Spruance graduated from the Naval War College in 1927 and spent the next two years in naval intelligence. Advancing through the ranks, he became a rear admiral in December 1939 and two years later, on the eve of the Japanese attack, assumed command of Cruiser Division 5 at Pearl Harbor. He also served as Halsey's cruiser commander in April 1942, when the latter escorted Jimmy Doolittle's B-25s across the Pacific to bomb Japan.

World War II

Spruance may have remained a gunship commander had Halsey not fallen ill before the Battle of Midway. Nimitz pulled Spruance from cruisers and put him in command of the *Enterprise* and the *Hornet* with Rear Admiral Frank Fletcher's carrier *Yorktown*, up from the South Pacific. Spruance used his dive bombers skillfully at Midway, sinking all four Japanese carriers. The enemy fleet withdrew, although Fletcher later lost the damaged *Yorktown* after a submarine attack.

Nimitz named Spruance chief of staff, promoted him to vice admiral, and put him in charge of the new Fifth Fleet. During Nimitz's island-hopping campaign, Spruance led assaults on Tarawa Atoll in November 1943 and the Marshall Islands from January to February 1944. Promoted to admiral in February, Spruance pushed westward and on June 15 invaded Saipan in the Marianas, followed by Guam and Tinian. Vice Admiral Marc A. Mitscher commanded Spruance's carriers and wanted to finish off the Japanese fleet lying to the west. Mitscher's aircraft had destroyed all the enemy planes in the area, but Spruance held the carriers off Saipan for beachhead protection. Spruance viewed his task as protecting the amphibious force, whereas Halsey, had he commanded, would surely have chased after the Japanese fleet.

After turning the fleet over to Halsey for operations in the Philippines, Spruance returned to Honolulu to plan the Iwo Jima and Okinawa campaigns. He relieved Halsey on January 26, 1945, and on February 19 landed marines on Iwo Jima. Leaving ships behind to support the operation, he moved the rest of the fleet across the Pacific and on April 1 assaulted Okinawa. When Spruance failed to use Mitscher's aircraft to stop kamikaze attacks,

Halsey returned to the area, assumed command of the fleet, and destroyed the kamikaze air bases.

What Made Him Great

Controversy lingers over which man was the best tactical admiral of World War II. Admiral King probably had it right when he said, "Spruance [should] be put in charge of landings...so Halsey could go out and fight." A gifted commander, Spruance functioned with different goals than Halsey. He concentrated on saving lives. Most historians agree that compared with Halsey, Spruance was probably the better commander.

10. MARC ANDREW "PETE" MITSCHER (1887–1947)

Despite the focus on the deeds of men like Nimitz, Halsey, and Spruance, "Pete" Mitscher became the leading tactical and operational U.S. carrier force commander of World War II.

Mitscher grew up in Oklahoma City, attended the Naval Academy, and in June 1916 earned his wings at Pensacola flight school. Although he spent time serving on cruisers, he preferred barnstorming in air shows until 1926, when the Navy transferred him to the first experimental aircraft carrier *Langley*. In November 1927, after the commissioning of the carrier *Saratoga*, Mitscher became her air commander. Promoted to captain in 1938, he had spent more time with aircraft than with ships.

World War II

Assigned to command the carrier *Hornet*, he steamed into the Pacific after the beginning of World War II and from her deck launched Jimmie Doolittle's B-25 bombers for the April 1942 raid on Tokyo. Mitscher commanded the *Hornet* during the Battle of Midway, but when Nimitz sent Halsey into the South Pacific, he also sent Mitscher as Halsey's fleet air commander.

Mitscher directed air operations for the army, navy, marines, and the New Zealand air force during the Solomons campaign. When he returned to sea as commander of the fast Carrier Task Force, no one in the navy, including Halsey, knew more about carrier air tactics than Mitscher. From January to June 1944 he performed brilliantly in the island-hopping campaigns, surpassing the expectations of even Nimitz. Promoted to vice admiral in March,

...The shortest, for Air Force recruits, is 61/2 weeks. The Army's is 9 weeks.

he directed carrier operations during the invasion of the Marianas and used his aircraft to obliterate every Japanese plane in what his pilots called the Marianas Turkey Shoot. His greatest disappointment occurred when Spruance refused to let him attack the Japanese fleet in the Philippine Sea.

When Halsey replaced Spruance and took command of the Third Fleet during General MacArthur's assault on Leyte, Mitscher warned him to not pursue the Japanese decoys off Luzon. Halsey ignored the advice, received a curt message from Nimitz, and returned to Leyte. Mitscher remained off Luzon with three carrier groups and destroyed the decoy squadron. When Spruance later replaced Halsey for the assault on Iwo Jima and Okinawa, Mitscher joined both campaigns. He once again became frustrated at Okinawa when Spruance would not turn the carriers loose to destroy kamikaze air bases. When Halsey resumed command of the fleet, Mitscher's aircraft clobbered the Japanese airfields and ended kamikaze attacks.

What Made Him Great

Mitscher often brooded over perceived tactical errors made by Halsey and Spruance. He cared for his carriers, and he cared for his men. He became the leading tactical and operational American carrier commander of the war, ranking as a top admiral with Halsey and Spruance.

* * *

SERVICE ACADEMY GRADUATES WHO BECAME PRESIDENT

• U.S. Military Academy: Ulysses S. Grant and Dwight D. Eisenhower. West Point was Eisenhower's second choice when the U.S. Naval Academy turned him away for being too old.

• U.S. Naval Academy: Jimmy Carter

• West Point Reject: Harry Truman was turned down because of his nearsightedness, and he had to settle for enlisting in Missouri's Army National Guard. He rose to the rank of captain during World War I, and eventually became a colonel in the Army Reserves.

JOE AND WILLIE GO TO WAR

They met during World War II and became best friends while serving in the European theater. Everyone who saw them liked them—except for the top brass.

LAUGHTER IS THE BEST MEDICINE

Bill Mauldin was one of the preeminent cartoonists of the 20th century. One of his best-known cartoons, published in the *Chicago Sun Times* after John F. Kennedy's assassination, was set at the Lincoln Memorial and showed a grieving Lincoln with his head in his hands. Anyone who saw it couldn't help but be moved.

But it was Mauldin's early work that made him famous. During World War II, he created two unshaven, rumpled, and slump-shouldered characters, infantrymen Joe and Willie. What made them so real was that Mauldin himself was an infantryman in the U.S. Army's 45th Division. He fought his way through the mud and muck of Europe and instilled his characters with his own real-life war experiences.

BILL'S STORY

Mauldin's grandfather was a cavalry scout and his father was an artilleryman in World War I. Bill grew up in New Mexico and Arizona and spent his time drawing. His grandparents scraped together money to send him to Illinois so he could take courses at the Art Institute of Chicago. But in 1940, the 18-year-old Mauldin joined the Arizona National Guard, which became part of the 45th Infantry Division. He volunteered to draw cartoons for the unit's newspaper, and eventually his work was picked up by *Stars and Stripes*, the official newspaper of the armed forces. He saw combat in Sicily and Anzio and received a Purple Heart for wounds suffered in Italy, but his greatest contribution to the war was his cartoons.

JOE MEETS WILLIE

In his 1945 book *Up Front*, which won a Pulitzer Prize, Mauldin wrote, "Willie and Joe aren't at all clever. They aren't even good cartoon characters, because they have similar features which are distinguishable only by their different noses. Willie has a big nose and Joe has a little one . . . few people know which is Willie and which is Joe."

Joe appeared first, a clean-shaven, well-scrubbed guy. He met Willie just after the attack on Pearl Harbor. Then the pair, like Mauldin, headed for the Italian campaign as riflemen. They ended up sitting in muddy foxholes, getting through each day without decent rations or dry clothes and enduring the sometimes questionable wisdom and authority of their superiors. One cartoon showed his bone-weary, disheartened GIs sloshing through the rain, with the caption: "Fresh, spirited American troops, flushed with victory, are bringing in thousands of hungry, ragged, battle-weary prisoners."

BRASS ATTACKS

The rear echelon didn't always get the frontline jokes, and the officers who were often the source of Joe and Willie's complaints had complaints of their own. Mauldin was chastised because the unshaven, bleary-eyed, morose-looking pair were too messy. General George S. Patton, Mauldin's loudest critic, wrote to *Stars and Stripes* to complain about Mauldin's "attempts to undermine military discipline." Historian Stephen Ambrose said of him, "More than anyone else, save only Ernie Pyle, he caught the trials and travails of the GI." Mauldin touched a chord with the common foot soldier; many GIs wrote to the cartoonist after the war to tell him how his humor helped them keep going in spite of adversity.

WAR AFTER WAR

Like most other World War II soldiers, Willie and Joe returned home after the war and disappeared into civilian life. Before they did, Willie appeared on the cover of *Time* in June 1945. Mauldin and Joe were pulled back into combat with the 1950 Korean War. Mauldin became a war correspondent for *Collier's*; Joe went back to war and wrote letters home to his buddy Willie.

After the Korean War, Mauldin worked as an editorial cartoonist for the *St. Louis Post-Dispatch* in 1958, and then was a syndicated cartoonist until his retirement in 1991. He also found his way

Operation War Bride (1946) brought 50,000 British women to the U.S. on passenger ships...

back to the combat zone in 1965 to visit his son Bruce, who was serving in Vietnam, and in 1991 to visit troops in Saudi Arabia during the Persian Gulf War.

PULITZER NUMBER TWO

That first Pulitzer he'd won in 1945 made him at 23 the youngest person to win the Pulitzer Prize. In 1959 his editorial cartoon commenting on the "voluntary" refusal of the Nobel Prize by Russian writer and poet Boris Pasternak won him a second Pulitzer. It showed Pasternak as one scrawny labor camp prisoner saying to another, "I won the Nobel Prize for Literature. What was your crime?"

A FAMOUS FAN

In Mauldin's later days, a newspaper column reported that he'd taken up residence in a nursing home. The news prompted more than 10,000 fan letters from grateful soldiers and veterans. *Peanuts* cartoonist Charles Schulz was grateful, too. Like Mauldin, he'd spent some time as an infantryman and like lots of other vets had drawn emotional sustenance from Mauldin's cartoons. Every Veterans Day from the 1980s until Schulz's retirement in 2000, flying ace Snoopy would dress as an Army vet and visit Bill Mauldin's house to "quaff a few root beers and tell war stories."

* * *

VARIOUS (NOW POLITICALLY INCORRECT) NAMES FOR THE ENEMY

During World War I, the traditional offensive slang for a German was *Kraut*, an abbreviation for what was regarded as a quintessential German food, sauerkraut. Another was *Heinie*, an abbreviation for the common German name Heinrich. A third was *Jerry*, either derived from the British nickname for chamber pots (which the German helmets resembled), or a shortening of "German." These terms survived, on a small scale, but again came into wider use during World War II, when Germany was again the enemy of the Allies.

TWIST ME A DIZZY

Does dealing with death and destruction on a daily basis make men loose with language? Apparently, yes. Here are a few colorful examples of wartime slang.

EGG BEATER
Helicopter (Korean War)

GIVE A DIRTY ORB
To give a dirty look (World War II)

CEILING WORK
High-altitude planes protecting airmen at lower levels (World War I)

BOOM-BOOM GIRL
Prostitute (Vietnam War)

HOT SKINNY
Rumors about important things (Vietnam War)

LATRINE TELEGRAM
A rumored report (World War II)

PLUTONIUM WINE
Moonshine brewed on a nuclear submarine (Cold War)

BRAIN BUCKET
Helmet (Korean War)

BONE JAR
Meaning "hello," a corruption of the French *bonjour* (World War I)

MESSY BUCKET
"Thank you"; from the French *merci beaucoup*, "many thanks" (World War I)

AGONY WAGON
Ambulance (World War II)

DEEP KIMCHI
In serious trouble (Korean War)

DINKY DAU
Crazy; from the Vietnamese *dien cai dau*, "ridiculous" (Vietnam War)

BEHAVIOR REPORT
A love letter reply (World War II)

SMOKE A THERMOMETER
To have your temperature taken (World War I)

BOTTLED SUNSHINE
Beer (World War II)

BOUGHT GUTS
Courage inspired by too much bottled sunshine (World War II)

TWIST A DIZZY
To roll a cigarette (World War II)

COMPLETELY CHEESED
Extremely bored (World War II)

APPLESAUCE ENEMA
Mild criticism of a subordinate so he feels less "chewed out" (Vietnam War)

BIG PICKLE
The atomic bomb (Korean War)

Silent Drill Platoon: A 24-man Marine rifle platoon that does a precision drill routine.

HOW THE PENTAGON GOT ITS SHAPE

The Pentagon, a.k.a. home of the Department of Defense, is the world's largest office building—but how did it get such an odd shape?

ORGANIZED CHAOS

In the 1930s, the War Department facilities were scattered among 23 locations throughout Washington, D.C., Maryland, and Virginia. Army Chief of Staff General Malin Craig saw the situation as dangerous and warned that "unavoidable delays and difficulties" could result in "serious consequences in the event of an emergency." Congress agreed, and approved the construction of a new War Department building in 1938. When World War II broke out in Europe in September 1939, the department proved just as inefficient as Craig had predicted. Lost time, lack of personal contact, and lack of supervision all contributed to the urgency to build a larger, more efficient headquarters. The newly built headquarters in the Foggy Bottom area of Washington, D.C., was inspected on April 25, 1941, but with a mere 270,000 square feet of office space, it would hold only about 4,000 of the 24,000 War Department workers—a number that was growing every day. They had outgrown their new building before they even moved in.

THE MAN IN CHARGE TAKES CHARGE

Brigadier General Brehon Somervell took command as the chief of the Army's Construction Division in December 1940. The following July, Somervell declared that the War Department needed a new headquarters—one that would house more than 40,000 people. Somervell met with prominent architect George E. Bergstrom and Lieutenant Colonel Hugh "Pat" Casey, chief of design for the Construction Division. The new structure Somervell had in mind would have four million square feet of air-conditioned office space, no more than four floors, and would remain relatively horizontal so as not to obstruct the view of the nation's capital. And one more thing: He wanted the plans on his desk on Monday morning. Never mind that it was already Thursday afternoon!

The U.S. Congress authorized the first paper currency, called "greenbacks," in 1862...

A FIVE-PART SOLUTION

Casey located an odd-shaped 67-acre tract east of Arlington Cemetery, called Arlington Farm. Perched on a hill over the Potomac and overlooking the Memorial Bridge, the land had been part of Robert E. Lee's estate, confiscated by the Union in 1861.

Bergstrom immediately set a team of engineers to drafting irregularly shaped designs to fit the Arlington Farm tract. By the end of the weekend they had a plan. The result wasn't pretty, nor was it symmetrical, but the pentagon shape they came up with fit the asymmetrical layout of the land.

The War Department staff approved the basic concept that Monday. The Secretary of War approved it on Tuesday; that same day, Somervell sent the plan to Congress. They moved quickly, along with President Franklin D. Roosevelt, to approve funding for the construction.

On August 14, 1941, the Senate authorized construction of the new building. After hearing some opposition to the Arlington Farm location (because it would obstruct the view between the Lincoln Memorial and Arlington Cemetery), Roosevelt directed the building to be moved three-quarters of a mile south. The new location was at the site of the old Hoover Airport, a brick factory, a pickle factory, a racetrack, and a low-income residential area known as Hell's Bottom.

Although the structure wouldn't be built on an odd-shaped tract any longer, the project was moving too quickly to make any costly or time-consuming design changes. Besides, Roosevelt liked the five-sided design. The new location did at least allow architects to make the odd-shaped structure more symmetrical.

WHO SAYS THE GOVERNMENT'S INEFFICIENT?

Groundbreaking took place in September 1941. Employees moved in seven months later. The whole construction was completed in 17 months, at an approximate cost of $83 million.

The building's official title, the "New War Department Building in Arlington," was too much of a mouthful for Army officers and employees, who began using the name "Pentagon" informally after a few months. In 1942 the Army threw in the towel and started using "Pentagon" as the official name.

Even today, the Pentagon is regarded as one of the most

efficient office buildings in the world. Although it has a total of 17.5 miles of corridors, it takes no more than seven minutes to walk between any two points in the building.

A SMALL CITY

The Pentagon has three times more floor space than New York's Empire State Building. With 6,500,000 gross square feet of space that occupies 29 acres of land, the building has five floors aboveground plus two basement levels. Each floor has five "ring" corridors: from the innermost "A" ring to the fifth and outermost "E" ring. The Pentagon's footprint could accommodate five U.S. Capitol buildings.

- Employees (both military and civilian): around 23,000
- Office space: 3,705,793 square feet
- Parking lots: 16
- Acres of parking: 67
- Stairways: 131
- Escalators: 19
- Water fountains: 691
- Restrooms: 284
- Daily phone calls: more than 200,000
- Miles of telephone cable: 100,000

A HOME AWAY FROM HOME

Employees can take advantage of the service of a variety of on-site vendors. There are more than a dozen restaurants, including McDonald's, Taco Bell, Starbucks, and Subway. Employees can visit their dentist or optometrist, do their banking, have their hair done, and their clothes dry cleaned. And the lines at the Pentagon Department of Motor Vehicles are probably a lot shorter than the ones most of us face.

UNOFFICIAL GROUND ZERO

Today, the site of the former World Trade Center is widely known as "ground zero," but the Pentagon long ago coined that phrase for the five-acre open plaza in the center of the building. The Pentagon's "ground zero" got its name during the Cold War based on the presumption that it would be the target for one or more Soviet nuclear missiles. At one time, the Ground Zero Café, a snack bar, was located at the center of the plaza.

THE REAL THING

On September 11, 2001—60 years to the day of the Pentagon's groundbreaking—within 30 minutes of two planes hitting the Twin Towers in New York, American Airlines Flight 77, a Boeing 757, crashed into the west side of the Pentagon property. The plane took out light poles in the parking lot, hit the ground just outside of the Pentagon, turned on its wing, and penetrated the outermost ring—the E ring. It then traveled through the D ring and into the C ring. All 58 passengers, four flight attendants, both pilots, 125 occupants of the Pentagon, and five hijackers died.

After the bombing of the federal building in Oklahoma City on April 19, 1995, the Pentagon decided that major renovations were needed to protect the building from similar terrorist attacks. The first and only phase of the work that had been completed was on the west side of the building, just five months before American Airlines Flight 77 slammed into it. There's no telling how much more damage would have been done if not for the new Kevlar-reinforced windows, the interlocking steel tubes and mesh behind the outer facade, not to mention the building's new—and only—sprinkler system. The damaged area held up for 30 minutes before collapsing, and the windows next to the impact site stayed intact.

PENTAGON FACTOIDS

• The Pentagon Tour Program was established on May 17, 1976, for America's bicentennial celebration. It was supposed to last only through July 4, but internal support and public demand were so great that it continues to host more than 120,000 visitors annually.

• The Pentagon was constructed out of reinforced concrete made from 380,000 tons of sand dredged from the Potomac River.

• The Defense Post Office handles about 1,200,000 pieces of mail monthly. Although the building is located in Virginia, the U.S. Postal Service requires that "Washington, D.C." be used in conjunction with one of six ZIP codes: for each branch of the service (Army, Air Force, Navy, Marine Corps) and the Secretary of Defense and Joint Chiefs of Staff.

• The Pentagon was constructed with twice the number of bathrooms needed for the number of employees because of racial segregation laws existing at that time.

NO-NONSENSE NAVY

Life was harsh in Admiral Nelson's Royal Navy. That tradition carried over to the American Navy and lasted for almost 100 years.

STARTINGS, FLOGGINGS, AND HANGINGS

In the old British navy, an enlisted sailor who got out of line by not moving fast enough got a "starting"—a good whack by the bosun's mate using a rattan cane or a short length of rope. If the enlisted man was insubordinate, he got a flogging, up to 72 lashes with a cat-o'-nine-tails whip. Floggings, as practiced in the British navy in the 18th and 19th centuries, were associated in the public's mind with the tough duty of serving on a man-of-war and the seaman's ability to withstand pain. Unlike punishments ashore where offenders could be locked up in prison, there was no room to do so in ships for any long period of time. Thus, corporal punishment became standard fare.

Under the British military code, a captain of a warship could order 12 lashes for infractions. It took a ruling by a court-martial to exceed that limit. However, the admiralty often looked the other way when extra lashes, as many as 72, were meted out to the hapless offender. Shipboard floggings in both the British and American fleets began with an order for all hands to muster on deck to witness the event. The sailor was stripped to the waist and tied to an upturned grate. Navy officers in full dress uniform stood on one side while Marines stood on the other to preserve order. The rest of the crew were onlookers. The commanding officer then read the specific infraction of the military code that the offender was accused and found guilty of. The captain then gave the order to a bosun's mate to lay down a dozen lashes. If there were more than 12 to be administered, a second bosun's mate would pummel the offender with the second set of 12, and so forth. The blows were of sufficient strength to ravage the flesh, turning it black. Worse yet was a flogging on the feet that tended to cripple the condemned. When in port, the number of lashes was divided by the number of ships anchored under one command. The offending seaman then was rowed between each of the ships so crewmen could see equal portions of the lashing as a warning.

Actor Robert Ryan was a Marine drill instructor at Camp Pendleton, California.

PITY THE POOR THIEF

For minor crime like thievery on a British or American ship, an offender often "ran the gauntlet," in which crewmen in two lines and armed with knotted ropes beat the thief as he passed through. In cases of major theft, the guilty seaman was flogged with a knotted cat-o'-nine-tails.

A favored punishment for minor crime for young enlisted seamen was to make them "kiss the gunner's daughter"—being bent over a cannon barrel and then caned on the rump. Another punishment was "seizing," whereby an offender was tied high in the rigging of a tall ship, leaving him to the whims of weather for as long as the captain deemed necessary.

Corporal punishment in the Navy was not carried out as often as it has been portrayed. At sea, sailors realized their lives depended on working together as a team in foul weather or in enemy action. As a result, discipline was relatively easy to maintain. At sea, the ship's captain was in total command. However, he was restricted by the British 36 Articles of War, which outlined the degree of punishment that could be carried out only through a formal court-martial. When officers exceeded their authority, consequences for them could be stern. For instance, a lieutenant of the sloop *Griffon* in 1812 was hanged from his own ship for killing a marine sergeant who had disobeyed his orders.

By the mid-18th century, European revulsion to floggings and other forms of physical punishment in the military put pressure on the British and Americans to change their ways. Germany had long banned the practice of corporal punishment, and France outlawed such treatment in the wake of the French Revolution. Eventually the British followed. In the United States, change came more slowly.

As early as 1797, excessive flogging in the military drew rebukes from Captain Thomas Truxtun and Surgeon Edward Cutbush. A proposal to abolish flogging was introduced in Congress in 1820 but failed to pass. Newspaper editorials condemned the practice, and some line officers in the Navy also campaigned to abolish floggings, though many more supported the tradition.

In 1840 the book *Cruise of the Frigate Columbia Around the World* recounted how sailors received 12 lashes for minor offenses like failing to close the toilet door or having dirty pots aboard.

The War Department became the Department of Defense in 1947 via the National Security Act.

Author William M. Murrell received 12 lashes on that voyage for accidentally spilling ink on deck and improperly marking a piece of clothing. Public revulsion ensued, fanned by other accounts of floggings or worse aboard U.S. vessels. The publication of Herman Melville's novel *White-Jacket, or The World in a Man-of-War* in 1850 contained a chapter on flogging and other punishments at sea and led to renewed vigor by the public and Congress to take action—which it did in 1850.

The legislation signed by U.S. president Millard Filmore abolished flogging in the U.S. Navy and Merchant Marine. In 1855 Congress established a system of lesser punishments for minor offenses. Solitary confinement, leg irons, and a diet of bread and water for a limited time became standard fare. Bad conduct discharges also were added. In 1862 Congress enacted into law a major revision of all regulations of the Navy that included a ban on corporal punishment.

* * *

GREAT WAR-MOVIE QUOTES

"We're all scared. You hid in that ditch because you think there's still hope. The only hope you have is to accept the fact that you're already dead. And the sooner you accept that, the sooner you'll be able to function as a soldier's supposed to function: without mercy, without compassion, without remorse. All war depends upon it."

—*Band of Brothers*, Episode 3: "Carentan"

"The first casualty of war is innocence." **—*Platoon***

"Improvise. Adapt. Overcome"

—Gunnery Sergeant Tom Highway,
Heartbreak Ridge

Some 6,000 battles, skirmishes, and engagements were fought during the Civil War.

THE SOUND OF MUSIC

Whether it's used to unite, for solace, to protest, or to rejoice, the music that war has produced has always been memorable. In today's world, the troops are never far from their tunes. Here then are the tales of some of the most enduring war music of all time.

WHISTLING "DIXIE"

If there's one song that's identified with the Confederate forces during the Civil War, it's "Dixie." So it's a little surprising to learn that it was written by an Ohioan living in New York City with no Confederate sympathies and whose father reportedly assisted escaped slaves on the Underground Railroad.

Daniel Decatur Emmett made his name on the stage in minstrel shows, in which white entertainers masqueraded as blacks by blackening their faces with burnt cork. Undeniably offensive by modern standards, minstrel shows were an accepted part of 19th-century vaudeville theater. Emmett's participation wasn't indicative of his political inclinations—in fact, he was deeply disappointed that his song became a rallying call for Southern soldiers.

The year was 1859 and Emmett was in New York appearing with a troupe known as Bryant's Minstrels. Emmett, who had already written a number of popular tunes, including "Old Dan Tucker," was asked to write a jaunty new song—the type known as a "walk-around"—for the act. As he looked out a rain-spattered window and recalled the mild weather of Virginia, where he had lived before moving to New York, Emmett thought to himself, "I wish I was in Dixie," and thus the seeds of the song were sown.

Originally titled "Dixie's Land," the song was a hit both north and south of the Mason-Dixon Line. Its first step toward becoming a Southern anthem occurred in New Orleans in 1861 when it was performed as the encore at a variety show, and its fate was sealed later that year when it was played at the inauguration of Jefferson Davis as the Confederate president. But as time passed, Emmett felt a little better about his most memorable composition, particularly when President Abraham Lincoln requested that the military band play "Dixie" after the surrender at Appomattox—a sign that the song once again belonged to all Americans.

You're 40 and decide you want to join the Coast Guard Reserve. Can you?...

THE COMPANY JUMPED WHEN HE PLAYED REVEILLE

No performers embodied the songs and spirit of World War II like the Andrews Sisters. Patty, Maxene, and LaVerne hailed from Minnesota and became national celebrities when their single "Bei Mir Bist Du Schöen" hit number one on the *Billboard* charts in 1938. They sang a number of World War II standards, including "Don't Sit Under the Apple Tree" and "Apple Blossom Time," but without question their most recognizable song of the World War II era was "Boogie Woogie Bugle Boy."

Written by Don Raye and Hughie Prince especially for the Andrews Sisters' cameo performance in the 1941 Abbott and Costello film *Buck Privates*, the lyrics tell the tale of a "famous trumpet man from out Chicago way" who is drafted into Company B and discovers that he can't jam the way he'd like to because his band is back in Chicago. How to solve the problem? Draft the rest of the band! The tune was irresistibly catchy and the performance brought the film—and the songwriters—an Academy Award nomination for Best Song. All this in spite of the fact that the production execs at Universal reportedly wanted to cut the number from the film!

Was there really a Boogie Woogie Bugle Boy? While it seems highly unlikely, more than one man has claimed to be the song's inspiration. In fact, "Boogie Woogie Bugle Boy" was a recasting of an earlier Raye-Prince collaboration, written along with songwriter Eleanore Sheehy, called "Beat Me Daddy, Eight to the Bar" (a reference to boogie woogie's eight beats to a measure rhythm). In the original, recorded by the Andrews Sisters in 1940, the musician in the lyrics is a piano player from Texas, but a bugle boy made much more sense for a song in a 1941 war picture, and that's what the fellow became.

HOW MANY ROADS?

The Vietnam War wasn't the first to inspire war protest songs, but at the time, when antiwar songs overshadowed popular music in support of the war. For every "Ballad of the Green Berets"—Staff Sergeant Berry Sadler's 1966 patriotic tribute to the U.S. Army's elite special force—there were handfuls of antiwar and peace songs on the radio, from Barry McGuire's "Eve of Destruction" (1965) to John Lennon's "Give Peace a Chance" (1969) to Edwin Starr's hit "War" (1970).

The most influential voices of the generation were those of the

...No. The age limits for the CG Reserve are 17–39, and for CG active duty, 17–27.

folk music community, and among their enduring standards was Bob Dylan's "Blowin' in the Wind," which, ironically, was not written as an anti–Vietnam War song at all. For one thing, the song was penned in 1962, before the United States entered the Vietnam War (even though the conflict had started a few years before). For another, Dylan insists that he did not write anti–Vietnam War songs per se, although he has allowed that some of his songs were protest songs. Dylan didn't appear at antiwar protest rallies and concerts; he never even stated that he was against the war. Much to the exasperation of fans and interviewers who tried to pin him down, the famously taciturn singer refused to commit to a particular political ideology and even asked one interviewer, "How do you know that I'm not . . . for the war?"

Dylan didn't even make the most successful recording of the song. That distinction goes to Peter, Paul and Mary, whose single went to number two on the *Billboard* pop chart in 1963 and whose album with the song went to number one. In 1966 Stevie Wonder recorded the song and hit number nine on the *Billboard* charts. By then, "Blowin' in the Wind" had become an anthem for peace and social change, particularly civil rights.

LIVE FROM IRAQ

Music from the home front didn't always have the same impact on the troops themselves. It's hard to imagine soldiers in the Vietnam War being galvanized by songs that implied—or even stated point-blank—that what they were doing was wrong. Sentimental favorites from World War II that spoke of families and sweethearts waiting for their soldiers' return probably wouldn't keep the troops' morale high.

Men and women in the field require a more energetic, driving beat to keep them on their game. In the 21st century, that beat is the beat of rap music and in some cases the soldiers are producing it for themselves. In 2004 Sergeant Neal Saunders and several of his fellow soldiers from the 1st Cavalry, Task Force 112, formed the rap group 4th25. Their songs are brutal, profanity-laced, and raw—and they resonate with soldiers because they are unquestionably authentic. Some incorporate the "ambient" sounds of gunfire in Baghdad into the mix; even the group's name, pronounced "fourth quarter," has an element of doom, referring to the fact that the "game"—of war or life—could end at any second.

Their album, *Live from Iraq*, was recorded during the men's tour of duty in Sadr City; many of the songs were written immediately after battles or bombings and all were recorded in a makeshift barracks studio. It charts the progress of a soldier's career from the tears and fears at deployment to the internal conflict, and the need to conceal from the folks at home what soldiers *really* encounter on a daily basis to the troops' frustration and outrage provoked by the media, politicians, and even commercially successful rappers posing as tough guys while living safely at home.

The album was released in 2005, just weeks after the men of 4th25 were back home at Fort Hood in Texas, and it continues to be a rallying cry for soldiers in Iraq and everywhere, because no one can tell a soldier's story like a soldier can.

* * *

ONE FOR FIGHTING

"Five for Fighting" might seem a bit misleading, since the "band" is really comprised of one man who writes the songs, sings, and plays three instruments including piano, guitar, and harmonica. Former SportsIllustrated.com hockey columnist John Ondrasik adopted Five for Fighting as his stage name as a phrase from when a hockey player receives a five-minute penalty for fighting during game.

No ordinary singer-songwriter, Ondrasik has a philanthropic bent towards helping various organizations¬—including Operation Homefront, an organization dedicated to providing emergency assistance and increasing morale to American troops—and in the spring of 2007 performed for military men and women on a USO/Armed Forces Entertainment tour of Guantanamo Bay and other bases in Cuba. He followed up a few months later with another tour, this time of Japan, Guam, and Hawaii.

During that same year, Ondrasik worked with the Army & Air Force Exchange Service (AAFES) and other artists to release 13 songs for US military members on an album called *CD for the Troops*. Ondrasik and the AAFES delivered more than 200,000 CDs to US troops around the globe—in Iraq, Afghanistan, military hospitals, USO centers, and troops support groups. In 2008 he released *CD for the Troops II*, and delivered 200,000 more.

The U.S. military's standard-issue flashlight has its head angled at 90° to the body.

TOP COAST GUARD FLICKS

The smallest branch of the armed forces is also the most overlooked when it comes to movies. Before airplanes replaced ships as the preferred mode of travel, daring feats on the high seas took center screen. Movies such as Perils of the Coast Guard *(1926) and* Coast Guard *(1939) showed "Coasties" battling pirates, tackling storms, and braving rugged conditions to get everyone home.*

UNSUNG HEROES OF THE SILVER SCREEN

That's not to say that the U.S. Coast Guard isn't still active in Hollywood. On the contrary, the service plays a primary role in many movies and television shows, but often not as the star. Consider *I Am Legend*, a 2007 sci-fi film starring Will Smith as possibly the last man on earth. A Coast Guard aircrew spent nearly a week filming an evacuation scene on the Brooklyn Bridge even as other units worked to ensure that real-life maritime operations were not disrupted during filming. With the Coast Guard playing an active role in everything from Hurricane Katrina to Operation Iraqi Freedom, there's bound to be some love left for the service in Hollywood. Until then, here are a handful of the good (and, perhaps, the not-so-good) to keep your boat afloat.

RUGGED WATER (1925)

Between 1902 and 1943, writer Joseph C. Lincoln penned nearly four dozen works of fiction and poetry, most of them showcasing the stories and people of Cape Cod. One of the most famous for its time was *Rugged Water*, the story of a life-saving station on the coast and the people who dared to brave the often rugged sea. Written in 1924, it was turned into a silent film the following year, one of six books by Lincoln that made it to the silver screen.

SEA SPOILERS (1936)

Among the seven films John Wayne made in 1936 is *Sea Spoilers*, in which he stars as the commander of a patrol boat in the waters off Alaska. Nothing to find up there, you say? Tell that to the smugglers and poachers that Wayne and company take head-on.

Airplanes were first used in war not for fighting or bombing, but for observation.

SEA DEVILS (1937)

Ah, those were the days. In its review, the *New York Times* reported that ushers "tricked out in chief petty officers' uniforms" seated guests for the premiere of *Sea Devils*, a story of iceberg patrols, sea rescues, and a tough old Coastie (Victor McLaglen) who tries to prevent his daughter from falling for a brash coastguardsman (Preston Foster) by pushing her toward a more respectable candidate.

TARS AND SPARS (1946)

Loosely based on the theater production of the same name, which toured across the country to rave reviews, this musical centers on a coastguardsman who has never been to sea. Where does the name come from? "Tar" is a nickname for a sailor, while "SPAR" was a term for a member of the U.S. Coast Guard Women's Reserve, one of many such groups created to free men from duty at home during World War II. Sid Caesar, a former Coastie, makes his film debut.

THE BEAST FROM 20,000 FATHOMS (1953)

In this film based on a story by Ray Bradbury, the beast is a dinosaur freed from a block of ice by an atomic blast. The Coast Guard does all it can to stop the beast, but it's an Army weapon that brings it down. If it sounds a lot like *Godzilla*, there's a reason. Taking a cue from this film, Japanese filmmakers released their movie the next year and the rampaging lizard became a cult hit.

ONIONHEAD (1958)

It's hard to believe a film with Andy Griffith and Walter Matthau would be poorly received, but critics still poke fun today. Perhaps fans of *The Andy Griffith Show* and *Matlock* should be happy that Andy's portrayal of a Coastie wasn't more popular. It's been said that the stink of *Onionhead* is what drove Griffith into television.

THE GUARDIAN (2006)

Borrowing a page from the Japanese, Hollywood tried to re-create a blockbuster from Asia that showcased rescue diver trainees from Japan's coast guard. They ended up with *The Guardian*, starring Kevin Costner as the salty senior chief petty officer and Ashton Kutcher as the youngster trying to get started. It didn't get much love from critics, but fans of military movies might be surprised.

Spitkit: Navy slang for a small, ramshackle vessel.

ARMY AVIATION TAKES WING

The story of Lieutenant Benjamin D. Foulois, who never lost faith in the airplane's military potential, and General John J. Pershing, who did—for a while.

THOSE MAGNIFICENT MEN

The Army showed no interest when, in 1903, Wilbur Wright flew his kitelike contraption powered by a small combustion engine for 59 seconds, but eventually President Theodore Roosevelt intervened to bring the parties together. On August 1, 1907, the Army Signal Corps established an Aeronautical Division, and on August 2, 1908, accepted delivery of its first aircraft, the Wright *Flyer*.

Lieutenant Benjamin D. Foulois accompanied Orville Wright on the *Flyer*'s final test flight and became one of the earliest pilots to recognize the potential of air power.

TRADED IN FOR A NEW MODEL

Producing the first flying machine gave the Wright brothers an early advantage, but their plane had steerage problems. Glenn Curtiss, who owned a bicycle shop in Hammondsport, New York, was building small combustion engines on the side. He entered the aircraft-building race and solved the steering problem by developing ailerons (hinged control surfaces attached to the wing of a fixed-wing aircraft). By then, the Wright brothers had opened a flight school in Dayton, Ohio, but Curtiss was producing better aircraft, which the Army designated as JN-1s, or "Jennies."

The differences between the Wright design and the Curtiss design were significant. The Wright B biplane had a huge wingspan, a pilot's seat but no cockpit, not much power, and could fly only in perfect weather. The Curtiss Jenny looked like a modern biplane with an open cockpit, and had more power, longer range, and better maneuverability. So after Foulois and others finished pilot's training at the Wright school, they switched aircraft and started flying Jennies.

1ST AND FOREMOST

The 1st Aero Squadron had been in existence since early 1913, but in name only because the Army's generals considered flying to be a waste of money. The War Department issued an order in September 1914 that made the unit official with 16 officers, 77 enlisted men, and eight Jenny flying machines. Under Captain Foulois, the squadron engaged in training and testing from 1914 to 1915. In the years preceding World War I, the squadron represented the total tactical air strength of the Army.

OPERATION OOPS

On July 15, 1915, Foulois moved the entire squadron of JN-2s by air from San Diego to Fort Sill, Oklahoma, to participate in field artillery fire-control operations—to be observed by General John J. Pershing. The pilots performed magnificently, but the planes, equipped with cranky 90-horsepower engines, didn't. One JN-2 flown by Lieutenant J. C. Morrow with observer B. Q. Jones in the front cockpit experienced turbulence at 1,100 feet and unexpectedly dropped 200 feet. When Morrow and Jones took off the next day, the JN-2 nose-dived and smashed into the ground. Lieutenant R. B. Sutton crashed his plane, killing the observer in the front seat. Pershing had seen enough. He discontinued further experiments and told Foulois to get better flying machines. Rankled by the setback, Foulois flew his remaining planes 439 miles to Fort Sam Houston at San Antonio to avoid winter weather and continue training his pilots until the new JN-3s became available.

THE INVASION OF AMERICA

On March 9, 1916, Francisco "Pancho" Villa, the notorious revolutionary leader, raided Columbus, New Mexico, and killed 17 Americans. Provoked into military action, the War Department sent Pershing and 10,000 troops to pursue Villa into Mexico and take him dead or alive.

Ordered to Columbus, Foulois arrived six days later with the 1st Aero Squadron: 11 pilots, 82 enlisted men, and eight Curtiss JN-3s, which were two-seaters originally designed for training and powered by Curtiss's new 90-horsepower engines. Foulois made sure that every one of his pilots knew that Pershing would be watching. War had already erupted in Europe, and Foulois knew

...He was severely wounded and was awarded a Silver Star and three Purple Hearts.

this would be the only opportunity to test the squadron under full field conditions.

THE INVASION OF MEXICO

The rickety and already battered Jennies never had a chance in the high winds blowing through the mountains in northern Mexico. The improved engines coughed and sputtered; the aircraft's extremely low rate of climb made operating on small fields tucked between high hills hazardous for takeoffs and landings. Nevertheless, Foulois intended to change Pershing's mind about the importance of air reconnaissance.

On the 125-mile flight from Columbus to Casas Grandes, Mexico, one plane turned back with engine trouble, one cracked up in a forced landing, and the other six were forced down by darkness. Six Jennies finally arrived at Pershing's headquarters for the ostensible purpose of locating Villa's roaming revolutionaries. Foulois soon discovered his Jennies couldn't cross over 12,000-foot mountain peaks, battle the terrific air currents and whirlwinds, or contend with dust storms and high-level blizzards. Extremely hot weather caused the engines to overheat and propellers to delaminate (separate into layers).

FLYING BY THE SEAT OF THEIR PANTS

Curtiss sent metal propellers, but the extra weight slowed climbing even more. A few handy mechanics carved propellers from dried native wood, which solved one problem. Thereafter, every pilot carried at least one extra propeller in a humidity-controlled box strapped to the side of the fuselage in case one broke during a forced landing. Most of the mechanics were familiar with motorcycle engines and did all they could to keep the Jennies flying, but the aircraft had been designed for training—not for combat.

Jennies carried no guns; if a pilot ditched, he had no weapon larger than a .22-caliber rifle or a .45-caliber pistol. Foulois had visions of aircraft someday becoming bombers and ordered a case of artillery shells. But the pilots were afraid they'd blow themselves up, so Foulois postponed the experiment.

Navigation problems contributed to the headaches. Nearly every plane carried a different style of compass, and maps of the area were useless. Pilots got lost, found themselves flying in the

Austria-Hungary's declaration of war against Serbia was the first delivered by telegram (1914).

moonlight, tried to navigate by the North Star, and often landed wherever they spotted a section of level ground. Lieutenant I. A. Rader had the latter experience during a 300-mile mission and was forced to land near Ojito, a hundred miles from the nearest U.S. outpost. The loss left Foulois with two planes, though more were on the way.

¡AY, CHIHUAHUA!

In early April, Lieutenant Herbert Dargue flew a scouting mission over Chihuahua with an observer, R. E. Willis, who carried a new Brock aerial camera capable of taking sequenced photographs. Twenty miles northwest of Chihuahua, the Jenny's engine seized and the plane crashed in the woods. Dargue climbed out of the rear cockpit unhurt, but Willis was pinned under the wreck with a broken ankle and a lacerated scalp. Dargue pulled Willis free, but the plane, camera, and photographic plates were all destroyed. Following Army rules, Dargue set fire to the wreckage. The two men traveled 65 miles by foot and mule to get back to headquarters.

On April 19, Pershing sent two Jennies to Chihuahua with important messages for the American consul; Foulois flew one, Dargue flew the other. When they landed, mounted *rurales* (policemen) fired on them and marched them off to jail. Meanwhile a crowd, angry at the invasion of their country, surrounded the machines, burned holes in the wings with cigarettes, slashed the fabric with knives, and loosened exposed nuts and bolts on the fuselages. The American consul bargained for the release of Foulois and Dorgue, and a few hours later both men rushed back to their planes to take off. The top section of the fuselage on Dargue's Jenny blew off and damaged the stabilizer, leaving him stranded in Chihuahua. Dargue had to be saved from the crowd by the Mexican army, after which he repaired his plane and rejoined Foulois at Army headquarters. The episode did nothing to boost Pershing's confidence in flying machines.

JENNY, YOU'RE GROUNDED

Foulois finally settled for short flights in good weather for carrying mail and dispatches between Columbus and wherever the Army went. By April 20, only two of the original Jennies were still oper-

The Battle of Frenchtown (War of 1812) was the largest battle ever fought on Michigan soil.

ational. They were flown to Columbus, where they were condemned and destroyed.

Foulois brought two new planes to Columbus, a Curtiss JN-4 and a Curtiss R-2, the latter being a large Jenny-style biplane with a more powerful engine. But the two planes were so poorly built that neither were of any use in the field. General Pershing publicly expressed his appreciation for the 540 missions flown and the pioneering efforts made by the 1st Aero Squadron in Mexico. Congress showed its faith in the future of wartime aviation by awarding the Air Service an appropriation of $13 million for the further advancement of aeronautical development.

COUP DE GRACE

Pershing knew talent when he saw it. When he went to France in 1917 as commander of the American Expeditionary Force, he asked for the men of the 1st Aero Squadron—but not their flying machines. For the balance of World War I, the squadron went on scouting missions in French planes, not Jennies.

"It is nothing short of criminal to send aviators up under such conditions as we meet here [in Mexico]."

—Lieutenant Herbert Dargue

* * *

NASCAR JOINS THE SERVICE

Since the 1950s, organizations have been paying to sponsor NASCAR race teams, placing their names and logos on race cars in exchange for the exposure of being associated with (hopefully) a winning team. But it isn't only companies paying millions of dollars to get into the sponsorship game.

In the past decade the Navy, Marines, and Coast Guard have sponsored cars. In 2009 the Army and Air Force got in the act and sponsored drivers Ryan Neuman and Reed Sorenson, respectively. Not to be outdone, the National Guard sponsored Jeff Gordon. So if you're a NASCAR fan, your tax dollars are helping to keep them in gas and new tires.

On March 31, 1995, the Coast Guard sent its final message by Morse code, then signed off...

DEVIL DOGS IN FRANCE

How the Marines made it to Belleau Wood and what they did when they got there.

DON'T LEAVE HOME WITHOUT US

When America entered World War I on April 6, 1917, the Marine Corps numbered just 511 officers and 13,214 men. Because it seemed unlikely that the Corps would be ordered to Europe, Major General George Barnett, commandant of the Marine Corps, pressed his case on Capitol Hill. When the next naval appropriations bill became law, it included funding for 30,000 Marines, a number that later increased to 70,000. The first brigades sailed in June from New York to Saint-Nazaire, France, for training with the combat-hardened French.

By early 1918, the war was stalemated by the hideous losses of both sides. Having knocked Russia out of the war in late 1917, the Germans decided to launch an all-or-nothing offensive aimed at defeating the French and British before an avalanche of fresh American troops arrived. They knocked the British army back 50 miles in March and April, and by May 31 had broken the French army and stood only 40 miles from Paris. The Allies were close to collapse when, on June 2, the untested 6th Marine Regiment under Colonel Albertus Catlin was ordered to establish a position to block the Germans just south of a little forest called Belleau Wood, about one square mile in size.

DON'T EVEN THINK OF RETIRING

Catlin's orders left no doubt as to the seriousness of the situation; they were to dig in and hold at all costs: "No retirement will be thought of on any pretext whatsoever." The German forces arrived the next day and attacked the untested Marines. Waiting until the Germans approached to within 100 yards of their lines, the Marines annihilated them with well-aimed rifle fire. For two days the Germans tried to break through the Marine lines, but the 6th Regiment had single-handedly halted the German advance on Paris.

On June 6 came an order to capture Belleau Wood for the Allies. By now the Germans knew they were fighting Marines, and decided that instead of moving laterally, they needed to teach these brash Americans a lesson.

INTO THE WOODS

Waves of Marines fixed their bayonets and walked through wheat fields to the forest as German machine-gun fire tore huge holes in their ranks. Catlin took a bullet in the lung, but continued to command his men. The Marine lines wavered but kept advancing, then slowed 50 yards from the woods. Gunnery Sergeant Dan Daly, already the holder of two Medals of Honor, stood up, waved his rifle, and shouted at his platoon, "Come on, you sons of bitches, do you want to live forever?" The Marines rushed the woods but left a trail of blood in the wheat behind them. By nightfall, they had a foothold in the forest despite losing more Marines that day (1,087) than in their entire 143-year history.

The Marines' advance continued the next morning. Fighting in the heavy woods was hand to hand and yard by yard, but after five more days, the Marines had kicked the Germans out of Belleau Wood. On the morning of June 13, the Germans counterattacked behind a heavy barrage of mustard gas and artillery fire. On a day of desperate fighting, the 6th Marine Regiment held its ground, and finally the Germans withdrew.

JUST WHEN YOU THOUGHT IT WAS OVER

To the surprise of the exhausted Marines, the fight wasn't over yet. As they were withdrawn on June 15 and replaced by the Army's fresh 7th Infantry Regiment, the Germans reinforced their troops; the Army was unable to hold the Marines' gains. After a week, the Marines replaced the Army in Belleau Wood, and after three more days of fighting, drove the Germans out yet again. On June 26, Marine Major Maurice Shearer sent out this report: "Woods now U.S. Marine Corps entirely."

MERCI BEAUCOUP

A grateful France announced that Belleau Wood would forever be known as "Bois de la Brigade Marine." The shocked Germans began to refer to the Marines as *Teufel Hunden*, or "devil dogs." The Marines had earned both names; they suffered 5,183 killed and wounded during the 20-day battle, a casualty rate of 51 percent.

The Pentagon's 5-acre center courtyard is the world's largest military no-hat, no-salute zone.

CODE TALKERS

In World Wars I and II, American Indians helped the U.S say, "Nin hokeh bi-kheh a-na-ih-la." (That's "We have conquered our enemies.")

A BRILLIANT PLAN

In October 1918, the American Expeditionary Force was in France and in trouble. They'd been sent to help the British and French in World War I but got bogged down in hilly terrain, were surrounded by Germans, and took heavy casualties.

To make matters worse, the American officers couldn't coordinate attacks or retreats without the Germans knowing their plans. If the Americans tried to communicate by telephone, the Germans listened and broke their code. Sending communications by runners was no better. About 25 percent of American runners were caught and their communiqués were easily deciphered by the Germans.

But then someone came up with an idea. According to Private Solomon Louis, he and a friend were conversing in Choctaw when an officer overheard them and realized he couldn't understand anything they were saying. The officer's confusion was the beginning of one of America's greatest military intelligence coups.

THANK THE CHOCTAW

In 1918 Native Americans weren't allowed to vote. They weren't even considered U.S. citizens, and most had been forced as children to attend boarding schools that punished them for speaking their native languages. But now they were asked to use their language to save lives.

Colonel A. W. Bloor, commanding the 142nd Infantry, 36th Division, assigned Louis, his friend, and six other Choctaw to manage the communications. They were so successful that 18 Choctaw code talkers got jobs with the military, telephoning messages, writing field orders for runners, and translating communications for English-speaking officers.

The men adapted their language into a code. Army companies were called different grains of corn—"one grain," "two grains," etc. A machine gun became "little gun shoots fast." As for casualties—they were translated as "scalps."

The USCGC *Ingham* in Charleston, South Carolina, is the official memorial site to...

The first successful test of the new code was a secret movement of American troops during the night; the second was a surprise attack on the Germans. Neither message was successfully intercepted. Thanks to the Choctaw, the United States finally had a code that stumped the Germans, and the tide of war immediately turned in favor of the Allies. In fact, the war ended only weeks after the Choctaw code breakers started managing Allied communications.

The men came home to zero recognition for their accomplishments, however, and very few people knew how much the Army had depended on them. The Germans knew, though. Adolf Hitler sent "students" to the United States to study Native Americans and their dialects. He didn't want German generals outfoxed by code talkers again.

HERE WE GO AGAIN

The Army hadn't forgotten the code talkers, either. Technology for coding military messages had improved by the 1940s, but it still had problems. The military used cipher machines to encrypt messages and make them unreadable to the enemy, but it was a slow process. One message could take nearly an hour to complete, and on the front lines, time mattered.

Looking for a better way to transmit coded messages, the Army again turned to Indian tribes. In 1941, 17 Comanche recruits at Fort Benning, Georgia, developed a coded language for use in Europe. They created a 100-word dictionary and adapted their language to translate military terms. The word for "machine gun" in Comanche code was "sewing machine" (they both made a racket), and a "pregnant airplane" was code for a bomber. As for Hitler, his code name was *posah-tai-vo*, meaning "crazy white man."

On D-day, the Comanche code talkers landed at Normandy, and despite Hitler's best efforts, the Nazis couldn't understand the messages they were sending. The Germans never broke the Comanche code.

TELL IT TO THE MARINES

U.S. troops in the Pacific relied heavily on their code talkers, too. These men were Navajo. The idea for using the Navajo language—

...members of the U.S. Coast Guard who were killed in action in World War II and Vietnam.

called Diné by native speakers—came from Philip Johnston, a city engineer from Los Angeles. Johnston wasn't Navajo, but he'd grown up on a Navajo reservation where his father was a missionary, and he'd learned to speak the language of his playmates.

With no connection to any European or Asian language, Diné had tonal variations and a complicated syntax that mystified people who hadn't grown up with it or studied it. It was also a language the Germans hadn't gotten around to learning.

To show how well Diné worked as a military code, Johnston and four volunteer Navajos gave a demonstration for Major General Clayton Vogel and his staff at Camp Elliot in San Diego. The men showed that Navajo could deliver a three-line message in under a minute; cipher machines needed at least 30. On Vogel's recommendation, Navajos were recruited into the Marines and sent to Camp Pendleton for training as radio signalmen.

WATCH OUT FOR FALLING BUZZARD EGGS

Navajo code talkers had eight weeks to learn the complex code. Because Indian words were lacking for standard military terms, they coined new terms, using Navajo words for the natural world. Planes were "birds," a bomber was a "buzzard," and its bombs were "eggs."

Eventually, the Navajo code talkers used more than 400 military terms. They also used a coded alphabet for spelling out words that were difficult to translate. For example, they could spell out Iwo Jima as "Ice-Weasel-Owl-Jackass-Itch-Mouse-Ant." But they did it by substituting the Navajo word for each English word. To make the code even more complicated, a talker had more than one choice for words that represented common letters and vowels. For example, to avoid repeating "ice" for the letter "i" in "Iwo Jima," the codebook gave the option of using the word "itch" or "intestine." The men memorized this so no books could fall into enemy hands.

When Navy intelligence was asked to break the Navajo code, they said it was a "weird succession of guttural, nasal, tongue-twisting sounds" that they couldn't even write down. Later, the Marines discovered that not even native Navajos could break the code. Joe Kieyoomia, held by the Japanese on Bataan, was tortured so that he would reveal the secrets of the messages coming over the radio.

74% of Vietnam veterans said they would serve again, even knowing the outcome.

But though Kieyoomia could pick up certain words, he had no clue what the words stood for.

TOUGH TALK

After training was over, the first Navajo code talkers began their job at Guadalcanal. Since their training had been top secret, when radio signalmen first heard Navajo code, they panicked, thinking the Japanese had hijacked their frequencies. Some code talkers were mistaken for Japanese (and nearly shot), so commanders gave them non-Navajo bodyguards. But the speed and accuracy of the Navajo soon led to requests for additional code talkers.

Before the war was over, about 420 Navajo Marines were transmitting communications in the Pacific. They served in every assault between 1942 and 1945 and consistently proved their worth. During the first two days of the Battle of Iwo Jima, six code talkers sent more than 800 messages without any errors.

One Navajo on Iwo Jima had a friend killed right beside him while they were working, but he still sent out an error-free message for help. And when the Marines (who were being fired at from Japanese atop Mount Suribachi) finally took the mountain summit and famously raised the U.S. flag, it was a code-talker message that reported their triumph. According to Major Howard Connor, the 5th Marine Division's signal officer, "Were it not for the Navajos, the Marines would never have taken Iwo Jima."

After the war, the Japanese chief of intelligence admitted that his soldiers had been able to decipher some codes used by the Army and Army Air Corps. But they never cracked the code of the Navajo Marines.

*   *   *

LONG TIME COMING

Navajo code talkers received Congressional Gold Medals in 2001. But it took until September 2008 for Congress to pass the Code Talkers Recognition Act and honor the Choctaw from World War I and the Comanche from World War II.

THE LOST BATTALION

They weren't really lost, but a series of command failures and tactical errors kept them trapped for days while the whole world wondered what would happen to them.

THE CAMPAIGN TO END ALL WARS

The final campaign of World War I was set for H-hour, 5:30 a.m. on October 4, 1918. General John J. "Black Jack" Pershing, commanding the American Expeditionary Force in Europe, had ordered the left wing of the U.S. 1st Army to push forward into the Argonne Forest on September 29. German artillery hidden in the forest had been clobbering American and French forces, and Pershing wanted the guns silenced before the massive Allied advance. Major General Robert Alexander's 77th Infantry Division drew the assignment; his orders were to push forward "without regard to losses."

The Argonne was different from other battlefields. A few trails meandered through the woods, but the enormous size of the forest and the density of the trees made it difficult to organize cooperative action among units, some of which quickly became separated. Brigadier General Evan Johnson, commanding the 154th Brigade, made it clear to the battalions under his command that "Any ground gained must be held . . . If I find anybody ordering a withdrawal from ground once held, I will see he leaves the service," meaning dishonorably. Major Charles W. Whittlesey's 1st Battalion of the 308th Infantry Regiment was part of Johnson's brigade and received the same message.

INTO THE FOREST

Whittlesey's composite battalion consisted of Companies A, B, C, E, G, and H from the 308th Infantry, Companies C and D from the 306th Machine Gun Battalion, and Company K from the 307th Infantry, which accidentally joined them later. All the companies were depleted from earlier losses when they entered the Argonne Forest. Whittlesey had been told not to worry about safeguarding his flanks because an American battalion with the French infantry would be on his left and two American battalions would be on his right. On October 2, he and his roughly 670 men plunged into the foggy, rain-drenched Argonne Forest, lost contact with the units on his flanks, but kept pressing forward.

By accident, Whittlesey's battalion found a gap in the German line, but lost about 90 men before resistance subsided. With nightfall approaching, Whittlesey moved the battalion into a ravine that ran along the side of a steep and rocky slope about 300 yards long and 60 yards wide with good defensive ground and protection from mortar fire. Whittlesey then waited through the night for the other units to make contact.

DAY TWO

The other units never arrived, and on the morning of October 3, German mortars opened fire. Whittlesey sent 50 men back through the forest to find General Alexander and ask for reinforcements. An hour later, 18 men returned and said they had been ambushed about a mile away. They also reported a more serious problem. The Germans had strung wire defenses between their battalion and the 77th Division—they were trapped. Whittlesey's only communication system was carrier pigeons; he handed a message to Private Omar Richards, the pigeon keeper, who sent the first of six birds off to division headquarters to report the battalion's position and to request reinforcements and supplies. They wouldn't know for hours if the message had reached headquarters.

SO NEAR AND YET . . . SO FAR

Meanwhile, the men were hungry and thirsty. To reach water, they had to crawl 50 yards to a small stream running along the base of the ravine—but the stream was covered by a German machine gun. Too many men had been hit trying to reach it, so Whittlesey posted guards with orders to shoot anyone attempting to fill their canteens.

During a mortar barrage, both Whittlesey and Captain George G. McMurtry had been hit by shrapnel. McMurtry's knee began to fester, but both officers continued to hobble among the men, stopping at each foxhole to assure them that help was on the way. The men knew their major would never surrender. Newspaper correspondents hanging around headquarters learned about the trapped unit and started writing daily accounts about the "Lost Battalion."

...It's how the acronym HF/DF, or High-Frequency Direction Finding, was pronounced.

ONE MORE DAY

On the morning of October 4, a mortar bombardment and firefight did more damage. The major sent a second pigeon, again asking for help and reporting 222 casualties, with 82 men dead. His machine-gun crews were decimated—only five were left with a little ammunition, and the medics were running out of bandages. General Alexander detached two companies, but they were stopped by the enemy and turned back after losing more than half of their men.

"FOR HEAVEN'S SAKE, STOP IT"

October 5 opened with another German mortar attack on the remaining machine-gun positions. Whittlesey sent another pigeon requesting artillery support—but with the wrong coordinates. American artillery opened at 1:15 p.m., and for four hours shells rained down on the Lost Battalion instead of the Germans. There were only two pigeons left, but when Private Richards opened the cage, one escaped. The other, Cher Ami, carried this brief message from the major: "Our own artillery is dropping a barrage directly on us. For heaven's sake, stop it." The pigeon flew to a nearby tree and settled on a branch. When throwing stones failed to dislodge the bird, Richards dodged howling artillery shells, climbed the tree, and shook the branch until the pigeon flew off and disappeared. No one expected much to come of it, but Cher Ami reached division headquarters at 4:00 p.m., with one leg and one eye missing.

THINGS COULDN'T GET WORSE, COULD THEY?

Finally, on October 6, artillery fire began to fall on the Germans, taking pressure off Whittlesey's battered men. Germans still lurked around the perimeter but were too busy to attack. New enemies intruded on morale—hunger, thirst, cold, battle fatigue, and the stench of putrefying corpses. With all the pigeons gone, Private Richards ate the birdseed.

Later in the day, a reconnaissance plane spotted the battalion and reported its position. An hour later, planes from the 50th Aero Squadron dropped supplies, dehydrated soups, and ammunition, all of which landed among the Germans. Whittlesey's men heard the enemy rejoicing over the bungled airdrop. Nine desperate men from the battalion were captured trying to rescue the parcels.

Length of Sherman's march: 285 miles (Atlanta to Savannah).

THE VOLUNTEERS

On the morning of October 7, Private Lowell B. Hollingsworth lay in his foxhole with a slight wound, weak with hunger, and feeling hopeless. When told that Whittlesey wanted eight volunteers to infiltrate through the German lines to contact nearby friendly forces who were searching for the battalion, Hollingsworth knew it could be his last chance to find food. Seven more volunteers stepped forward, including Private Carl Rainwater, a full-blooded Indian from Montana, who the volunteers chose as their guide and leader. The eight men worked silently through the forest, stopping frequently to let the wounded rest. After less than a mile, Rainwater halted and raised his hand for the others to stop. A machine gun opened fire, and Hollingsworth fell unconscious. When he came to, there was a German gun pointed at his head. Four of his buddies were dead and the other three wounded.

Hollingsworth was taken prisoner and fed, then the Germans returned him to his battalion with a note encouraging Major Whittlesey to surrender. Whittlesey read the note but didn't reply. When the men learned of the contents of the message, they shouted rude things in German back across the lines.

LOST AND FOUND

Early in the evening, elements from the 77th Division broke through the German lines and located the Lost Battalion. Of Whittlesey's original 600 men, only 191 were able to walk. Five men from the battalion received the Medal of Honor, including Whittlesey and McMurtry, and 26 men were awarded the Distinguished Service Medal.

The carrier pigeon, Cher Ami, was awarded the French Croix de Guerre for heroic service delivering 12 important messages to his headquarters in Verdun. His stuffed body is on display in the National Museum of American History at the Smithsonian Institution in Washington, D.C.

* * *

"The nation which forgets its defenders will be itself forgotten."

—Calvin Coolidge

RELUCTANT HERO

Alvin York had the most important qualities of a war hero. He wasn't scared of anything, he was well schooled in the art of hunting, and he could shoot the fleas off a dog's back from a mile away.

Alvin Cullum York was born on December 13, 1887, in a two-room log cabin in Pall Mall, Tennessee. His father was a farmer and a blacksmith, and Alvin was one of 11 children. Like most people of that time who lived in a mountain region, Alvin learned to hunt at an early age. He grew into a tall, red-headed youth who was an expert shot; he often won the weekly shooting matches that were held in his town on Saturdays. He was a wild young man who did a lot of drinking and fighting, but in 1914, after one of his best friends was killed in a bar fight, he realized the error of his ways and joined a fundamentalist church with a strong moral code that forbade violence of any kind.

NICE TRY, ALVIN

So when the United States declared war on Germany in 1917, York wrote on his draft notice "Don't want to fight." But the Army denied him conscientious-objector status, and during his training, his commanders managed to convince him that going to war to save lives was a moral thing to do. Relieved that his moral dilemma had been resolved, he became an outstanding soldier. York was such an excellent marksman that he was promoted to corporal and assigned to train other men.

ON THE BATTLEFRONT

On October 8, 1918, in France's Argonne Forest during the last major battle of World War I, Corporal York and 16 other soldiers led by acting Sergeant Bernard Early crept around the left flank of the German lines. Their mission: to capture machine-gun positions and a rail line that was supplying the German front.

York and the others crawled undetected through the heavy brush and got themselves situated well behind the front lines. They quietly approached a group of about 20 Germans, who were eating breakfast in a small valley surrounded by hills.

The Battle of the Rice Boats was a 1776 patriot victory against the British Royal Navy.

The Americans took the enemy completely by surprise; the Germans immediately surrendered. The position they'd captured was a headquarters for a machine-gun company, and when the Germans on the surrounding hills realized what was going on, they turned their machine guns around and started firing. Everyone dove for the ground, but six Americans were killed and two were wounded—among them Sergeant Early, who turned over his command to York.

IN HIS OWN WORDS

The battle still raged. York was crouching on the ground, trying to use the prisoners as cover. He later recounted in his diary:

> The Germans were what saved me. I kept up close to them, and so the fellers on the hill had to fire a little high for fear of hitting their own men.
>
> As soon as the machine guns opened fire on me, I began to exchange shots with them. In order to sight me or to swing their machine guns on me, the Germans had to show their heads above the trench, and every time I saw a head I just touched it off. All the time I kept yelling at them to come down. I didn't want to kill any more than I had to. But it was they or I. And I was giving them the best I had.

A TURKEY SHOOT

As he picked off the Germans one by one, he thought of the turkey shoots back home in Tennessee. A turkey would be tied up behind a log and the only way to hit him was to aim for his head whenever he was foolish enough to raise it up above the protection of the log. The German soldier's heads made much better targets. York later recalled:

> Suddenly a German officer and five men jumped out of the trench and charged me with fixed bayonets. I changed to the old automatic and just touched them off, too. I touched off the sixth man first, then the fifth, then the fourth, then the third, and so on. I wanted them to keep coming. I didn't want the rear ones to see me touching off the front ones. I was afraid they would drop down and pump a volley into me.

Once again, York's training as a hunter had kicked in. He explains in his autobiography that as a boy he'd learned when hunting geese in flight to shoot the birds in the rear first and work your way to the front, so that the others don't spook and scatter.

THE WHITE FLAG

A German major who had already been taken prisoner had seen enough. He called to his men and ordered them to surrender. The eight remaining Americans now had more than 80 prisoners. Problem was, they were still behind German lines. York put the German major at the head of the line of prisoners and held a gun on him, as he and the other American soldiers escorted the prisoners toward the front.

Whenever they come across German soldiers, York would have the major order them to surrender. When one refused, York had to shoot him. By the time they reached the American lines, they'd taken 132 German prisoners, including three officers. Surveyors of the battle scene a few days later reported that York had killed 28 Germans. Word of his exploits quickly spread throughout the entire Allied armies—and to newspapers around the world.

SERVING UP THE "FRUIT SALAD"

The commander of the American Expeditionary Forces, General John J. "Black Jack" Pershing, called York "the greatest civilian soldier of the war," presented him with the Medal of Honor, and promoted him to sergeant. Marshal Foch, the Supreme Allied Commander, said, "What York did was the greatest thing accomplished by any soldier of all the armies of Europe," and awarded him France's medal for bravery—the Croix de Guerre.

When York returned to the States, New York City threw him a ticker-tape parade. He was inundated with offers to endorse this and endorse that, but he refused them all, saying, "Uncle Sam's uniform ain't for sale."

THE RETURNING HERO

When he finally returned to his hometown in Tennessee, his neighbors presented him with a home and a farm. He quickly married and settled back into the quiet and simple life he'd dreamed of while he was gone. He also reverted back to his pacifist nature, and during the 1930s when war clouds were gathering once again, he spoke out against U.S. involvement. He even went so far as to renounce America's involvement in World War I—*his* war.

Eventually he realized that America couldn't stand by while Germany enslaved Europe. He started traveling the country on bond tours and recruitment drives. He even tried to enlist, but was turned down because of his age.

YORK GOES HOLLYWOOD

Filmmaker Jesse Lasky approached York about making a movie of his life. At first, the retired sergeant refused, but he finally consented. The film, *Sergeant York*, was a smash hit in 1941 and won Gary Cooper an Academy Award for Best Actor that year.

UNHAPPY ENDINGS

York used all the movie income to support the school he had helped to fund in his hometown. And even though he was totally on the up and up, the IRS accused him of tax evasion in 1951. It turned out that York owed money because he'd gotten some bad advice from his tax lawyers. The penalties, interest, and fees he owed were more than his total net worth. When word got around that York was in serious financial trouble, some friends in Congress established a relief fund for him that paid off his debts.

In 1954 he suffered a stroke that left him paralyzed from the waist down. Alvin York died at the Veterans Hospital in Nashville, Tennessee, on September 2, 1964, and was buried with full military honors in his hometown.

A REAL MAN

Alvin York was a humble man who wore the mantle of "war hero" with a quiet dignity, and who used his fame to help the people of Tennessee. The school he founded, now called the Alvin C. York Institute, is still in operation today. Though he was honored throughout his life for his bravery on that fateful day in 1918, he said just before he died that he preferred to be remembered for what he did after the war, "for helping improve education in Tennessee, bringing in better roads, and just helping my fellow man."

Actor James Earl Jones graduated from U.S. Army Ranger School at Fort Benning, Georgia.

WHERE CAN I SEE . . . ?

A rich array of museums across the country are filled with items from wars fought by the U.S. military. Here are some interesting Civil War artifacts.

CIVIL WAR CARBINE: This carbine has carvings on its stock reflecting ownership by both Union and Confederate soldiers. Provenance says the carbine was issued to a Union cavalryman, then later was possessed by a Confederate cavalryman. *Parris Island Museum, Parris Island*, SC, *www.pimuseum.us*.

Ironclad: Remains of the largest ironclad to survive the Civil War, the CSS *Jackson*, which was built in Columbus, Georgia, and burned by Federal troops when the city was captured in 1865. The hull alone weighs more than 560,000 pounds. *National Civil War Naval Museum at Port Columbus, Columbus*, GA, *www.portcolumbus.org*.

Stonewall's Raincoat: Raincoat worn by Confederate Civil War General Thomas J. "Stonewall" Jackson, mortally wounded in May 1863 during the Battle of Chancellorsville, Virginia. He was shot three times by friendly fire, and the raincoat shows two bullet holes in the left sleeve. His arm was amputated. *Virginia Military Institute Museum, Lexington*, VA, *www.vmi.edu/museum*.

General Robert E. Lee's Frock: Worn by Confederate commander-in-chief General Robert E. Lee at the surrender at Appomattox in 1865. *Museum of the Confederacy, Richmond*, VA, *www.moc.org*.

Colliding Bullets: Two Civil War .89-caliber minié balls that collided in midair and became fused. Found on a battlefield. *Marietta Museum of History, Marietta*, GA, *www.mariettahistory.org*.

***Monitor* Turret:** The turret from the ironclad USS *Monitor*, which fought against the Confederate CSS *Merrimack* during the Civil War. The turret was raised from the bottom of the Atlantic Ocean and is being restored. *Mariners' Museum, Newport News, VA, www.mariner.org.*

Double-Barrel Cannon: This Civil War cannon was built in Athens, Georgia, with two barrels—designed to fire two six-pound cannonballs connected with a chain. Scholars debate whether it was ever successfully fired in combat. *Athen's City Hall, Athens,* GA, *http://ngeorgia.com/ang/Athen's_Double_Barrel_Cannon.*

Sherman's Hat Pin: As General William Tecumseh Sherman's Union troops marched through the South during the latter part of the Civil War, they tore up Confederate railroads and made them unusable. *Marietta Museum of History, Marietta,* GA, *www.mariettahistory.org.*

Grant's Cigar Butt: According to legend, Ulysses S. Grant dropped this cigar butt while walking through Galena, Illinois, after the Civil War (in 1880) and a local kid picked it up and saved it. *Galena History Museum, Galena, IL, www.galenahistorymuseum.org.*

Bloody Rail: Perhaps the only surviving full-length fence rail from the "Bloody Lane" at the Battle of Antietam during the Civil War. It was collected from the battlefield in 1872 and contains several iron artillery canister balls embedded in the wood. *National Civil War Life Museum, Fredericksburg,* VA, *www.civilwarlife.org.*

Submarine *Hunley*: This Civil War submarine, which was recovered only a few years ago, is on display along with a gold coin retrieved from the captain's body when the ship was brought to the surface. The coin is bent—supposedly from a bullet that hit the captain in a previous engagement and saved his life. *Hunley Museum, Columbia, SC, www.hunley.org.*

General's Leg: During the Civil War, at the Battle of Gettysburg, Union General Daniel Sickles had his leg amputated from a wound. Supposedly, he visited it often after the war. *National Museum of Health and Medicine, Washington, DC., www.roadsideamerica.com.*

...killed in action: Desmond Doss (World War II); Thomas W. Bennett (Vietnam).

HOW AMERICA GOT AN AIR FORCE

Among the many things that makes the U.S. Air Force unique is that, for its first 40 years of existence, the U.S. "Air Force" was part of the U.S. Army.

READY FOR TAKEOFF

Attempts to separate the United States' airpower from the Army had been initiated before World War I, but not everyone supported the split. Creating a new administrative structure would be time-consuming and costly. Only when aviation technology was developed to the point that it played a more significant role in war did people realize the importance of giving aviators the support they needed to be effective.

The first step came in August 1907 with the formation of a military aerial unit within the U.S. Army: the Aeronautical Division, established by Brigadier General James Allen and staffed by one officer and two enlisted men responsible for "all matters pertaining to military ballooning, air machines, and all kindred subjects." The only things it didn't have were airplanes.

A GROWING CONCERN

In 1914 Congress created the Aviation Section to replace the Aeronautical Division, which had been operating within the Army's Signal Corps. Only a few airplanes had been acquired over the years, training for combat was inadequate, and manpower was lacking. In April 1917, the evolving air unit was manned by 131 officers and 1,087 enlisted men in seven squadrons that flew 55 aircraft, most of which were obsolete. Essentially, American airpower didn't exist.

By May 1918, the War Department had recognized the importance of aviation in warfare; the unit was renamed the Division of Military Aeronautics, then the U.S. Army Air Service. Brigadier General William "Billy" Mitchell's armada of nearly 1,500 airplanes was flying over the trench-bound stalemate of World War I. Americans shot down more than 750 enemy aircraft and dropped more than 130 tons of bombs while flying approximately 35,000 hours during the war. In operations near the end of the war, Americans commanded and participated in the first mass aerial attacks in history.

By 1920, two years after the war had ended, the Air Service was elevated to a combatant arm of the Army. Over the next few years, pilots trained with what little equipment was left over after the mass demobilization that gutted the Army following victory in World War I.

UNDER NEW MANAGEMENT

The Air Corps Act of 1926 changed the unit's name yet again to the U.S. Army Air Corps (AAC). Over the next 10 years, the AAC established a training center and primary flying school in San Antonio, Texas. What is today Randolph Air Force Base remains the "West Point of the Air" as envisioned by AAC leadership in the 1930s. But it wasn't until 1935 when the General Headquarters (GHQ) Air Force was formed that the first hint of an independent air arm appeared. The GHQ Air Force was responsible for the first truly independent mission within the Army—strategic targeting. The tactical (ground support) versus strategic (long-range bombardment) argument between surface forces and air forces was resolved with the establishment of the GHQ Air Force as part of the U.S. Army's combat structure.

When Major General Henry "Hap" Arnold officially took command of the AAC in September 1938, he immediately accelerated research and development efforts that were already under consideration, including radar, rocket boosters to assist takeoffs, and a host of aircraft and engine design modifications.

By the dawn of the 1940s, the AAC had made large leaps in technology, had developed policies in the use of its new weapons, and established contacts with scientists and industrialists who would make the expansion of aeronautical research and aircraft production run smoothly when the need arose.

HAP TAKES COMMAND

As the Air Corps expanded, reorganization and restructuring of the War Department became an obvious necessity. When the U.S. Army Air Forces was established in June 1941, General Arnold

Merci! **The French supplied the American colonies with 90 percent of their gunpowder...**

was named overall commander and acting deputy chief of staff for Air. Under the War Department General Staff reorganization in March 1942, the Army Air Forces were recognized as being equal in status to the Army Ground Forces and the equally new Army Services of Supply branch. Arnold became a member of the Joint Chiefs of Staff, directly responsible to the secretary of war and to the Army's chief of staff for all Army air operations.

BACK DOWN TO EARTH

The 2.4 million airmen who had flown some 300,000 aircraft in World War II were the product of a global necessity—America's air forces would never again be as large. The combination of weapons technology, aircraft capability, and the need for large crews on each aircraft resulted in these huge numbers. But immediately after the Japanese surrendered in 1945, the Army Air Forces began to demobilize, and in less than one year had released 1.7 million airmen. General Arnold once said, "Of all the Air Force's faults, its greatest has always been the fact that it has made its work seem too easy." To Hap, it was untiring hard work that made it *look* easy.

A BREECH BIRTH

The establishment of the U.S. Air Force seemed inevitable after World War II, but the Navy wasn't happy about it. Arguments reached a flashpoint when monies were cut from the Navy's aircraft carrier budget and transferred to the AAF's heavy B-36 Peacemaker program. The postwar interservice fighting over budgets and missions was typified by the "Revolt of the Admirals," a well-publicized rebellion by some of the Navy's top brass who felt the Navy was being stripped of its powers by Congress, the secretary of Defense, the Joint Chiefs of Staff, and the president.

The 1947 National Security Act and Executive Order 9877 created the independent U.S. Air Force, but it left broad holes (which would eventually be filled) in the definition of roles and missions expected of each service. Since then, the U.S. Air Force has cemented its place as a vital component of the nation's armed forces through combat, reconnaissance, cargo transport, and even humanitarian missions.

BURIAL AT SEA

One of the oldest traditions in naval history is burial at sea. The ceremonial disposal of the body or ashes of the deceased has evolved with quite a few restrictions over what can and cannot be done today.

ANCIENT TRADITION

Since mankind first went to sea in ships, burials at sea have followed. In ancient Egypt, the dead were often set adrift in some sort of watercraft in anticipation of them reaching the afterlife. The Vikings followed the same ritual, but did so after setting the vessels afire. So ingrained was the custom in Viking culture that archaeologists have uncovered evidence that some Vikings were buried on land in a ship set afire while others were cremated and set into a ring of stones shaped like a ship. In later days, entombing bodies below the surface of the sea was a preferred practice for many nations. The deceased were sewn into a sailcloth or some other form of canvas that was weighted to make the shroud sink when it was sent overboard following a memorial ceremony. During World Wars I and II, there were many burials at sea of those lost in battle.

PROCEDURE IN THE U.S. NAVY

To qualify for a burial at sea by the United States military, one must be an active duty, retired, or honorably discharged veteran. Their family members, U.S. civilian marine personnel of the Military Sealift Command, or other U.S. citizens deemed eligible by the Chief of Naval Operations because of notable service or contributions to the government may also qualify. Anyone desiring burial at sea must indicate so in a will or other legal document. Due to environmental considerations, burials of bodies at sea in the United States must occur in waters at least 600 feet deep and at least three miles from shore.

Prior to burial of a body at sea, the ship is stopped and the casketed remains are brought on deck attended by casket bearers. The foot of the casket is positioned for launch on a stand, with the foot extending overboard at right angles to the ship. The casket is draped with the U.S. flag, with the stars placed at the head. The

Desertion during the Civil War was called "taking French leave."

captain then issues an order, "All hands bury the dead." The ship's flags are displayed at half-mast as officers and crew assemble on deck and are called to attention by the adjutant. The massed formation assumes parade rest for the burial service, which is presided over by the ship's chaplain, the commanding officer, or another designated officer.

The burial service consists of the reading of scripture, saying prayers, and committing the remains to the ocean as the assembled crewmen and officers salute. The benediction ends the service with heads bowed, followed by the firing of three volleys by a firing party of seven and the playing of "Taps." The ship then resumes its course and speed.

In the case of cremations, the urn is placed on a small table or platform, with a folded flag next to it. The commanding officer or an appointed substitute opens the urn and scatters the remains at the designated time during the service. If the urn is not to be opened, it is positioned for launch into the ocean by tilting the platform. Flowers often accompany the urn as it slides into the sea, or they can be tossed into the sea after the burial. Cremated remains have occasionally been scattered at sea from naval aircraft. Burials at sea from submarines have also occurred, including firing the remains from a boat's torpedo tubes.

The commanding officer or the chaplain must, within 10 days, contact the next of kin through a personal letter to advise them indicating when and where the burial was accomplished, giving the date and time of the burial service as well as photographs or a videotape of the proceedings, if available.

* * *

WHAT HAPPENS TO OLD DOGS?

Just like their human counterparts, canine soldiers receive emergency treatment on the battlefield. If they need more advanced treatment, the Military War Dogs are transported to the $15 million "Walter Reed of the veterinary world" facility that opened at Lackland Air Force Base in October 2008. Older military war dogs often find second careers with stateside law-enforcement agencies or retire to civilian life with their handlers or other caring individuals.

TOP 10 GENERALS, PART II

We carry on with America's best generals. For Part I, go to page 100.

6. DWIGHT D. EISENHOWER (1890-1969)

"Ike" was born in Denison, Texas, and grew up in Abilene, Kansas. He graduated from West Point in 1915, and played football there. Unlike most officers, Eisenhower rarely served in the field. After performing a variety of training duties during World War I, he graduated at the top of his class from the Command and General Staff School in 1926 and from the Army War College in 1928. He was on General Douglas MacArthur's staff from 1933 to 1939, and in September 1941 he received a promotion to brigadier general while serving as chief of staff to the 3rd Army. Attached to the Army War Plans Division from December 1941 to June 1942, Eisenhower advanced to major general and was put in charge of U.S. forces in Europe.

World War II—Eisenhower assumed command of Operation Torch, the November 8 invasion of French North Africa, and the invasion of Tunisia one week later. It took Allied forces six months to drive the German and Italian armies out of Africa.

On July 9, 1943, Eisenhower commanded the invasion of Sicily. Once the Allies secured a strong holding position in Italy, President Franklin D. Roosevelt moved Eisenhower to England to plan the cross-channel invasion of France. Appointed Supreme Commander of the Allied Expeditionary Force, Eisenhower directed Operation Overlord, the Allied amphibious assault on Normandy, France, on June 6, 1944.

It was at this point that Eisenhower's role became extremely political: he had to placate Great Britain and the other Allies while making decisions regarding the war in Europe. He also had problems with some of his generals and made political concessions that produced poor results. Yet he made extremely sound decisions when reacting to setbacks, such as the German Ardennes offensive (Battle of the Bulge) from December 1944 to January 1945. When the Allied offensive resumed in February, he planned and implemented the crossing of the Rhine and the push into Germany.

After Germany's surrender on May 7–8, 1945, Eisenhower commanded the Allied occupation forces until November. He returned home and replaced General George C. Marshall as chief of staff, the highest-ranking officer in the U.S. Army.

What Made Him Great?

Eisenhower became a man of exceptional ability. He retired in February 1948 to become president of Columbia University, but in December 1950 President Harry S. Truman made him the first supreme commander of NATO. Eisenhower retired again in 1952, ran for president, and won. Part of his foreign policy was to protect Middle Eastern countries from Soviet aggression and to avoid getting the United States involved in countries like Vietnam.

7. DOUGLAS MacARTHUR (1880–1964)

MacArthur was the son of Medal of Honor recipient Lieutenant General Arthur MacArthur Jr., and followed in his father's footsteps. He graduated from West Point in 1903, first in his class, and began his career serving under his father in the Philippines.

During World War I, he went to France and commanded a brigade at Saint-Mihiel and a division during the Meuse-Argonne campaign. After the war, he returned to the Philippines as a major general. He retired from the Army in August 1936 to become the Philippine government's field marshal. As war with Japan became imminent, President Roosevelt reinstated MacArthur as a lieutenant general commanding U.S. forces in the Far East.

World War II—Though he was warned repeatedly that the Philippines could be struck by Japan, and was provided with B-17 bombers to defend against an attack, MacArthur believed the islands would not be invaded before the spring of 1942. This miscalculation led to faulty vigilance and would have resulted in the removal of any other commander but MacArthur. Instead, he was ordered to Australia to stem the Japanese advance, awarded the Medal of Honor for the defense of the Philippines, and became the supreme commander of Allied forces in the Southwest Pacific.

Always a superb strategist, MacArthur stopped the Japanese drive on New Guinea and recovered western New Britain. In November 1942 he began leap-frogging forces along the northern coast of New Guinea to Morotai in the Molucca Islands, which reopened the way to the Philippines. On October 20, 1944, he led the invasion of Leyte, fulfilling his promise to return to the Philippines. President Roosevelt raised MacArthur to general of the armies and put him in charge of planning the invasion of Japan, which was preempted by Japan's surrender. MacArthur remained in Tokyo as supreme commander of the occupation forces and administered the defeated country with benevolence. He was still there when North Korea invaded South Korea in June 1950.

The Korean War—As supreme commander of United Nations forces in Korea, MacArthur conceived one of the greatest double envelopments in military history. Using a force strong enough to hold a perimeter in the southeastern corner of Korea, he sent a strong amphibious force to assault Inchon in the northwestern corner of the country. The resulting "pincers" movement virtually destroyed the North Korean army. He followed this brilliant move with perhaps his biggest mistake when he attempted to unify Korea and stepped on the toes of Communist China. Neither President Truman nor the United Nations wanted China drawn into the Korean War, but MacArthur, mainly from arrogance, allowed it to happen. After he was recalled to the United States and replaced by Lieutenant General Matthew Ridgway, MacArthur retired.

What Made Him Great?

Though egotistical and controversial, MacArthur was nevertheless one of the greatest generals of World War II and of history. His amphibious campaigns were masterpieces of strategy and boldness, and were noted for their efficiency and low casualty rates. Despite his flamboyance, MacArthur cared for his men and believed thorough planning would save lives—and it did.

8. GEORGE S. PATTON (1885–1945)

Patton was descended from an old Virginia military family but was born in San Gabriel, California. He attended the Virginia Military Institute and went on to West Point, graduating in 1909. After placing fifth in the modern pentathlon at the 1912 Olympics, Patton joined the cavalry when men still rode horses, and he never left the branch after it became mechanized. He learned a great deal about fighting while serving under General John J. Pershing, and during World War I he organized and led the 1st Tank Brigade during the Saint-Mihiel and Meuse-Argonne campaigns late in 1918. During the postwar years, Patton spread his time between studying and advancing tank technology (a series of tanks were named for him), serving on the general staff, and attending the Army War College. By April 1941 he had risen in the ranks to major general and was in command of the 2nd Armored Division. By then, Patton had earned the reputation of having a uniquely gifted military mind, immense energy, and a penchant for being blunt.

WORLD WAR II—Patton participated in the planning of Operation Torch and in November 1942 commanded the landings in French Morocco. He replaced Major General Lloyd Fredendall following the defeat at Kasserine Pass on March 3, 1943, and assumed command of the 2nd Army Corps. Temporarily relieved of duty after a minor quarrel with the British, Patton subsequently took command of the 1st Armored Corps, which later became the 7th Army. His brilliant campaign in Sicily during July and August of 1943 was overshadowed by a highly publicized face-slapping incident in a hospital on August 3. Patton despised cowardice, and when he found a soldier skulking in a hospital bed with no evidence of an injury, he called him "a damned coward" and slapped his face in the presence of reporters. After the incident made national news, General Eisenhower brought Patton to England and tried to keep him out of trouble until the Normandy campaign.

Patton sulked for five months before Eisenhower gave him command of the newly formed 3rd Army. He landed in France on July 6, 1944, broke out of Normandy with his tanks, advanced east across France, wheeled suddenly north, and struck the southern flank of the German army. When the German Ardennes offensive in December 1944 threatened to swallow up a surrounded American division at Bastogne, Patton pushed the 3rd Army through mud and snow and relieved Bastogne on December 26, 1944. He pressed on to the Rhine under stiff resistance, crossed it on March 22, and pushed through central Germany into Bavaria. By May 8, when Germany surrendered, his spearheads had reached into Czechoslovakia.

Now without a war to fight, Patton's inappropriate political

One of many U.S. Marines slogans: "Pain is temporary. Pride is forever."

comments once again put him at odds with Eisenhower. Removed from command of the 3rd Army, Patton moved to the 15th Army, which had few troops and existed mainly on paper. With one day to go before his return to the United States, a car he was riding in was hit by a truck. Patton was paralyzed from the neck down and died less than two weeks later.

What Made Him Great?

Like many field commanders, Patton was a warrior and not a politician. His tactics were brilliant. By any measure, he became America's greatest leader of heavy-armor forces, as well as one of America's outstanding field commanders.

9. MATTHEW B. RIDGWAY (1895–1993)

Best known for saving the UN effort in the Korean War, Ridgway was also a celebrated leader in World War II. He was born at Fort Monroe, Virginia, and graduated from West Point in 1917. During World War I, Ridgway served with the 3rd Infantry Regiment but did not go overseas. During the postwar years, the Army sent Ridgway to China and the Philippines. He periodically returned stateside to attend high-level military training. In December 1941 he joined the 82nd Infantry Division, which he later commanded as the 82nd Airborne, one of the Army's new airborne divisions.

In early 1943 Major General Ridgway brought the division to the Mediterranean and on July 9–10 made the first American airborne assault on Sicily. He led elements of the division during the September 9 amphibious assault on Salerno. On D-day, June 6, 1944, he parachuted into France with his troops. In August he moved up to command the 18th Airborne Corps, which consisted of the 82nd and 101st Airborne divisions, and led his men in the airborne assault at Arnhem on September 17. He played a major role in stemming the German Ardennes offensive in December 1944 and later participated in the Rhineland and the Ruhr campaigns, during which he received his third star.

The Korean War—Ridgway's greatest hour came during the Korean War, when the Joint Chiefs of Staff sent him to Korea to clean up MacArthur's mess. The Chinese had sent MacArthur's UN forces reeling back from the Manchurian border in December 1950, recaptured the South Korean capital of Seoul, and threatened to drive UN forces completely out of Korea. Ridgway stopped the counteroffensive 75 miles south of Seoul and gradually reestablished control of the area, fighting his way back to the original border between the two Koreas. For the next several months, he fought a battle of containment, forcing the enemy to throw hundreds of thousands of men into his stubborn mincing machine before agreeing to truce talks. Ridgway's strategy of containment became the adopted policy of the United States throughout the Cold War.

After serving briefly as Supreme Allied Commander in Europe, Ridgway returned to the United States in October 1953 to become the Army's chief of staff during Eisenhower's administration. Because of his personal policy of Communist containment, he probably kept the United States from becoming involved in the Vietnam War for 10 years.

What Made Him Great?

Ridgway did not believe in massive retaliation to Communist threats, but he did sanction "flexible response," which is the strategy he followed that ended the Korean War. With the exception of Vietnam, it is the same policy American presidents followed until the Iraq War in 2003.

10. H. NORMAN SCHWARZKOPF (1934–)

Born in Trenton, New Jersey, Schwarzkopf was an Army brat whose father served in both World Wars. Like his father, he graduated from West Point, and in June 1956 he became a second lieutenant in the infantry.

Vietnam War—The man who became known as "Stormin' Norman" served two tours in Vietnam, first as an advisor to the South Vietnamese in 1965 and later as commander of the 1st Battalion, 6th Infantry, in the 23rd Infantry Division, where he earned the first of three Silver Stars and two Purple Hearts. Promoted to colonel, he returned to the United States in a body cast due to war injuries. After reaching home, Schwarzkopf was shocked by the public's hostility to the war and considered resign-

...She helped pave the way for the feminist movement of the 1960s and '70s.

ing. He privately blamed the government for becoming involved in a war with unclear objectives and a misconceived strategy.

Between the Wars—Schwarzkopf remained in the Army and for the next 20 years worked his way up the ladder by commanding the 172nd Brigade in Alaska and the 1st Brigade, 9th Infantry Division at Fort Lewis, Washington. After serving as deputy director of plans for the Pacific command in 1978–80, he eventually became a major general and commanded the 24th Mechanized Infantry Division at Fort Stewart, Georgia. He returned to Fort Lewis in 1986 as a lieutenant general and took command of the 1st Corps. With his elevation to U.S. Central Command in 1988, he was responsible for planning Desert Shield, which became Desert Storm in January 1991, the ousting of Iraqi forces from Kuwait.

Desert Storm—In this capacity Schwarzkopf planned, organized, and executed the largest U.S. mechanized combat operation since 1945. Between August 1990 and January 1991, he assembled 765,000 troops—of which 541,000 were American—from 28 countries, hundreds of ships, and thousands of tanks and aircraft. When a six-week aerial bombardment failed to bring Saddam Hussein to the negotiating table, Schwarzkopf drew Iraqi forces out of position with a fake amphibious landing and performed what he termed an "end run" around Iraq's vaunted Republican Guard. He cut the enemy's communications, destroyed their supply lines, and in 100 days forced Saddam to accept a cease-fire. Total U.S. casualties were 293 killed and 467 wounded.

Schwarzkopf could have marched into Baghdad with little resistance, and he expressed a willingness to do so. But UN resolutions did not include the capture of Iraq, so Schwarzkopf stood down. Somewhat annoyed by not finishing the job, he retired from the Army in 1992.

What Made Him Great?

Schwarzkopf executed a classic campaign and left no messes within the scope of his task. He understood his orders and performed them with few casualties and received much praise from the world community.

Drone: A land, sea, or air vehicle that is remotely or automatically controlled.

GUERRILLA WARFARE, PART III

The U.S. Army Rangers during World War II.
(Part II is on page 75.)

In 1942 the 1st Ranger Battalion was created after Major General Lucian Truscott convinced General George C. Marshall, the Army chief of staff, of the need for large, all-volunteer, and highly trained commando units that could be used for special operations. "Rangers Lead the Way" was and is their motto.

DARBY'S RANGERS

The 1st Ranger Battalion was nicknamed "Darby's Rangers" after their commander, Lieutenant Colonel William O. Darby. They first saw action during the invasion of North Africa, at the Battle of El Guettar, where U.S. forces handed legendary German general Erwin "the Desert Fox" Rommel his first solid defeat. During the invasion of Sicily, Darby led his Rangers in an attack on the town of Gela. Darby's men suffered heavy losses, including one platoon that was completely wiped out. During a counterattack by Italian tanks, Darby and one of his captains took control of a captured antitank gun, knocking out several of the tanks and forcing the surrender of more than 200 Italian soldiers.

THE DEVIL'S BRIGADE

The Devil's Brigade, also known as the 1st Special Service Force, was a Canadian-American unit trained in mountaineering, airborne, and close-combat skills that operated mostly in Italy and France. They excelled at close-quarters combat with numerically superior forces. At Monte la Difensa, Italy, they wiped out a strategic enemy defensive position high atop a mountain surrounded by steep cliffs. They got their nickname from a captured diary of a German officer who wrote of the American commandos (whose faces were camouflaged in black paint for the nighttime raid), "The black devils are all around us every time we come into line and we never hear them."

According to the Military Channel, the top chopper is the Apache Longbow.

RUDDER'S RANGERS

The 2nd Ranger Battalion was commanded by Lieutenant Colonel James Earl Rudder and is best known as the unit that scaled the cliffs at Pointe du Hoc during the D-day invasion. Their mission was to neutralize a battery of six 15-mm coastal artillery pieces that were capable of hitting the Allied ships participating in the invasion. The Rangers hit the beach and immediately began scaling the cliffs with rope ladders while under constant rifle and machine-gun fire from the Germans on the cliffs above. Once they made it to the top of the cliffs and eliminated the Germans, they were shocked to find out that Allied intelligence had been faulty. The guns had obviously been removed sometime before the invasion. Two hundred and twenty men attempted the climb up the cliffs. After the Germans were routed, only 90 Rangers were still battle-ready.

MERRILL'S MARAUDERS

Named after their leader, Brigadier General James Merrill, the 5307th Composite Unit (Provisional) operated in the Burmese jungle. The United States was supporting China by supplying them with war materials, but when the Japanese occupied Burma, they cut off the land route. The Marauders' mission was to pave the way for the construction of the Ledo Road—a connection between the Indian railway and the old Burma Road to China—and capture Myitkyina Airfield, the only all-weather landing strip in northern Burma.

Merrill's Marauders traveled more than 1,000 miles in dense jungle, destroying Japanese supply lines, disrupting communications, and defeating the Japanese in 35 separate engagements. Every member of the Marauders was awarded the Bronze Star.

Turn to page 212 for Part IV.

* * *

"People sleep peaceably in their beds at night only because rough men stand ready to do violence on their behalf."

—George Orwell

Potato masher: World War II slang for a German hand grenade, because of its shape.

TOY SOLDIERS

"The toy soldier game is not really about war . . . these are all little friends." —Peter Johnson, former curator of the Museum of Military Miniatures

A MINIATURE HISTORY

Toy soldiers have been around since people have been fighting battles, and some models date back as far as ancient Egypt to Prince Emsah, who was buried with painted wooden statuettes 4,000 years ago. Today, instead of guarding the prince's tomb and serving as a reminder of his military achievements, the unique collection stands proudly at the Cairo Museum . . . in a storage room.

Originally fashioned from materials such as wood, clay, or stone, toy soldiers were handcrafted for only the most noble of children and collectors. They weren't mass-produced until the 1890s, when new manufacturing techniques allowed for inexpensive production and collection.

CRAFTING A BETTER TOY SOLDIER

In 1893 an Englishman named William Britain, one of the best-known makers of authentic and highly detailed metal toy soldiers, figured out how to spin the miniature molds in such a way that would allow the lead to stick to the sides and leave the center hollow by pouring the molten metal out before the entire figure could set, leaving just a "skin" on the inside of the mold— thereby inventing the hollow-cast method of production. Not only were these soldiers lighter, but they were also much cheaper to make.

Britain dominated the toy soldier market until Louis Marx, a former U.S. Army private, went back to his life as a toymaker. In the 1930s and 1940s, Marx created his toy soldiers from metal alloys. However, the U.S. government needed spare metal during World War II for real military weapons and not just toy ones. Following World War II, inexpensive and child-friendly plastic became the popular choice for some manufacturers. By the mid-1950s, these simple, unpainted soldiers were readily available and

Battle bowler: British military slang for an officer's steel helmet. To the troops, a tin hat.

affordable (less than a dollar a bag for a troop of 20 men) to the masses of children who wanted to play their own war games—along with melting them, tying them to fireworks, and experimenting in just about every destructive way you can imagine.

During the early 20th century, many of the little military figures had been made of lead. In 1966 concerns about lead poisoning caused many toymakers—including Britains, Timpo, Crescent, and Cherilea—to stop production of lead figures altogether and focus solely on plastic ones. By this time, Louis Marx and Company was back in the game with its own line of plastic figures, but later went out of business in 1978. The antiwar protests during the 1960s and 1970s took its toll on the American public, and people generally shied away from military toys. But popular science-fiction movies and video games gave rise to action figures with movable parts and accessories like G.I. Joe, and toy soldiers made a comeback. Marx sold many of its patents and molds to the Mego Corporation, which in the 1980s created a collection of their own military action figures called "Action Jackson," which some considered a G.I. Joe imitation.

TOY SOLDIERS VS. GREEN ARMY MEN

Army men, not to be confused with the more expensive toy soldiers and miniature replicas, have certain attributes that qualify them as genuine army men. Toy soldiers often have movable parts and are painted with more detail. A genuine army man stands approximately 2 inches tall and is molded of one piece of solid-colored, unpainted soft plastic. Army men come equipped with various weapons, usually molded directly onto the toy. They are usually some shade of green, and are widely understood to be American soldiers. The packages of other colors—reds, blues, yellows—represent the "other" side. There are some painted plastic soldiers preferred by collectors and enthusiasts because of their historically correct uniforms.

FROM THE TOY BOX TO THE TERRAIN

Some of these little plastic army men have ventured a long way from the corners of children's rooms and the clutches of shag carpeting. Mouths Wide Open, a small collective of civilians committed to ending the war in Iraq, started the Army Men Project. The ad hoc group encourages people to stealthily place little green army men everywhere—grocery stores, gas stations, public restrooms, on the hood of a car—with "Please bring me home" stickers attached at their bases to remind people of the ongoing horrors of war and "to serve as tools to foster dialogue, action, and resistance to the war."

The Army Men Project was the catalyst to March First, a group of four women who wanted to "blur the line between protesting and public art" instead of choosing a side. Less a protest and more an artistic demonstration, on March 1, 2006, the group placed 4,500 green plastic army men along a five-mile stretch of Lincoln Avenue's sidewalk in Chicago. (That's one army man every 14 inches.)

At Flagler Palm Coast High School in Florida, some students created a memorial project designed to offer students a better idea of the large numbers of soldiers lost in the war. Inside large glass display cases stand thousands of the little green men, each figure symbolizing a fallen troop in the war in Iraq. After the students each donated one miniature figure, they had to rely on donations from the community in order to get more people involved and to promote awareness. Their plan worked and donations came from as far away as New Jersey and Arizona, and then from the whole country after their story aired on CNN.

NOT JUST FOR KIDS

Author H. G. Wells and British wartime prime minister Sir Winston Churchill have each been photographed with their miniature armies, and Churchill purportedly housed one of the greatest collections of Lucotte soldiers, produced in France. In his biography *My Early Life*, Churchill describes his army: "I had almost 1,500 of the same size, all British and organized in an infantry division and a cavalry brigade. I had 15 fieldpieces but lacked a train. My father's old friend, Sir Drummond Wolff, noticed this and created a fund, which to a certain extent remedied this." Others who were known to collect: Robert Louis Stevenson, Jerome K. Jerome, and G. K. Chesterton.

Malcolm Forbes—a famous publishing giant who acquired extravagant items such as Fabergé eggs, a fleet of motorcycles, and an island in the Pacific—also collected more than 50,000 little soldiers over the course of three decades. In 1997 his diverse and pristine collection that used to be housed at the Forbes Magazine Museum of Military Miniatures in Tangier, Morocco, was sold off in a two-part auction at Christie's for approximately $700,000.

But the most expensive toy soldier in the world sold to date is a 1963 G.I. Joe prototype—11½ inches tall with 21 movable parts, and wearing a hand-stitched sergeant's uniform—designed by Hasbro's creative director, Don Levine. The buyer, Baltimore businessman Stephen A. Geppi, purchased Joe on August 7, 2003, at an auction performed by Heritage Comics Auctions of Dallas, Texas, for $200,000. Yo, Joe!

* * *

THE BEST PART OF WAKING UP

Seven-year-old Jackson decided to serve his mom breakfast in bed for Mother's Day. She was delighted, of course, but after she'd drunk some of her coffee, she found three little green army men in the bottom of the cup. "Honey," she asked, "Are these little guys in here for a reason?" "Sure, Mom," said Jackson, "I heard it on TV: the best part of waking up is soldiers in your cup!"

* * *

GENERAL CONFUSION

A general was standing by the classified-document shredder with a piece of paper in his hand. A young officer walked by and asked if he could help. The general asked, "Do you know how to work this machine? My secretary's out today."

"Sure thing, sir," said the young officer. He took the paper and fed it into the machine.

"Great," said the general. "Now, can you make me two copies of it?"

...He received the Silver Star, Bronze Star, and two Purple Hearts.

PROFILES IN COURAGE

"One man with courage makes a majority."
—Andrew Jackson

LIEUTENANT MICHAEL P. MURPHY, U.S. NAVY, AFGHANISTAN

Kunar Province, June 28, 2005

Deep behind enemy lines on the Afghan-Pakistani border, a four-man Navy SEAL team was conducting a reconnaissance mission in the Hindu Kush's unforgiving 10,000-foot altitude. The four-man team of Lieutenant Michael Murphy, Gunner's Mate Second Class Danny Dietz, Sonar Technician Second Class Matthew Axelson, and Hospital Corpsman Second Class Marcus Luttrell was compromised when the team was spotted by local nationals, who reported their presence and location to the Taliban.

A fierce firefight erupted between the four SEALs and a much larger enemy force, estimated at more than 50 insurgents who not only outnumbered the SEALs but also held the higher ground. The Taliban launched a well-organized, three-sided attack on the SEALs and the firefight continued relentlessly as the Taliban's overwhelming numbers pushed the team deeper into a ravine.

Trying to reach safety, the four men, all wounded, began bounding down the mountain's steep sides, making leaps of 20 to 30 feet. Approximately 45 minutes into the fight, pinned down by overwhelming forces, Dietz tried to place a distress call back to the base, but before he could move to a clear area, he was shot in the hand, shattering his thumb. Despite the intensity of the firefight and suffering grave gunshot wounds himself, Murphy then risked his own life to save his teammates. With radio communication blocked by the steep mountainsides, Murphy "unhesitatingly and with complete disregard for his own life" moved into the open, where he could call for assistance.

His deliberate and heroic act made him a target for the enemy, but even while he was being shot at, he was able to contact his Quick Reaction Force at Bagram Air Base. Murphy passed them his unit's location, as well as an estimate of the size of the enemy forces arrayed against them. Shot in the back while making the

Kirk Douglas was a U.S. Navy communications officer in antisubmarine warfare.

radio call, he dropped the transmitter—yet picked it up, completed the call, and continued firing at the still-attacking enemy. Severely wounded, Murphy then returned to his men and continued to fight.

An MH-47 Chinook helicopter with reinforcements aboard was sent to pull out the four wounded SEALs. The MH-47 was escorted by heavily armored Army attack helicopters. But the heavy weight of the attack helicopters slowed their flight, prompting the MH-47 to outrun their armored escort. They knew the tremendous risk going into an active enemy area in daylight without their attack support and without the cover of night. But knowing that the SEALs were surrounded and severely wounded, the rescue team opted to directly enter the oncoming battle in hopes of landing someplace on the brutally hazardous terrain. As the Chinook raced to the battle, a rocket-propelled grenade struck the helicopter, killing all 16 men aboard.

On the ground and nearly out of ammunition, Murphy and the other SEALs continued the fight. By the end of the two-hour gunfight that careened through the hills and over cliffs, Murphy, Axelson, and Dietz had been killed. An estimated 35 Taliban were also dead.

The fourth SEAL, Luttrell, was blasted over a ridge by a rocket-propelled grenade and was knocked unconscious. Regaining consciousness some time later, Luttrell managed to escape—badly injured—and slowly crawled down the side of a cliff. With a bullet wound to one leg, shrapnel embedded in both legs, three vertebrae cracked, and dehydrated, Luttrell walked seven miles as he evaded the enemy for nearly a day. Local nationals came to his aid, carrying him to a nearby village. The villagers kept him for three days, defending him from the Taliban. One of the villagers made his way to a Marine outpost with a note from Luttrell, and U.S. forces finally rescued him four days later.

By his courage, fighting spirit, and devotion to his men in the face of certain death, 29-year-old Lieutenant Michael Murphy was able to relay the position of his unit—a selfless act that led to the rescue of Luttrell and the recovery of the remains of the three SEALs killed in the battle. Murphy was awarded the Medal of Honor on October 22, 2007.

War of 1812: There's no evidence that any of the rockets fired at Fort McHenry ever hit it.

CODEBREAKERS

More than 1,000 women worked in the spy business during World War II, many without really knowing what they were doing.

WELCOME TO OHIO

In April 1943, about 600 "Women Accepted for Volunteer Emergency Service" (or, Navy WAVES) arrived at the National Cash Register Company in Dayton, Ohio. They were there, they thought, to train on tabulating machines for their work helping the war effort . . . except there were no tabulating machines. Instead, there were rooms guarded by armed Marines. On eight- hour shifts, 24 hours a day, women reported to work to create one small part of a mysterious machine. The women were only allowed to speak about their work with the others assigned to their room. Although they may have wondered if the wheels with 26 unmarked keys they were putting together were code machines, most women didn't talk about their work at all. And according to their letters home, they continued to claim that they were learning how to operate the tabulating machines.

YOUR SECRET'S SAFE WITH ME

The women were actually building huge decoding machines that were seven feet high, ten feet long, and two feet wide. At 5,000 pounds, the machines were officially called "Bombes," but were nicknamed the "gray elephants." The women in Dayton built 121 Bombes to break messages the Germans enciphered in their Enigma code.

The finished machines and their WAVE operators were then sent to Washington, D.C. In the chapel of the Naval Communications Annex (NCA), the WAVES received this ominous welcome from an anonymous officer: "If you ever tell what you are doing, you are committing treason. And don't think that just because you are young ladies you will be treated any differently than the men who commit treason. If you ever tell, we will shoot you."

Two floors at the NCA were divided into bays of four machines, four operators, and one supervisor who worked eight-hour shifts, 24 hours a day, just like in Dayton. Secrecy and division of labor were the norm. There were operators for the Bombes, operators for the machines that verified the messages, cryptologists who used codebooks if messages were double-encoded, translators, and messengers. And no one was trained in more than one job, making it impossible for one person to completely decode a message on her own.

By June 12, 1943, the U.S. government had used the decoded messages to launch attacks on German U-boats. Thanks to the Bombes, U.S. forces sank 95 U-boats by the end of the war.

SPY SCHOOL

The Bombes weren't the only decoding machines women worked on during World War II. Both the Army and the Navy had military personnel and civilians working in their cryptology departments: intercepting and decoding messages, solving codes, sending coded messages, and making American codes more secure. To find many of these cryptologists, the military searched colleges for people (women especially, since most young men would be off fighting) who were gifted in math or languages. The Navy's Enigma Office was also called the "Office of College Professors" because so many of the officers held PhDs or were teachers. But candidates also had to be judged as invulnerable to recruitment by the enemy. Women with relatives in Axis countries or who had financial problems were rejected no matter how many degrees they'd earned.

And like everything else in cryptology, even the training was secretive. Budding cryptologists taught by English professor Ola Winslow at Baltimore's Goucher College found themselves in a locked and guarded classroom. There, students learned languages like *katakana* (a syllabic form of Japanese writing), analysis, decryption, and translation.

WELCOME HOME

When the United States entered the war, just over 1,000 men and women were involved in the cryptology departments of the Army Signals Intelligence Service and the Navy's Code and Signal Section. By the war's end, those departments included more than 5,000 women. Some of them stayed with the cryptology departments into the postwar years, working to decode Soviet messages, but 75 percent returned to their hometowns.

They took an oath of secrecy upon discharge, so these women returned home with vague stories of the filing and typing they did

A Rhino Runner is a fully protected armored bus used to transport press and VIPs in Iraq.

in Washington to help win the war. Then, in 1974, when Royal Air Force Captain F. W. Winterbotham wrote about England's World War II work with the Enigma decoders, the U.S. government declared World War II cryptology work declassified, and the women could finally get credit for the crucial intelligence they'd provided the Allies.

THREE CODEBREAKERS

• Agnes Driscoll, who had degrees in math and physics, worked for the Navy for almost four decades, beginning in 1918. She participated in several key breakthroughs, including solving Japanese codes in 1930, breaking the "Blue Book" (the Japanese navy's operations code), and helping to develop cipher machines to decode Japanese messages.

• In 1940 Genevieve Grotjan of the Army's Signals Intelligence Service wrote a key to solving the Japanese "Purple" code (a diplomatic code, the Japanese government's most secure) and helped build that decoding machine.

• Mary Louise Prather began working for the Signals Intelligence Service in 1938 doing clerical work but rose through the ranks. She eventually identified the relationship between two Japanese messages, which helped uncover a new Japanese code.

* * *

A WAC-KY MOVIE

The 1943 movie *Women at War* provides a glimpse of what it was like to be a female in the service in World War II. Here three characters discuss job options.

> **Anastasia "Stormy" Hart:** I figured on goin' in the motor transport. I used to drive a five-ton tractor on the farm. You reckon' I can wrassle them Army trucks?
>
> **Sgt. Ramsey:** Well, you should give one plenty of competition anyway. You know, girls, the WACS offer a great opportunity for every woman that wants to specialize. You'll be serving your country, and at the same time, you'll be learning something that may to be of great value to you after the war.
>
> **Anastasia "Stormy" Hart:** How do you get to be a sergeant, anyway?
>
> **Lorna Travis:** [sarcastically] You buy a whistle.

SHE, HE, OR IT... WHAT IS A SHIP?

For centuries, ships in the English-speaking world have been referenced by a feminine pronoun. Women becoming sailors in what was once an all-male military service has helped put the issue of gender in focus: Is it sexist to call a ship a "she"?

NO CONFUSION IN OLDEN TIMES

For at least four centuries, a ship of European origin has been considered a "she." That tradition was based on the lore of ancient mariners dating back 2,500 years when sailing was a very dangerous profession and a ship represented a sailor's livelihood, his love, and, in times of peril, his salvation as his "mother ship." Those who sailed the seas often named their vessels after women as a reminder of their love when separated, often for months or years. That custom of referring to a ship as a "she" caught on.

THE TIMES ARE CHANGING

The U.S. became more sensitive to political correctness in the 1970s when feminists began campaigning to abolish gender in reference to objects like ships. One of the first targets was the government's habit of naming tropical storms after women, a tradition started by Australian meteorologist Clement Wragge in the late 19th century. In 1978, the practice of naming all major storms after women ended; male names were added to the list of Pacific typhoons and in 1979 the same was done for tropical storms in the Atlantic and Gulf of Mexico.

Along the way the prestigious *Chicago Manual of Style* and the Associated Press decided that ships should be gender neutral. Both guides declared that a ship or boat would in the future be referred to as "it." In 2002 Lloyd's Registry of Ships also began using "it" rather than "she" in referring to ships. In Russia, a ship is known as a "he," whereas it is still a "she" in German, French, Slavic, and other Indo-European languages. Still, the U.S. Navy and British Royal Navy aren't budging. A ship is still a "she" and tradition backs that up. Thus, the ship—she lives on.

The U.S. Army Reserve, headquartered in Atlanta, GA, consists of about 200,000 soldiers.

WHAT'S SO FUNNY ABOUT WAR?

Before World War II, cartoons with war themes attempted to use humor or satire to sway public opinion. The spread of military newspapers and the inclusion of cartoons as a feature designed to boost morale changed all that.

UP FRONT

Arguably the most well-known of the World War II cartoonists, Bill Mauldin (see page 126) created the characters Willie and Joe, who were depicted as rank-and-file soldiers dealing with the realities of war without the sugarcoating that some leaders, including General George S. Patton, would have preferred to see. Mauldin's caricatures, which he began in 1940 when he was an 18-year-old in the U.S. Army's 45th Infantry Division, were initially published in the division's newsletter and soon became hugely popular with the soldiers on the front lines. In 1943 Mauldin's cartoon was picked up by *Stars and Stripes*, and was then distributed domestically by United Feature Syndicate as *Up Front*, thanks in part to the war correspondent Ernie Pyle, who helped bring the cartoons to the attention of the general public.

Mauldin did not attempt to glorify the fighting in any manner; rather, he used wry humor to demonstrate the absurdities of war. For example, to make an exaggerated commentary on the practice of sending increasingly younger soldiers to the front lines, Mauldin showed Willie and Joe in a bunker, reading a notice handed to them by an adolescent dressed in a soldier's uniform. One says to the other, "I guess it's okay. The replacement center says he comes from a long line of infantrymen."

SAD SACK

At the time that he was drafted into the U.S. Army in June 1941, George Baker was a struggling animator on the verge of losing his job with the Walt Disney Company in Los Angeles. Although the war in Europe had been raging for several years, the possibility of the United States entering the war seemed remote to many at the time. Baker and other soldiers went through the motions of their training with little sense of purpose, waiting for their one-year enlistment to be up so they could get on with their lives. To break up the monotony of Army life, Baker began to create drawings on his own time, attempting to explain pictorially what life was like in the armed forces. After taking his drawings to several New York publishers and being rejected, a despondent Baker put his cartoons away and tried to forget about them. However, a few months later, the armed forces sponsored a cartoon contest for servicemen. Baker decided to enter one of his drawings in the contest—and won first prize. This caught the attention of the editor of the Army's *Yank* magazine, Major Hartzell Spence, who secured Baker a position on *Yank*'s staff. Baker worked for *Yank* for the duration of World War II, moving from one training camp to another as a salesman for the magazine while also being exposed to the many facets of Army life, which he then used as a basis for his cartoons.

Baker's character, named the Sad Sack, was a stumbling, bumbling soldier trying to fit into an Army comprised of stereotypes: trim and well-dressed men in perfect marching lines, belligerent drill sergeants, and unsympathetic cooks, barbers, and doctors. The Sack represented the common man trying to live up to the perceived ideal of what a soldier should be, and usually without success. Baker tried to show situations that troops in all branches of the Army—situated in any theater or at any training base—would recognize. One famous cartoon, titled "Drill," shows the Sack in a marching drill, repeatedly bumping into taller, neatly groomed men lined up in perfect formations, and then getting trampled and carted off on a stretcher. (Neither the Sack nor anyone else in the cartoons spoke a word.) Baker took a more lighthearted approach with his illustrations than did Bill Mauldin, which may be why Baker did not get in much trouble with his superiors.

After the war, Baker returned to civilian life and continued to draw *Sad Sack* until 1958, but Sack the civilian was not as popular as Sack the soldier, in part due to the younger audience for comic books. Baker had to use entirely new settings and use less suggestive material—and in the comic books, the Sack engaged in conversations, which changed the style of the cartoon considerably. Although *Sad Sack* (illustrated by other artists after 1958 and distributed by Harvey Comics) lasted into the 1990s and produced

...that Japan might attack the United States.

several spin-offs, it never matched the popularity of the cartoons done by Baker during World War II.

MALE CALL

Prior to World War II, *Terry and the Pirates*, produced by Milton Caniff, was one of the most popular comic strips in American newspapers. The serial comic followed the exploits of a young boy, Terry, and his adult sidekick, Pat Ryan, in the Far East, and the supporting cast included a beautiful blonde woman named Burma. When the war broke out, Caniff, who was unable to enlist due to a childhood illness that damaged his lungs, wanted to contribute in his own way to the war effort. He created a special version of *Terry and the Pirates*, with Burma as the star, for the military's newspapers. When civilian newspapers complained about not having access to the "unauthorized" version of the comic strip, Caniff changed it completely (including revising the format from serial to stand-alone) and renamed it *Male Call*. The new star was Miss Lace, a dark-haired woman who visited men on military bases and addressed everyone as "General." *Male Call*'s intended audience was comprised exclusively of men in the military, so it was raunchier than what would appear in civilian newspapers, and contained numerous double entendres of a sexual nature. One of the strip's notable features is that it showed injured soldiers in a genuine manner, including those who had been blinded or had lost a limb. *Male Call* last appeared in military newspapers in 1947.

Another of Caniff's creations was the serial comic *Steve Canyon*, which he began in 1947 and continued until his death in 1988. The title character started out as a civilian pilot but joined the Air Force during the Korean War. *Steve Canyon* did not reach the heights of popularity seen by *Terry and the Pirates* and contained less-suggestive material than *Male Call* to appease the general public, but it achieved a wide circulation and lasted four decades, much longer than a typical comic strip.

G.I. JOE

Before Hasbro created the G.I. Joe action figures in 1964, Dave Breger introduced the original G.I. Joe to his comic strips in 1942. Begun upon Breger's enlistment in 1941 and originally titled *Private Breger*, it was distributed domestically by King Features Syndi-

Korean peace talks lasted two years and 17 days, and involved 575 meetings.

cate. In order to have the strip published in military newspapers, Breger had to rename his character. Joe was an ordinary private who attempted to be respectful of his superiors but often ended up doing something that was good for a chuckle. By no measure was the boyish-looking Joe even close to being the gruff hero idealized by the more well-known Hasbro action figures. *G.I. Joe* caught on with the troops so much that it became a name given to the common foot soldier. The 1945 movie *The Story of* G.I. *Joe*, which was about correspondent Ernie Pyle, and Hasbro's action figures simply pirated the name. After the war, Breger—both the cartoonist and the character—returned to civilian life. The new comic, *Mister Breger*, began to appear in newspapers, and continued until 1969.

TODAY'S MILITARY COMICS

As the World War II–era comics were phased out and others that had a military theme, such as *Sgt. Rock* (see page 274), came and went, more comic books focused on the exploits of superheroes, and newspapers tried to make their funny pages, well, funnier. The unpopularity of the Vietnam War was another contributing factor to the decline of military-themed comics in the public eye. One exception was *Beetle Bailey* (see page 252), which debuted in 1951 and has continued to this day, seemingly stuck in time and never engaged in combat (which may help explain its long tenure), but still good for a laugh.

Does that mean that military comics are becoming extinct? Not at all—they have simply become modernized via the Internet, and continue to be printed in military newspapers wherever U.S. troops are stationed. Today's military comics aren't just for the soldiers, either—one of the more popular is Julie Negron's *Jenny the Military Spouse*, which revolves entirely around the lives of Air Force spouses and makes little mention of the enlisted men and women. Other comic strips focus on a certain service branch, as the ease of distributing a comic through the Web means that any artist with a bit of skill and a computer can be successful without the direct support of the armed forces. Reading the funnies has long been a means for soldiers to share a daily laugh, to relieve a bit of the stress that comes with the military lifestyle, and to realize that they are not the only ones who want to roll their eyes when the red tape becomes almost overwhelming.

Every Special Forces graduate is issued a coveted combat knife known as the Yarborough.

TOP NAVY FLICKS

Be sure to pack these ten Navy movies into your bag before you head off on that long sea voyage to distant shores.

THE FIGHTING SEABEES (1944)

John Wayne stars as Wedge Donovan in this dramatized retelling of the origin of the U.S. Navy's Construction Battalions (CBs, or "Seabees") during World War II. The Duke and his newly trained fighting Seabees work to hold off the Japanese, but will their efforts be enough? Amid all the training and fighting, Donovan develops a romantic interest in war correspondent Constance Chesley (Susan Hayward). The film was nominated for an Oscar for Best Music but lost to *Since You Went Away*, another film that used World War II as a backdrop.

THEY WERE EXPENDABLE (1945)

Following up on the success of *The Fighting Seabees*, John Wayne returned the following year alongside Donna Reed and Robert Montgomery for this story of tiny torpedo patrol boats taking on the massive Japanese fleet in World War II. Considered by many to be one of the Duke's finest performances, the film was nominated for a pair of Academy Awards for Best Sound and Best Special Effects, but won no Oscars.

MISTER ROBERTS (1955)

After six years as a Broadway smash, *Mister Roberts* hit the big screen with Henry Fonda reprising his Tony-winning role as Lieutenant Doug Roberts, whose assignment to the USS *Reluctant* during World War II provides moments of both humor and drama as the ship seemingly misses out on the war. The film's all-star cast, which included James Cagney and Jack Lemmon, was movie gold. *Mister Roberts* was nominated for three Academy Awards, with Lemmon winning his first Oscar, for Best Supporting Actor.

THE CAINE MUTINY (1954)

Based on Herman Wouk's Pulitzer Prize–winning novel of the same name, this movie stars Humphrey Bogart as the eccentric and dis-

Actor Steve McQueen (*The Great Escape*) served in the Marines from 1947 to 1950.

liked Lieutenant Commander Philip Francis Queeg of the fictitious destroyer/minesweeper *Caine* during World War II. After the unstable Queeg is relieved of his command by two of the ship's officers, the officers are later court-martialed for mutiny on the high seas. The film was nominated for seven Academy Awards but didn't win in any category—partially because of the competition, which included Marlon Brando's classic *On the Waterfront*, which was named Best Picture.

TORA! TORA! TORA! (1970)

This epic retelling of the Japanese attack on Pearl Harbor was a combined effort by American and Japanese filmmakers and actors, told from both sides' point of view. Although most of the cast were relative unknowns, a notable exception is Jason Robards, who would later win two Academy Awards. One famous line in the movie gave rise to the idea that the Japanese had "awakened a sleeping giant." These days, historians argue over whether the statement was historical fact or an enduring Hollywood invention. The film was nominated for five Academy Awards in technical categories, and won for Best Special Visual Effects.

MIDWAY (1976)

Exactly six months after the attack on Pearl Harbor, the Japanese navy remained undefeated and apparently invincible. Then came the Battle of Midway, a tiny atoll situated between Hawaii and Japan, which proved to be a resounding loss for the Japanese forces. The turning point of World War II combat in the Pacific made for a great movie with an all-star cast that included Charlton Heston, Henry Fonda, and James Coburn. Critics were less impressed, however, and the film was not nominated for any major awards.

AN OFFICER AND A GENTLEMAN (1982)

Richard Gere stars as Zack Mayo, a loner who ends up in the Navy's Aviation Officer Candidate School with aspirations of becoming a pilot. But first he must survive his stern drill instructor, Gunnery Sergeant Emil Foley, portrayed by Louis Gossett Jr. The drama unfolds through a tale of love and loss as Mayo strug-

More than 95 percent of all jobs in military service are open to women.

gles to find his place under Foley's relentless pressure. The film was nominated for six Academy Awards, with Gossett earning an Oscar for Best Supporting Actor, and the Joe Cocker and Jennifer Warnes hit "Up Where We Belong" winning for Best Original Song.

TOP GUN (1986)

Tom Cruise stars at Lieutenant Pete "Maverick" Mitchell, a hot-shot fighter pilot who takes his "need for speed" to the U.S. Navy Fighter Weapons School, better known as "Top Gun," where he falls in love with civilian instructor Charlotte Blackwood, played by Kelly McGillis. Although it has often been criticized as campy and overacted, the film was such a hit with audiences that the Navy set up recruiting booths in many theaters to capitalize on the crowds. The film was nominated for four Academy Awards, and won the Oscar for Best Original Song for "Take My Breath Away," performed by Berlin.

THE HUNT FOR RED OCTOBER (1990)

Author Tom Clancy may be well known these days, but it was this 1984 novel that put him on the map. Six years later, the book was turned into a film starring Sean Connery as Soviet navy Captain Marko Ramius, who attempts to defect to the United States with the USSR's most advanced ballistic missile submarine. Alec Baldwin plays Jack Ryan, the CIA analyst determined to help Ramius succeed. Though well-received by the public, the film was panned by critics. Nevertheless, it won one of the three Oscars for which it was nominated, Best Sound Effects Editing.

CRIMSON TIDE (1995)

If mutiny and nuclear submarines make epic Navy films, does that mean the story of mutiny aboard a nuclear submarine equates to an instant hit? It did for *Crimson Tide*, which starred Denzel Washington and Gene Hackman as officers aboard the USS *Alabama* who are ordered to launch their missiles in a preemptive strike on Russia. When their sub loses its communications, Washington and Hackman go toe-to-toe over whether to carry out the order or wait for further guidance. *Crimson Tide* was nominated for Academy Awards in three technical categories.

Average age of the 58,148 Americans killed in the Vietnam War: 23.11 years.

NOW YOU SEE ME...

The introduction of air warfare during World War I brought about a need to rethink soldiers' attire. To keep troops healthy and stealthy, they and their artillery, vehicles—even buildings—had to be invisible from above. And so modern military camouflage was born.

DUDE, WHERE'S MY TANK?

Camouflage was first employed not for people but to conceal field artillery and tanks that would immediately reveal a key strategic position if spotted. Painting heavy weapons dull gray, green, or brown helped them blend into the landscape, but a disruptive pattern of dark and light tones created a more natural sun-dappled appearance that more effectively blurred the outlines of otherwise discernable objects. Camouflage artists—many of whom were professional artists in civilian life—were put to work hand-painting equipment with random blocks of color. They also built decoy soldiers and tanks out of wood and masked heavy artillery with blankets of foliage and camo-painted tarps. Then things started to get really creative.

During World War I, the British navy employed a camouflage system for ships known as "dazzle." Created by Lieutenant Commander Norman Wilkinson, an artist by trade, dazzle used zigzagging lines of dark and light colors to break up the ship visually into an unidentifiable collection of shapes that an enemy could not detect and follow from a distance. By 1918 American naval forces were employing dazzle (also known as razzle-dazzle) camouflage as well, covering ships with great swaths of ultramarine, black, and green, and striving to make each one unique from others in the fleet. From a distance, dazzle-painted ships were a visual puzzle; up close, they resembled a Picasso masterpiece.

AND SPEAKING OF PICASSO

Pablo Picasso and the French Cubist painters realized that the seemingly random blocks of color used in camouflage painting stemmed directly from their chockablock painting style. Cubism's abstract style blurred the distinction between foreground and background and made three-dimensional objects appear two-dimensional; one could argue that camouflage accomplished the same things.

The writer Gertrude Stein told an oft-repeated story of walking down the street in Paris with Picasso during World War I. When they spotted a camouflage-painted truck—the first one they'd ever seen—she said that Picasso reacted by crying out, "We made that! That is Cubism!" Lucien-Victor Guirand de Scévola, the acknowledged father of modern camouflage—the *premier camoufleur*—would not have argued with Picasso.

Guirand de Scévola, a successful painter who was serving as a military telephone operator for a French artillery unit in 1914, is considered to be the first to propose the use of camouflage to his military superiors. The story goes that they were so impressed with his idea, they promoted him to lieutenant and put him in charge of the first known designated military camouflage unit. Serving under Guirand de Scévola was a staff of some 1,200 soldiers and 8,000 civilian women, all put to work painting field artillery, vehicles, buildings, and other battlefield accoutrements. Oddly enough, Guirand de Scévola was not a Cubist. He was a highly regarded portraitist and painter of the pre-Raphaelite school—all golden-haired women depicted in a romantic, gauzy haze—and by some accounts he retained the dandyish habit of wearing white kid gloves while he supervised his painters. (Guirand de Scévola's works still come up for sale at major auction houses like Sotheby's and Christie's and fetch prices in the tens of thousands of dollars.)

The fact that camouflage for artillery came about before camouflage for individuals was purely practical: During World War I, the technology did not exist to make fabric with woven camouflage patterns, and it simply wasn't possible to hand-paint combat uniforms. By the 1930s, weaving and dyeing technology had progressed so that camouflage fabric for uniforms could be produced efficiently; the German SS entered battle as the first to wear camouflage, with Allied troops very close behind. Some accounts say that the earliest camouflage worn by the opposing sides was so similar that the soldiers couldn't tell friend from foe.

Camouflage developers went back to their respective drawing boards and sorted themselves out, devising distinctive camouflage patterns, like the so-called frog skin worn by U.S. Marines in the Pacific during World War II, which was inspired by amphibians

...women in blue who perform 90 minutes of music, dance, and comedy.

and created by an editor at *Better Homes and Gardens* magazine. Most German World War II camouflage took its inspiration from trees and plants, and even generations later the German military returned to the forest for its five-color dappled pattern known as *Flecktarn* (splotch camouflage), which the armed forces of a reunited Germany wore in the 1990s.

Different battle conditions required different camouflage patterns, like the beige and brown "chocolate-chip" pattern worn by U.S. ground forces during the first Gulf War. And some countries worked symbolic motifs into their camouflage, like the tiger-stripe patterns worn by South Vietnamese troops—and U.S. Special Forces—during the Vietnam War. Not only were the camouflage patterns distinct, eventually they were copyrighted. In November 2008, Finland noticed that the camouflage uniforms worn by Russian troops invading Georgia was too similar to the copyrighted Finnish pattern M/05. The Finns considered suing the Russians for violation of their design rights, but in the end decided not to.

GOING DIGITAL

Camouflage is moving away from the artist's paintbrush and toward the computer screen. The Finnish pattern M/05, introduced in 2007, was derived from digital photographs of forests taken by the Finnish Forest Research Institute and analyzed using infrared technology by the Finnish Defense Forces Technical Research Institute. Computerized design has also led to the development of reflective camouflage inks that can be specifically adapted to different locations, such as forests or deserts. Most recently, camouflage uniforms have been made from fabric that suppresses human heat signatures to foil thermal vision equipment used by soldiers in the field. Specialized paints and decals that mask the heat from field artillery are in use as well.

As detection technology advances, camouflage technology evolves with it. Yet sometimes the old ways are still best. During the Kosovo conflict in the late 1990s, NATO bombers succeeded in driving back Serbian troops, but they didn't destroy much weaponry. Mostly they blew up decoy tanks and guns hand-painted on wood and tarps—not a terribly sophisticated camouflage technique, but enough to fool modern radar for the time being.

Navy SEALs in Vietnam sometimes wore pantyhose...to keep leeches off.

SOLDIER'S BOOK CLUB

Whether depicting the valor of one or many, or highlighting war's horrors, great books convey the emotions of the victor and the vanquished along with details of the battles and put the reader in the middle of the action.

THE RED BADGE OF COURAGE, Stephen Crane (1895)

Crane's masterpiece is often considered to be the first modern war novel. Following its initial serial appearance in the *Philadelphia Press* in December 1894, *The Red Badge of Courage* was published as a complete novel in 1895. The story tells of a young Union soldier's experiences in the Civil War's Battle of Chancellorsville in 1863. The narrative is a brilliant psychological representation of the fears and emotions of Private Henry Fleming, a farm boy facing his first battle. Union and Confederate veterans praised the book for its accurate retellings of combat, and reviewers were astonished to discover that Crane had not seen combat prior to writing his book but had instead used his imagination and discussions with old soldiers to present the battle scenes.

Today's readers may find the writing style and some expressions quaint, but Crane's vivid battle stories could be dropped into a recounting of any modern conflict and be considered completely authentic. *The Red Badge of Courage* quickly became a best seller in the United States and abroad, and remains widely read today.

THE KILLER ANGELS, Michael Shaara (1974)

This historical novel recounts the Battle of Gettysburg as seen through the eyes of both the Union and Confederate generals. Shaara takes the reader through each stage of the three-day battle as it rages around the small Pennsylvania town. General Robert E. Lee leads Confederate commanders George Pickett, James Longstreet, and Lewis Armistead on a plan to invade Pennsylvania in order to shorten the war, but Union generals George Gordon Meade and Winfield Scott Hancock engage him at Gettysburg instead. The unlikely hero of the battle is the Union's Colonel Joshua Chamberlain, a professor from Bowdoin College whose 20th Maine Regiment barely held the North's flank at Little Round Top on the battle's second day. Shaara does an excellent

The Luger was adopted by the German army in 1908. It became the world's most used pistol.

job in describing a three-day battle that encompasses 140,000 soldiers, and his very readable dialogue conveys the thoughts and concerns of officers and enlisted men at war. *The Killer Angels* won the 1975 Pulitzer Prize for Fiction, and Shaara's son Jeffrey later wrote a prequel and a sequel to complete the trilogy.

ALL QUIET ON THE WESTERN FRONT, Erich Maria Remarque (1928)

"Wars are started by politicians, but are fought by young men" has long been a popular saying. *All Quiet on the Western Front* tells the story of a few young men in a German infantry squad in World War I. They may be German, but the soldiers could just as easily be American, British, or French; the stories and personalities of the young men living and dying in the poison gas and mud of the western front transcend nationality. In Remarque's gripping tale, written in the first person, the reader gets to know each member of the German infantry squad as they live, die, and try to survive while performing their duties as honorable soldiers. Long hailed as one of the most definitive war novels by literary critics, this book needs to be on the shelf of every military enthusiast.

A FAREWELL TO ARMS, Ernest Hemingway (1929)

Hemingway served in World War I as both an infantryman and ambulance driver in the Italian army; his war novels carry the grittiness earned by someone who has seen combat firsthand. A master of simple yet elegant prose, Hemingway excels at giving the reader the personal stories of the people fighting—and how they are affected by the suffering around them. *A Farewell to Arms* tells the story of Lieutenant Frederic Henry, an American volunteer fighting for Italy in World War I, who meets Catherine Barkely, an English nurse. As the war flows up and down the Italian peninsula, Henry narrates how they are touched by the conflict.

THE MOON IS DOWN, John Steinbeck (1942)

A novella that was translated into different languages and published by resistance groups across Europe in the dark early days of World War II, this may be one of Steinbeck's finest books. A traitor in a Norwegian village has suckered their local militia away for a weekend as the Nazis invade the country. The townspeople are initially cowed by the Germans and appear complacent, but soon

The average U.S. Army soldier is a 22-year-old E4 (corporal or specialist) and is married...

regain their courage and fight back. Initially working solo, but soon in concert, the citizens fight a guerrilla war against the Nazis, which leads one of the German enlisted men to complain, "The flies have conquered the flypaper." After the town's mayor is sentenced to death by the Nazis as punishment for the guerrilla operations conducted by his townspeople, a debate over liberty, freedom, civil disobedience, and courage begins among the mayor, his old friend the doctor, and the German officer commanding the occupation. Such debates remain relevant even today, and the mayor demonstrates that courage in wartime comes in many forms.

THE LONGEST DAY, Cornelius Ryan (1959)

Based on interviews with civilians and soldiers from both sides, this classic account of the Normandy invasion is one of the most thoroughly researched books about World War II. Ryan spent almost five years writing, researching, and interviewing hundreds of civilians and soldiers, from enlisted men to generals. *The Longest Day* weaves the many small actions that made up the invasion into the larger scenario of tactics and strategy. Ryan succeeds in personalizing a battle that encompassed more than 200,000 troops on both sides in an interesting and historically accurate book. It's been called one of the best books on the D-day invasion.

IF YOU SURVIVE, George Wilson (1987)

"If you survive your first day, I'll promote you." Anyone who saw the opening scenes of the film *Saving Private Ryan*, when the soldiers landed on Omaha Beach, can appreciate what author George Wilson faced as his commanding officer addressed his squad when they were sent as replacements for the first day's horrific losses. But not only did Wilson survive, he fought his way through France, Belgium, and into Germany for the next 250 days in some of the war's worst battles. Wilson was the only officer who survived from that small group of replacements on Omaha Beach, and his memoir is one of the better first-person accounts of the land war in Europe. An Army volunteer, Wilson is an unintentional representative of the American fighting man: resourceful, brave, and willing to sacrifice himself for the greater good. *If You Survive* gives the reader an inkling of the intensity of the fighting in the last violent months of the war against Nazi Germany, as well as an understanding of the character of the soldiers who defeated them.

...He (85%) or she (15%) is a high school graduate and makes $1,978.50 a month.

THE BRIDGES AT TOKO-RI, James Michener (1953)

One of Michener's shorter novels, *The Bridges at Toko-Ri* is about Navy aviators flying combat missions off an aircraft carrier in the Korean War. Lieutenant Harry Brubaker is a Denver-based attorney and World War II veteran who has been recalled to fight in Korea, and he bitterly resents being uprooted from his family to fight in an unpopular war. "Nobody at home even knows there's a war except my wife," he tells the admiral who interviews him after he is shot down and rescued—yet he continues to fly his missions to the best of his ability. The heavily defended bridges at Toko-Ri must be destroyed in order to halt the North Korean supply line, and Brubaker and his squadron fight hard to take them down. With Michener's usual extensive attention to detail, *The Bridges at Toko-Ri* is a riveting snapshot of the Korean conflict, but an even better snapshot of men who make up our military and rise to the occasion time and again.

WE WERE SOLDIERS ONCE . . . AND YOUNG, Lieutenant General Harold G. Moore and Joseph L. Galloway (1993)

The story of the U.S. Army's 1st Battalion, 7th Cavalry, is told by two who survived the vicious four-day Battle of Ia Drang in November 1965 after being air-dropped into the middle of a large North Vietnamese force.

Written by the 7th Cavalry's commanding officer, Lieutenant Colonel Harold Moore, and an embedded reporter, Joe Galloway, *We Were Soldiers Once . . . and Young* is a no-holds-barred recap of the battle. Ia Drang was the first time the Americans faced the North Vietnamese regular army. Both sides tried their utmost to win, but U.S. helicopter gunships and airpower finally turned the tide. Moore and Galloway interviewed more than a hundred survivors to record their stories of how courage under fire enabled the 7th Cavalry to hang on and wait for American airpower to come through. The fighting was so intense that Galloway needed to drop his camera and pick up a rifle to help defend against the determined North Vietnamese. In a blunt style, Moore and Galloway write as much about the emotions of the soldiers as they do of the tactics that helped them win. The book is considered by many to be one of the better books written about the U.S. Army in the Vietnam War.

The first permanent Coast Guard air station was commissioned at Cape May, NJ, in 1926.

UNCLE SAM NEEDS YOU! PART II

During the Cold War and after, the draft changed dramatically. Resistance to it—as well as the changing nature of warfare—caused the military to rethink how it filled its ranks.
Part I of this story can be found on page 38.

THE KOREAN WAR

When North Korea invaded South Korea in June 1950, Congress quickly extended the Selective Service Act; more than 200,000 men were drafted by the end of the year. The Universal Military Training and Service Act replaced the Selective Service Act in 1951, but it was more of a means of amending the previous law than an entirely new system. Among the new features of the 1951 act were:

- A new system of deferments, including exemptions for fathers and certain types of professionals, as well as for college students who, based on a review of grades and a standardized test score, could receive a deferment until graduating or reaching the age of 24, whichever came first.
- A lowering of the draft age from 19 to 18½ years.
- An increase in the period of service from 21 to 36 months.
- Lower mental and physical standards.
- A limit of 5 million personnel on active duty in the armed forces.

Of the 2.8 million men who served in Korea, 1.3 million were conscripts—about 46 percent of the total.

WHAT ELSE IS NEW?

The complex system of deferments seemed to favor those who had the money or resources to get exemptions, but the short-lived nature of the war (it ended in 1953) may have prevented opposition to the draft from gaining much steam. All the same, General Lewis Hershey, head of the Selective Service System, urged Congress to keep the draft mechanisms up and running to meet future

Frenchman Marquis de Lafayette was a general in the Continental Army at age 19.

needs. Hershey's theory was that because draftees had no choice about their assignments, for every man drafted, three or four would be scared into volunteering so they could get preferential placement within the military.

THE VIETNAM WAR

Many people associate the military draft with the turmoil surrounding the Vietnam War in the 1960s and early 1970s. Approximately 500,000 eligible men were classified as draft offenders during the Vietnam era; another 100,000 dodged the draft by fleeing to countries such as Canada, Mexico, and Sweden. (Of those 600,000, only 10,000 were convicted of draft dodging.) The military focused on increasing recruitment of volunteers, many of whom were attracted to noncombat services such as the Coast Guard and National Guard to avoid the likelihood of being sent into battle.

According to the Veterans Administration, out of the 3.5 million men who saw combat duty in Vietnam, 2.2 million, or roughly 63 percent, were draftees. Other military reports indicate that as many as 50 percent of the volunteer enlistees did so to gain preferential placement rather than risk being drafted and almost certainly being assigned to combat duty.

CALIFORNIA SCREAMIN'

As in other 20th-century conflicts, exemptions were granted to students, clergymen, and professionals whose services the government deemed useful. Besides the conscientious objectors, some tried to get themselves disqualified by getting married and having children to gain a paternity exemption, or claiming a medical condition or homosexual orientation. Resentment arose among the poor and working classes, who didn't obtain as many exemptions and/or weren't as knowledgeable about working the system.

One of the first public draft protests took place at the University of California, Berkeley, in May 1965, where 40 students burned their draft cards; similar protests broke out across the country. In August 1965, President Lyndon B. Johnson signed a law that made it a crime to burn a draft card. As the antiwar movement escalated, more protests and the corresponding media coverage led to widespread public disapproval of the war.

In use from 1969 to 1999, the USS *Narwhal* was the quietest submarine of its time.

THE END IS NEAR

In 1969 a lottery system that used randomly chosen birth dates rather than age groups (with the oldest being called first) to determine the order in which men were drafted did little to ease resistance to the draft. Statisticians who investigated the results suggested that the draft lottery system wasn't truly random, further fueling public distrust of the government. The lottery system was tweaked over the following years, but support for the draft continued to decline.

In December 1972, the final group of conscripts was inducted into the U.S. armed forces. President Richard Nixon allowed the Selective Service Act to expire in 1973, and the U.S. military converted to an all-volunteer organization.

In 1980 tensions with the Soviet Union over Afghanistan prompted President Jimmy Carter to reestablish draft registration for all men aged 18 to 25 as insurance against any future crisis in which the military finds itself in need of additional manpower. The requirement remains in effect, although no one has actually been drafted under the legislation.

IF THERE'S NO DRAFT, WHY REGISTER?

The U.S. military has been composed entirely of volunteers since 1973, and the feeling at the Department of Defense is that warfare has become so specialized and complex today that the time and resources it would take to select, train, and deploy draftees would hamper efficiency. Still, many in Washington subscribe to the old adage of "expect the unexpected," and so draft registration remains in effect. Congressman Charles B. Rangel (D-NY), a veteran of the Korean War who was awarded the Purple Heart and Bronze Star, introduced legislation to reinstate the draft in 2003 as a way to make the military more representative of the American public at large, only to see the bill rejected overwhelmingly by the House of Representatives. (Even Rangel voted against his own bill.)

In 2005 former Defense Secretary Donald Rumsfeld told Congress, "There isn't a chance in the world that the draft will be brought back." The 70 percent of the general population that are opposed to a military draft hope he was right.

DUSTWUN: Military acronym meaning "Duty Status—Whereabouts Unknown."

CARBINE WILLIAMS

The ex-con whose weapon helped win World War II.

Shots rang out on July 21, 1921. The sheriff of Cumberland County and his deputies had just destroyed a liquor still in the mountains of North Carolina when a volley of gunfire from the woods killed Deputy Alfred Pate. Three men were spotted at the site before the raid began. One of them, the owner of the whiskey still, David Marshall "Marsh" Williams, was charged with murder. He pled guilty (though he always claimed he was innocent, and there were conflicting stories of where he was when the shots were fired).

NOT MAKING LICENSE PLATES

Williams had always had a talent for machinery, especially firearms. While serving out his 30-year sentence in the Caledonia Correctional Institute, his talent got noticed. He was eventually put to work fixing farm machinery. Warden H. T. Peoples and Williams developed a relationship of mutual trust—a lot of trust. After the talented prisoner was given a job in the machine shop repairing guards' weapons, the warden let Williams take the next step: designing guns. Williams made a semiautomatic rifle that worked on the short-stroke gas piston system. A gas piston was located under the middle of the rifle's barrel. When the gun was fired, the gases from the ejected bullet exploded and propelled the piston violently to the rear. The slam of the piston initiated a slide-bolt action in the gun and automatically loaded another bullet into the ejection chamber.

LIGHTENING THE BURDEN

After eight years in prison, Williams went home and started working on more designs and getting patents. The folks at the Winchester Repeating Arms Company noticed and hired him as a weapons designer.

In 1941 war was looming, and the Army had a problem. The traditional M1 rifle, or Garand rifle, weighed about 10 pounds. These were too cumbersome for medics, radio operators, vehicle drivers, and officers—basically, any troops who weren't frontline

The U.S. Naval Observatory is a major authority in timekeeping and celestial observation...

riflemen. These "second-line" troops usually carried the M1911A1 .45-caliber handguns. At 3 pounds when loaded, the handguns were lightweight, but they didn't have the range or firepower needed for defense.

So the Army held a competition to design a lightweight, semi-automatic shoulder weapon, which Winchester intended to win by providing a lightweight carbine. (Carbines, developed for cavalry troops, were shorter than standard rifles.) It was Marsh Williams who suggested using the short-stroke piston system he'd developed in prison. The result was the M1 Carbine.

It weighed in at 5 pounds, 7 ounces; some well-stocked purses are heavier. But its accurate range and firepower was much greater than any pistol. The Army accepted Winchester's design less than three months before December 7, 1941, when the Japanese attacked Pearl Harbor and the United States went to war.

KEEP IT SIMPLE, STUPID

The first M1 Carbines were delivered to the Army in 1942. Six million would be produced by 1945. Standard issue during World War II, and used in Korea and even Vietnam, the carbine became "the war baby," the most-produced small-arms weapon in American military history. (The Soviet Kalashnikov AK-47 is the most-produced small-arms weapon in the world.)

The M1 took on mud, rain, rust, and rough treatment—and kept on shootin'. General Douglas MacArthur, head of the United States armed forces in the Far East, called the M1 Carbine "one of the strongest contributing factors in our victory in the Pacific."

THEY'RE SHOOTING IN HOLLYWOOD

After the war, Marsh Williams got a new nickname—he was now known as Carbine Williams. He kept designing guns well into old age, and he eventually held more than 50 patents for gun improvements. He made a small fortune—and lost it again with bad investments and hard living.

In 1952 the movie *Carbine Williams*, starring Jimmy Stewart, brought the ex-con nationwide fame and ensured that his legacy would not be forgotten. Williams died in 1975 in Raleigh, North Carolina.

...The voice of the late Fred Covington has been announcing USNO time since 1978.

THE ORIGINAL FLYING TIGER

Claire Lee Chennault's ideas about aerial warfare helped the Chinese people fight the Japanese, and after that the Communist Chinese. In the process, he helped create a legendary group of fighter pilots.

THE LIEUTENANT GENERAL AS A YOUNG MAN

Although he did not attend West Point, Claire Chennault was commissioned as a first lieutenant in the U.S. Army Infantry Reserve in 1917. When he became a second lieutenant, he was unable to obtain overseas duty, so he joined the Aviation Section of the Army Signal Corps and became a pilot. Chennault spent the next 15 years flying pursuit planes, studying tactics, and writing a textbook: *The Role of Defensive Pursuit.* Between 1932 and 1936, he commanded the Air Corps exhibition group known as Three Men on a Flying Trapeze—a primitive version of today's Blue Angels—and developed techniques for close-formation flying. The Army forced him to retire in 1937 with the permanent rank of lieutenant colonel due to a combination of hearing loss from flying open-cockpit fighter planes and chronic bronchitis stemming from aerial exposure as well as smoking two packs a day.

CHENNAULT MEETS MADAME CHIANG

Japan had invaded Manchuria in 1931, but July 7, 1937, marked the start of World War II in the Far East when Japan invaded China proper. Madame Chiang Kai-shek, a graduate of Wellesley College and wife of General Chiang Kai-shek, was put in charge of reorganizing the Chinese air force. Looking for a man of experience to direct the Chinese air defenses, she hired the 44-year-old Chennault. Madame Chiang had read Chennault's textbook and knew the savvy tactician had been forced into retirement.

Two volunteers joined Chennault: "Luke" Williamson and Billy McDonald, former wingmen from the Flying Trapeze. They taught Chinese pilots "defensive pursuit," a tactical approach to shooting down the enemy without being shot down themselves. The slow but maneuverable Chinese biplanes cut a murderous path through enemy bomber squadrons flying without fighter escorts. But when Japan introduced the Mitsubishi A5M monoplanes with two rifle-caliber machine guns, Chinese aircraft could no longer compete. Chennault concluded that China needed modern pursuit planes as well as trained pilots to fly them. He returned to America and reached an agreement with the government to borrow planes and pilots from the U.S. Army Air Corps.

CHINA ON $600 A MONTH

Madame Chiang promised good wages in U.S. dollars, and during the summer of 1940 Chennault returned to Kunming in southern China with a group of pilots and mechanics enticed by promises of adventure, $600 a month in regular pay—a sum that could buy a new car in the United States—plus a bonus of $500 for each kill. Madame Chiang called them the American Volunteer Group; Chennault called his team of mercenaries the Flying Tigers.

THE FLYING TIGERS

Chennault was distantly related to Sam Houston and Robert E. Lee, which might have given him an advantage, because his predecessors were, like him, forced to fight with few resources. Chennault never had enough planes, pilots, fuel, or spare parts. He became one of those gutsy, gritty, and egocentric characters of the China-Burma-India theater who didn't let anything stand in his way. The pilots, crews, and the first shipment of Curtiss P-40C Tomahawks, which had been diverted from a shipment destined for England, began arriving at a Royal Air Force base near Taungoo, Burma, which was the only Allied air base near China with the facilities to train and support combat pilots. Chennault began training the flyers in tactics. In December, he moved the 1st and 2nd squadrons to the new base at Kunming to begin operations. The 3rd squadron remained at Taungoo with the impossible tasks of keeping the 2,000-mile Burma Road open so supplies could be transported from Rangoon to China, and intercepting air attacks out of Japanese bases in Hanoi, the capital of French Indochina.

THE TIGERS ATTACK

On the morning of December 20, 1941—just after the bombing of Pearl Harbor—10 twin-engine Mitsubishi bombers carrying incendiaries and 500-pound bombs took off from the Japanese air base at Hanoi on a 300-mile flight to bomb Kunming, which lay at the terminus of the Burma Road. Japanese pilots expected a routine mission; they had been regularly bombing Kunming on clear days for over a year. The bombers flew without escorts because they had never encountered any military resistance at Kunming.

Alerted by outposts of the approaching attack, Chennault sent up his P-40C interceptors. The Japanese were shocked to see four Tomahawks bearing down on them. Taking no chances, the Japanese crews jettisoned their loads to gain speed and swung back to Hanoi. They seemed to be getting away when 10 more P-40s appeared from above and dove through the Japanese squadron with guns blazing. One after the other, the bombers exploded or fell smoking to the ground. Only one made it to Hanoi. The Flying Tigers had struck and flown their first combat mission. In two air battles on December 23 and 25, 18 P-40 pilots shot down 17 enemy planes, mostly heavy bombers, losing just two pilots and six Tomahawks. The air war in Burma and western China had begun.

CHENNAULT'S ACES

On December 25, the Flying Tigers' Hell's Angels 3rd Squadron waited on alert at Rangoon because Radio Tokyo promised a Christmas surprise. Sixty Japanese bombers were within 10 miles of the air base when the squadron received the warning. The Flying Tigers were ready with their engines warmed. They bumped off the corrugated field and climbed to gain altitude. After dealing with the enemy escort fighters, they dived for the kill and riddled the bombers with .50-caliber tracers, knocking down one after another. Another 20 bombers and eight fighters appeared out of the east. Using Chennault's diversionary tactics, the pilots climbed, rolled, and cut a swath through the enemy formation with scythelike precision, pulled up, and repeated the tactic. Robert "Duke" Hedman downed six enemy planes in one day.

Over the next five months, Robert Neale scored 13 victories and David Lee "Tex" Hill, George Burgard, Robert Little, and Charles Older each scored 10. Neale rose from obscurity to capture worshipful attention from the Chinese. In all, 19 Tiger pilots became aces (i.e., shot down more than five enemy planes) before most American flyers scored their first victories in the Pacific.

CHIANG'S ANGELS

Madame Chiang referred to the pilots as "angels with and without wings." The mercenaries did more than get rich shooting down enemy planes. They served as guinea pigs for Chennault's tactics, which saved planes and kept pilots out of harm's way well above Japanese formations. From aloft and with the sun to their backs, they dove at high speeds, riddled the enemy with bullets, climbed to get back into formation, and did it all again—a tactic that eventually became part of the Japanese fighter's playbook as well.

COMING IN FOR A LANDING

The Flying Tigers were a combat unit only until July 1942. Chennault never had more than 55 planes and 70 pilots in service at once, and only had a handful of operable planes when the unit disbanded. After seven months of aerial combat, the Tigers had destroyed nearly 300 enemy planes and killed more than 1,000 Japanese airmen at a cost of 16 Americans killed or captured.

The Flying Tigers' performance was the first time Japan's pilots had been bested in the Far East. The press lauded the mercenaries as superhuman to the extent that "Generalissimo" Chiang Kai-shek began to believe U.S. airpower could defeat Japan. That was before the U.S. Army recalled Chennault to active duty on July 4, 1942, as a colonel and absorbed the Tigers into the Army Air Forces (AAF) in China. Only five Tigers followed Chennault. The others went home and rejoined their old units.

CHENNAULT MEETS STILWELL

By becoming part of the AAF, Chennault's squadron became part of Lieutenant General Joseph W. "Vinegar Joe" Stilwell's army, which encompassed China, Burma, and India. The two men seldom agreed. Vinegar Joe did not get his nickname by being a sweet guy. He and Chennault disagreed, for one thing, on Chiang Kai-shek; Chennault had the highest regard for the man, whereas Stilwell detested him. When Stilwell tersely informed Chennault, "It's the men in the trenches that will win the war," the latter snapped back, "Goddammit, Stilwell, there aren't any trenches." As Stilwell soon discovered, the bitter fighting lurched through Burmese jungles and butted up against enemy air attacks, ambushes, booby traps, and pillboxes.

...Gen. Dwight D. Eisenhower never commanded troops in combat or saw action himself.

DIFFERENT STROKES

The differences between the two dated back to the military philosophy of World War I, when aircraft were a novelty and not overly useful. Stilwell came from West Point and had served during the 1918 Meuse-Argonne offensive. He believed war could be won only on the ground and thought an air force could do little more than "knock down a few Japanese planes." Chennault felt hamstrung, reporting to a man who did not understand air warfare. Although the two consistently disagreed on strategy, the Army boosted Chennault to major general in March 1943 and put him in command of the 14th Air Force, which eventually curbed enemy air operations in China and sent bombing raids into Japan.

OLD SOLDIERS NEVER DIE

Chennault ignored Stilwell as much as possible, and being assigned to China, he preferred to work with Chiang Kai-shek. Although Stilwell proved to be proficient at driving Japanese ground troops out of Burma, he was eventually recalled out of China because of his refusal to cooperate with Chiang.

For his part, Chennault finally complained one too many times and lost the confidence of his superiors. When General Henry H. "Hap" Arnold suggested Chennault "take advantage of the retirement privileges now available to physically disqualified officers," the quarrelsome air commander took the advice and retired.

FAREWELL TO A HERO

When Chennault left China on August 1, 1945, an outpouring of grateful Chinese numbering in the hundreds of thousands filled the streets of Chongqing. They stopped his car and told the driver to cut the ignition so they could push the vehicle to the airport.

Chennault loved the Chinese for their simplicity and courage. He returned in 1946 to help the Nationalists fight the Communists. When the Nationalists took refuge in Taiwan, Chennault followed and built another air force like the Flying Tigers but with better aircraft. At the age of 67 and after 12 years in China and Taiwan, he returned to America and died on July 27, 1958, of lung cancer; the Army promoted him to lieutenant general a day before his death. A brilliant tactician and indefatigable organizer, Chennault will always best be remembered as the original Flying Tiger.

Five U.S. Navy ships have been named USS *Farragut* after the admiral, David Farragut.

GUERRILLA WARFARE, PART IV

The Green Berets (Part III is on page 176).

The U.S. Army Special Forces had its genesis during World War II, when the Office of Strategic Services (OSS) was created. The OSS mission definition was intelligence gathering, support of resistance movements, and sabotage. Toward these ends, the OSS created Jedburgh teams (named after the town in England where they trained) consisting of three men: a leader, an executive officer, and a radio operator. Normally, the radio operator was American, one officer was American, and the other was a member of the French Resistance.

They parachuted into Nazi-occupied France to conduct sabotage and guerrilla warfare, and to lead French guerrilla forces (called the maquis) against the Germans. They provided advice, expertise, and leadership, and they arranged airdrops of arms and ammunition.

THE COLD WAR

It wasn't until 1952 that the Army Special Forces were formed by recruiting former OSS officers (with Jedburgh experience) and veterans from the elite Rangers and Airborne Army units. Captain Aaron Bank was recruited from the OSS and became the first leader of the Special Forces. Headquartered at Fort Bragg, North Carolina, the unit's mission was "to infiltrate by land, sea, or air deep into enemy-occupied territory and organize the resistance/guerrilla potential."

Candidates were required to speak more than one language. They were trained in at least two of the basic Special Forces skills: intelligence, communications, demolitions, weaponry, and medical aid, as well as how to operate behind enemy lines with little or no outside support. Special Forces units were organized into A teams, consisting of two officers and ten enlisted men.

During the 1950s, the Special Forces carried out plenty of Cold War missions, supporting rebels fighting against their Communist governments and helping friendly countries battle Communist

Japanese kamikazes were suicide pilots and human bombs. *Kamikaze* means "divine wind."

insurgencies. But they weren't well known outside the military establishment because nearly all of their missions were secret.

The Green Beret headgear was designed by Major Herb Brucker in 1953, based on the berets worn by elite troops in European armies. But the beret wasn't officially authorized Army headgear until President John F. Kennedy—a big supporter of elite Special Forces—helped persuade the Army to make it so in 1961.

VIETNAM

After World War II, the French reoccupied South Vietnam in an ill-fated attempt to resurrect their prewar empire. The North Vietnamese wanted to reunify their country, so they fought a guerrilla war to convince the French to leave. In 1956 Green Berets were sent to Vietnam to assist the French and train South Vietnamese soldiers in modern warfare and counterinsurgency techniques.

The Green Berets won 17 Medals of Honor, 814 Silver Stars, and more than 13,000 Bronze Stars in the war. They also provided medical care and built schools and hospitals as part of the program to win the hearts and minds of the local populace.

A book about their exploits, *The Green Berets*, by journalist Robin Moore, was published in 1965; Green Beret staff sergeant and medic Barry Sadler wrote and recorded the hit song called "The Ballad of the Green Berets" in 1966; and in 1968 John Wayne produced, directed, and starred in a movie called *The Green Berets*.

On November 20, 1970, a rescue mission was launched to rescue 75 American POWs from a North Vietnamese prison camp in Son Tay, about 23 miles from Hanoi. The mission was executed brilliantly, and no Green Berets were lost. Unfortunately, no prisoners were rescued, either—the prisoners had been moved a couple of days earlier. The raid did help the prisoners' morale though, because the North Vietnamese decided to move all the prisoners to a central facility in Hanoi, where they were no longer kept in isolation.

After the United States withdrew from Vietnam, budget cuts in the late 1970s forced the Army to rethink its dependence on large conventional forces and to consider the use of more elite units. It was thought that in the future, wars could be fought with air power and small units of highly trained men.

General Robert E. Lee was a descendant of *Utopia* author Sir Thomas More.

PANAMA

The Army put this plan into effect during Operation Just Cause, the invasion of Panama to remove its leader, Manuel Noriega, and stop him from allowing Panama to be used as a way station for drug runners. The invasion and capture of Noriega was carried out entirely by Green Berets, Rangers, and Navy SEALs.

IRAQ I

During the first war against Iraq, Special Forces went into Kuwait early to train resistance forces. Once the air war was launched, Green Berets operated well behind enemy lines, providing intelligence and targeting data to direct air units to hidden and elusive targets, like the Iraqi mobile SCUD missiles.

Before the ground war began, Special Forces were instrumental in clearing lanes through minefields and trenches that blocked invasion routes for U.S. conventional forces. After Kuwait was liberated, Special Forces helped reconstitute the Kuwaiti armed forces.

AFGHANISTAN

The ground war in Afghanistan was fought almost entirely by Special Forces and Rangers leading, or in cooperation with, Afghan forces. The war was over quickly, but as of this writing, terrorist leader Osama bin Laden has yet to be captured. He's believed to be hiding in the border region between Afghanistan and Pakistan, where the rugged terrain makes military operations difficult to sustain; Special Forces continue to hunt for him there.

IRAQ II

Special Forces spearheaded the invasion of Iraq on March 20, 2003. The war lasted approximately three weeks, but securing the peace has been far more difficult. As of this writing, Special Forces are now training the new Iraqi army and police force, as well as providing humanitarian aid to the people of Iraq.

ELSEWHERE

The Green Berets' motto is De oppresso liber (To free the oppressed), and today, Special Forces troops are stationed in trouble spots all over the world, fighting terrorism and training local forces in counterterrorism tactics, techniques, and procedures.

Turn to page 409 for Part V.

Scud Stud: Nickname given to Canadian journalist Arthur Kent during the 1991 Gulf War.

MR. ZIPPO GOES TO WAR

How a crafty businessman kept his company up and running during the war and created an icon in the process.

MEET MR. ZIPPO

George G. Blaisdell was 46 and too old to serve when the United States entered World War II, so he sent the next best thing—everything manufactured in his Bradford, Pennsylvania, factory.

Blaisdell invented the Zippo lighter in his garage in 1932. He wanted a lighter that was sturdy and that you could light in the wind using one hand. He named his windproof lighter after the word "zipper" because he thought it sounded "modern." The first Zippo sold for $1.95 and came with a lifetime guarantee. The original design called for a shiny metallic nickel-plated case, but with World War II came shortages, including the brass and chrome used for Zippo lighters. So Blaisdell used porous steel coated with black paint instead. The result was a black, crackled cover.

THE GI'S FRIEND

From 1943 through 1945, Zippo lighters, with that distinctive click they made when flipped open, were available only to military personnel at U.S. Army exchanges and naval ship stores around the world. Soldiers liked to personalize their Zippos by scratching the surface of the lighters with their names, places they'd been, messages to loved ones, or simple pictures. The lighter was so popular it was nicknamed "the GI's friend," and after the war, the vets came home to civilian life as dedicated Zippo customers.

We'd like to say that Mr. Blaisdell sent all his lighters to the military because he was patriotic, but that was only part of it. Mr. Blaisdell didn't want Zippo Manufacturing shut down for the war's duration as "unnecessary to the war effort" or refitted to make parachutes or fatigue caps. By working with the government, he could keep his factory at full production levels.

A ROUND OF ZIPPOS FOR MY FRIENDS

George Blaisdell became Mr. Zippo with the help of war corre-

Most Civil War cannons had a range of only about one mile.

spondent Ernie Pyle, who was embedded with troops in England, Italy, Sicily, Africa, and the Pacific. Pyle's columns dealt mostly with the civilian soldiers and their day-to-day lives. Blaisdell enjoyed the column and sent the correspondent a Zippo lighter with Pyle's signature engraved on the side. He sent 50 more for Pyle to give away, even though, as he wrote in his letter, "You probably know nothing about the Zippo lighter." In fact, Pyle knew all about the Zippo, as did every other American GI. "If he only knew how soldiers coveted them! Why, they're so popular I had three of them stolen from me in one year," wrote Pyle in his column. He finished the column by giving Blaisdell his nickname: "The fifty others went like hot cakes. I found myself equipped with a wonderful weapon for winning friends and influencing people. All fifty-one of us were grateful to Mr. Zippo."

IF YOU'VE GOT A WAR, WE'VE GOT A ZIPPO

Today Zippo produces several lighters for all the branches of the armed forces and for specialty branches such as the Top Gun school, Navy SEALs, Seabees, and Army Rangers. Since World War II, every Navy ship has had its own lighter that includes a picture of the ship, its name, and its number.

Zippos commemorate leaders and battles of World War II: Generals Dwight D. Eisenhower, Omar Bradley, and George Patton, as well as France's General Charles de Gaulle and British Field Marshall Bernard Montgomery have their profiles on Zippos. The Battle of Britain, the Battle of the Bulge, the Battle of Midway, the raising of the flag at Iwo Jima, and the Japanese surrender on the USS *Missouri* are all captured in finely detailed pictures. Several designs honor D-day and its 50th and 60th anniversaries.

The Korean War is commemorated with a map of Korea and the 38th parallel, as well as a picture of the Korean War Veterans Memorial in Washington, D.C.

The company has produced two lighters that have views of the Vietnam War Memorial. The lighters for Operation Desert Shield and Operation Desert Storm use a background of the tan-colored desert camouflage. Designs available to recent warriors include maps of Iraq, helicopters, and Humvees. Another has the red, white, and blue ribbon that symbolizes support of American troops. One even has a finish the color and texture of sand.

A first class petty officer in the Navy is equal to the rank of a staff sergeant in the Army.

MORE SITUATION: COMEDY

From 1960 on, military-themed sitcoms had some hits . . . and some misses.

HOGAN'S HEROES

It is so small feat, but somehow someone made a sitcom—a wacky, zany sitcom no less—about the daily life of American soldiers held captive in a World War II Nazi prison camp, and their attempts to escape. Bob Crane played Colonel Hogan, an American officer who led his cohorts in their attempts to escape, and who were always foiled by the bumbling commandant Colonel Klink. The grim subject matter was something many cast members knew firsthand. Werner Klemperer (Klink) was Jewish and had fled the Nazis during World War II. John Banner (Colonel Schultz) was also Jewish, and Robert Clary (French prisoner LeBeau) had been held in a Nazi concentration camp as a child. It is hard to imagine that a TV show set in a Nazi prison camp would make it on TV today. It remains controversial because of its setting in spite of the fact that it was a top-20 show for most of its original run (1965–71), it was nominated for Best Comedy Series at the Emmys twice, and it has been aired in syndicated reruns for years. In 2002 *TV Guide* named *Hogan's Heroes* the fifth-worst TV show of all time.

M*A*S*H

Predicted by many critics to fail because it had to live up to the beloved 1970 Robert Altman movie it was based on, *M*A*S*H* went on to become one of the longest-running and most successful TV shows in history. The show follows the 4077th Mobile Army Surgical Hospital near the front lines of the Korean War. (Length of *M*A*S*H*: 11 years; length of the Korean War: three years). The show did okay in its first season (1972–73) but became a phenomenon in year two, when it aired between hits *All in the Family* and *The Mary Tyler Moore Show*. *M*A*S*H* evolved greatly over the years; cast members came and went,

Peak American troop strength in Vietnam: 543,482, on April 30, 1969.

including, shockingly, when McLean Stevenson's Colonel Potter was killed trying to leave Korea to return home. Company clerk Radar (Gary Burghoff) eventually returned to his farm, but before he departed he trained Klinger as his replacement. Jamie Farr (Klinger) up until then had been a part-time cast member whose character had been trying to get a discharge by dressing in women's clothes.

Most notably, *M*A*S*H* transformed from a wry sitcom with dramatic moments about war to a stark drama about the horrors of war with the occasional comic moment. Credited with the shift is Alan Alda, who starred as Hawkeye Pierce and took over as the creative force of the show in the sixth season. Alda won Emmys for acting, writing, and directing *M*A*S*H*. Alda cowrote and directed the landmark final episode of the series in 1983, "Goodbye, Farewell and Amen." Watching the Army doctors finally go home (and Hawkeye deal with a mental breakdown) were more than 106 million people—the largest audience in TV history.

ROLL OUT

To complement *M*A*S*H*, CBS rolled out another war-themed sitcom in the fall of 1973 called *Roll Out*. Like *M*A*S*H*, many episodes were written by the creator of both shows, Larry Gelbart. Also like *M*A*S*H*, *Roll Out* was allegorical—*M*A*S*H* used the Korean War to discuss the Vietnam War; *Roll Out* used World War II to comment on present-day race relations. In fact, *Roll Out* was one of the first predominantly African American shows in TV history. The plot concerned a mostly black Army supply unit fighting in Europe in World War II. Characters all had colorful names, such as Sweet Williams, Phone Booth, High Strung, and Wheels (portrayed by a pre–*Saturday Night Live* Garrett Morris). The hoped-for *M*A*S*H* bounce didn't happen. *Roll Out* lasted just 13 episodes—it was trounced in the ratings by its competition, ABC's *The Odd Couple*.

C.P.O. SHARKEY

Legendary comic Don Rickles was given this sitcom vehicle in 1976; he played chief petty officer (C.P.O.) Otto Sharkey, a veteran drill instructor in charge of training a ragtag band of new naval

The answer: Yes—Commander Charles E. "Chuck" Brady, MD, flight surgeon...

recruits. The show revolved around Rickles's ethnic- and gender-based insult humor—his assistant was African American, his commanding officer was a woman, and some of his trainees were Polish, Jewish, and Italian. The show was not a ratings hit and was canceled at the end of the 1976–77 season. But when the *Sanford and Son* spinoff *Sanford Arms* unexpectedly bombed, *C.P.O. Sharkey* was rushed back into production to fill the hole on CBS's schedule, where it ran for another season.

OPERATION PETTICOAT

Yet another military sitcom in which an unwitting commander, in this case Lieutenant Commander Sherman (John Astin, Gomez on *The Addams Family*) is put in charge of a motley bunch of hard-to-control, misfit troops. In this case, it's onboard the *Sea Tiger*, a pink submarine staffed mostly by women in the World War II era. Though based on the classic 1959 Cary Grant movie of the same name, the show was a flop. It ran for half a season in 1977 before it was taken off the air, revamped, and most of the cast replaced. It returned in the fall of 1978 and lasted another half season to little fanfare. *Operation Petticoat* is notable for being the first widespread exposure of Jamie Lee Curtis and Jim Varney (the *Ernest* movies).

MAJOR DAD

At work, Major John "Mac" McGillis (Gerald McRaney) is the fierce, imposing, no-nonsense (and extremely tall) commander of an infantry training school on a Marine base in California. Then he falls in love with and marries a single mom who is a liberal journalist with whom he has many fundamental political disagreements. But despite his strict leadership abilities, the major finds it nearly impossible to reign in his three new stepdaughters, who pay him no respect. In fact, the daughters were so disrespectful that the Marine Corps had a problem with the show. *Major Dad*'s original opening-credit sequence in 1989 depicted the youngest daughter removing the major's military-issue hat and placing it on her own head. At the USMC's request, the footage was dropped from the rest of the show's four-year run.

SUPER PLANE!

The Barling was the largest plane built in America until the XB-15 came along in 1935. However, bigger is not always better.

MUCH BIGGER THAN A BREADBOX

The XNBL-1 (Experimental Night Bomber, Long Range), more commonly referred to by the name of its designer, Walter H. Barling, was built by the Witteman-Lewis Aircraft Corporation of Teterboro, New Jersey, in 1923. Its most vocal advocate was Brigadier General William "Billy" Mitchell, who's been called "the father of the U.S. Air Force." Mitchell had pushed hard for the plane's development, thinking that the only way to wage offensive air actions behind enemy lines was to utilize massive bomber planes that could carry massive bomb loads. The necessary technology was in its infancy, but at the time it was built, U.S. Army Air Service planners saw the 27,000-pound Barling as only a stepping-stone to massive 200,000-pound bombers.

THE BARLING BOMBER BY THE NUMBERS

• Three wings—two with flight control surfaces and a middle wing to help lift the mammoth plane into the air.

• Wingspan of 120 feet—as long as the distance of the Wright brothers' first flight. (By way of comparison, the B-17 had a 104-foot wingspan.)

• Three stories tall and 65 feet long.

• Six Liberty engines—four tractors and two pushers provided enough thrust for a cruising speed of 100 mph.

• A landing gear system that consisted of two "trucks"—one more toward the nose for landing, and another near the rear of the plane for taxiing around on the ground.

• A 2,000-gallon fuel capacity that allowed the plane to fly for a full 12 hours when not loaded with bombs. With a payload of 10,000 pounds, it was restricted to only two hours in the air.

• Seven defensive guns mounted at five locations, requiring a crew of four to operate them.

The USCGC *Acushnet* is the oldest Coast Guard cutter in service, since February 5, 1944.

GROUND CONTROL TO MAJOR FIASCO

The Barling was assembled and flown for the first time at McCook Field in Dayton, Ohio, on August 22, 1923. Its performance was so poor that it couldn't fly directly between Dayton and Washington, D.C., while fully fueled because the Appalachian Mountain range was higher than it could climb. When fueled and loaded with simulated bombs, it was so heavy that only two runways in America could support its tremendous weight without cracking and breaking. Normal hoses would have required excessively long ground delays for refueling, so large-volume fuel hoses were created to fuel it faster.

In 1924 the Barling (in some circles known as "Mitchell's Folly") became Billy Mitchell's pulpit for spreading the gospel of strategic bombing. The one-of-a-kind monster made the air show circuit, during which Mitchell demonstrated the bomber's massive payload capacity by establishing altitude records based on weight carried aloft. The publicity brought the bomber, its huge costs, and its poor performance to the attention of the House Military Appropriations Committee, which cut the funding for the program in early 1925. The lone Barling didn't fly much in 1925 or 1926. After that, it was taken apart and put away in an old storage hangar at Wilbur Wright Field near Dayton, Ohio.

The Barling wasn't a total loss. Its wind-tunnel tests and construction provided valuable data, and it helped solve aeronautical engineering problems in aircraft development. In that way, the Barling influenced the design of the B-17, B-24, and B-29 bombers that became the backbone of America's strategic bombing campaign of World War II.

The Barling cost the U.S. Army Air Service $375,000, and put the manufacturer out of business when the cost overrun of $150,000 surpassed the company's liquid assets. The Witteman-Lewis Company had won the bid for the bomber, but in those days there were few provisions that excused overruns of that magnitude.

A "HAP-PY" ACCIDENT

It was still lying there disassembled alongside vintage World War I planes when it was discovered by Major Henry H. "Hap" Arnold during an inspection. The War Department's books still carried the Barling as a flyable Air Corps airplane. Having the Barling on the books prevented the Air Service from building more modern, technologically advanced aircraft—there was a limit to the total number of planes that the Army could own. Arnold wanted it destroyed, but couldn't convince the Air Service to give it up.

The airplane finally met its end after Arnold, future commander of the Army Air Forces during World War II, took charge at the Fairfield Air Depot. An old Arnold family story describes his frustration with the Air Corps' hopelessly bureaucratic logistics system. Arnold had been at home in the middle of a working day—a rare occurrence for him. He had been on the phone with Washington all morning trying to get rid of the Barling bomber.

AT HOME WITH THE ARNOLDS

As Arnold's wife Bee and his young son Bruce ate lunch with him, Arnold looked carefully at his wristwatch, then looked up and said, "There's gonna be a fire." Just about then, the wail of the airfield fire brigade siren rose in the distance. The scream echoed off the walls of nearby military housing. The sound grew louder as the fire brigade raced to the blazing fire that was billowing from one of the old storage hangars. Major Arnold never looked up from his lunch.

Bee suspected what had just happened but still had to ask, "What was in that old hangar?"

"Well, Beadle," said Arnold as he lifted his head in the direction of the fire without shifting his eyes, "it looks like the hangar where we kept that old Barling bomber. What a shame. I'll have to notify Washington." He finished his lunch, his famous grin stretched wide across his thin, boyish face.

BYE-BYE, BARLING

The reality was probably not very different from the family's recollections. Documents authorizing the destruction of "one heavy bomber" have not survived, but Arnold probably had tacit permission to destroy an outdated bomber—but not specifically the Barling. The story likely has been exaggerated over the years, perhaps to show Arnold as a fiery, get-things-done officer. No disciplinary action was ever taken against the staff after the incineration of the hangar. All that remains of the Barling bomber are two of the ten large tires from its revolutionary landing gear, housed at the U.S. Air Force Museum at Wright-Patterson AFB near Dayton.

"Mickey Mouse" was the Allied password on D-day.

TELL IT TO THE MARINES

Advertising Week *inducted the United States Marine Corps into its Madison Avenue Walk of Fame, where it enshrined their recruiting slogan, "The Few. The Proud. The Marines." The Corps has always been quote-worthy.*

"The more Marines I have around, the better I like it!"

—General Mark Clark, U.S. Army

"We're surrounded. That simplifies the problem!"

—Chesty Puller, USMC

"We're not retreating, hell! We're just attacking in a different direction!"

—General Oliver Smith, USMC

"Retreat, hell! We just got here!"

—Captain Lloyd Williams, USMC

"Being ready is not what matters. What matters is winning after you get there."

—Lieutenant General Victor H. Krulak, USMC

"The deadliest weapon in the world is a Marine and his rifle!"

—General John J. Pershing, U.S. Army

"The Marines I have seen around the world have the cleanest bodies, the filthiest minds, the highest morale, and the lowest morals of any group of animals I have ever seen. Thank God for the United States Marine Corps!"

—Eleanor Roosevelt

"Sometimes it is entirely appropriate to kill a fly with a sledgehammer!"

—Major I. L. Holdridge, USMC

"A ship without Marines is like a garment without buttons."

—Admiral David Porter, U.S. Navy

"Once a Marine, always a Marine!"

—Credited to Master Sgt. Paul Woyshner, USMC

"Some people spend an entire lifetime wondering if they made a difference. The Marines don't have that problem."

—President Ronald Reagan

Initially called a "landship," the first British tank was dubbed "Little Willie."

FIVE FOR FIGHTING

In 1942 five brothers made a sacrifice that showed just how much a family could give to the war effort.

PATRIOTIC FERVOR

January 3, 1942: After ringing in the New Year, the five Sullivan brothers from Waterloo, Iowa, enlisted in the Navy. The brothers were George, 28; Francis, 27; Joseph, 24; Madison, 23; and Albert, 20. The brothers all joined the Navy, which (along with the rest of the military) discouraged family members from serving together in a highly dangerous area. It was not forbidden, though, and the brothers wanted to stay together. So they requested permission to serve on the same ship, the USS *Juneau,* a new light cruiser. It first took them to fight in the North Atlantic and the Caribbean, and then set off for Guadalcanal in September.

FIGHTING SPIRIT

The Battle of Guadalcanal was one of the most important fights of World War II. Japan wanted control of the island to build a strategic base, and U.S. and Allied forces waged a campaign to stop them. The entire battle lasted months, and the USS *Juneau* was just one of the ships involved.

An intercepted Japanese message revealed that a large battalion of enemy ships were coming. The Allies prepared themselves for their arrival—five cruisers, including the *Juneau,* and eight destroyers stood ready. On November 13, just after midnight, the Japanese brigade arrived: one light cruiser, two battleships, and 11 destroyers. Outnumbered and outgunned, the Allies also suffered poor radar reception that failed to show the location of the enemy ships.

DAMN THE TORPEDOES

The intense battle that followed didn't take long. It was only 15 minutes before two Japanese destroyers, a Japanese battleship, three American cruisers, and five American destroyers were felled. The *Juneau* was hit by a torpedo, so it cruised away to seek repairs at Pearl Harbor.

But the massive boat could only make speeds of 18 knots, and reaching Pearl Harbor seemed impossible. So a few hours later, the *Juneau* turned around and rejoined the battle. The bloody confrontation raged until almost noon, when the Allied forces retreated. The *Juneau* limped along at a speed of 13 knots before it was hit again. This time, the torpedo split the cruiser in half; it sank almost immediately.

About 600 men on board were killed right away, including Francis, Joseph, Madison, and Albert Sullivan. The eldest brother, George, was severely wounded but made it into a lifeboat. More than 100 men from the *Juneau* were also still alive, but the odds were greatly stacked against them.

IN THE WATER

Finally, the Japanese left, and with the surviving men of the *Juneau* in need of rescue, the captain of the USS *Helena* radioed the sinking ship's position and asked for aircraft assistance. Unfortunately, that message never reached its intended audience.

For a full week, the remaining servicemen had to fight exposure, exhaustion, and sharks. Many died from the wounds they had already suffered. Only three crowded lifeboats were available for the entire remaining crew, and sharks circled each of them, waiting for anyone to fall overboard.

George's wounds were serious but not life-threatening. He might have made it, but was attacked by a shark when he attempted to quickly clean himself in the ocean. The last remaining Sullivan brother had perished. And by the time a rescue ship returned to the area, just 10 survivors remained.

Back in Waterloo, Iowa, the Sullivans' parents did not know of their sons' deaths. The U.S. military, in an effort to keep the Axis from knowing how much damage its forces had sustained, did not make the cruiser's destruction public. The Sullivan parents suspected something was wrong only when they stopped receiving letters from their sons. They did not receive an official notice until January 12, 1943.

HEROES REMEMBERED

The nation mourned the loss of all aboard the *Juneau*, but especially the sacrifice of the Sullivan family. The brothers' parents, Thomas and Alleta, were left behind, as was a sister, Genevieve,

Osama bin Laden's al Qaeda declared war on America in 1996, five years before 9/11.

and Albert's widow and son. Pope Pius XII sent his condolences. President Franklin D. Roosevelt wrote a letter to the Sullivan parents in which he said, "I am sure that we all take heart in the knowledge that they fought side by side." President Roosevelt also asked Mrs. Sullivan to christen a new naval destroyer, the USS *The Sullivans*, in San Francisco in April.

The Navy awarded the brothers several posthumous medals, including the Purple Heart; the American Defense Service Medal, Fleet Clasp; the Asiatic-Pacific Campaign Medal; the World War II Victory Medal; and the Good Conduct Medal.

Thomas and Alleta remained staunch supporters of the war effort, and they began a tour to promote the buying of war bonds. Genevieve joined the WAVES (Women Accepted for Volunteer Emergency Service), a female service corps employed by the Navy during the war.

The house the Sullivan brothers grew up in has since been torn down. In its place stands a park dedicated to the family. Waterloo, Iowa, also hosts the Five Sullivan Brothers Convention Center, and the city's Grout Museum opened a wing called the Sullivan Brothers Iowa Veterans Museum in 2004.

THE LEGACY LIVES ON

The first USS *The Sullivans* served the U.S. Navy through the Korean War. After the conflict, it was decommissioned and now resides in Buffalo, New York, as a tribute to the brothers. A second USS *The Sullivans* was launched on August 12, 1995, and is still in service.

A movie about the Sullivan brothers' sacrifice, *The Fighting Sullivans* (originally titled just *The Sullivans*), was released in 1944 and was nominated for an Academy Award. The film *Saving Private Ryan*, which won five Academy Awards, was partially inspired by the brothers' deaths but did not directly tell any part of their story.

Today, there is widespread belief that a law was enacted after the death of the five Sullivan brothers to prevent family members from serving together on the same ship, but it's not true. No such law exists, and it never has. The Navy does, however, continue to recommend against it, as do the other branches of the military. Still, if enlisted servicemen and women fill out a request form, the rule can be bent.

Primary U.S. military sidearm: the Beretta M-9 pistol, a 9-mm semiautomatic.

AN UNCOMMON BROTHERHOOD

Four heroes who never saw a battlefield, but who left an impression on the people who witnessed their bravery.

A RABBI, TWO MINISTERS, AND A PRIEST

The men who are known as "the Four Immortal Chaplains" came from varied religious backgrounds in an era when religions didn't mix, so it was somewhat unusual that they became close friends at Chaplain's School at Harvard University in 1942. They did have at least these things in common: three of the four had served as Boy Scout leaders, each held the rank of lieutenant in the U.S. Army, and each was a member of the Chaplain Corps.

The official duties of the Army's Chaplain Corps were to serve their country through spiritual leadership, to minister to soldiers and their families, to lead worship, to visit the wounded, and to raise morale. A few months after their meeting, the four chaplains were appointed to accompany more than 900 soldiers and civilians who were being transported to Europe on the USAT *Dorchester* during World War II.

Colonel Frederick Gillespie Sr. was in charge of choosing the chaplains who would sail on the *Dorchester*. He'd completed his list, but at the last minute was forced to fill two spots when two chaplains were pulled from his roster. With a Protestant minister and rabbi already on the list, Gillespie's superior told him to find a second Protestant and a Catholic. For the latter he chose John Washington, whom he didn't know personally but who happened to be from his own hometown of Newark, New Jersey. The colonel's other choice was Clark Poling, who was the son of a famous Baptist evangelist.

THE CHAPS WHO WERE CHAPLAINS

Rabbi Alexander Goode, 31, was the son of a rabbi. Born in Brooklyn, Goode was an all-around athlete in high school. He graduated from the University of Cincinnati in 1934 and earned a doctorate in Oriental languages from Johns Hopkins University in 1940. He and his wife, Theresa—the niece of singer Al Jolson—had one daughter. He was one of the 309 rabbis who served during World War II.

Reverend Clark Poling, 32, born in Columbus, Ohio, was a seventh-generation Protestant minister whose father had served in the Chaplain Corps in World War I. A Yale Divinity School grad, the younger Poling was a Dutch Reformed minister, married with one child. A second child was born three months after his death.

Father John P. Washington, 35, grew up in New Jersey, the oldest of six children in a middle-class Irish immigrant family. He earned diplomas from New Jersey's Seton Hall University, and attended seminary in Darlington, New Jersey. His poor eyesight didn't stop him from enlisting in the service; he tricked the Army into letting him serve by cheating on his eye exam.

Reverend George L. Fox, 41, from Pennsylvania, first enlisted in the Army at age 17, serving as a medical orderly during World War I. After the war, he completed high school and studied at Moody Bible Institute and Illinois Wesleyan University. Ordained as a Methodist minister in 1934, Fox reenlisted as an Army chaplain in 1942, on the same day that his son, Wyatt, enlisted in the Marine Corps.

All four men were sociable, and the friendship forged at Chaplain's School continued. They told jokes among themselves, ate and prayed together, and were eager to tend their shipboard flock.

DANGEROUS WATERS

The *Dorchester* was a retired luxury liner that had been converted into an Army transport ship, one of three being escorted by three Coast Guard cutters (the *Tampa*, the *Escanaba*, and the *Comanche*) en route to Greenland. With a capacity load of 902 servicemen, merchant seamen, and civilian workers, the *Dorchester* was less than 150 miles from its destination on the night of February 3, 1943, when it cruised into the crosshairs of the German submarine *U-223*. The U-boat fired three torpedoes at the *Dorchester*. Only one hit the ship, but it hit on the starboard side below the waterline and knocked out the ship's power.

The captain gave the order to abandon ship, but panic had set in, disrupting any possibility of orderly evacuation. Men stood dazed on the deck. Others jumped into lifeboats, overcrowding and capsizing them. Rafts were tossed from the ship into the icy waters, but drifted away before anyone could board them. In the midst of pandemonium, the chaplains remained composed. They spread out among the soldiers to calm them down, tend to the wounded, and guide disoriented men toward safety. Soldiers and crew lined up and the chaplains handed out life jackets from a storage locker. When the supply ran out, the chaplains removed their own life jackets and gave them to the next four men in line.

As the ship sank, the chaplains linked arms and braced themselves against the slanting deck, singing hymns and praying in Latin, Hebrew, and English. Survivors floating in life rafts heard their songs and prayers above the chaos. In less than 20 minutes, the *Dorchester* sank beneath the Atlantic waters. Two of the cutters, the *Comanche* and the *Escanaba*, had responded to the explosion, and picked up 229 survivors.

GONE BUT NOT FORGOTTEN

On December 19, 1944, the four chaplains were posthumously awarded the Purple Heart and the Distinguished Service Cross. Congress has designated February 3 as "Four Chaplains Day." To commemorate their service and sacrifice, the U.S. Postal Service issued a three-cent stamp in 1948.

To honor his deceased son, and to celebrate the four chaplains' courage, Reverend Daniel Poling organized the Four Chaplains Memorial Foundation, a nonprofit organization honoring people whose deeds symbolize good will and cooperation as demonstrated by the four chaplains—a list that has included four presidents (Harry S. Truman, Dwight D. Eisenhower, Jimmy Carter, and Ronald Reagan), and famous figures like Bob Hope, John Glenn, and Congresswoman Shirley Chisholm.

The Chapel of the Four Chaplains, an interfaith chapel at Temple University in Philadelphia, was dedicated by President Harry S. Truman on February 3, 1951.

Several books have also kept the story alive, including *Sea of Glory* by Ken Wales and *No Greater Glory* by Dan Kurzman. A 2004 TV documentary, *The Four Chaplains: Sacrifice at Sea*, also told their remarkable tale of courage and selflessness.

...and got a Purple Heart for wounds received in Guam.

WORLD WAR II IN THE 1960s

One of the biggest fads in television in the 1960s: loud and violent weekly dramas that took place on the front lines of World War II.

THE GALLANT MEN (1962–63)

The first of the 1960s World War II shows to debut, *The Gallant Men* depicted an American infantry unit fighting in Italy, as told through the eyes of embedded war reporter Conley Wright (Robert McQueeney), who also narrated the show. It was not a ratings hit and was not critically acclaimed; the characters were well-worn stereotypes, including an Italian-American ladies' man and a no-nonsense sergeant, and the good guys never got hurt or ever seemed to actually be in danger. Despite the show bombing, a line of action figures was produced for the show.

COMBAT! (1962–67)

Starring classic big-screen tough guy Vic Morrow as Sergeant Saunders, *Combat!* followed a U.S. Army platoon (King Company) fighting on the front lines in France. The show was notable for its stark realism and brutal violence. Main characters and guest stars, who portrayed German soldiers, French citizens, or peripheral King Company members, were routinely killed. *Combat!* ran for five years; the actual ground war in Europe in World War II lasted just 11 months. Nevertheless, King Company never fought its way out of France. Bonus: cast members Morrow, Jack Hogan, Dick Peabody, and Shecky Greene had all fought in World War II, although they had all served in the Navy, not the Army.

TWELVE O'CLOCK HIGH (1964–67)

Based on the 1949 film, this show followed the 918th Bomb Group, an American bomber unit stationed in Archbury, England. Robert Lansing starred in the first season as Brigadier General Frank Savage, but when ABC executives decided they wanted a younger-looking actor at the center of the show (as well as a new time slot for the series), Lansing protested; his character was killed

"Sewer trout" is military slang for bland fish served at mess.

off. His replacement: Paul Burke as Colonel Joe Gallagher (ironically, in real life, the youthful-looking Burke was two years older than Lansing). Color film was available, but *Twelve O'Clock High* was filmed in black and white in order to utilize actual battle footage from World War II supplied by the Air Force.

CONVOY (1965)

Today, TV shows with lots of characters and long plot arcs are commonplace—*Lost, The Wire, The Sopranos*, and *Mad Men*, for example. *Convoy* was ahead of its time. Truly massive in its scope, *Convoy* was about a group of 200 American ships heading across the North Atlantic to fight in World War II in Europe. This created the opportunity for hundreds of characters and hundreds of stories. Unfortunately, *Convoy* lasted just 13 weeks on the air. *Convoy* was also one of the last TV series ever shot in black and white.

COURT MARTIAL (1966)

A midseason replacement show about the U.S. Army's Judge Advocate General Corps, otherwise known as military court, which handles tribunals and court-martial cases. The first episode—which aired three years earlier as an episode of *Kraft Suspense Theater*—actually took place during the Korean War. The setting was shifted to World War II when the series came to fruition. *Court Martial* starred Peter Graves as the prosecutor and Bradford Dillman, a former Marine in real life, as the defense. Produced in England, the show was critically acclaimed there, where it won the BAFTA TV award (the British Emmy) for Best Dramatic Series. In the United States, the show lasted just 26 episodes. Just a year later, Graves would go on to massive success on *Mission: Impossible* and the concept of a JAG drama would be revived in 1995 with the megahit series *JAG*.

THE RAT PATROL (1966–68)

Erwin Rommel's Afrika Korps terrorized northern Africa during World War II, but an Allied unit called the Long Range Desert Group terrorized them. Made up of troops from England, New Zealand, and Rhodesia, the Long Range Desert Group used reinforced, machine gun–armed trucks to "attack, harass, and wreak havoc on Field Marshal Rommel's vaunted Afrika Korps." In 1966 the story of "the desert rats" came to television on *The Rat Patrol.* One big change was made for American television: all but one of the soldiers were Americans. The show was one of the most popular new series of 1966, but expensive, difficult shoots in Spain led to a truncated two-year run. *The Rat Patrol* did not fare as well on English television. The real-life LRDG were well-known, home-grown heroes there, and the British viewership resented how the series had made the outfit a mostly American operation. It was pulled after just a handful of episodes.

JERICHO (1966–67)

In this short-lived series, the James Bond/1960s spy movie treatment was applied to World War II. *Jericho* depicted three Allied secret agents working behind enemy lines to thwart the Nazis. Franklin Shepherd (Don Francks) was an American expert on psychological warfare; Nicholas Gage (John Leyton) was a British demolitions master; and Jean-Gaston Andre (Marino Masé) was a French munitions expert.

GARRISON'S GORILLAS (1967–68)

Inspired by *The Dirty Dozen*, *Garrison's Gorillas* has a similar plot: federal prisoners are recruited by the government to fight in secret World War II missions in Europe. If they succeed, they eventually get full pardons; if not, executions. Among the criminals were a pickpocket, a master thief, and a knife enthusiast. After one season, the show was canceled and replaced with *The Mod Squad.* But in 1981, *Garrison's Gorillas* was one of the first American shows purchased to air in China, though it was canceled after a few months because of reports it riled up too many Chinese teenagers.

* * *

RADIO POETS

Two patrols in the jungle were checking in with each other. The first radioed:

"Eeny, meeny, miney, mo, how do you read my radio?"

Not wanting to be outdone, the receiving operator replied:

"Fe, fi, fo, fum, loud and clear with a little hum."

Motto of the 104th Infantry Division (WWII): "Nothing in Hell can stop the Timberwolves."

BING BONG: ACE OF ACES

Medal of Honor recipient Richard Ira "Bing" Bong became America's highest-scoring ace by shooting down 40 Japanese aircraft during World War II.

HEAD IN THE CLOUDS

Little did Richard Bong's parents know that one of the nine children they were raising on their Wisconsin farm would grow up to be the top American ace of all time. Bong's childhood fascination with building model airplanes might have given them a clue: It led to his enrollment to study engineering at Superior State Teachers College, where he entered the local Civilian Pilot Training Program. Two years later, he'd earned a private pilot's license flying a Piper Cub.

In June 1941, Bong enlisted in the U.S. Army Air Forces Aviation Cadet Program at Luke Field, Arizona, where instructor (and future presidential nominee) Captain Barry Goldwater described him as "a very bright gunnery student." Seven months later, Bong earned his wings as a second lieutenant and became a gunnery instructor. But the future ace really wanted to be a fighter pilot, so he joined the 49th Fighter Squadron at Hamilton Field, California, where he was trained to fly a Lockheed P-38 Lightning.

The Lightning had been around since 1937, but the latest version, the P-38E, could clock nearly 400 mph at a 25,000-foot altitude. Two 1,425-horsepower engines on separate hulls with the cockpit mounted in between meant that Bong didn't have to look through a spinning propeller spewing grease anymore. The single 20-mm cannon and four .50-caliber machine guns fit snugly in the aircraft's nose below the cockpit. A P-38 couldn't maneuver as well as Japan's Mitsubishi A6M Zero, but its armored cockpit and fuel lines gave pilots protection that Japanese flyers didn't have.

A PILOT GETS HIS WINGS AND HIS BING

When the officer in charge at Hamilton Field—Major General George C. Kenney—was tapped by General Douglas MacArthur to lead the Fifth Air Force in Australia, he selected 50 of his best pilots to accompany him, Bong among them. Lieutenant Bong celebrated by looping his P-38 around California's Golden Gate Bridge and buzzed the base at a dangerously low altitude. He was grounded for recklessness and didn't do much flying before getting to Port Moresby, New Guinea.

Bong claimed his first two kills on December 27, 1942, shooting down a pair of Japanese fighters during MacArthur's Buna-Lae campaign on New Guinea's northeast coast. Two miniature red-and-white Japanese flags were stenciled below the cockpit, signifying his first two kills. Three more would qualify him as an ace. He shot down two on January 7, 1943, and another the next day. In 13 days he had bagged five kills and earned the Silver Star, the third-highest decoration for combat heroism. Fellow officers nicknamed him "Bing" because it fit with "Bong," and it stuck.

Bong admitted to being a marginal aerial gunner; he compensated for his bad aim by flying directly at his targets, sometimes flying through the debris left from his hits. No one questioned his shooting after he knocked down 18 fighters, two medium bombers, and one heavy bomber. At least 16 of his victories resulted from head-on duels. After his 10th kill, Bong was awarded the Air Medal. Three months later, after shooting down four Zeros over Lae, he received the Distinguished Flying Cross. With three other aces—Thomas J. Lynch, Neel Kearby, and Thomas B. McGuire—Bing Bong shared the top echelon of General Kenney's professional gunfighters. He rebuffed an offer to become a squadron leader; he wanted to be a fighter pilot, nothing more.

TIME-OUT

After Bong's 21st victory, Kenney sent him home for three months to relax. At a college homecoming event, Bong met Marjorie Vattendahl. He named his P-38 "Marge" and pasted her photo above the guns mounted in the plane's nose.

Back at the base, Lynch, Kearby, and McGuire had closed in on his record, but Bong had set his sights on a higher goal—to smash Eddie Rickenbacker's record of 26 kills in World War I. Between February 15 and April 12, 1944, Bong disposed of seven more Japanese planes, downing three in one day. Kenney promoted his top gun to major, and Rickenbacker sent a letter, which read, "I hasten to offer my sincere congratulations with the hope that you'll double or triple this number." Bong would've tried if

General Henry H. "Hap" Arnold hadn't decided to send him on a 15-state tour to promote war bonds. Bong fretted through the summer, then convinced the general to take him off the tour and put him back in the cockpit. But Kenney didn't want his number-one ace chasing enemy aircraft anymore and assigned him as an advanced gunnery instructor. Bong was instructed not to engage enemy aircraft while conducting training maneuvers unless attacked. The restless ace followed orders until October 27, 1944.

YOU CAN'T KEEP A GOOD MAN DOWN

Bong lifted off Tacloban Airfield in the Philippines and between October 27 and December 7 scored eight kills, bringing his total to 38. On December 12, General MacArthur looked him straight in the eye and said, "Major Richard Ira Bong, who has ruled the air from New Guinea to the Philippines, I now induct you into the society of the brave, the wearers of the Congressional Medal of Honor of the United States." Bong had fulfilled his tour as a combat pilot and could've gone home, but in mid-December he flew without permission and scored two more victories, bringing his total to 40. When Kenney heard about the two unauthorized sorties, he ordered Bong to park his P-38L. He sent Bong home and turned the competition over to others. McGuire finally tallied 38 kills, but died in combat on January 7, 1945.

HOME AT LAST

Richard and Marge married in 1945 before a gathering of 1,200 guests. A few weeks later, the Army Air Forces assigned Bong to Lockheed to test the P-80 jet fighter. On August 6, in its 11th flight, the jet stalled at 400 feet. Bong was ejected and the plane nose-dived; Bong's body landed a hundred yards away.

After flying more than 500 combat hours and receiving the Medal of Honor, Distinguished Service Cross, Silver Star with oak leaf cluster, Distinguished Flying Cross with six oak leaf clusters, and Air Medal with 14 oak leaf clusters, Bong died on a routine test flight, a month short of his 25th birthday. Today, in the Richard I. Bong World War II Heritage Center in Superior, Wisconsin, visitors can see a restored P-38L with a picture of Marge painted on its side—just like the ace of aces would have wanted.

...On a visit to France, his horse rolled on top of him and broke his pelvis.

IN THE CROSSHAIRS

The word "sniper" derives from snipe shooting—the snipe being a small, fast bird that's extremely difficult to hit.

STEADY, AIM, FIRE

In modern warfare, the enemy is usually faceless and the violence is impersonal—a roadside bomb, a land mine, artillery fire, an aerial rocket or bomb, or even armed drones. But a sniper selects individual targets, sees them up close and personal through a rifle scope, and then, with scientific detachment, factors in weapon specifics, range, wind, trigger pull, breathing—and only then fires from a concealed position that can be thousands of yards away.

PIP-PIP, TALLYHO—AND DUCK!

The first significant well-documented sniping took place in 1643, during the English Civil War, when the Parliamentarian commander, Lord Brooke, was killed by John Dyott, a Royalist sniper, from 300 yards using a smoothbore musket and a homemade musket ball. This was a remarkably difficult shot because smoothbore guns of that time fired with an unpredictable trajectory beyond 100 yards.

Although the military in mainland Europe had been using sniping from the early sixteenth century, the shooting of Lord Brooke was considered an outrage because, except in the heat of battle, the prevailing etiquette of engagement dictated that mere rank and file does not single out officers.

A CLOSE CALL

Etiquette also prohibited shooting an officer in the back, a fact that saved George Washington's life when British officer and sharpshooter Patrick Ferguson had the general in his sights. Since Washington's back was turned, the sniper didn't shoot, possibly turning the tables of history. Later in the Revolution, ironically, Ferguson himself was killed by a sniper at the Battle of King's Mountain.

Airwing Alpo: A meal containing corned beef hash and meatballs with barbecue sauce.

ETIQUETTE, SCHMETTIQUETTE

Americans relied heavily on sharpshooters during the Revolution. Instead of formal battles, most encounters were hit-and-run skirmishes in which a few well-aimed musket balls could have a significant disruptive effect. And the colonials—long dependent on their marksmanship to feed their families—were particularly good shots. The tactical situation left little room for gentlemanly behavior. As the war continued, the potential impact of snipers became increasingly apparent to the Americans.

One sharpshooter, Timothy Murphy of Daniel Morgan's Sharpshooter Corps, may have changed the course of the Battle of Bemis Heights when he shot British general Simon Fraser out of his saddle. Largely as a result of Fraser's death and that of British general John Burgoyne's aide-de-camp Sir Francis Clarke, the British retreated to Saratoga, where the Americans forced Burgoyne's surrender.

MASON-DIXON SNIPING

In 1861, during the Civil War, the Union army was persuaded by a well-known sporting marksman, Hiram Berdan, to form two regiments of handpicked, specially trained sharpshooters who were given license to move freely around the battlefields. Over the course of the war, their devastating effectiveness turned back many attacks. A total of six Confederate generals fell to the guns of Berdan's snipers.

Confederate marksmen were no slouches, either. Following the example of Berdan's sharpshooters, the Confederates formed sniper units in early 1862. At the Battle of Spotsylvania, they killed a Union colonel and General John Sedgwick, and seriously wounded Brigadier General William Morris. Prior to that, at the Battle of Chickamauga, a Confederate sniper fatally wounded General William Lytle.

THE SNIPER EVOLVES

It was during the Civil War that the role of snipers expanded to include what it does today—notably independent operations, infiltration, and intelligence gathering.

By the early 20th century, sniper teams—a shooter and a spotter—were part of the standard order of battle in most armies of the

U.S. Air Force mission: "To fly, fight and win...in air, space, and cyberspace."

Western world. Some teams had a third member who acted as a replacement if needed and was tasked with hauling equipment and acting as a defensive backup so the sniper team could concentrate on its primary mission. Increasingly, snipers' skill at concealment, stealth, patience, initiative, and willingness to work alone were applied to other roles such as intelligence gathering, countersniping, deep-penetration sabotage, and kidnapping.

SNIPING IN 20TH-CENTURY EUROPE

During World War I, snipers had a very active role on both sides of the front. A Canadian native, Corporal Francis Pegahmagabow, was credited with 376 kills. Sergeant Alvin York of Tennessee became a legend for his sharpshooting. And on November 11, 1918, Canadian private George Price was the last Allied soldier killed in World War I—shot by a sniper.

The Winter War of 1939–40, when Russia attempted to invade Finland, confirmed for the Russian military the immense value of snipers, for it was the expert Finnish riflemen who turned the outcome of the war. One Finnish sniper, Simo Häyhä, accounted for more than 500 confirmed kills.

The Russians put the lesson to successful use against the Germans, notably at the siege of Stalingrad, which commanders on both sides called "a snipers' war." The 2001 movie *Enemy at the Gates* was based on the Stalingrad siege, and, while substantially fictional, it highlighted the exploits of Vasily Zaytsev, one of Russia's most decorated snipers.

Throughout World War II, the Russians recruited and trained many women as snipers, based on the prevailing idea that women were more limber, cunning, and less prone to stress. According to the Russians, their 1,000-plus women snipers and their instructors accounted for more than 12,000 German fatalities.

SNIPING SUPERSTAR

In Vietnam, two-man sniper teams often worked alone for weeks in jungles nominally controlled by the North Vietnamese. Emerging from the Vietnam experience was Gunnery Sergeant Carlos Hathcock II, who was instrumental in developing the USMC sniper training program. Hathcock often worked behind enemy lines, stalking high-ranking North Vietnamese officers and collab-

About 30,000 died from gas attacks in World War I, including 2,000 Americans.

orators. He was so effective that the North Vietnamese put a $30,000 price tag on his head. As a result, many of his 93 confirmed kills were enemy snipers. By then, countersniping had become a very important part of a sniper's role.

WHAT HAVE YOU SNIPED FOR ME LATELY?

In Iraq, where fighting often takes place in densely populated urban areas and is very fluid, snipers sometimes work from Humvees, enabling them to move quickly to neutralize opposition, protect troops, and, particularly, isolate enemies from civilians.

NOT YOUR GRANDPA'S MUSKET

Sniping techniques haven't changed much, but technical advances have been profound, including night-vision scopes, silencers, computerized and laser range finders, and thermal imaging. One advance that's still in the experimental stage is a compound to negate a body's heat signal and thwart thermal imaging, which would render the sniper nearly invisible.

A DANGEROUS PROFESSION

Given the distance a sniper is from the target, and a sniper's hidden positioning, you might think they're pretty much out of harm's way. But snipers have always incurred a high casualty rate. Add to that, when a soldier is captured holding a rifle with a scope, the Geneva conventions are often ignored—that rifle usually becomes an immediate death sentence. It's all part of the fear they inspire, as much by their skill as their mystique.

Perhaps the reason can be found in the old Chinese proverb, "Kill one man, terrify a thousand."

* * *

SIGN LANGUAGE

The following sign was spotted at the exit to an Air Force base:

ENTERING DANGER AREA. PUBLIC HIGHWAY.
GOOD LUCK!

THE ONE AND ONLY

Canadian-born Douglas Munro became a U.S. citizen when he was a toddler, then grew up to be one of the greatest American heroes of World War II.

SMALL-TOWN BOY

Growing up as he did in Cle Elum, Washington, a town situated between two national forests in the Cascade Range, Douglas Munro might have become a logger, or a railroad man like his father, but a life at sea was his calling. In 1939, at age 19, he joined the Coast Guard and set sail on the 327-foot cutter *Spencer*.

JOINING THE NAVY

In June 1941, President Roosevelt transferred part of the Coast Guard to the Navy to man four large naval transports and to serve in mixed crews on 22 smaller naval transports. When Munro, now a signalman third class, learned those ships needed signalmen, he transferred to the *Hunter Liggett*, a 535-foot, 13,712-ton attack transport, one of the largest of its kind in the Pacific. The ship carried 700 officers and men; 33 Landing Craft, Personnel (LCPs); and two Landing Craft, Tank (LCTs).

MAN WITH A PLAN

When a Japanese seaplane base on the island of Tulagi and a major airbase under construction on nearby Guadalcanal were discovered, Pacific Fleet commander Admiral Chester W. Nimitz made preparations to counter any Japanese advances there. The Japanese wanted those bases so they could disrupt supply routes between the United States and its allies Australia and New Zealand, but they were only lightly defended. So Nimitz targeted the two islands for the first amphibious assault of World War II.

Eighteen of the 22 boats participating in the campaign carried Coast Guard sailors, many of whom had come from lifesaving operations and were expert small boat handlers—just what the Navy needed. They would be in charge of the landing boats. As the task force approached Guadalcanal, the commander of Transport Division 17 sent Munro from ship to ship instructing coastguardsmen and preparing them for the landings.

ODDS AGAINST

On August 7, 1942, the main force approached the beaches of Guadalcanal while Munro put a section of LCPs filled with Marines onshore at Tulagi. The Guadalcanal landings went uncontested, but in days of stubborn fighting on Tulagi, 80 percent of the Marines' first wave was wiped out. Two weeks later, Munro took his boats 20 miles across Ironbottom Sound (named for the sunken warships that littered its waters) and landed at the joint Navy–Coast Guard base on Guadalcanal's Lunga Point.

A LOT OF GOOD MEN

Heavy reinforcements arrived in September. Working west through the jungle, Lieutenant Colonel Lewis B. Puller's Marines were stopped on the eastern side of the Matanikau River by heavy Japanese resistance. Puller returned to Lunga Point and asked the Coast Guard to take his 500-man battalion around Point Cruz and land the men on the west side of the river. Munro took charge of ten LCPs and LCTs and landed the first wave of Marines at 1:00 p.m. in a small cove west of Point Cruz. Leaving one landing craft behind to remove anyone who might be wounded, Munro returned to Lunga Point.

A BIG HELP

Colonel Puller immediately encountered enemy troops, and the advance stalled. The Japanese began driving the Marines back to the beach. Using their undershirts, the Marines spelled out the word "HELP" on a ridge. A Navy plane spotted the message and radioed it in. When word reached Lunga Point, Munro volunteered to take the same boats back to retrieve the Marines. Made of plywood and armed with only two .30-caliber machine guns, the LCPs weren't exactly well protected. As soon as the boats approached the beach, the Japanese opened fire from three positions. But that didn't stop Munro, who led the boats ashore two or three at a time and began herding the Marines on board. As one boat filled up and backed away from the beach, he signaled another to come ashore.

...in the greatest air assault of World War I at the Battle of Saint-Mihiel.

EVERY LAST MAN

The firing intensified, so Munro interposed his boat between the enemy and the departing LCPs to provide cover. After every Marine, including 25 wounded, got safely off the beach, Munro followed, his LCP pockmarked with bullet holes.

Approaching Point Cruz, Munro noticed that an LCP filled with Marines was grounded on the beach. He steered toward it and signaled a nearby LCT to pull it off. Twenty minutes passed before the LCP was freed, giving the Japanese enough time to get to the beach, set up machine guns, and begin firing on all three boats.

The roar of the boat's engine prevented Munro from hearing a shouted warning from a shipmate, and a single bullet struck him at the base of his skull. Before his LCP got back to Lunga Point—and two weeks before his 22nd birthday—Munro died. His last words were, "Did they get off?"

THE ONE AND ONLY

Because of his extraordinary heroism and outstanding leadership and gallantry, Munro received, posthumously, the first and only Medal of Honor awarded to a member of the Coast Guard. In fact, his mother received the medal directly from President Roosevelt. Weeks later, Edith Munro joined the SPARs—the United States Coast Guard Women's Reserve. (The name is an acronym of the Coast Guard motto *Semper paratus* and its English translation, "Always ready.")

Edith Munro went directly to the Coast Guard Academy for officer's candidate training. Being in her mid-40s, she became a lieutenant—and the oldest SPAR in the Coast Guard. She is buried next to her son at the Laurel Hill Memorial Park in Cle Elum, Washington.

The Douglas Munro grave site is a Washington Historical Monument. As Munro's relatives left the area, his grave fell into disrepair. A veterans' organization took on its upkeep as a cause. They installed a flagpole and arranged for lighting on the flag so that no one need raise and lower the flag each day. Eventually, they managed to get it designated as a Coast Guard Operating Facility so they would no longer have to worry about the site's upkeep.

Starting date of World War II: September 1, 1939, when Germany invaded Poland.

HERE IS YOUR WAR

That's the title of a 1943 book written by World War II embedded journalist Ernie Pyle. His stories put the folks back home as close to the war as words could—and contained the warning that the boys who'd gone off to war would be different when they returned.

LAST DISPATCH

All of America mourned the passing of 44-year-old journalist Ernie Pyle when he was killed by a Japanese sniper in April 1945. By then he'd traveled with American soldiers in North Africa, Sicily, Italy, and France, from Normandy to Paris. Then came Okinawa and, days later, death. Like the soldiers he wrote about, he too had changed.

SMALL-TOWN AMERICA

In 1941, when the United States entered the war, Ernie Pyle was already a well-respected, widely read journalist. He'd perfected an appealing, simple, and straightforward writing style and an approach to his topics that would carry over into his 600 newspaper reports from the battle lines. From 1935, he'd been writing a travel column for the Scripps-Howard newspaper chain. He traveled the United States by car, going off the beaten track to meet people in out-of-the-way small towns. The towns and their people were his subjects. His columns read almost like diary entries but focused on the small details of life.

Pyle went to war in 1942 as a correspondent for Scripps-Howard. He wrote his first overseas column in November 1942 and continued—six columns a week with few interruptions—until his death. The columns, which appeared daily in more than 800 newspapers, were the most widely read reports of the war.

By the end of 1943, Pyle was the country's foremost war correspondent. In 1944 he was awarded the Pulitzer Prize for Journalism. And his story was the basis for the 1945 movie *The Story of G.I. Joe*, starring Burgess Meredith.

BEARING WITNESS

Pyle's articles put a human face on war. He let people know that

Operation Just Cause: the 1989 U.S. invasion of Panama to depose Manuel Noriega.

the great battles weren't merely abstract strategies of remote generals and heads of state plotting victories with stickpins on maps. Of the transition from young man to soldier, he wrote:

> The last of the comforts are gone. From now on you sleep in bedrolls under little tents. You wash whenever and wherever you can. You carry your food on your back when you are fighting. You dig ditches for protection from bullets and from the chill north wind off the Mediterranean. There are no more hot-water taps. There are no post exchanges where you can buy cigarets [*sic*]. There are no movies.

He wrote about individual soldiers, quiet heroism, and solitary doubt and pain. Pyle's soldiers were husbands, fathers, sons, and brothers from across America, from small towns and farms and big cities. His soldiers' concerns were mundane—their next meal, sleep, a real bath—and focused on getting the job done, surviving, and getting home. Overriding these concerns was fierce loyalty to the men beside them, men with whom they were sharing this intense horror, minute by minute, day by day. Deeply touched by their experiences on the front lines, Pyle successfully lobbied to have troops be given combat pay, just as airmen received flight pay. The bill approving the funding became popularly known as the "Ernie Pyle Bill."

UP CLOSE AND PERSONAL

Worried that the soldiers would be unrecognized—if not forgotten—by people back home, Pyle threaded his articles with the names and hometowns of the soldiers he encountered and the violent realities they were facing. This practice also helped drive home Pyle's core message—that these soldiers were now much different from the men and women America had shipped to North Africa, Europe, and the Pacific. In his April 22, 1943, article, he wrote:

> They have made the psychological transition from the normal belief that taking life is sinful, over to a new professional outlook where killing is a craft. To them now, there is nothing morally wrong about killing. In fact, it is an admirable thing.

NO ONE LEAVES UNSCATHED

Ernie Pyle was human, too. Although riding high on the crest of public acclaim, he experienced personal tragedy. His troubled marriage to an alcoholic wife (since diagnosed as a probable manic-depressive) collapsed. The two were divorced in 1942, but stayed in contact. In a 1945 letter to his ex-wife, he sounded like a battle-weary soldier: "I am very sick of the war and would like to leave it, and yet I know I can't. I've been part of the misery and tragedy of it for so long that I feel if I left it, it would be like a soldier deserting."

In the last column he wrote from the European theater, he told his readers: "I've been immersed in it too long . . . it seemed to me that if I heard one more shot or saw one more dead man, I would go off my nut." All the same, a few months later he was reporting from the Pacific theater. The few columns he wrote there seemed uninspired, and none of them are among his famous ones. He was a man doing his duty, just like the soldiers he wrote about. Just like them, he'd changed. He'd lost his taste for battles and longed for the war to be over.

And soon it was for him when, on the island of Ie Shima, near Okinawa, a jeep he was riding in was hit by machine-gun fire. Everyone dived for the dirt. Pyle raised his head to see if any of his party had been hit and was shot in the temple by a sniper. He was first buried on Ie Shima, and later reburied in 1949 at Punchbowl Cemetery in Honolulu, Hawaii.

* * *

NOW HEAR THIS!

Talking G.I. Joe, introduced in 1967, didn't have a huge vocabulary, but what he did say could fire up a kid's imagination:

"G.I. Joe, U.S. Army, reporting for duty."

"Enemy planes, hit the deck!"

"All units commence firing!"

"Medic, get that stretcher up here!"

"Take the jeep and get some ammo, fast!"

"This is Charlie Company, send reinforcements!"

"Cover me. I'll get that machine gun!"

"Take Hill 79. Move out!"

...but Army personnel often use the terms "Sir," "Ma'am," or—most commonly—"Chief."

KILROY WAS HERE

His most daring appearance was in the bathroom reserved for President Harry Truman, Josef Stalin, and Prime Minister Clement Atlee during the "Big Three" conference in Potsdam, Germany, in July 1945. Stalin returned from the bathroom in an agitated state and asked his translator, "Who is Kilroy?" That's what we wanted to find out.

WHO IS KILROY?

World War II's best-known GI didn't earn any medals or carry a weapon, but he did get around. The cultural hero was spotted at the Statue of Liberty, at the Arc de Triomphe, near crumbling walls in Italy, and even in Hitler's Eagle's Nest retreat. And there are more than a few stories of pregnant women being wheeled into delivery rooms with "Kilroy was here" written on their swollen bellies.

Kilroy was a simple graffiti cartoon of a bald man with a long nose peeking over a wall. Sometimes Kilroy grips the top of the wall with his fingers. The sad-looking little guy is usually accompanied by the words "Kilroy was here" or variations such as "Kilroy slept here" or "Kilroy passed through."

Something about Kilroy appealed to the GIs. Maybe they liked the idea that one of them was everywhere, always ahead of the enemy as well as the dreaded military brass. So they left his imprint everywhere.

BUT WHERE DID HE BEGIN?

There are plenty of stories to explain Kilroy's existence—some plausible, some not, but all interesting.

• At least 62 men with the surname Kilroy served in the military during World War II. One of them might have drawn the first image and the idea exploded from there. At least one, Sergeant Francis J. Kilroy Jr., points to himself as the inspiration for Kilroy. While posted at the Boca Raton Army airfield, Sergeant Kilroy was hospitalized with the flu. He claims a fellow soldier posted the first Kilroy cartoon along with the words "Kilroy will be here next week" on the barracks bulletin board. But Sergeant Kilroy never could pinpoint which of his buddies was the budding cartoonist.

About 25 percent of veterans admitted to VA hospitals are homeless.

• Another rumor says that the real Kilroy went AWOL and had his friends draw the cartoons in various places to throw the MPs off his trail.

• There's a theory that Kilroy was a GI copycat of a similar graffito, Mr. Chad (drawn by cartoonist George Edward Chatterton), who first appeared in Britain in the 1930s, then faded away. Another character started showing up in Britain in 1944 with mottos like "Wot, no bread?" and "Wot, no petrol?" Since Kilroy's first appearance in Britain dated to 1942, it's thought that the "Wot?" fellow is a copycat of Kilroy and that the resemblance to Chatterton's comic is a coincidence. But the three characters look so much alike (bald guy with big nose looking over a wall) that some people (mostly Brits) insist that Kilroy was a copy of Mr. Chad. Maybe . . . but it's unlikely that American GIs would've heard about a British cartoon from the previous decade. And why would they change his name to Kilroy?

• Then there's the ever-popular "secret agent communicating with other spies through the Kilroy cartoon" story? Hmm.

• The most widely accepted origin is a real live Kilroy from Halifax, Massachusetts. James J. Kilroy inspected riveting work at the Fore River Shipyard in Quincy, then marked it as approved with a check mark. Welders were paid by the number of riveted sections checkmarked, so some of them began to erase the inspector's mark after a section was approved, hoping to get a second payment. So Kilroy began marking his sections "Kilroy was here"—a mark that couldn't be erased without being noticed. The mystery began weeks or months later when a sailor doing repairs half a world away would find "Kilroy was here" in what seemed like an inaccessible or sealed compartment. In 1946, during a radio contest to uncover the origins of Kilroy, Fore River Shipyard workers backed up Mr. Kilroy's story about his unique inspection mark.

IS KILROY STILL LEAVING HIS MARK?

Kilroy continued to show up after World War II and during the Korean War. As younger men unfamiliar with Kilroy entered the service, he became a rarity—but did not become extinct. Besides being sighted at the World War II Memorial in Washington, D.C., he's been seen more recently in Iraq and Afghanistan.

IF YOU CAN'T STAND THE HEAT...

Avoiding KP duty has always been a soldier's best reason to stay out of the kitchen.

KITCHEN PATROL

Dodging enemy fire, hunkering down in a foxhole, living with the perpetual threat of air attack—definitely not enjoyable. But ask former enlisted personnel, from World War I to the present day, what they disliked most about their service and they will probably answer you with two letters: KP.

KP—which stands for "kitchen patrol" or "kitchen police"—was arguably the most dreaded duty of a soldier's career. This might seem peculiar to civilians, who would probably figure that combat conditions would be a bit more distasteful than peeling potatoes, setting the table, serving food, or mopping the mess hall floor. Yet KP ranks at the top of the "what I hated about military life" list for plenty of soldiers, sailors, and airmen, and many did whatever they could to avoid it. One member of the World War II Women's Army Corps fessed up decades later that during basic training she hid under her bunk with a book to avoid being assigned to KP.

Hated though it might have been, KP has long been one of the more universal experiences of military life. Army, Navy, Air Force, Marines—whatever branch of service you chose, if you were an enlisted man (or woman), you could expect to take your turn on KP. It was simply a matter of manpower—to keep a camp or a shipful of personnel fed three times a day, you needed extra hands to pitch in. Chefs and kitchen staff handled the cooking, but the KP was responsible for helping with the food prep, sweeping and scrubbing floors, washing and rinsing all the silverware and plates, and handling the garbage (more on that later)—three times a day! If you pulled KP, you could figure on working from 5:00 a.m. to 7:00 p.m., and that included weekends.

WHAT A MESS!

The term "KP" came into use in 1918, around the end of World

War I, but KP duty itself really came into its own during World War II; by the Vietnam era, fewer soldiers were assigned KP duty and in today's U.S. armed forces, almost all kitchen work is contracted to private firms.

The "police" part of "kitchen police" had little to do with crime and punishment. It refers instead to the definition of "police" that means "to put in order and keep clean," which is what personnel on KP were supposed to do, in addition to menial food prep chores such as peeling potatoes and plucking chickens.

Officially, KP was known as "mess duty," and even *that* doesn't mean what you think it does. Believe it or not, the word "mess" started out with positive connotations. It comes from an old French word for a morsel of food and it evolved to mean a dish of food, then a whole bunch of food, then a place where food is served . . . and finally it came to mean what you've made when you spill food on the floor! But for most recruits who pulled KP duty, it was a mess any way you looked at it.

Take the potatoes, for starters. You've seen the cartoon depictions of a fellow on KP with a potato peeler in one hand and a mountain of spuds in front of him. Stereotypical, maybe, but not far from the truth for generations of servicemen. The *General Mess Manual and Cookbook* of the U.S. Navy, 1902 edition, called for 80 pounds of potatoes to make mashed potatoes for a crew of 100 men aboard ship (only 60 pounds were needed for boiled potatoes). Figure that three medium potatoes equal one pound. That's 240 spuds to make mashed potatoes for 100 crew members. But you're not done yet! A mess hall on an Army base could be expected to serve thousands. For instance, the World War II training facility at Camp Santa Anita in California fed 3,500 soldiers per meal—that's 8,400 spuds, all for a side dish.

GARBAGE IN, GARBAGE OUT

Worse than peeling potatoes, scrubbing pots, or mopping the floor was handling the trash. It all had to be separated, and if someone on KP before you hadn't done it right, you just had to reach in and fix it—pulling out handfuls of vegetable waste from the trash cans full of used cooking oil and grease and dropping them where they needed to go. That kind of dirty, smelly, exhausting work was positively punishing . . . as some recruits quickly found out.

...A *simoom* is a desert wind.

WHAT DID I DO TO DESERVE THIS?

Usually reserved for low-ranking or enlisted personnel—and of course for all the recruits in boot camp—KP was also inflicted as a punishment for anything from breaking curfew to brawling to being late for inspection. And incredibly, KP duty was so disliked that the punishment was often enough to deter bad behavior. There was even a pecking order among those assigned KP: show up late, and you could count on being the one who had to scrub the pots and pans or deal with the trash.

In some cases during World War II, Italian or German prisoners of war were put on what amounted to permanent KP duty. Considering what they might have had to endure, kitchen patrol probably wasn't that bad.

On the downside, KP duty presented opportunities for abuses of power. Officers assigning KP duty sometimes made sure that the enlisted men they liked the least spent the most time on KP duty. There were also numerous reports of blacks and other minorities being assigned "permanent" KP duty simply because of their race.

There was an occasional bright side, however. For one thing, those with KP duty had access to the kitchen and the food stores, which meant they ate well and, occasionally, that they took a few "souvenirs" from the pantry back to their quarters.

And for those who didn't mind a case of dishpan hands, KP presented a financially rewarding opportunity. There were always soldiers around who would take on their comrades' KP duty—for a price of, say, $10 a pop. If you were earning around $50 a month, as many World War II enlisted personnel were, that extra money was awfully welcome.

WOMEN'S WORK

When the members of the Women's Army Corps, or WACs, were deployed during World War II, male personnel of all ranks saw this as their opportunity to escape the chores they loathed. At the top of the list was KP. In fact, there are plenty of tales of WACs being placed on permanent KP duty, so much so that Colonel Oveta Culp Hobby, director of the Women's Army Corps, had to create a regulation in 1944 specifying that WACs were not to be assigned permanent KP duty, but were to be placed on the duty roster as any other enlisted soldier and were to take their turn in the kitchen when called.

Male personnel, officers in particular, argued that they could find plenty of women who were perfectly suited to permanent KP—and who, in fact, didn't mind it all that much. They focused largely on the WACs considered to be "unskilled" (many of the "skilled" WACs wound up working as secretaries and office assistants!), and on the women of color who were part of the corps. Yet the fact is, scrubbing pots, scraping carrots, and dishing out grub to hundreds of soldiers three times a day isn't a whole lot of fun for anyone, man or woman. In a history of the Women's Army Corps published by the Center of Military History of the United States Army in 1954, author Mattie E. Treadwell notes a WAC song, sung to the tune of the 1918 chestnut by Geoffrey O'Hara, "K-K-K-Katy":

> K-K-K-KP, beautiful KP,
> You're the only Army job that I abhor.
> When the moon shines over the mess hall,
> I'll be mopping up the K-K-K-kitchen floor.

TAKE THIS JOB AND OUTSOURCE IT

Post-Vietnam, it was decided that a ground force's time was better spent on tactical training than on kitchen patrol, and the requirement of KP was slowly reduced. (To the detriment of the troops, some old hands argued; if nothing else, they insisted, KP was a character-builder.) By the time of the Bosnia and Kosovo conflicts in the 1990s, civilian contractors ran the food-service operations at many military facilities, a trend that continues to grow. Plenty of the civilian contractors are working stateside, but many are making their way to combat zones.

For instance, the "dining facility" (they don't even call it a mess anymore!) that opened in 2007 at Camp Striker, part of the Victory Base Complex in Baghdad, is staffed by 300 workers, most of whom are civilians. In its first days of operation, the facility, which supports the 2nd Brigade Combat Team, was serving 9,000 people per meal with pizza, gyros, stir-fry . . . and whole lot of potatoes!

The standard-issue canteen has a capacity of one U.S. quart.

BEETLE BAILEY

Cartoonist Mort Walker has been bringing us the hijinks of Camp Swampy since 1950. Yet Beetle, Sarge, General Halftrack, and the rest have never seen combat—except in newspaper boardrooms and editorials calling for the comic strip's ouster.

CITIZEN BEETLE

Before he was Private Bailey, Beetle was a college student—originally named "Spider"—who was based on Mort Walker's own experiences at the University of Missouri. The comic strip was not an instant success when it debuted in September 1950, and Walker (himself a World War II vet who served in Italy) was in danger of losing his yearly contract to produce the comic for King Features Syndicate, the nation's leading distributor of comic strips to newspapers. To give *Beetle Bailey* a new twist that might endear it to more readers who were concerned about the escalating conflict in Korea, Walker had Beetle duck into an Army recruiting office—in an attempt to avoid his two girlfriends, neither of whom knew about the other—on March 13, 1951. From there, Beetle was off to Camp Swampy and would soon meet his nemesis, Sergeant Orville P. Snorkel, known to readers as Sarge.

WORKING HARD AT NOT WORKING HARD

Today's readers of the comic strip know Beetle as a lazy private who will do anything to avoid his responsibilities, whether it's going on a march, peeling potatoes, or scrubbing the floors. The long-running theme of the strip involves Beetle trying to get away from Sarge, who will beat him to a pulp for the slightest infraction. Although the two are often seen interacting in a cordial manner, the possibility always exists that Beetle will light Sarge's short fuse and end up on the floor with a black eye (or worse).

Beetle's obvious disdain of his superiors and his unwillingness to exemplify the U.S. Army ideals of teamwork, effort, and discipline have led to some well-publicized events off the funny pages. In 1954 the Tokyo edition of *Stars and Stripes*, the newspaper of the U.S. armed forces, dropped the strip due to its apparent engendering of disrespect toward officers. Back in the United States,

Manfred von Richtofen, the "Red Baron," the most famous air ace of World War I...

where the strip had been growing in popularity, this action resulted in a round of mockery from the comic-reading public. Despite the minor setback (*Stars and Stripes* later reintroduced the strip), *Beetle Bailey* continued its rise; today, it is printed in more than 180,000 newspapers in over 50 countries.

CHANGING WITH THE TIMES

One of the criticisms that has been voiced over *Beetle Bailey* is that it is too stagnant. After all, the characters are still wearing 1950s-style uniforms, drive open-top jeeps rather than Hummers, and have never been to Korea, Vietnam, Iraq, or Afghanistan. But don't ask Walker to introduce the grim realities of warfare to his comic strip. Instead, the men and women of Camp Swampy have been transformed over the years to reflect the changing face of today's military. In 1970 the comic saw the arrival of Lieutenant Jack Flap, the first African American character in an otherwise all-white comic strip. Lieutenant Flap's arrival caused some Southern newspapers to drop *Beetle Bailey*, but a hundred other publications saw fit to add it to their funny pages. Corporal Konishiki Yo, the first Asian character in the strip, debuted in 1990. The most recent addition is Specialist Chip Gizmo, the camp's computer whiz, who was given his name in a 2002 contest sponsored by Dell Computers that also raised more than $100,000 for the Fisher House Foundation, which provides housing for the families of wounded soldiers while they undergo treatment at hospitals.

New characters can be introduced, but can those who have been around for more than 50 years ever change? In response to concerns that General Halftrack's constant ogling of Miss Buxley encouraged sexism, Walker had the general undergo sensitivity training in 1997. Since then, Halftrack's behavior has been toned down noticeably, but readers can still glimpse the underlying sexism and double standards that persist at Camp Swampy—not too much unlike what goes on at many military bases today. And Sarge continues to beat up Beetle whenever he has the chance, something that would lead to criminal charges in today's military.

DISCHARGE PAPERS?

When the *Chicago Tribune* dropped *Beetle Bailey* in 2002, some speculated that it was due to the comic strip's repeated portrayal of

...became even more famous as the imagined foe of Snoopy in the *Peanuts* comic strip.

sexism in the military, or perhaps that the jokes or the setting had simply gotten old. Among the younger demographics, the comic has lost some of its luster, but it remains popular with older readers. Despite its outdated setting, *Beetle Bailey* continues to tickle our funny bones because it shows people reacting in bizarre ways to both everyday and unusual situations and also reminds us that war is not always the be-all and end-all of the armed forces.

Mort Walker continues to oversee the daily operations of his studio in Connecticut, which is said to have more than 10,000 unused jokes in its vault. Six of his children are involved in the business; after Walker does the initial pencils for a strip, his son Greg will do the inking to complete it. One of the characteristics that makes *Beetle Bailey* so appealing to a wide range of people is that the gags are simple, effective, and stand on their own each day. A reader of *Beetle Bailey* does not need to know what happened the day before, and does not need to know if any sort of statement is being made—unlike with some other comic strips that have become focused on real-life situations such as terminal illness, strained relationships, and politics. Walker has said that being funny is his top priority, and he has stayed true to his word for more than half a century.

* * *

THE DUCK SALUTES

During World War II, Donald Duck starred in several short films, but it was *Der Fuehrer's Face* that won a 1942 Academy Award for Best Animated Short Film.

In the film, Donald works in an artillery factory in "Nutzi Land" (Nazi Germany). Forced to salute Hitler every time he sees his face, Donald becomes exhausted when the parts on his assembly line bear Hitler's resemblance. Eventually, Donald suffers a nervous breakdown.

Donald is relieved when he wakes to find that it was only a dream. At the end of the short, Donald looks to the Statue of Liberty and American flag with renewed gratitude.

EGADS stands for "Electronic Ground Automatic Destruct System."

WHEN "AHOY THERE!" ISN'T ENOUGH

The International Code of Flags and Pennants enables anyone who speaks the language to communicate from ship to ship and from ship to shore.

NO ROOM FOR INTERPRETATION

In the seafaring universe, there's no disputing what certain flags of a uniform color mean:

- White: truce
- Black: piracy
- Red: a mutiny or a revolution is underway
- A national flag flown at half-mast: the crew is in mourning
- A flag flown upside down: distress—help is needed

More complicated messages are sent using the alphanumeric flags for letters of the alphabet and numbers from zero to nine, used in combination with one another to spell out messages.

The system dates back to the dim recesses of naval history. Among the first groups to use signal flags were the Knights Hospitaller during the Crusades, when they defeated the Ottoman naval fleet in 1571. Captains of the Hospitallers' ships used as many as 15 flags to relay secret codes so they could coordinate ships manned by sailors from all over Europe who spoke different languages.

SAY WHAT?

Over time, other systems of communicating with flags developed to regulate ship movements near shore. However, confusion inevitably crept in, so the British decided to address the problem: a system of flag signals was established as a standard for use on every ship and in every port throughout the world. The first International Code of Signals was drafted in 1855 and published by the British Board of Trade in 1857.

The code, with definitions written in English, contained 17,000 signals using a mere 18 signal flags. Modified at the International Conference of 1889 in Washington, D.C., the system was

Captain Ronald Reagan signed Major Clark Gable's discharge papers in 1944.

gradually adopted by most maritime nations. It was revised in 1932 and again in 1961 to include nine languages: English, French, German, Italian, Japanese, Spanish, Russian, Greek, and Norwegian.

HOW IT WORKS

Today, there are 40 flags and pennants recognized by the code. The international code recognizes 26 square flags for letters of the alphabet, 10 pennants for numerals, and four pennants for special messages. Five colors were chosen based on their visibility at sea: red, blue, yellow, black, and white.

Each flag or pennant stands for a letter of an alphabetic message or a number. Individual flags have their own specific meanings. Here are some examples:

- A white flag with a large red diamond is the letter F in combination with other flags, or when standing alone means "I am disabled, communicate with me."
- A white flag with a blue cross is the letter X in combination with other flags, or standing alone communicates "Stop carrying out your intentions and watch for my signals."
- A white flag with a red X does triple duty: in combination with other flags it is the letter V, standing alone it means "I require assistance," and with one or more numeral pennants signifies speed in kilometers per hour.

1, 2, 3, OR MORE

The number of flags is significant, too:

- A single flag stands for either urgency or a particular message.
- Two-flag signals usually mean a vessel in distress or maneuvering.
- Three-flag signals represent directives such as points of the compass, relative bearings, standard times, verbs, punctuation, or general code and decode signals.
- Four flags stand for geographical signals and names of ships.
- Five flags strung together communicate the time and position of a vessel.
- Six-flag signals indicate longitude and latitude.

Sailors string the signal flags end to end and hoist them on the rigging, going from bow to stern. Of course, it's imperative that lookouts memorize the signal flags and have keen eyesight.

FLAG SHORTHAND

The U.S. Navy adopted the international code in 1913, adding a variation in World War II in the form of "governing flags." Using the A, I, N, O, and P flags as a sort of shorthand between ships, the Navy could convey extra information (affirmative, interrogatory, negative, optional, and preparatory) based on their position in a string of flags. Governing flags were used only among the fleet and reverted to traditional meanings when communicating with ships of other nations. Some organizations use other flags or give existing ones additional meanings; NATO, for instance, uses an extra set of flags to convey specific messages, akin to the Navy's use of governing flags.

JUST FOR SHOW

Of course, signal flags are still in use today. And you've probably seen them as decorations during boating festivals or special events. They're used in yacht racing, too: the international P flag (blue with a white rectangle) is used to signal an imminent start to a race and the S flag (white with a blue rectangle) signals a shortened sailing course.

* * *

"SWINGING THE LEAD"

This phrase is still frequently used to imply someone who's lazy or work-shy. It comes from the method that ships used to measure their speed through the water. A long piece of hemp rope was tied with knots at equal distances along its length and a lead weight was tied to the end to help it sink. The rope was then thrown out to sea and pulled in after a set time; the number of knots that disappeared underwater showed the speed at which the ship was traveling. "Knots" remains the official measure of speed for all sailing vessels.

An unfortunate deckhand (usually someone being punished) performed this backbreaking task, and had to swing the leaded rope around his head to create enough momentum to get it over the wake of the ship. If he wanted to avoid the really hard work of dragging the sodden rope back in, he'd keep swinging the rope around his head, until a whip from the boatswain's cat-o'-nine-tails made him stop "swinging the lead."

...He had accidentally grabbed her coat as he was running out of the house they were in.

AUDIE MURPHY'S RÉSUMÉ

Get familiar with the accomplishments of this American hero.

Name: Audie Leon Murphy
Date of Birth: June 20, 1924
Original Home Address: Sharecropper's shack near Kingston, Texas
Present Address: Arlington National Cemetery, Virginia

1928–42: COTTON CHOPPER, HEAD OF HOUSEHOLD

Hit the fields—picking cotton barefoot at age five. Great Depression in full swing. Shot rabbits and squirrels and other small game to feed family. Good at school, but didn't go much; needed at home to keep everyone else fed and such. Worked hard, often went to bed hungry.

1942: U.S. MARINES

Got sent home. Said I was too young at 17, and too short at five feet seven inches.

1942: ARMY PARATROOPERS

Sent home the first day. Same reason as the Marines.

1942–45: REGULAR ARMY INFANTRY

Successfully enlisted in Greenville, Texas, when I turned 18. Got off to a shaky start. Passed out during my first basic training close-quarters drill at Camp Wolter. Superiors didn't want to send me overseas; didn't think I could handle it. But I finally talked them into it.

Highlights:

- Received advanced training at Fort Meade, Maryland.
- Fought for assignment to North Africa (Company B, 15th Infantry Regiment, 3rd Infantry Division).

• Killed a total of 240 enemy soldiers single-handedly throughout service.

• Received battlefield promotion to second lieutenant.

• Became the most-decorated combat soldier of World War II. Won every single medal that the United States could give a soldier for valor, including: Distinguished Service Cross, Silver Star, Legion of Merit, Bronze Star, Purple Heart, U.S. Army Outstanding Service Medal, Good Conduct Medal, Distinguished Unit Emblem, American Campaign Medal, European-African-Middle Eastern Campaign Medal, and World War II Victory Medal.

• Received five medals from France and Belgium: French Croix de Guerre with Palm, French Croix de Guerre with Silver Star, French Fourragere (in colors of the Croix de Guerre), French Legion of Honor (Grade of Chevalier), and Belgian Croix de Guerre (1940 Palm).

• Awarded the Medal of Honor for fighting near Holtzwihr, France. Wounded in action, but managed to kill or wound 50 German soldiers in less than 30 minutes. It was called a "one-man stand." The French erected a small memorial to me as the soldier who best exemplified the courage, valor, and sacrifice that Americans soldiers had made there.

1945–49: STRUGGLING ACTOR, WRITER

• James Cagney saw my picture in *Life* magazine; invited me to Hollywood. Moved out there, went to audition after audition. After a few years, landed some bit parts. In 1949, got a starring role in a movie called *Bad Boy*, a juvenile-delinquent drama.

• While waiting for my big break, I wrote *To Hell and Back*, the story of my own personal war experience. Also wrote poetry and song lyrics.

1950–69: HOLLYWOOD STAR

• Made 45 films, mostly Westerns: played Billy the Kid in *The Kid from Texas*, Jesse James in *Kansas Raiders*, Tom Destry in *Destry* (a remake of *Destry Rides Again*).

• In 1955, starred as myself in the movie version of *To Hell and*

Professional boxing brothers Leon and Michael Spinks both served in the Marines.

Back, Universal Studios' highest-grossing film until *Jaws* was released 20 years later.

• In 1958, played "the American" in *The Quiet American.*

• In 1960, was third-billed (after Burt Lancaster and Audrey Hepburn) in *The Unforgiven.*

• Came full circle in 1969; played Jesse James again in my last film, *A Time for Dying.*

1959–71: BUSINESSMAN, GAMBLER

Made more than $3 million making movies; invested a lot of it. Owned ranches, bought Thoroughbred horses, played high-stakes poker. In 1971 on a business trip, my private plane crashed into a mountain. I was 46.

POSTHUMOUS HONORS

Of the many memorials to me in Texas, the citizens of Farmesville dedicated one right in the middle of town. The inscription reads:

> In Memory of
> Audie L. Murphy
> 1924–1971
>
> And all American men and women of all races and creeds—military and civilians—who have loyally and proudly served this nation in times of war and peace. To their courageous sacrifices and their unselfish devotion to duty without regard to personal preference or safety, we owe our liberty and our right to the pursuit of happiness.
>
> "Greater love hath no man than this that a man lay down his life for his friends." St. John 15:13

In 1999 then-governor George W. Bush proclaimed June 20 to be Audie Murphy Day in Texas.

SEA CHANGE

Five minutes during the Battle of Midway changed control of the Pacific, the course of World War II, and the fate of the world.

THE EMPEROR'S EMPIRE

After the attack on Pearl Harbor, Japan conquered the American-governed islands of Guam, Wake, and the Philippines. They'd also taken control of the British colonies of Hong Kong, Borneo, Malaya, and the Dutch East Indies. In just a few months, Japan had established an empire in the Pacific.

To protect that empire, Admiral Isoroku Yamamoto, commander in chief of the Japanese fleet, knew he'd have to finish off the Americans. His plan centered on a surprise attack at the U.S. base at Midway, a group of tiny islands about 1,000 miles west of Hawaii. If Yamamoto's plan succeeded, the Japanese would destroy the U.S. Pacific Fleet and gain a base from which to take Hawaii and raid America's West Coast. Instead, during five minutes of a battle that lasted days, the American forces turned the tables. They so damaged Japan's naval air power that the Japanese never launched another offensive operation and eventually lost the war. What led to those decisive five minutes that changed history?

DOWN IN THE DUNGEON

Admiral Yamamoto planned a diversionary strike on the U.S. base in the Aleutian Islands near Alaska on June 3, 1942. Then, while the U.S. Navy sped to Alaska, Vice Admiral Chuichi Nagumo (who'd led the bombing on Pearl Harbor) would stage a surprise air attack on Midway on June 4. That same day, Vice Admiral Nobutake Kondo would bring in a landing force to invade the base. When the U.S. ships turned away from Alaska and came back to defend Midway, Yamamoto's battleships would ambush them.

Unfortunately for Japan, its naval officers weren't the only ones studying the daring plan. The first stage of the Battle of Midway took place in "the dungeon"—a basement of the Old Administration Building in Pearl Harbor. It was here that the U.S. Combat Intelligence Unit, known as Station Hypo, studied Japan's naval

...It was once commanded by General George S. Patton.

radio transmissions and worked on breaking "JN-25"—the cryptanalysts' name for the Japanese navy's code.

JN-25 consisted of 45,000 five-digit numbers, each representing a code word or phrase. To make JN-25 harder to crack, each word was enciphered with added random numbers. Hypo's team used mathematical equations to separate the coded words from the random numbers. There were no computers in 1942, so every coded message was entered on punch cards and fed into IBM tabulators that kept track of each "word" (or set of numbers) so that the cryptanalysts could find matching numbers and patterns of numbers within the messages. It was slow, painstaking work, but by April 1942, Hypo had decoded quite a bit of JN-25.

SURPRISE, SURPRISE

Usually, the Japanese changed their code every month, but in May, Japan's new codebooks were delayed and Hypo was able to read a flurry of radio communications about an invasion of "AF." As head of Hypo, Lieutenant Commander Joseph Rochefort studied thousands of Japanese radio messages. He guessed that "AF" was Midway, but to test his theory, Rochefort asked Midway to radio Pearl Harbor with an uncoded message about problems at the desalination plant that provided the island with fresh water. Soon after, Hypo intercepted Japanese radio messages relaying the news that "AF" was short of water. Bingo!

Hypo worked day and night to decode messages with details about the coming invasion. By May 27, they were able to tell the head of the U.S. Pacific Fleet, Admiral Chester Nimitz, that Japan's first attack would come in the Aleutians on June 3, but most of the enemy fleet would be heading to Midway from the northwest to strike on June 4. Hypo gave Nimitz the order of Yamamoto's battle plan, and explained how his fleet would be divided. One day after transmitting the battle details, the Japanese changed their code, but the damage had been done. Before the fighting even started, U.S. intelligence had scored the first victory. When the Japanese got to Midway, they would be the ones who were surprised.

THE UNDERDOG

Knowing where and when an attack would take place was an

At age 23, George Armstrong Custer was the youngest general in the Union army.

advantage, but that didn't help with the scarcity of ships and planes. Nimitz had two aircraft-carrier task forces for Midway's defense: one led by Admiral Raymond Spruance, the other by Admiral Frank Jack Fletcher. Spruance's task force had two carriers, the *Hornet* and the *Enterprise*. But Fletcher had no carriers at all. Technically, he commanded the *Yorktown*, but she was too damaged to go to battle. Nimitz ordered about 1,300 men to work on the *Yorktown* around the clock so that three aircraft carriers would be available for Midway. They would be supported by eight cruisers and 15 destroyers.

Yamamoto had a big advantage here. Along with his landing force, he had four large and two light aircraft carriers, 21 cruisers, 11 battleships, and 53 destroyers. Besides that, Japan's Zero fighter aircraft were faster and more maneuverable than any American planes, and their pilots were more skilled and experienced.

Nimitz prepared Midway for the onslaught by sending antiaircraft guns, tanks, and extra planes. While new bunkers and beach fortifications were being built, Nimitz pressed his one advantage—information. Admirals Fletcher and Spruance rendezvoused about 325 miles east of Midway at a spot called Point Luck because Hypo believed that would put them near the approaching Japanese. Nimitz gave his two admirals a simple battle plan: ambush the enemy carriers.

ZEROS HOUR

At about 9:00 a.m. on June 3, a patrol plane from Midway spotted a large flotilla of Japanese ships 700 miles away. Three hours later, nine B-17s left Midway and flew out to bomb what would turn out to be the Japanese landing force. The Japanese ships zigzagged to avoid the bombs. They knew that the B-17s came from Midway, but they still had no idea that the carriers were nearby.

On June 4, at 4:30 a.m., Vice Admiral Nagumo launched 100 planes from his four carriers—*Kaga*, *Akagi*, *Hiryu*, and *Soryu*—expecting the Americans to be asleep. Instead, 50 of Midway's planes were already in the air to intercept the Japanese. Outnumbered and outmaneuvered by the Zeros, many American planes were shot down. They managed to slow but not stop the Japanese. The Japanese bombs and bullets that hit the island started fires in oil tanks and damaged buildings, but didn't disable the airfield.

At about 7:00 a.m., Nagumo got word from his pilots that Midway would need to be attacked again. This was the first unraveling of Yamamoto's plan. The surprise strike could have decimated Midway—just like Pearl Harbor—but in this case, the Americans hadn't been surprised, and their base was still operational.

DECISIONS, DECISIONS

Half of Nagumo's planes hadn't gone out on attack and were still on the carriers. They were loaded with torpedoes, ready to strike any U.S. ships that might be in the area. A second attack on Midway meant that the torpedoes that had been set aside for use against ships would have to be replaced with land bombs.

While Nagumo was weighing his options, his fleet was attacked by U.S. bombers from Midway. Although their bombs didn't do a lot of damage, Nagumo decided that he wanted Midway finished off. He ordered the planes reloaded with land bombs; the crews scrambled to follow his orders. But when a Japanese scout plane spotted the *Yorktown*, Nagumo reversed his decision and the crews rushed to undo everything they'd just done. Now Nagumo's planes were rearmed with torpedoes, ready to destroy the *Yorktown* before she could attack.

Ready? Well, not quite. Nagumo had to make one more tough decision. The pilots returning from the attack on Midway were low on fuel and would have to ditch in the water if they couldn't land on the carriers, so Nagumo delayed the attack on the *Yorktown* to let his pilots land. It was a good decision, but the wrong one at the time. How could Nagumo know that planes from the *Yorktown*, *Hornet*, and *Enterprise* were headed right for him?

THE WINNING NUMBER IS ZERO

The American plan was for a coordinated air assault. Fighter planes would escort low-level torpedo bombers and high-level dive-bombers that together would overwhelm the enemy. But communication between units was poor, the Pacific was vast, and the skies were cloudy. American squadrons got separated and some squadron leaders, like the *Enterprise*'s Lieutenant Commander Clarence Wade McClusky, and the *Yorktown*'s Lieutenant Commander Maxwell Leslie, simply got lost.

At 9:15, while the Japanese were still rearming, torpedo

bombers from the *Hornet* found the enemy. With no fighter escort, the bombers were an easy target for the Zeros; by 9:30 all but one bomber was shot down. Almost as soon as the *Hornet*'s planes were overpowered, torpedo bombers from the *Yorktown* attacked, but the Zeros got them, too. By 10:24 the Japanese had defeated every attack the Americans had thrown at them. His planes finally ready, Nagumo prepared to destroy the *Yorktown* and any other American ships in the area.

SHOT WITH LUCK

About a minute later, the previously lost Lieutenant McClusky and his squadron of dive-bombers found the Japanese carrier fleet. And, to their surprise, they had a clear shot. The Zeros had been concentrating on low-flying torpedo planes, so they were far below McClusky's high-flying squad. Just as McClusky swooped in to hit the *Kaga*, Lieutenant Leslie's dive-bomber squadron from the *Yorktown* also found the enemy.

It was pure accident that McClusky and Leslie launched a perfect attack at the right time. Not only did they squarely hit the *Kaga*, *Akagi*, and *Soryu*, but also the decks of the carriers were still filled with planes, fuel lines, and bombs—all of which exploded into flames. As Admiral Spruance would later say, the Americans "were shot with luck." In about five minutes, Japan lost three carriers, the planes on the decks, and most of its best pilots. By 10:30, the Battle of Midway wasn't over, but Japan's ability to protect its empire was.

AFTERMATH

The *Hiryu* escaped the dive-bombers and, a few hours later, its planes crippled the *Yorktown*. Several hours after that, American planes sank the *Hiryu*. On June 5, the Americans also sank two Japanese cruisers; on June 6, a Japanese ship sank the *Yorktown*. Admiral Yamamoto tried but failed to find and destroy the other American carriers. Finally, he retreated.

The Battle of Midway was Japan's first decisive naval defeat in more than 300 years. It never recovered from the loss of its carriers and pilots. After Midway, the Allies took the offensive until Japan was finally defeated.

...replicates the look and instruments of Continental Army musicians of about 1781.

BRASS FACTS

Admiral Nimitz was one of the first high-ranking naval officers to realize the importance of U.S. intelligence. The Battle of Midway marked the beginning of its use to help determine naval strategy.

Admiral Yamamoto tried to destroy the U.S. fleet while it was still weak because he feared Japan could never match the power of America's industry or its ability to mobilize its citizens for war. The admiral believed that after Pearl Harbor, Japan had about six months to "run wild" in the Pacific before the United States regrouped to become the superior force. In fact, America's Midway victory came six months after Pearl Harbor.

* * *

WHICH SERVICE IS BEST?

While waiting outside the Pearly Gates, a soldier, a sailor, an airman, and a Marine get into an argument about which of the armed forces is the best. Saint Peter butts in and tells them to cool it—he'll ask God and get back to them. The next time they see Saint Peter, he's got a letter in his hand, and he reads to them aloud:

FROM: God
TO: Soldiers, sailors, airmen, and Marines
RE: Which service is best

Dear members of the armed forces,

I've been watching and here's what I think. All branches of the United States armed forces are truly honorable, courageous, well trained, and capable.

Therefore, there is no superior service.

Sincerely,
God, USMC (Ret.)

THIS SPUD'S FOR YOU

Who would think that lowly potatoes could save a warship? But that's exactly what happened at the height of World War II.

ASLEEP AT THE WHEEL

On April 5, 1943, the destroyer USS *O'Bannon*, on patrol near the Solomon Islands, was sent to investigate a blip on the radar. The blip turned out to be a Japanese submarine casually floating on the surface. The Japanese sailors, unaware that they had been discovered, were sleeping on the deck—even the lookouts were asleep on their watch.

The Americans were poised to ram the sub, but at the last minute the captain, worried that the sub might be filled with explosives, gave the order to swing the rudder hard to avoid a collision. With the *O'Bannon* so close to the sub, an explosion would have dispatched both vessels at the same time.

A RUDE AWAKENING

When the sleeping sailors opened their eyes, they were startled to find an American warship alongside them. The two ships were so close that the *O'Bannon*'s guns could not be lowered enough to fire upon the sub. For a time no one seemed to know what to do; sailors on both sides just stood and stared at one another.

Suddenly, the spell was broken and the Japanese made for their guns. Unwilling to be sitting ducks, the American sailors looked for something, anything, that could be used as projectiles. What they found were measly potatoes in a nearby storage locker. In a stroke of genius, some sailors reached into the storage bins and started pelting the enemy with the tubers. The Japanese, probably thinking that the potatoes were grenades, busied themselves catching them and throwing them back at the *O'Bannon* or overboard into the water. They were kept so busy battling the potatoes that they had no time to man their guns.

With the enemy occupied, the *O'Bannon* was able to maneuver into a position from which her guns could be used. Several shots were fired and the sub's conning tower—the compartment that houses the periscope—was hit. Nevertheless, the sub was able to

The 1991 Persian Gulf War lasted 42 days, from January 16 to February 27.

get below the surface, but it was too late for the Japanese. The destroyer moved into a position just above the sub and set off a depth charge. The sub was sunk, and the potatoes were credited with the victory.

When the Association of Potato Growers of Maine heard the story of the *O'Bannon*'s exploit, they had a commemorative plaque made, which read:

A TRIBUTE TO
THE OFFICERS AND MEN
OF THE
U.S.S. O'BANNON
FOR THEIR INGENUITY IN
USING OUR NOW PROUD POTATO
TO "SINK" A JAP SUBMARINE
IN THE SPRING OF 1943
PRESENTED BY
POTATO GROWERS
OF THE STATE OF MAINE
JUNE 14, 1945

The plaque was awarded to the *O'Bannon*, where it was proudly displayed near the mess hall—where the sailors thereafter put the spuds to more peaceful (and hopefully more delicious!) purposes. It was perhaps the only time in history that a potato was credited with winning a naval encounter.

* * *

PRESIDENTS WOUNDED IN COMBAT

During his time with the 23rd Ohio Volunteer Infantry Regiment in the Civil War, Rutherford B. Hayes was wounded four times! He returned to battle after each injury and was fighting Confederate troops in Virginia when the war ended. John F. Kennedy exacerbated an existing back problem while rescuing a fellow crewman when his torpedo boat was rammed by a Japanese destroyer during World War II.

The MQ-1 Predator, an unmanned recon plane, can fire two laser-guided Hellfire missiles.

HERSHEY GOES TO WAR

The Hershey Corporation supplied World War I doughboys with milk chocolate bars, but it wasn't until World War II that the Hershey bar officially became known as "the GI's chocolate bar."

BETTER THAN A BOILED POTATO

In 1937 the U.S. military began quietly preparing for a war they believed they would eventually enter. One of the preparations was a meeting of Army Quartermaster Captain Paul Logan, Hershey Chocolate Corporation president William Murrie, and Hershey's chief chemist, Sam Hinkle. Captain Logan had four simple requirements for what was originally known as the "Logan Bar":

1. It should weigh 4 ounces.
2. It should be able to withstand high temperatures.
3. It should have 600 calories.
4. It could serve as a starvation ration.

The Army wanted the soldiers to save the candy bars as an emergency ration, so, in Logan's words, "They should taste just a little better than a boiled potato."

TESTING, TESTING

In June 1937, the Hershey Corporation produced a test batch of the new Logan Bar. The thick paste made of chocolate liquor, sugar, oat flour, powdered milk, and vitamins was "like clay when we got it from the mixing room," according to a production worker. Each bar was made by pressing the chocolate clay into the molds by hand. It took three weeks to produce 90,000 bars. The bars were then tested at military posts in the Philippines, Hawaii, Panama, and at the Texas border. Some were even sent with Admiral Richard Byrd to Antarctica in 1939. When it became apparent that the Logan Bar would withstand extreme climates, the Army quartermaster awarded the Hershey Corporation a contract to manufacture their new chocolate bar.

NEW AND IMPROVED

In the years leading up to America's entry into World War II, some changes were made to the Logan Bar. First, it was renamed Field Ration D. In anticipation of tropical warfare, Hershey added thiamine to prevent beriberi. The company also developed packaging to keep the bar dry even after it was submerged in water for one hour: first, individual bars were encased in cellophane and heat-sealed, then each bar was placed in a cardboard carton, the ends glued, and the entire box dipped in wax.

Automated machinery speeded up production, but employees occasionally had to stop the production line to dig the extra-thick chocolate paste out of the molds and the machinery. The new and improved machinery raised production to 100,000 bars a day and, by war's end, to 3.4 million a day. Production of Field Ration D took up three factory floors operating seven days a week, 24 hours a day.

HERSHEY BAR II

In 1943 the Army requested a heat-resistant bar with improved flavor, so Field Ration D was followed up by the Hershey's Tropical Bar, in one- and two-ounce sizes, providing America's armed forces—and many of the civilians they met—with a much-needed chocolate high. And it tasted like a real candy bar.

OVER ONE BILLION SERVED

By war's end Hershey had supplied the military with over one billion Field Ration D bars. They were including three bars in one package as a daily ration of 1,800 calories and providing the military with tins of cocoa. With approximately 70 percent of Hershey's production going directly to military personnel, enjoying Hershey's chocolate in any form was a rare thing for most civilians.

For their achievements, the Hershey Corporation received five Army-Navy E Production Awards for excellence, more than any other military supplier with the exception of Bausch & Lomb, which received six awards (for supplying three million pounds of optical glass, binoculars, periscopes, and gas masks—not to mention General Douglas MacArthur's signature Ray-Bans).

Hershey received its first award after less than a year of full-scale production of the Field Ration D: an E flag to fly above the factory and a gold-toned E lapel pin for each employee. Already in his 80s and less active in the day-to-day operations of the company, founder Milton Hershey called the company's military work "the finest thing I have ever seen accomplished here."

THE DESERT BAR DIVE-BOMBS

Hershey continued making the military bars developed for World War II into the 1970s. In 1971 its Tropical Bar went to the Moon with the astronauts of *Apollo 15*. In the 1990s, with war in the Persian Gulf approaching, the company developed a new ration bar code-named the Desert Bar. It tasted more like the original Hershey's chocolate bar and was heat-resistant up to 140 degrees. Instead of liquefying in heat, it turned "soft and fudgy." In late 1990 and early 1991, the company shipped almost one million one-ounce Desert Bars to soldiers free of charge. Borrowing from the slogan for M&Ms, which are made by their competitor the Mars Company, Hershey called the Desert Bar "a candy bar that melts in your mouth, not in the sand."

But Mars had the final laugh. In August 1991 the military awarded a contract to Mars for 6.9 million heat-resistant M&Ms and Galaxy Block Chocolate. Hershey's Desert Bars were left in the dust . . . or was it the sand?

* * *

PX, I LOVE YOU

The PX (for Post eXchange) system dates back to July 1895 when the War Department directed Army post commanders to establish an exchange (a kind of general store for soldiers) at every post where possible. The first documented PX was at Fort McKinley in the Philippines in the early 1900s.

The Army's PX is the Air Force's BX (for Base eXchange), the Navy has its NEX (for Navy EXchange), and the Marine Corps Exchange is abbreviated MCX. All of them are run by or with the Army & Air Force Exchange Service (AAFES) out of the Department of Defense. The AAFES entered the consumer age with a vengeance: Today their retail stores, catalogs, and online store offer everything a military man or woman could want, from a double caramel latte at a Starbucks counter to a brand-new Jeep Grand Cherokee. And if you're not happy with the merchandise, there's even a virtual complaint department for disgruntled customers.

...by the Civil War's end, 180,000 black men made up 10 percent of the Union army.

ON SILENT WINGS

The valiant glider pilots will not be forgotten. On October 19, 2002, the Silent Wings Museum opened its doors at Lubbock International Airport (formerly South Plains Army Airfield) in Texas.

G IS FOR GLIDER

An Army Air Forces uniform sporting silver wings with a "G" for "glider" was a one-time phenomenon during World War II. These tough, independent men flew fragile craft—"throwaways" constructed of metal, wood, and fabric—that had no engine. When tow planes "snatched" the glider into the air, one veteran pilot described it as being "violently bounced on the end of a nylon rope 350 feet back of the tow plane." Once released near the landing area, glider pilots hedgehopped in at treetop level to deliver soldiers or equipment on silent wings while bullets often ripped through the fabric. "It was like flying a stick of dynamite through the gates of hell," the pilot said. No wonder these men, all volunteers who dared to fly with no engine, no parachute, and no second chance, claimed the "G" stood for "guts."

WHY GLIDERS?

Germany turned to gliders after the Versailles treaty in 1919 forbade their building motorized airplanes. By 1922 Germany had constructed the first true sailplane, and until the early 1930s, all gliding records were held by Germany and Austria. Although the U.S. Army experimented with gliders in 1923 and the Navy in 1930, both programs were abandoned long before World War II. Since the United States had concentrated on the development of powered aircraft, the Soaring Society of America, a recreational group, wasn't established until 1932.

To fly without power, gliders use air mass currents for lift. While soaring, the glider can travel a surprisingly long distance. When gliding, it descends on an inclined path toward the ground. Unlike paratroops spread over a large drop zone, glider pilots could make a silent, concentrated landing in the target zone. The pilots were expected to maneuver their craft as close as possible to an open space near the front lines that was often mined or under fire.

When Germany's secretly rebuilt air force attacked Belgium, the Netherlands, and Luxembourg in 1940, transport planes towed glider trains, with each glider carrying six soldiers apiece. A year later, General Henry H. "Hap" Arnold and the United States War Department created the American Glider Program.

GLIDER PILOT TRAINING

Early gliders used for training were off-the-shelf commercial sailplanes and training pilots to fly them at Twentynine Palms in California was a problem. There were few experienced instructors among the volunteers, and many trainees were enlisted men with no flying experience or washouts from powered airplane pilot programs. The first class only graduated six students. General Arnold upped the number, six other states offered their airfields, and by early 1942, over 6,000 glider pilots had earned their "G" wings.

MILITARY GLIDERS

Manufacturers, including piano companies and casket factories, that had the necessary material, joined the effort and began turning out military gliders. By late 1944, over 14,000 had been built. Military gliders came in a variety of models: combat assault and bomb gliders, cargo gliders for carrying troops or equipment, and training gliders, built from 1941 to 1948. The Waco cargo glider was the most widely used by American glider pilots.

In July 1943, gliders participated in the first Allied airborne invasion in Sicily. Two-man crews ferried combat-equipped troops, jeeps, or armament to the front lines from D-day to March 24, 1945, when Operation Varsity at Wesel, Germany, was the last glider mission in the European theater. A total of 1,348 American and British gliders participated in the Rhine River crossing.

Glider pilots, along with airborne forces, were part of all major invasions behind enemy lines. They also served in Luzon, the Philippines, and Burma. By the end of World War II, 221 glider pilots had been killed in action and 151 more in training or other noncombat operations. During the Korean War, military gliders were replaced by helicopters, which could not only extract soldiers but dropped light tanks by parachute. Although the U.S. Air Force continues to train cadets in sailplanes, the Defense Department ended the glider pilot program in 1952.

In 1780 West Point—as a military fort—was under the command of Benedict Arnold.

SGT. ROCK

World War II produced plenty of real-life heroes to inspire future generations, but Sgt. Rock is possibly the most recognizable and admired comic-book soldier to emerge from the conflict.

THE MAKING OF A WAR HERO

When Frank Rock made his first appearance (as simply "the Rock") in DC Comics' *G.I. Combat* #68 in January 1959, hardly anyone thought he'd grab enough attention to become the most popular World War II character in the history of comic books. Even in his second appearance a few months later in DC's *Our Army at War* #81, the details of his identity were still to be fleshed out; he was called "Sgt. Rocky" in that story. Finally, in the next issue of *Our Army at War*, Sgt. Rock's name was established for good, and the details of his life would gradually be revealed over the course of the next three decades, until the July 1988 publication of the final issue of *Sgt. Rock* (the title of *Our Army at War* was changed to reflect Sgt. Rock's popularity in 1977). Rock has appeared in other comic books and graphic novels since 1988, but they weren't written by Robert Kanigher, who created the original *Sgt. Rock* stories.

TOUGH ENOUGH

Frank Rock was the quintessential World War II hero: he grew up in Pittsburgh, where he worked at a steel mill; enlisted in the Army as a private following the attack on Pearl Harbor; rose rapidly through the ranks to become a sergeant; and led the men of Easy Company through numerous confrontations with the Axis forces, repeatedly putting himself through great tests of suffering and endurance to serve his country for the ultimate goal of justice and freedom. He was an expert marksman, a skilled hand-to-hand combatant, and—even though he wasn't a superhero like many comic-book characters of his time—he possessed a remarkable ability to survive gunshot wounds, shrapnel, and exposure to the elements.

His creators, Kanigher and artist Joe Kubert, made no concessions to the growing popularity of superheroes; the only character in the stories who had any sort of superhuman power was the Iron

Paul Newman was disqualified from the Navy's pilot training because he was color-blind.

Major, a Nazi officer with a hand made of iron. Everyone else fought with pure humanity.

THE PERFECT SOLDIER

At a time when the real world was watching the escalation of conflict in Korea, *Sgt. Rock* provided readers of comic books (many of whom would soon be old enough to serve) with the perfect reminder of why the United States needed men of fighting age to join the armed forces and support the cause of democracy. The fact that *Sgt. Rock* continued to do well through the Vietnam era, when the military lost favor with much of the general public, provides some insight into how a war hero was defined at the time.

World War II was perhaps the last major global conflict in which the "good guys" and "bad guys" were clearly identified, and Sgt. Rock—the frontline soldier who did anything, anywhere—espoused the ideals of the good guy in a way that no soldiers of the Cold War era ever could. His heroics earned him several offers of promotion, all of which he turned down; if he were an officer, he'd likely be assigned a position behind the front lines and wouldn't be able to lead his men onto the battlefield.

THE SARGE'S SIDEKICKS

Sgt. Rock's Easy Company was a mixed group that consisted of several regular characters and a large number of anonymous grunts (many of whom would invariably be killed off early in a story for dramatic purposes). Among the regulars were Bulldozer, Sgt. Rock's second in command, a big but not overly bright corporal; Wildman, a former professor who became ferocious in battle; Ice Cream Soldier, who earned his nickname as a private when the veteran members of the unit teased him that he'd melt under fire (he didn't); and Four Eyes, a bespectacled sharpshooter.

Why all the nicknames? In the 2003 graphic novel *Between Hell and a Hard Place*, written by Brian Azzarello and illustrated by the aforementioned Joe Kubert, Sgt. Rock explains that the nicknames are needed on the battlefield because the men may have to do things that would be unthinkable back home, so when they returned to civilian life after the war, they'd be able to leave their assumed identities behind.

In the attack on Pearl Harbor, 217 planes were destroyed—188 U.S. planes...

MAKING STATEMENTS WITH COMICS

One groundbreaking member of Easy Company was Jackie Johnson, an African American infantryman who was a former world heavyweight boxing champion. He made his first appearance in *Sgt. Rock* in 1961, at a time when the civil rights movement was near its boiling point. In the story, Jackie and Wildman, both injured, rely on each other to escape the Nazis and reunite with Easy Company. Jackie returned to Easy Company as a regular character in 1965. DC Comics was well aware that units weren't integrated at the company level during World War II, but Kanigher and Kubert had no qualms about using their comic books as a social platform, and, according to Kubert, the inclusion of Jackie Johnson as one of the first nonstereotypical black characters in a comic book generated a lot of positive feedback from readers.

THE REAL WORLD

Sgt. Rock wasn't alone in using the medium to make social commentaries, nor was it the first. While war-themed comic books published during World War II tended to show superheroes such as Captain America helping the Allied cause, the comic books of the 1950s were more rooted in reality, showing the darker side of war and human suffering. One historian, William Savage Jr. of the University of Oklahoma, suggests that, with the war still fresh in their minds when the Korean War broke out, World War II participants in the comic-book industry wanted to show the world what war was really like. According to Savage, the comic books of the 1950s can be considered the only antiwar literature at the time, before the Vietnam years ushered in a new age of free speech. In 1971, after the court-martial of the officers responsible for the My Lai massacre in Vietnam, Kanigher wrote a Sgt. Rock story called "Head Count" for *Our Army at War* #233, which dealt with a similar atrocity in a World War II setting. The story's conclusion leaves it to the reader to decide whether the GI is a hero or a murderer, and also shows a seal that was seen in other DC Comics titles at the time: "Make war no more."

ROCK, ROCK, AND MORE ROCK

Sgt. Rock continued to be in high demand, even after Kanigher's death in 2002. Over the years, Sgt. Rock has appeared in other

DC Comics releases, including *The Brave and the Bold* (in which he met Bruce Wayne, a.k.a. Batman) and *Swamp Thing*, as well as several recent graphic novels. Called "crossovers," these appearances have created some contradictions regarding Sgt. Rock's ultimate fate. In some storylines, he's said to have become a general; in others, he is seen at the Tomb of the Unknowns in Arlington National Cemetery after the conclusion of the war.

According to Kanigher, Sgt. Rock and Easy Company didn't survive the closing days of the war (although he never wrote a story about it). But comic-book readers are accustomed to seeing characters killed off in one story and then revived in another. As an iconic hero of a war in which American patriotism reached new heights, Sgt. Rock stands little chance of ever being written off for good.

* * *

NAME, RANK, SERIAL NUMBER

Anyone who's ever watched a war movie is familiar with the prisoner of war who stoically invokes the Geneva convention and refuses to give anything but his name, rank, and serial number. But there's more to the rules of war than that. First, the Geneva convention is actually the Geneva conventions.

The first Geneva convention was held in 1864, the result of Swiss citizen Henry Dunant's horror after witnessing the War of Italian Unification in 1859 and then founding the International Committee of the Red Cross. Additions were made over two dozen times, the most recent being the Protocol of Explosive Remnants of War in 2003. Although we usually associate the Geneva conventions with rules of conduct regarding prisoners of war, they cover many other aspects. The rights, behavior, and protection of fighting soldiers, wounded soldiers, those shipwrecked at sea, medical personnel, clergy, spies, civilian journalists, civilians, and children under age 15 are all outlined as well as rules governing the use of some types of warfare such as nuclear weapons, terrorism, and biological weapons. With 194 nations accepting the rules, the Geneva conventions have gained universal acceptance. Sadly, despite official agreement, many nations ignore certain sections of the Geneva conventions.

WATCH YOUR STEP!

A short history of land mines and what's being done to get rid of them.

DEADLY HISTORY

The Chinese invented gunpowder and fireworks, so it is not surprising that they were the first to use land mines in the late 13th century. Europe caught on by the early 16th century, using their first explosive mines to defend city and fortress walls under siege. During the American Civil War, Confederate forces laid thousands of "land torpedoes" around key Southern cities like Richmond, Charleston, and Savannah. (In fact, five were discovered, still live, near Mobile, Alabama, in 1960.)

All major participants of World War I used them. It was during major wars like the two World Wars that land mine locations were documented so that the mines could be removed when peace came. But regional insurrections and civil wars since 1945 have changed all that. The ease of manufacture and low cost of land mines make them attractive weapons—and laying them takes almost no skill.

NAVIGATING THE MINEFIELDS

In 1995 the United Nations estimated that there were 110 million land mines in 64 countries; about 10,000 people a year, mostly civilians, are killed by them and countless thousands are severely injured, usually in countries that are at peace.

In 1997 more than 100 countries signed a global treaty opposing the use of antipersonnel mines. By 2007, only one country, Myanmar, was reported to be using them, as were nonstate groups like FARC in Colombia, Sri Lanka's Tamil Tigers, and Somali rebels. Nevertheless, a few countries—notably the United States, China, and Russia—still reserve the right to use them if they choose. And millions of mines are warehoused worldwide, many simply waiting for the highest bidder.

Unexploded mines not only endanger life and limb; in agricultural areas, they bring farming to a dead stop, which in poor countries can lead to famine. Poor countries have two other problems: They can't afford medical assistance for land mine victims, nor can

The U.S. was part of the eight-nation alliance against China in the Boxer Rebellion.

they afford the cost of demining their countrysides, which can cost up to $1,000 per mine.

In some countries—Vietnam among them—mines planted more than 30 years ago are still killing or injuring people. Unexploded but live ordnance, including mines, are still being turned up by archaeologists and military historians excavating World War I and II battle sites.

A NOT-SO-SIMPLE SYSTEM

Mine clearance is specialized, labor intensive, time consuming, and always dangerous. By the end of 2006, the U.S. Department of Defense had developed the Handheld Standoff Mine Detection System, which can differentiate between mines and detritus, thus accelerating the clearance process by more than 600 percent. Unfortunately, except for a modest international aid program, this equipment is used primarily by military personnel. Not only is the equipment too expensive for poor countries—and those with the highest density of land mines are among the poorest of the poor—but effective use of the system requires considerable training.

The United States has been providing training to civilian organizations in Cambodia, Afghanistan, Thailand, and Angola since 2006. As effective as these devices are, they're not enough. That's where other techniques come in.

SNOUTS AND ALL

Dogs have been used to sniff out mines since the 1970s. Today, more than 200 are in use in Afghanistan. But dog training takes a long time, and retraining is often required, so land mine hunters are trying other, more efficient critters.

The Mozambiquans use the Gambian giant pouched rat, which, at six pounds, is too light to detonate a mine if it steps on one. It's easier to train than a dog and, best of all, is native to Mozambique. Formerly a scourge, the rat is now a lifesaver. It is trained to associate the smell of explosives with food; the rat covers far more ground in a day than does a human with a metal detector.

In Sri Lanka, mongooses are attached to a remote-controlled robot that enables the operator to direct the mongoose from a safe distance. As with the pouch rat, they are trained to respond to the odors of explosives.

The World War I song "Keep the Home Fires Burning" was written by Ivor Noello...

In Israel, experiments are under way using boars to sniff out mines. The pigs can be trained twice as quickly as dogs and stay more focused on the job, probably because food is their primary interest.

THE TINIEST HUNTERS

Bees are being studied, too, the theory being that bees can be conditioned to associate explosives with food, and can then be tracked as they go about gathering pollen. When they return to their hives, the dust sticking to them can be analyzed for trace explosive components that leached into the soil.

Another experimental approach is blanketing an area with a microorganism (bacteria) that fluoresces when it comes in contact with vapors from explosives.

THE BOTTOM LINE

When a mine is located, it still has to be detonated or disarmed, a process that requires extensive training in the hundreds of configurations of land mines. Most demining experts have been trained in military branches of engineering or ordnance corps, but in recent years, aid agencies have begun their own training programs. Still, most agree that the problem will probably require decades to clean up.

* * *

GAS ATTACK

Gas warfare was first used in World War I, with as many as 17 different kinds of gases tried out by both sides. There were three kinds of gases, of which only the lachrymator (tear gases, from the Latin *lachrima*, "tear") were combatible by gas mask. The other two varieties included asphyxiant, or poisonous, gases such as chlorine, and the dreaded blistering gases, such as mustard gas, which produced burns on contact. A contemporary news report of the use of poison gas:

> "[The] vapor settled to the ground like a swamp mist and drifted toward the French trenches on a brisk wind. Its effect on the French was a violent nausea and faintness, followed by an utter collapse. [The] Germans, who charged in behind the vapor, met no resistance at all." *New York Tribune*, April 27, 1915

AMERICAN FLYERS IN THE ROYAL AIR FORCE

America mourned its first World War II casualty on August 17, 1940. No, that isn't a typo Uncle John missed. Pilot Officer William M. L. Fiske died after being burned when his airplane was hit almost 16 months before the Japanese attack on Pearl Harbor.

RECRUITMENT IN ENGLAND

Most Americans listened to Edward R. Murrow's rooftop radio reports about Germany's relentless bombing of England's fighter airfields, radar stations, aircraft factories, and London neighborhoods during the summer and fall of 1940. But, along with Fiske, nine other American flyers flew during the Battle of Britain as members of England's Royal Air Force (RAF). By the war's end, over 200 American men had served with the RAF and over 8,000 with the Royal Canadian Air Force. How did these men end up flying for his majesty's air force instead of the U.S. Army Air Forces (AAF)?

As they saw how swiftly neighboring countries fell to Hitler's troops, many Londoners realized that they needed all the help they could get to protect their vulnerable island. Charles Sweeney, an American millionaire living in London, quietly began to recruit American pilots to fight for the Allies.

Originally he began to recruit pilots to help protect Finland from the Soviets, until Finland fell in early 1940. Next, the French Armee del l'Air received his attention. But in June, when the French signed an armistice with the Nazis, Sweeney began sending pilots to the England. RAF Squadron No. 609, which fought in the Battle of Britain, included Sweeney's American recruits Vernon C. Keough, Andrew Mamedoff, and Eugene Q. Tobin.

FLYERS FROM CANADA

Some Americans realized that the United States would eventually enter the war and wanted to avoid years of service as infantrymen. Flying seemed a better alternative—if you could get into the training program. Even men who already knew how to fly couldn't always meet the Army Air Force's strict requirements for the pilot program: two years of college and 20/20 vision.

The RAF offered a less stringent option: no college and 20/40 vision if it could be corrected to 20/20. The RAF also required that volunteers be single, and have a birth certificate, high school diploma, pilot's license, and 300 flying hours. The RAF was so desperate for pilots that even these requirements (especially the number of flight hours) could be embellished and go unchallenged by RAF officers.

American pilots made their way to Canada, talked their way into the Royal Canadian Air Force (RCAF), and eventually into transfers to the RAF and overseas combat. William Dunn had already been denied a transfer to flight school because he had no college education when he was in the U.S. Army in the late 1930s. He left the Army and, after 160 hours of flying time, went to Canada in late 1939 to enlist in the Seaforth Highlanders. He received advanced training in Hurricanes and, despite lacking the college education the Army Air Force required, went on to become the first American ace—flying with the RAF.

KNIGHT COMMITTEE

One small group of World War I veterans decided not to sit by quietly hoping Americans would come to the aid of Britain even though the United States wasn't in the war yet. Just one day after Great Britain and France entered the war, Air Vice Marshall William Bishop of the Royal Canadian Air Force contacted two friends who had flown with him during World War I. Both Clayton Knight, an American author and illustrator, and Homer Smith, a wealthy Canadian, agreed to quietly reach out to American pilots to train Canadian pilots and fly in combat even though it violated the American Neutrality Acts. In the beginning the Knight Committee invited pilots and aviation technicians to local hotels, asked their feelings about the war, and—if they seemed open to the hypothetical idea of aiding Canada and England—gave them money for a "vacation" to Canada. Of course, their indefinite vacation consisted of instructing other pilots, learning how to fly English fighter planes, or caring for RCAF planes.

Recruitment by the Knight Committee became more open after

the fall of France. Refresher schools were opened for future RCAF pilots in the United States and the Knight Committee even had a recruiting booth at Alabama's Maxwell Field to sign up AAF washouts. By the fall of 1941, 50,000 Americans had applied and 6,700 were accepted by the RCAF. When Great Britain's RAF eventually formed squadrons made up solely of Americans, 80 percent of the flyers came to the Eagle Squadrons through the Knight Committee.

EAGLE SQUADRONS

By the summer of 1940, the RAF had welcomed dozens of American pilots, but the idea of forming strictly American squadrons within the RAF was rejected. The air minister found the Americans "loud and unruly." He was certain the behavior of these American squadrons would be unbearable. Prime Minister Winston Churchill had another viewpoint. These American squadrons were just the PR he needed to help encourage the Americans to support Britain against invasion. Between September 1940 and October 1941, three American squadrons, named Eagle Squadrons, were formed within the RAF. Squadrons No. 71, 121, and 133 initially had English squadron leaders, but Americans eventually took over. Beginning with convoy escort duties before switching to fighter sweeps across France, these "unruly" pilots were credited with 7,312 enemy aircraft destroyed, 12 Distinguished Flying Crosses, and one Distinguished Service Order. Although they normally worked different missions, all three Eagle Squadrons participated in the Dieppe raid of August 19, 1942, which was seen by many as a practice run for the invasion of France at Normandy.

In late autumn 1942, when the Yanks arrived in England, the Eagle Squadrons were transferred to the 8th U.S. Air Force and became the 4th Fighter Group. It wasn't just the uniforms that were changing. Despite promises to keep the units together, the American leaders swiftly transferred most of the original Eagle Squadron members to other units or stateside to train new pilots. Their aircraft were also changed from Spitfires to P-47 Thunderbolts, an aircraft twice as large and more difficult to handle. For many former Eagle Squadron members, joining the AAF was a disappointment.

AN RAF FLYING ACE VIA TEXAS

Not every American pilot traded in his RAF uniform for that of the AAF. British squadron leader Lance C. Wade, a Texas farmer, not only chose to remain with the RAF but became one of their most decorated and successful pilots. When he realized his lack of education would keep him from flying for the AAF, Wade took his pilot's license and 80 hours of flying time to the RAF in December 1940. He spent most of his time in North Africa flying his plane with the memorable nose art of a rooster standing in front of an American flag before returning to the United States in September 1942. It was a busy trip that included not only a visit home but also a meeting with President Franklin D. Roosevelt, a press conference at Rockefeller Center, and an interview with the *New York Times*. The AAF also came calling, promising better rank and pay if he would join, but Wade replied, "Thanks, that's mighty fine, but I'd rather keep stringing along with the guys I have been with so long now."

He returned to North Africa to command Squadron No. 145 before being promoted to wing commander and serving on the staff of Air Vice Marshal Harry Broadhurst, air commander for the RAF's Mediterranean theater. On January 12, 1944, when leaving Italy after visiting his old squadron, Wade's plane went into a spin and crashed; Wade was killed instantly. In his time with the RAF, Wade reached the equivalent of the rank of lieutenant colonel in the AAF, shot down 40 Axis planes (25 confirmed), and was awarded two Distinguished Flying Crosses and a Distinguished Service Order.

* * *

FAMOUS FLYBOY

Actor Jimmy Stewart—that's Major James Maitland Stewart to you—did his bit during Big Week. He flew his B-24 bomber on the Gotha mission, was group leader on Nuremberg, and led the wing to Brunswick, for which he was awarded the Distinguished Flying Cross.

But Jimmy Stewart didn't stop serving when World War II was over. In later years, he joined the Air Force Reserves and flew several missions over Vietnam. He was awarded the Presidential Medal of Freedom in 1985. When he died, Brigadier General James Stewart was buried with full military honors.

...as the heaviest in Britain's military history.

"BRAVO ZULU"

In the modern U.S. Navy, "Bravo Zulu" is an accolade much appreciated by those who serve well. But where did the expression come from?

A LOT OF BULL

An active Navy myth is that Fleet Admiral William "Bull" Halsey Jr. originated the expression "Bravo Zulu" in complimenting the performance of Task Force 38 during combat against Japan in the Pacific when Halsey commanded the U.S. 3rd Fleet during World War II. Halsey was known for his quips and slogans such as "Hit hard, hit fast, hit often" and "Before we're through with 'em, the Japanese language will only be spoken in hell."

But the British navy has its own legends regarding the term's origin. One story is that the expression was improvised as a "well done" signal to HMS *Zulu* for an accomplishment during World War II. Another is that "Bravo Zulu" was a signal flag used in the Royal Navy meaning "Issue an extra tot of rum to the crew."

All three stories are false. "Bravo Zulu" didn't become a naval term until many years later. It began as a system of communication between foreign allied navies that developed after World War II.

FROM "TARE VICTOR GEORGE" TO "BAKER ZEBRA"

The original expression for "well done" in the U.S. Navy before the war was to hoist signal flags indicating "TVG," or "Tare Victor George" in the phonetic alphabet of the Navy used over voice radio at that time. After World War II, "Tare Victor George" evolved into "Baker Zebra." The change came from the Allied Naval Signal Book, known as the ACP 175 series, adopted after the North Atlantic Treaty Organization was founded in 1949. Wartime experiences convinced commanders that a uniform system of communication involving signal flags was necessary to ease communications when so many foreign languages were involved among allied navies working together.

ACP 175 codified visual flag signals between ships. Signals with the letter "B" coming first indicated administrative signals. Flags with "BZ," the last of a series of administrative codes, represented "well done"—or, expressed orally, "Baker Zebra."

U.S. Navy submarines are either ballistic (carrying missiles) or attack submarines.

In the 1950s, the International Civil Aviation Organization (ICAO) adopted English as the international language for air traffic control. Some expressions taken from the ACP 175 series were difficult to say for some foreign pilots and controllers. One of them was "Baker Zebra." Thus, the ICAO devised a more "pronounceable" signal code using a new radio alphabet beginning with "Alpha, Bravo, Charlie, Delta," and so on. In 1956 the Navy realized the benefit of the new command code and adopted it. As a result, "Baker Zebra" became "Bravo Zulu." Well done!

MAKE THAT A NEGAT!

Over the years, "Bravo Zulu" has become a colloquialism for anything done right. Some opera buffs, however, bristle in thinking the Navy and ICAO have co-opted the term from the Italian *bravo*, meaning "brave, skillful, clever, and/or bold" and heard for centuries in the form of applause for great performances. Naturally, not everything is praiseworthy, so today there is an expression for "not so well done"—"Negat Bravo Zulu."

* * *

THE ACADEMY RING

The official class ring that Navy midshipmen wear contains the United States Naval Academy's coat of arms. The seal has four elements: a hand grasping a trident, a shield bearing the image of an ancient galley ship, an open book representing college, and a banner with the Latin motto "Ex scientia tridens"—"from knowledge, seapower." Traditionally, first classmen (academy seniors) wear their rings on the third finger of their left hands with the Naval Academy seal facing out. But for graduation, they turn the seal inward, closest to their hearts.

The coat of arms was designed by Park Benjamin, who graduated from the Academy in 1867. It was formally adopted by the Navy Department in 1899, due to the construction of a University Club in New York City—the coats of arms of American colleges were going to be used to decorate the building's exterior. Benjamin, learning of this and realizing the academy had no coat of arms, presented several suggestions to fellow alumni who were members of the club and a final design was determined and approved by the Navy Department.

The only mutiny on a U.S. warship occurred in 1842 aboard the USS *Somers*.

PROFILES IN COURAGE

"Courage is the price that life exacts for granting peace."
—Amelia Earhart

PETTY OFFICER SECOND CLASS MICHAEL A. MONSOOR, U.S. NAVY, IRAQ

Ramadi, September 29, 2006

Mike Monsoor was one of about 32 Navy SEALs fighting with U.S. Army, Marine Corps, and Iraqi troops to regain control of the insurgent-controlled city of Ramadi in September 2006. While their role was to provide reconnaissance and cover for other troops as they fought in the city, they were often attacked directly by the insurgents.

On the afternoon of September 29, Monsoor was lying on a rooftop between two SEAL snipers. The three were providing cover to an Army patrol stringing concertina wire in the rail yard. The two snipers were lying prone, aiming their rifles through holes blasted in the wall, with Monsoor kneeling behind the low rooftop wall, when a grenade sailed onto the rooftop and hit Monsoor in the chest.

Monsoor was up on one knee, and he was the only man on the roof who could have dived away and escaped the grenade's blast. Instead, he dropped on the grenade and absorbed the blast with his body, thereby saving the lives of the two SEALs with him.

Monsoor was still alive, but barely. Both SEALs on the roof were wounded, and one of them, Lieutenant John Seville, called a nearby SEAL team for assistance. They were on a building 150 meters away, called for casualty evacuation, and fought their way through the streets to Monsoor's position, but it was too late for Mike Monsoor—he died on the way to the hospital at Camp Ramadi.

For prior courage under fire, he'd already been awarded a Silver Star. For this action, "above and beyond the call of duty," 25-year-old Petty Officer Second Class Michael Monsoor was awarded the Medal of Honor on April 8, 2008.

PRIVATE FIRST CLASS ROSS McGINNIS, U.S. ARMY, IRAQ

Baghdad, December 4, 2006

Private First Class Ross McGinnis was a 19-year-old soldier who died saving the lives of four comrades in Iraq by jumping on a grenade tossed into their military vehicle. The young soldier "gave all for his country," President George W. Bush said somberly.

McGinnis was manning the gunner's hatch when an insurgent tossed a grenade from above. It flew past McGinnis and dropped down through the hatch before lodging near the radio. "McGinnis yelled, 'Grenade! It's in the truck!'" said his platoon sergeant, Cedric Thomas. "I looked out of the corner of my eye as I was crouching down and I saw him pin it down." His status as the youngest soldier in Company C, 1st Battalion, 26th Infantry Regiment, was immaterial. "He had time to jump out of the truck," Thomas added. "He chose not to." Promoted posthumously to specialist, Ross McGinnis had been in the Army only 18 months.

For his actions, McGinnis was awarded the Medal of Honor on June 2, 2008.

* * *

MORE GREAT WAR-MOVIE QUOTES

"If it weren't for the Japanese and Germans, we wouldn't have any good war movies."

—Stanley Ross

"Gentlemen, you can't fight in here! This is the War Room."

—President Merkin Muffley, *Dr. Strangelove or: How I Learned to Stop Worrying and Love the Bomb*

"Let me see if I've got this straight: In order to be grounded, I've got to be crazy, and I must be crazy to keep flying. But if I ask to be grounded, that means I'm not crazy any more, and I have to keep flying."

—Captain John Yossarian, *Catch 22*

...machine gun. It could fire over 1,200 rounds a minute and sounded like a saw.

DRESSED TO KILL, MARCH, OR PEEL POTATOES

Today's U.S. Army has some of the best-dressed soldiers in the world, but it took a while to get there.

MOTLEY CREW

When George Washington took command of the Continental Army, he couldn't distinguish one unit from another: some wore colorful militia uniforms or buckskin, but most wore homespun, faded brown hunting clothes.

When Washington appealed to Congress for standard uniforms, the legislators responded with the first military dress code—but no funding for it. They decided that Continental soldiers would wear brown coats with different-colored trim to identify their regiments, and a cocked hat—but each soldier had to buy the uniform himself.

WHERE'S BETSY ROSS WHEN YOU NEED HER?

On June 3, 1784, one year after the official end of the American Revolution, Congress authorized the first fully funded peacetime regular army—the 1st American Regiment, which over time became the 3rd Infantry Division (based today at Fort Stewart, Georgia). The uniforms consisted of blue coats faced with red, cocked hats, clean white waistcoats, and belts. Faces were clean-shaven, hair powdered, and weapons clean and polished. Congress could afford only one regiment and barely that—the clothes the government purchased were badly cut and poorly made of cheap material.

GRAY, IT'S THE NEW BLUE

In 1807 Congress organized the Regular Army (professional soldiers versus militias) and created a new regiment under the command of Lieutenant Colonel Winfield Scott. While some units continued to wear the old blue uniforms, Scott dressed his men in gray. When the British army stopped blue-attired American forces at Chippawa, Ontario, on July 5, 1814, Scott arrived with his "handsome little army" of four infantry regiments and two artillery companies dressed in gray. British general Phineas Riall gasped when he saw clumps of gray approaching with sunbeams reflecting off bayonets and said, "These, by gad! These are regulars!" The British broke and retreated. The tradition born at Chippawa remains alive and well today; the West Point cadets' dress uniform is copied from the outfits worn by Scott's regiment.

FROM ARMY BLUES TO PROJECT RUNWAY

The gray uniforms worn by Scott's regiments during the War of 1812 finally gave way to a standard dark blue wool uniform for enlisted men and, during the Mexican War, a fancier uniform with a blue coat, red sash, white leggings, cockade hat, and black boots for officers. The uniforms underwent few changes until the Civil War, when volunteer and regional militias introduced a staggering variety of cuts and colors.

• Borrowing from the French Zouave soldiers, regiments on both sides of the conflict sported gaudy uniforms featuring bright blue embroidered jackets, baggy red trousers, white gaiters, and a turban or fez.

• The 79th New York Highlanders' ethnic dress included kilts, sporrans (purses that hang from a belt or chain), and glengarry caps.

• The 7th and 8th New York wore West Point cadet-gray uniforms similar to those worn by the Confederate soldiers.

• The 39th New York (nicknamed the "Garibaldi Guard") wore Italian-style uniforms with a broad flat hat topped with chicken feathers.

Stylish they may have been, but in battle, commanding generals couldn't differentiate between a friendly regiment and an enemy regiment, so in 1862 the Federal government standardized the blue uniform worn by the Regular Army. By the winter of 1863, every soldier on the battlefield could distinguish between Union and Confederate soldiers. The dress code established during the Civil War became the most comprehensive yet—everything from buttons, vests, sashes, gloves, cap insignia, epaulettes, belts, swords, and cravats was governed by extensive uniform regulations.

The average man working in a U.S. wartime plant in World War II made $54.65 per week.

THE BOYS IN BLUE

Chevrons identified an enlisted man's rank and shoulder boards identified an officer's rank. Enlisted men wore dark blue single-breasted frock coats hanging to mid-thigh, but those worn by junior officers had a single row of gold buttons. Sergeants wore a 1½-inch stripe down the outer seams of their trousers; corporals wore a ½-inch stripe. The stripe's color identified the wearer's branch of service: yellow for cavalry, scarlet for artillery, sky blue for infantry, emerald green for mounted infantry, and crimson for ordnance. Officers of the rank of major and above wore double-breasted coats with two rows of gold buttons arranged to show their rank. In cold weather, all soldiers wore dark blue overcoats with a short cape. A simple kepi with a leather visor (like a baseball cap with a higher, flat-topped crown) replaced a variety of hats worn at the outset of the war.

SHADES OF BROWN

Fast-forward to the Spanish-American War in 1898, when khaki coats began to replace army blues among officers. Most infantry enlisted men still wore dark blue wool shirts, but with light blue trousers and light brown hats and leggings. The cooler, lighter-weight khakis designed for the tropics didn't become available until after the war. The knapsack also made its first appearance, but the soldiers rejected it in favor of the more comfortable blanket roll used during the Civil War.

Enlisted men hated the new regulation brown uniforms issued during World War I because, besides being ill-fitting, the heavy woolen material it was made of was neither water- nor wind-resistant, irritated the skin, and was uncomfortable on hot days. The tunic's high, coarse collar scuffed the neck, and the pants became tight and uncomfortable because they shrank. Boots didn't fit, so men who could afford to purchased their own. The typical soldier also wore spiral puttees—a long strip of woolen fabric wound around the legs from the ankles up—a gas mask bag over the shoulder or the hip, and, later, a metal helmet that helped reduce casualties. The same uniform was used for parades.

WHAT THE WELL-DRESSED GI WAS WEARING

Everything began to change in 1939 with the development of

olive drabs. The cotton twill shirt and trousers were conceived as fatigues—work and field clothing. Over those, a soldier wore a field jacket, which was probably the best item in the GI's abundant wardrobe. First issued by the Army after the draftee went through the processing center, the wardrobe contained both brown dress clothing and shoes for formal and off-base affairs, olive drab work clothes and boots for drill and fighting, light khaki clothing for summer, heavy wool clothing for winter, a formal cap and a fatigue cap, and a helmet. A soldier pulling sentry duty one bitterly cold night during the Battle of the Bulge in December 1944 wrote:

> I wore a set of cotton underclothes, a wool undershirt, a set of work shirt and trousers, a wool knot sweater, a set of fatigue shirt and trousers, a field jacket, an overcoat, a wool cap under my helmet, gloves, at least two pair of wool socks, boots, and galoshes. It was almost impossible to wear another article of clothing, and it did not give me much freedom of movement, but I wouldn't have parted with a single thread.

FROM THE GROUND UP

The Army was paying attention to the comfort of its soldiers—at least more than it had in previous wars. Footwear became a priority: When the soles of boots rotted in jungles, the Army quartermaster developed a jungle boot for operations in New Guinea and the Solomon Islands. Extra socks were issued in Italy to prevent trench foot, which occurred when feet inside boots were constantly wet. When the weather turned cold, the Army issued a shoepac—a high moccasin with a leather top and a rubber foot.

Many draftees had never owned as many clothes as the Army dispensed at the beginning of basic training. Private James Gilpin declared after receiving his wardrobe, "I just took my civilian clothes out and threw them in the trash can. It was my supreme gesture of acceptance. Why struggle any more. I was in the Army now."

THE BEST-DRESSED SOLDIERS IN THE WORLD

Today's enlistee receives a *Soldier's Handbook* emphasizing "Personal Appearance and Uniform." Every soldier is expected to be neat

...in a letter to President Theodore Roosevelt.

and well groomed. Forbidden are common civilian adornments like visible tattoos and body piercings while in uniform. Male haircuts must be kept short, and fully shaven heads are now acceptable. Female hair must not fall over the eyes, although cornrows and braided hairstyles are allowed. Unnatural colored hair is not allowed and nail color is limited to soft, natural colors. Contact lenses cannot be color-tinted. Anything that's bright or distracts from the uniform must be avoided.

Insignia must be placed exactly halfway between the shoulder and the elbow, and Army insignias must be sewn above the left pocket of the camouflage shirt and jacket, and the last name of the wearer sewn over the right pocket. A rank insignia pin must also be worn on both collars of shirts, jackets, and coats.

The camouflage set, which is worn in the field or at work, is only a small part of the enlistee's wardrobe. The Army issues green, white, and blue uniform coats, plus different outfits for men and women and an enormous array of formal wear.

THE BARE ESSENTIALS

The only items recruits require when they arrive at the processing center are soap and a soap case, toothpaste, dental floss, two locks, two towels and washcloths, three sets of underwear, six pairs of white socks, an athletic supporter (males), a comb or hairbrush, and the clothes on their backs. Before they reach basic training they will have a duffel bag with more clothes, including some of the ones they brought along. A drill sergeant informs them that every article of Army issue must be properly cared for, including clothes, boots, shoes, belts, and accessories. A simple poster serves as a constant reminder:

REMEMBER, YOU ARE AN AMERICAN SOLDIER
TAKE PRIDE IN YOUR UNIFORM
LOOK LIKE A SOLDIER
THINK LIKE A SOLDIER
ACT LIKE A SOLDIER

SPECIAL OPERATIONS

Small, clandestine, and unorthodox military teams involved in high-risk operations have played an important role in the history of warfare. "Pain is weakness leaving the body." —Special Ops Instructors

"The only easy day was yesterday."

—Navy SEALs

"Death waits in the dark."

—U.S. Army Task Force 160 "Night Stalkers"

"Any time, any place"

—USAF 16th SOW

"These things we do that others may live."

—USAF Pararescue

"Elite of the elite"

—2nd Force Recon (USMC)

"*De oppresso liber.*" ("To free the oppressed.")

—U.S. Army Special Forces

"*Sua sponte.*" ("Of their own accord.")

—U.S. Army Rangers

"There is no 'I' in TEAM."

—Navy SEALs

"First there . . . that others may live."

—USAF 720th Special Tactics Group

"Anyone can just go in there and kill someone, but you can't get information from a corpse."

—Navy SEALs

"*Lo que sea, cuando sea, donde sea.*" ("Anything, anytime, anywhere.")

—7th Special Forces Group (Airborne)

"We ain't making no d*mn cornflakes here."

—Colonel Charlie Beckwith, Delta Force

"We want to be in a situation under maximum pressure, maximum intensity, and maximum danger. When it's shared with others, it provides a bond which is stronger than any tie that can exist."

—SEAL Team Six Officer

In 1917 basic training for American soldiers could last as long as six months.

TOP ARMY FLICKS

Given that it's the largest branch of the armed forces, it should come as no surprise that the Army leads the services in appearances on the silver screen. Even with so many options available, some films inevitably rise to the top.

SERGEANT YORK (1941)

Gary Cooper stars as Alvin York, who initially tried to avoid World War I by applying for conscientious objector status. After his request was denied, he went on to became the most decorated soldier of the war and earned the Medal of Honor for capturing 132 German soldiers in a single attack. *Sergeant York* was nominated for an impressive 11 Academy Awards, winning two: Best Actor for Gary Cooper, and Best Film Editing.

THE LONGEST DAY (1962)

Running just shy of three hours, the story of the D-day invasion at Normandy nearly lives up to its title. The all-star cast included Eddie Albert, Richard Burton, Sean Connery, Henry Fonda, and John Wayne. The producers used actual participants from both sides of the battle as set consultants, and the film's characters speak their lines in their own languages (with on-screen subtitles), lending the film a sense of authenticity. Nominated for five Academy Awards, including Best Picture, it took home awards for Best Special Effects and Best Black-and-White Cinematography.

THE GREEN BERETS (1968)

At the height of the Vietnam War, John Wayne turned down a chance to star in the ensemble World War II film *The Dirty Dozen* and instead chose to create a stylized tribute to the troops fighting overseas at the time. *The Green Berets* is significant for its portrayal of troops in a war without defined front lines and its stance against the antiwar movement of the 1960s. However, it was not the critics' favorite. The film wasn't nominated for any major awards, but it let Oliver Stone direct *Platoon* as a counterpoint 20 years later.

PATTON (1970)

This film tells the story of irascible General George S. Patton—

More than twice as many Americans died at Antietam as perished on D-Day in World War II.

famously portrayed by George C. Scott—and his legendary campaigns in World War II. "The very thought of losing is hateful to Americans," says General Patton, standing onstage in front of a gigantic American flag in the memorable five-minute opening monologue. The movie won over critics, too, despite the antiwar sentiment that was raging across the country due to the Vietnam War. *Patton* was nominated for 10 Oscars and won seven, including Best Picture and Best Director, as well as Best Actor honors for Scott—whose disapproval of competition among actors led him to refuse the award; he was the first actor to do so.

MASH (1970)

The Korean War is often referred to as "the Forgotten War," but it's not for Hollywood's lack of trying. Director Robert Altman's comedy about a Mobile Army Surgical Hospital (MASH) during that conflict combined the reality of war with the dark humor that naturally accompanies troops in battle. That combination turned the film, which starred Donald Sutherland, Tom Skerritt, Elliot Gould, and Robert Duvall, into a runaway hit. *MASH* was nominated for five Academy Awards, and won for Best Screenplay. The film launched one of the most popular television shows in American history, which ran for 11 seasons.

APOCALYPSE NOW (1979)

Widely regarded by critics and industry insiders as one of the greatest movies ever made, Francis Ford Coppola's tale of a soldier sent deep into Vietnam to track down and assassinate a rogue Special Forces colonel continues to resonate decades after its release. Based on Joseph Conrad's equally brooding novel *Heart of Darkness*, it features Martin Sheen (who had a heart attack during filming) as Captain Benjamin Willard, who is on the hunt for Colonel Walter Kurtz, famously portrayed by Marlon Brando. Nominated for seven Academy Awards, the film earned Oscars for Best Cinematography and Best Sound. *Apocalypse Now Redux* was released in 2001 with nearly an hour of additional footage.

PLATOON (1986)

The film tells the gripping story of an Army platoon in Vietnam as seen from the perspective of its newest member, Private Chris

Private Daniel Hough was the first soldier to die in the American Civil War...

Taylor, played by Charlie Sheen. *Platoon*'s realism and conflicted look at the war made it a sensation among aging Vietnam War vets. This brutal honesty is generally credited to the wartime experiences of writer/director Oliver Stone, who was an infantryman in Vietnam, and resulted in eight Oscar nominations, winning for Best Director, Best Picture, Best Film Editing, and Best Sound.

GLORY (1989)

Glory recounts the experiences of the 54th Massachusetts Volunteer Infantry, one of the first all-black regiments in the Union army of the Civil War. The 54th was led by white officers, including regimental commander Captain Robert Gould Shaw, portrayed by Matthew Broderick. The film takes liberties with some of the history but does an otherwise impressive job of depicting the initial attempts at integrating the military during the Civil War. The film won Oscars for Best Supporting Actor (Denzel Washington), Sound Mixing, and Cinematography.

SAVING PRIVATE RYAN (1998)

Director Steven Spielberg fires every round in his magazine in this gritty World War II drama about a team of soldiers sent to find a missing paratrooper—and bring him home alive—after all three of his brothers are killed in the war. The cast is led by Tom Hanks as Captain John H. Miller and Matt Damon as Private James Francis Ryan. Generally remembered for its brutal opening scenes of the D-day landings at Omaha Beach, *Saving Private Ryan* was nominated for 11 Academy Awards and won five, including Best Director.

BLACK HAWK DOWN (2001)

The 1993 Battle of Mogadishu was a brutal fight in the heart of Somalia. Directed by Ridley Scott, the film tells how a Special Operations team comprised of Delta Force soldiers and Army Rangers undertook a mission to snatch a pair of Somali men from the city; the mission devolved into brutal chaos, especially after one of the team's Black Hawk helicopters was taken out by a rocket-propelled grenade. The film is loud and bloody, a gritty portrayal of a battle that killed as many as 1,500 people and wounded up to 4,000. Nominated for four Academy Awards, it took home Oscars for Best Editing and Best Sound.

...He was killed at Fort Sumter when a pile of cartridges exploded by accident.

THE COAST GUARD'S TOP 10 RESCUES

In 2007 the U.S. Coast Guard released a list of its top 10 rescues of all time. Here are the stories of those exciting and daring rescues by these heroes of the armed forces.

Rescue: Hurricane of 1888
When: November 25–26, 1888
Where: Off the coast of Massachusetts
Lives saved: 28
During the great hurricane that hit New England in November 1888, volunteer life-saving station keeper Joshua James and his crew rescued 28 people from five different vessels. Probably the most celebrated lifesaver in the world, James had a hand in rescuing a total of 626 people in his career. The Coast Guard's Joshua James Keeper Award honors longevity and outstanding performance in Coast Guard boat operations.

Rescue: Overland Expedition
When: 1897–98
Where: Near Point Barrow, Alaska
Lives saved: 260
The Coast Guard cutter *Bear* was sent on an expedition to rescue eight whaling ships trapped in the Arctic ice near Point Barrow, Alaska. Unable to navigate the ice, Lieutenant David H. Jarvis led a party of five other men, along with sled dogs and reindeer, on an overland expedition of 1,500 miles to rescue the stranded whaling crews.

Rescue: Sailing ship *Priscilla*
When: August 18, 1899
Where: Gull Shoal, North Carolina
Lives saved: 10
Rasmus S. Midgett, a Coast Guard surfman (a highly trained boat handler) from the Gull Shoal Life-Saving Station, North Carolina,

was patrolling the beach on horseback at 3:00 a.m. when he saw the *Priscilla* run aground. With no time to contact his station, Midgett shouted instructions for the stranded men to jump overboard one at a time as the waves receded. As they did, Midgett dragged each of the seven men from the waves. Three men on board were too weak to get off the boat, so Midgett went into the water and carried each of them to the beach.

Rescue: Schooner *John R. Noyes*
When: December 14–15, 1902
Where: Lake Ontario
Lives saved: 5
After hauling their surfboat via horse-drawn sled for miles, clearing a path through snowdrifts as high as six feet to the shores of Lake Ontario, George N. Gray and his crew from the life-saving station in Charlotte, New York, searched the fog for possible survivors of the wreck of the *John R. Noyes*. The crew rowed nearly 60 miles in icy waters for 15 hours before finding and rescuing four men and one woman from the schooner.

Rescue: Mississippi River flood
When: January 1937
Where: Mississippi and Ohio rivers and environs
Lives saved: 43,853
The flood was the worst natural disaster of the 20th century—it rained for 27 out of 31 days that January. Tens of thousands of people were removed from perilous positions to places of safety by 674 coastguardsmen and 128 Coast Guard vessels. The Coast Guard also saved 11,313 head of livestock and furnished transportation for 72 persons in need of hospitalization. According to the Coast Guard, the immense scope of the effort in 1937 eclipsed the number of persons that the Coast Guard rescued in the 2006 Hurricane Katrina operations.

Rescue: U.S. Army transport ship *Dorchester*
When: February 3, 1943
Where: Off the coast of Greenland
Lives saved: 230

All U.S. Navy destroyers since the USS *Bainbridge* are named for naval heroes and leaders.

The Coast Guard cutters *Comanche* and *Escanaba* responded to the torpedoing of the *Dorchester* in the frigid North Atlantic. Knowing that the survivors had only minutes to live in the icy waters, the crew of the *Escanaba* used what was then the new "retriever" rescue technique: rescue swimmers in wetsuits swam to victims and secured a line to them so they could be hauled onto the ship. The *Escanaba* saved 133 men (one of whom died later) and the *Comanche* saved 97.

Rescue: Flying boat *Bermuda Sky Queen*
When: October 14, 1947
Where: North Atlantic Ocean
Lives saved: 69
Facing strong headwinds on a transatlantic flight from Foynes, Ireland, to Gander, Newfoundland, the *Bermuda Sky Queen* was running low on fuel. The *Queen*'s captain decided to turn around and land the huge airship among the massive rolling waves near the cutter *Bibb* at Ocean Station Charlie in the North Atlantic. When the idea of passing a line from the *Bibb* to the *Queen* was tried, the two craft collided in the heavy seas. The *Bibb* backed off and sent a 15-man rubber raft and a small boat to do the job. The 62 passengers and seven crew members jumped from the escape door of the aircraft into the raft, which was then pulled to the small boat. The rescue made international headlines.

Rescue: Oil tanker *Pendleton*
When: February 18, 1952
Where: Off the coast of Cape Cod, Massachusetts
Lives saved: 33
During a severe winter storm, the tankers *Fort Mercer* and *Pendleton* broke in half within 40 miles of each other. In 60-foot seas, a 36-foot Coast Guard motor lifeboat with a crew of four rescued all but one of the *Pendleton*'s 34-man crew by maneuvering their boat under the *Pendleton*'s stern and pulling each man aboard as they jumped into the water. U.S. Coast Guard vessels, aircraft, and lifeboat stations rescued 62 people that day with a loss of only five lives.

What is Breed's Hill famous for? It's where the Battle of Bunker Hill actually took place.

Rescue: Cruise ship *Prinsendam*

When: October 4, 1980

Where: Off the coast of Ketchikan, Alaska

Lives saved: 520

Coast Guard and Canadian helicopters and three cutters were among the responders to the *Prinsendam* after a fire broke out on board. The passengers, many of whom were elderly, had to leave the ship in lifeboats. The Dutch cruise ship was 130 miles from the nearest airstrip and was ordered to be abandoned; it later capsized and sank. The rescue is particularly important because of the distance traveled by the rescuers, the coordination of independent organizations, and the fact that all passengers and crew were rescued without any loss of life or serious injury.

Rescue: Hurricane Katrina

When: August 29, 2005

Where: New Orleans and the Mississippi Gulf Coast

Lives saved: 33,545

More than 5,000 coastguardsmen served in Katrina operations. Seventy-six Coast Guard and Coast Guard Auxiliary aircraft took part in the search-and-rescue operations that saved 24,135 lives from danger, mostly the people on the roofs of their homes. Coastguardsmen also evacuated 9,409 patients from local hospitals. Flying 1,817 sorties, the aircrews saved more than 12,000 lives; 42 cutters and 131 small boats rescued more than 21,000. *Time* magazine noted: "The Coast Guard was saving lives before any other federal agency—despite the fact that almost half the local Coast Guard personnel lost their own homes in the hurricane."

* * *

WHAT'S WITH "AWEIGH"?

In Old English, the term "weigh" is defined as completing the action of heaving, hoisting, or raising something. Thus, the anchor of a ship is "aweigh" when it is hoisted off the seafloor. According to Navy protocol, the exact time and location of each aweigh must be noted in the ship's official log.

THE BIG GAME

The annual Army-Navy game of 1942 was almost canceled, but President Franklin D. Roosevelt and the former assistant secretary of the Navy decided that it was important to the morale of the nation and the students of the military academies.

GAME ON

With gas rationing in effect, people were encouraged to avoid unnecessary travel. Spectators were limited to those within a 10-mile radius of Thompson Stadium in Annapolis, Maryland; Naval Academy employees; girlfriends of midshipmen; and 210 reporters. West Point's Army cadets, who traditionally piled on buses to travel to the game, were also allowed to attend.

Nevertheless, the stadium was relatively empty, with just 11,700 spectators—the smallest crowd since 1893. In the spirit of patriotism and sportsmanship, the midshipmen refused to let the Army side remain empty and silent. Third- and fourth-year midshipmen were designated "Army" for a day and learned the traditional Army cheers and songs. After the national anthem was sung, the "Army" fans roared "Beat Navy!" and cheered for their team, but it wasn't enough. Navy won 14–0.

The 1943 game was held at Michie Field in West Point and, with gas rationing still in place, some Army cadets became "Navy" for a day. Their cheering must have been more inspiring: this time Navy walloped Army 13–0.

In 1944 travel restrictions were eased enough so that Army cadets could take a slow steamer to Baltimore's Memorial Stadium—with five Navy destroyers protecting them. At the suggestion of House Minority Leader William Martin, the game was used as a war fund-raiser. More than 100,000 people attended and paid from $25 to $1,000 a seat. Fifteen people even paid $1 million each for private luxury boxes on the 50-yard line. This was in 1944 dollars, when a bottle of Coca-Cola cost five cents, a movie cost 20 cents, and an Electrolux vacuum cleaner cost $16.95. When the final whistle blew, the game had raised $58 million for the war effort and spectators witnessed Army win their first national championship since 1914 by defeating Navy 23–7!

By 1945 the Quartermaster Corps had trained almost 10,000 dogs for the U.S. armed forces.

DOOLITTLE'S RAID

After Japanese airpower dealt a stunning tactical blow to the U.S. military forces at Pearl Harbor, a retaliatory strike against the Japanese was a priority for President Franklin D. Roosevelt, who challenged his general staff to devise a way to attack the heart of Japan.

PAYBACK PLANS

By mid-January 1942, a carrier-based air strike against Japan was accepted as the most plausible solution to FDR's request. When Admiral Ernest J. King, chief of Naval Operations, was asked to evaluate the possibilities, he passed the idea to General Henry H. "Hap" Arnold, commander of the Army Air Forces, who in turn asked Lieutenant Colonel Jimmy Doolittle to work out the details with the Navy. In the days immediately after Pearl Harbor, service rivalries took a backseat to striking a blow against the enemy.

After preliminary test flights, the North American B-25 Mitchell bomber was selected for the mission. Eighteen B-25s flew from their Oregon home base to Indiana for modifications. The range of an unmodified Mitchell was only 1,300 miles on a favorable day, so additional internal tanks were added to allow for more fuel. At the last second, 10 five-gallon cans of gas were stowed in the radio operator's seat. The heavy guns were removed, along with the highly secret Norden bombsight, whose classified technology couldn't fall into Japanese hands. In the planned scenario, the Norden bombsight wouldn't have been very accurate at the low altitude that would be flown anyway, so it was replaced with a simple metal aiming sight. Aircraft radios were also removed, since the mission would be executed under strict radio silence. These changes allowed each aircraft to carry just over 1,100 gallons of usable fuel, which under typical flight conditions would allow for a range of 2,400 miles. After all of these radical modifications, four 500-pound bombs barely fit into the bomb bay.

The Army and Navy finally agreed on a near-dusk takeoff and night raid on Tokyo as the plan that stood the best chance of achieving complete surprise. The plan depended on a fast carrier run-in at night to get as close to the mainland as possible just prior

Navy cruisers (large warships) have largely been replaced by destroyers.

to launch. After the planes were away, the fleet would make an immediate turn back toward Hawaii and a run for waters beyond the range of Japanese land-based aircraft to preserve the limited fleet that remained in the Pacific. On April 13, Naval Task Force 16 gathered near Hawaii and proceeded toward the Japanese mainland with 16 ships, including Vice Admiral William F. "Bull" Halsey's flagship, the aircraft carrier USS *Enterprise*.

THE BEST-LAID PLANS

Doolittle's plan was to lead 16 planes with five-man crews ahead of the rest of the aircraft, to attack Tokyo with incendiary bombs, and to set fires that the others could follow to the city. But the B-25 crews were forced to launch early when the nighttime attack plan was disrupted by Japanese picket boats that spotted Task Force 16 early on the morning of the 18th. There were no other acceptable options; the mission had to launch immediately.

Owing to the added distance at the takeoff point, there was no plan for how or where to land these aircraft when Doolittle took off at 8:20 a.m. Doolittle recognized that the mission was already in jeopardy and might end with a parachute bailout at sea. Halsey and Doolittle shared the responsibility for the launch decision, with the clear intention of completing the mission.

OFF WE GO INTO THE WILD BLUE YONDER

The USS *Hornet* steered into the wind while the deck pitched in heavy seas. Engines roared to life and Doolittle taxied his plane forward a few feet onto three cork pads that provided enough friction for the tires to hold the B-25 as the engines were pushed to full throttle. Minimum-distance takeoff procedures practiced on dry land in Florida worked as advertised on the deck of the ship.

After traveling more than 700 miles, miniscule errors in heading control were amplified, putting the pilots many miles off course. Several of the B-25 crews were totally lost when they finally made landfall around noon. Doolittle himself flew well north of his planned route, but quick work by his navigator steered him back on course. Those following him were much relieved at the rapid course correction. The sun was shining brightly about half past noon when Doolittle became the first pilot to bomb the Japanese homeland in fulfillment of FDR's orders.

DOOMED FROM THE START

Unknown to Doolittle's Raiders, the aircraft carrying the homing radio beacons for the landing fields in China had crashed, and with it any chance of finding the strips at night and in bad weather. Fortunately, the original targets planned for night recognition and attack were large industrial zones, so hitting at least part of the complex would be much easier in broad daylight.

The attack was not intended to do maximum damage; rather, it was intended to make a spectacle. The attack was designed so that the Japanese people would clearly know that a foreign enemy had bombed Tokyo. In the original plan, Doolittle had hoped to set fires to serve not only as beacons to the following 15 B-25s, but also to dramatically—and undeniably—announce that the capital city had been bombed. An order forbidding the bombardment of the radio towers near Tokyo indicated that immediate dissemination of the news by Japanese radio was desired and expected.

TRIUMPH FROM TRAGEDY

In almost every case, primary targets were bombed. The damage done far exceeded expectations largely as a result of highly inflammable Japanese construction, the low-altitude attack, the clear weather over Tokyo, and the careful target study that the crews had done. All 16 planes had descended to extremely low altitudes, attacked, and egressed the target area at high speed. All 16 crews began to calculate how much fuel they had left and how far they could fly. Initial calculations were not encouraging. Navigator Lieutenant Eugene F. McGurl halfheartedly joked, "Hey, I don't think we're gonna have to swim more than one hundred miles."

Doolittle's Raiders got another lucky break that evening. A stiff tailwind had developed between Japan and China and, much to the surprise of the navigators, several of the planes appeared to be getting pretty good gas mileage and making good time. Only one bomber had insufficient fuel to make the Chinese mainland and diverted to Russia instead. That plane's five crewmen were interned in Russia until they managed to escape into Iran in May 1943.

Once the raiders made landfall over China, luck ran out. The Chinese, fearing air raids by the Japanese and not knowing of the timing of Doolittle's raid on the Japanese capital, extinguished all ground lights when the B-25 engines were heard. In addition, bad

...personal courage. Note that the first letters form the acronym LDRSHIP (leadership).

weather over the China coast made safe landings impossible and all of the planes either landed in the water near the coast or the crews parachuted out. Four were killed during bailout or ditching and eight were captured by the Japanese. Four of those who were captured survived until they were freed by U.S. troops in 1945.

FIRST TIME'S THE CHARM

The Tokyo raid was the first and, at that time, the only combat mission flown by these 80 men. In the weeks following the raid, American morale soared. For the planning, execution, and leadership during the raid, Doolittle received the nation's highest military award. On May 19, 1942, President Franklin D. Roosevelt, the man who had ordered the mission, personally decorated the newly promoted Brigadier General James H. Doolittle with the Medal of Honor in a private White House ceremony.

* * *

I SPY WITH MY LITTLE EYE . . .

U-2 pilot Francis Gary Powers of the U.S. Air Force was shot down over the Soviet Union while he was on a top-secret mission to photograph denied territory. With both plane and Powers intact, the Soviet government confiscated his photographs and obtained enough information to learn more about the technology it needed to launch countermeasures against the United States. This little spy mission caused the U.S. great embarrassment and began a decline in relations with the Soviet Union—including setting back peace talks between Soviet premier Nikita Khruschchev and U.S. president Dwight D. Eisenhower. But it also cost Powers time in prison, an American reception as frigid as the Cold War itself, and never receiving in his lifetime the medals that he deserved for his service. Powers was sentenced to 10 years in a Soviet prison, but his term was shortened when the United States swapped a Soviet spy—Colonel Vilyam Fisher, a.k.a. Rudolf Abel—for him. In 2000 Powers's family was presented with his Prisoner of War Medal, Distinguished Flying Cross, Silver Star, National Defense Service Medal, and the Intelligence Star for extreme fidelity and extraordinary courage in the line of duty—posthumously awarded 40 years after the fateful U-2 mission.

Bouncing Betty: A shrapnel mine that pops up a few feet and explodes at groin level.

WETTING DOWN A COMMISSION

Once upon a time in the old U.S. Navy, the phrase "wetting down a commission" brought certain nods of understanding. Today, though, there is a lot of confusion about the origins of that time-honored tradition.

LET'S PARTY

According to the Naval Historical Center in Washington, "wetting down a commission" stemmed from the practice of having a party with friends and shipmates to celebrate the commissioning of a naval officer or his promotion. By custom, the officer would appear before his assembled guests for the first time in his new uniform with its stripes to signify his status in the Navy. At that point, the guests christened him, his uniform, and his commission with whatever libations were available, normally paid for by the man being honored. As time went by and gold braid and uniforms became increasingly expensive, the tradition was frowned on by the admiralty and eventually disappeared.

PASS ME THE COMMISSION, PLEASE

An older explanation traces the expression back to when commissions were conveyed on heavy parchment. The newly anointed officer appeared at a special dinner with his shipmates where the achievement was recognized. As the festivities ensued, the commissioning document was rolled into a cone with the narrow end folded, becoming a de facto conical cup. It was then filled with a preferred alcoholic beverage and passed around as a kind of communal offering and toast to the new officer. So, in the course of the evening, the commission was literally "wetted down." Because commissions were signed by the nation's president and conveyed great legal authority, this explanation is doubtful.

TRADITION LIVES ON

However, wetting down newly promoted officers is alive in the armed forces in the modern Navy and Marine Corps. "Wetting down" parties are quite the norm. When more than one officer is commissioned, it is customary for them to retire to a tavern and use their first pay raise on their friends. During the subsequent party, the officer's new grade insignia bar is placed in the bottom of a glass filled with alcohol that the officer must drink dry, thus "wetting down" his commission.

Other, more imaginative wetting-downs have also occurred. In one example, a U.S. Navy Seabee crew doing construction work in Iraq in 2005 paused to honor the commissioning of new officers by pouring more than 100 gallons of cold water in the bucket of a front-end loader over the uniformed officers to properly "wet them down."

* * *

ENSIGN ME UP!

The United States Coast Guard Academy may be the smallest of the U.S. federal military academies, but its reputation is certainly big. *U.S. News & World Report* ranked the prestigious academy as one of "America's Best Colleges" for 2009. And why shouldn't it be? Among high academic, athletic, and community achievements, their 2008 class had a median combined SAT score of 1,256; a third of who had graduated in the top 5 percent of their high school class. Eighty percent of their students go on to receive advanced degrees, usually paid for by the Coast Guard.

While the average Ivy League school enrolls anywhere from 4,000 to 14,000 undergraduates and costs around $35,000 per year, the highly selective United States Coast Guard Academy enrolls only around 200 students annually—and is free. In fact, the academy pays each cadet $8,760 for uniforms, equipment, textbooks, and other training expenses. In exchange for their four-year Bachelor of Science degree, students must then commit to serving for five years as a commissioned Coast Guard officer upon their graduation.

The academy's stats are pretty impressive when you consider that the first class had only nine cadets who hopped aboard the schooner Dobbin in 1876, which sailed from Baltimore, Maryland, for a two-year training mission.

HOORAY FOR HIGGINS

Battleships, carriers, and submarines dominate naval tales of World War II, but it was small Higgins boats carrying only 30 to 40 men that were the key to Allied victory.

THE LITTLE BOATS THAT WON THE BIG WAR

Dwight D. Eisenhower credited four things with helping the Allies win the war—the Sherman tank, the C-47 transport, the jeep, and Higgins boats. The boats were officially known as Landing Craft, Vehicle, Personnel (LCVP) but were often called Higgins boats, after their inventor, Andrew Higgins.

Higgins boats put troops on the Pacific beaches of Guadalcanal, Iwo Jima, and Okinawa. And they brought the soldiers to Normandy beaches in the critical invasion of Europe. Higgins boats brought more Allied troops and equipment to shore than all other landing craft combined. All of these landings were done on open beaches, and none of the sites had wharves or piers that would allow large vessels like troop carriers, which could move only in deep water, to dock and unload. Instead of being forced into attacking a port city that was fortified with heavy artillery, Higgins boats gave the Allies the ability to move troops from large ships onto an isolated strip of coastline that was easy to invade and hard for the enemy to defend. The ability to land troops by surprise was an advantage that the Allies desperately needed.

HELPING OUT THE RUMRUNNERS

Andrew Higgins was a New Orleans entrepreneur known for his love of good bourbon and fast boats. In the 1920s, he formed the Higgins Lumber and Export Company. Higgins acquired a fleet of ships to move their products, along with a shipyard to build and repair the fleet. When his lumber-importing business crashed, Higgins turned to the business of building boats, specializing in small craft that could navigate the local swamps and bayous. His new company, Higgins Industries, designed boats with protected propellers that could operate in waters filled with floating logs and debris and even submerged sandbars—waters where other motorboats quickly ran into trouble.

Higgins's most famous boat was the Eureka. It could jump logs, turn in its own length, and run up on a beach without damaging the hull. Its shallow-water abilities made it an ideal boat for local trappers, oilmen, and lumbermen. But rumrunners were some of his best customers. Higgins designed motorboats that were so fast they could help a smuggler outrun the Coast Guard.

SORRY, THE NAVY ISN'T INTERESTED

The fact that Higgins made boats that could outrun government vessels didn't go unnoticed. By 1937, the U.S. Coast Guard and the Army Corps of Engineers were purchasing boats from Higgins. Meanwhile, Colonel Holland M. Smith of the U.S. Marine Corps became interested in developing the Eureka into an amphibious landing craft. He and other Marine Corps officers were frustrated that the Navy had no small motorized boats that could power through surf, hit the sand, and put troops on the beach. Smith asked Higgins to help design a personnel carrier that could do the job. Higgins adapted the Eureka to the needs of the Marine Corps. In 1938 and 1939, tests by the Navy and Marine Corps showed that Higgins's boats surpassed the performance of the Navy-designed personnel carriers, but every time Higgins approached the Navy about buying his boats, they turned him away.

Higgins was competing with northern boatyards with long-established ties to the Navy's Bureau of Ships. He was also competing with the Navy itself. The Navy's Bureau of Ships was designing their own landing craft, and naval bureaucrats didn't like being shown up by a small shipbuilder. But Andrew Higgins wasn't a man who gave up easily. In 1942 he testified to a Senate committee that his boats were superior to those produced by the Navy. After an investigation, the committee agreed and Higgins got a contract to produce LCVPs. They were so successful that they became the standard landing craft of World War II. Higgins Industries factories in New Orleans went into full-out production, turning out more than 22,000 Higgins boats during the war.

THE LITTLE BOATS THAT COULD

Constructed of plywood, wood, and steel, the LCVPs were just over 36 feet long. Described as "floating cigar boxes," they had flat bottoms and could navigate in as little as 18 inches of water. Their job was to get to shore, quickly unload men and materials, and then immediately head back for more men and materials. Military changes made the LCVP heavier and slower than the Eureka, and it traveled at only moderate speeds of 9 to 12 knots. The boats had plated steel armor on their sides and were armed for combat with two machine guns in the rear of the boat. They could carry cargo loads of up to 8,100 pounds. Perhaps the most important adaptation that Higgins made to the LCVPs was a movable steel bow ramp. Instead of personnel scrambling over the sides to get out of the boat, the bow came down as a ramp to allow soldiers to rush out. The ramp also allowed vehicles like jeeps to roll in and out of the boats and made it easier for wounded soldiers to be carried onto the boats in stretchers. To ensure a fast getaway, LCVPs were supplied with a remote-control reversal mechanism that allowed them to back up and leave the beach almost as fast as they'd slammed onto it.

HITTING THE BEACHES

During an invasion, LCVPs normally carried a crew of three to four men, as well as up to 36 troops. The boats could also ferry a half-ton jeep and 12 armed soldiers. Troops often found getting on the Higgins boats trickier than getting off. The landing craft were lowered into the water, nets were thrown over the sides of the transport ships, and the men scrambled down the nets to their boats. Once the boats were manned, they typically traveled eight boats at a time, in two groups, or "waves," of four boats each, one behind the other, to carry the landing team. After the team was ashore, more LCVPs returned with equipment.

The LCVPs weren't the only Higgins landing craft used in landings. Higgins Industries also developed Landing Craft, Mechanized (LCMs) that moved medium-size tanks. They also developed Landing Craft, Personnel (Large) (LCPL), a lighter version of the LCVP specifically designed for the Navy. All three forms of landing crafts were used in the Normandy landings.

HIGGINS BOATS SINK HITLER

On June 6, 1944, D-day, the largest fleet in history crossed the English Channel. More than 5,000 ships carried the Allied troops to the beaches of Normandy. Along with men and weapons, the ships carried about 1,500 Higgins boats to bring the invasion force to shore.

On D-day, the Higgins boats ferried in assault teams of 30 troops. They carried 29 enlisted men and one officer on each boat. At Utah Beach, the first wave of 20 Higgins boats brought in the 8th Regiment. In other waves, landing craft brought in more troops, combat engineers, and demolition teams. They ferried in tanks, jeeps, supplies, and even carried captured German prisoners back to the main fleet for interrogation. D-day was the largest single-day amphibious invasion in history, and despite heavy fire and high casualties, about 130,000 troops made it into France.

The day after the invasion, Hitler was briefed on the huge Allied landing. During the explanation of how such a large landing took place without any access to French port cities, Hitler was informed of Higgins and his thousands of LCVPs. Hitler is said to have commented bitterly, "Truly this man is the new Noah." That just might have been the best compliment that Higgins and his little boats ever received.

"Andrew Higgins is the man who won the war for us. If Higgins had not designed and built those LCVPs, we never could have landed over an open beach. The whole strategy of the war would have been different."

—General Dwight D. Eisenhower, Supreme Allied Commander

* * *

FAMOUS BURIALS

On the list of famous people buried at sea are actress Jean Arthur, explorer Edmund Hillary, author L. Ron Hubbard, singer Janis Joplin, U.S. senator John F. Kennedy Jr., and actors Rock Hudson, Steve McQueen, Robert Mitchum, and Vincent Price. The cremains of Adolf Eichmann, the Nazi who oversaw the extermination of millions of Jewish prisoners during World War II, were scattered over the Mediterranean Sea in international waters by the government of Israel, which tried and convicted him. The Israelis did not want him buried on their soil and wanted to avoid the existence of a grave anywhere that might become a Nazi icon for followers.

In 1976 the Coast Guard Academy became the first service academy to admit women.

GET YAMAMOTO

"If we are to have war with America," Fleet Admiral Isoroku Yamamoto declared, "we will have no hope of winning unless the U.S. fleet in Hawaii is destroyed." These words sealed the fate of the Japanese empire and elevated the admiral to America's most-wanted list.

A SPY IN OUR MIDST

Having studied two years at Harvard, followed by three years of service in 1925–28 as naval attaché at the Japanese embassy in Washington, Isoroku Yamamoto understood the mind of most Americans. Many naval attachés performed espionage, and Yamamoto was among the best. Japan intended to expand its empire in the Far East, and the future admiral's assignment was to befriend members of the U.S. Navy and extract intelligence on America's program for sea power.

Yamamoto's task went smoothly because the United States and Japan had been allies during World War I, making for friendly diplomatic relations. Being a superb poker player as well as a skilled judge of character, he joined in high-stakes games and through observation could tell who in the ranks of the Navy were natural leaders, strategists, and risk takers—and who were not. Besides making a lot of money, Yamamoto also learned about the Navy's plans for naval aviation, which in the 1920s was still in its infancy. He knew that Japan would never become a Pacific power without a large navy, fast aircraft carriers, and long-range maneuverable planes with superior weapons.

SETTING THE STAGE

Yamamoto returned to Tokyo in 1928 and for two years served as captain of the *Akagi*, Japan's first fast carrier and the most advanced in the world. The ship carried 60 planes and was one of the six that would eventually take part in the attack on Pearl Harbor. Yamamoto used his time on the *Akagi* to develop carrier air tactics, which he applied over the next four years while serving as chief of Japan's naval technology division. In 1933, at his own request, he assumed command of the 1st Air Fleet to perfect the development of carrier aircraft, after which he convinced the ministry that carriers should become the principal weapon of the navy. It was Yamamoto's foresight that doomed the supremacy of battleships among the nations of the world, and he was correct.

ASKING FOR TROUBLE

In 1939, Yamamoto became commander in chief of the Imperial Navy's Combined Fleet and, despite opposition from admirals who doubted the wisdom of bringing the United States into the war, he conceived and carried out the December 7, 1941, surprise attack on Pearl Harbor. After Admiral Chester W. Nimitz arrived in Honolulu and saw the massive devastation, he assumed command of what was left of the Pacific Fleet—with the intention of avenging the attack. Nimitz knew the task would be enormous because he needed carriers and planes, and the United States had only begun to mobilize its shipyards and aircraft plants.

Meanwhile, Nimitz put a small staff of Navy cryptanalysts to work on breaking the Japanese naval code. Intercepting all of Japan's radio communications, they eventually succeeded in decoding them. By March 1942, the code breakers began to change the course of the naval war, first by preventing the Japanese invasion of New Guinea by turning back the enemy in the Coral Sea on May 7–8, and then by providing intelligence that enabled the Pacific Fleet to defeat Yamamoto on June 6–7 at Midway.

WHAT'S JAPANESE FOR "HUBRIS"?

On April 14, 1943, while monitoring Japanese radio chatter, cryptanalysts decoded an unusual message not normally transmitted over the radio. Despite their unaccountable losses in the Coral Sea and at Midway and because the Japanese navy believed their naval code could not be broken, they continued to use it. The commander of the U.S. intelligence unit hurried to Navy headquarters and handed Nimitz a freshly decoded message that read, "The Commander in Chief Combined Fleet will inspect Ballalae, Shortland, and Buin on April 18..."

TOO GOOD TO PASS UP

The message contained Yamamoto's complete itinerary, including the exact hours of his arrival and departure, and information about

The U.S. Seventh Fleet is the largest of the Navy's forward-deployed fleets...

the two medium bombers on which he would fly, as well as his escort of six Zero fighter planes. Nimitz studied his wall chart of the Solomon Islands and realized the inspection tour would bring Yamamoto to within 300 miles of Guadalcanal's Henderson Field. He turned to Layton and asked, "What do you say? Shall we try...?" The commander replied, "Aside from the Emperor, probably no man is so important [to Japan]...and if he is shot down, it would demoralize the fighting navy [and]...stun the nation."

Nimitz agreed, and with a smile said, "It's down in [Vice Admiral William] Halsey's bailiwick. If there's a way, he'll find it." He informed Secretary of the Navy Frank Knox and President Roosevelt of his plan and received the green light. Two words flashed through the channels: "Get Yamamoto."

Halsey forwarded the intelligence to Rear Admiral Marc A. Mitscher, who commanded the air operations for the Solomon Islands from Henderson Field. Mitscher ordered out Major John W. Mitchell's 339th Fighter Squadron, which consisted of 16 twin-hulled, twin-engine P-38 Lightnings, the Army's only long-range fighter aircraft in the Solomons.

GETTING YAMAMOTO

On April 18 at 8:00 a.m., Yamamoto and his staff boarded two "Betty" medium bombers at Rabaul, New Britain, and took off for Buin's Kahili airfield on Bougainville Island. Mitchell's fighters were already flying low along the west coast of New Georgia and looking for Yamamoto's expected arrival over Buin at 9:35. Almost to the minute, two Bettys with a six-plane fighter escort began making the approach at Kahili. Captain Thomas G. Lanphier, with both engines throbbing at maximum speed, dashed in under the Zeros just as the two bombers dropped their landing gear. Lanphier shot down one Betty and Lieutenant Rex T. Barber dropped the other. The first bomber, carrying Yamamoto, crashed in the jungle north of Buin. The other bomber, carrying Vice Admiral Matome Ugaki, Yamamoto's chief of staff, plunged into the sea and sank. Ugaki was critically wounded; the six staff members with him on the plane were killed. As Lanphier and Barber eased off, the trailing P-38 pilots shot down three Zeros, losing only one of their own in brief dogfights.

..."Forward-deployed" means in close proximity to a conflict or potential conflict.

GOT YAMAMOTO

A member of Yamamoto's staff who had been delayed at Rabaul arrived later and recovered his chief's body from the jungle. He cremated the remains and carried the ashes to Tokyo. Shocked by the loss of Yamamoto, the Japanese government did not announce the fleet commander's death until May 21. Because of the delayed announcement, Nimitz could not say for certain whether the admiral was dead. Six months passed before the Imperial Japanese Navy named Yamamoto's successor: Admiral Mineichi Koga. According to Vice Admiral Shigeru Fukudome, there "could be only one Yamamoto and nobody could take his place."

As naval historian Samuel Eliot Morrison observed, "This neat, planned kill was equivalent to a major victory." Without the genius of Yamamoto, the Japanese navy never recovered from the loss of its admiral, proving that one man can make a difference.

* * *

STRIKING THE FLAG

As early as the reign of King John in the early 1200s, England claimed sovereignty over the seas around the British isles. If commanders of any of his majesty's ships encountered vessels of other nations in territorial waters and they did not lower their flags in deference to the British, those enemy ships could be attacked and seized as prizes of war. By the 1500s with the growing power of the English armada, it was common etiquette for a ship of one nation visiting Britain to lower their topsails as well as their national flag as a sign of respect. Furling a nation's flag at such moments came to be known as "striking the flag," also "striking the colors." If the captain of a ship did not do so, it invited attack.

By the 1700s, "striking the flag" had taken on an entirely new meaning that related to the outcome of battle between warships. By then, European naval powers had agreed to require a ship to fly its national flag before attacking another ship as a means of identification to the enemy. By terms of international maritime law, whoever lost the engagement was required to "strike the flag"—lower the ensign as a sign of surrender. The rules of nautical warfare still insist on "striking the flag" to announce surrender.

First major military use of GPS: finding Scott O'Grady in Bosnia (1995).

BIG WEEK

In February 1944, Big Week signaled a transformation in the American air campaign in Europe and the beginning of the end of the war for Germany.

AIR SUPREMACY

If D-day was going to be a success, the Allies had to gain operational air supremacy over the Luftwaffe before then. The plan that came to be known as Big Week (officially known as Operation Argument) was to lure the Luftwaffe into the skies by targeting German aircraft plants. Killing German pilots in the process would make aircraft production irrelevant—Germany would not be able to train replacement pilots at a fast enough rate. It would be the first time that Luftwaffe planes and pilots were targeted as the number-one priority, versus Allied aircraft being used for defensive purposes.

WAITING FOR WEATHER

By February 1944 there were enough bombers and escort fighters to begin the massive raids against Germany that General Henry H. "Hap" Arnold, commander of the Army Air Forces (AAF), had requested. But the weather over Europe wasn't right for sustained combat missions until Army meteorologists finally delivered a favorable forecast for Sunday, February 20—an extended period of clear weather that would be perfect for visual bombardment.

PLANS INTO ACTION

General Carl "Tooey" Spaatz, the American air commander of the European theater, personally issued the order to begin the raids. Lieutenant General Jimmy Doolittle's 8th Air Force contributed the majority of the attack forces on this first mission, which consisted of more than 1,000 bombers, the first time that the AAF had launched that many bombers on a single raid. (Technically, only 971 of the bombers received mission credit, but more than 1,000 were launched.) Accompanying the bombers would be more than 900 long-range American fighter planes. In all, 16 bomber wings, 17 fighter groups, and 16 Royal Air Force (RAF) fighter squadrons darkened the skies over Europe.

The Spanish-American War lasted less than four months—from April 25 to August 12, 1898.

BIG PLANS FOR BIG WEEK

The attack plans were complex. Six of the bomber wings flew a diversionary attack—without fighters—to Poland on a northern route, hoping to draw some of the German fighters away from the main bomber force. The rest of the bombers attacked aircraft industry targets around Leipzig and Brunswick in central Germany. The damage inflicted was heavy; the only downside was that machine tools used in aircraft construction escaped significant destruction.

This daylight raid on February 20 had been preceded by an RAF night attack on Leipzig and would be followed each night by coordinated RAF nighttime bombing raids on targets that would be attacked again by American bombers the following day.

THE REST OF THE WEEK

The raids flown on February 21 and 22 were less successful; on the 23rd, the entire 8th Air Force was grounded due to low clouds and icing conditions while the 15th Air Force, launching from bases in Italy, flew only 102 bombers against some ball-bearing factories in Austria. On the 24th, the clouds broke and more massive attacks on Germany were launched. More than 800 bombers of the 8th and 15th Air Forces attacked Augsburg, Stuttgart, Schweinfurt, and Regensburg under clear skies. On the 25th, more than 1,300 bombers and 1,000 fighters struck airplane factories in Germany. The 8th had dropped 10,000 tons of bombs—equaling the total tonnage dropped during the entire first year of its operation. In general, Allied losses were light and damage inflicted during these raids was severe—largely the result of a precision visual attack. When the participants in these last missions landed, Big Week officially came to an end.

SOMETHING LOST, SOMETHING GAINED

Roughly 2,600 airmen were killed, wounded, or captured during the operation. Of the 3,800 8th and 15th Air Force bombers that flew that week, losses totaled 6 percent—less than predicted by American commanders. RAF attacks against five German cities were equally massive: more than 2,300 bombers dropped nearly 10,000 tons of bombs. And the RAF suffered similar losses.

The effects on German industry were difficult to assess, but of

U.S. aircraft dropped 437 bombs and missiles in Iraq in the first six months of 2007.

greater impact was the damage done to the Luftwaffe, which lost a third of its single-engine fighters and 20 percent of its pilots. German losses continued into March, and by April the Luftwaffe was unable to effectively defend against the Allied air offensive. Big Week signaled a transformation in the air campaign against Germany. In the end, the Luftwaffe lost the "Argument" and Germany lost the war.

> "I could see the omen of the war's end when I lay in my sickbed and watched the bombers of the American Fifteenth Air Force fly across the Alps from their Italian bases to bomb German industrial targets and there wasn't a German fighter plane anywhere in sight."
>
> **—Albert Speer, Germany's Minister of Armaments**

* * *

FOR THE BIRDS

In spring 1922 a San Francisco newspaper issued a challenge to any aviator to race homing pigeons from Portland, Oregon, to San Francisco, California. A young Air Service major, Henry H. Arnold, who would eventually become General "Hap" Arnold, rose to the occasion. Carrier pigeons had been used to transmit important messages during World War I; Arnold's plane, an old DH-4 biplane powered by a Liberty engine, had seen some action, too.

"War Bird," "Miss Oregon'" and "Miss California," were among the feathered entrants. Oregon governor, Ben W. Olcott, a staunch advocate for soldier's rights and military aviation, flew with Arnold. The morning was so damp that it took nearly an hour to start up the old biplane's engine. By 9:22 the pigeons had been sighted over Eugene, Oregon, and Major Arnold was still behind. The Liberty caught up with the pigeons and passed them, then lost the lead during refueling in Medford, Oregon. After getting the engine started once again, Arnold took off for the final leg of the race, eventually beating the pigeons by a handsome margin—and sparing the fledgling Air Service any loss of face—or funding.

Singer Kate Smith helped sell $600 million worth of war bonds during World War II.

CHEESE IT! THE MP!

They do a lot more than round up AWOLs and break up fights in bars.

A STEP BACK IN TIME

The U.S. Army's Military Police Corps didn't achieve permanent status until September 26, 1941, but the history of military police in America goes back a lot farther than that. You've heard of "provosts"? That's what the privates in the military police were called through most of their history.

PARDON MY FRENCH

The first American MP unit, the Troops of the Marechaussee (styled after a French provost corps of that name), was authorized by Congress in May 1778. The unit had 63 men, including officers, two trumpeters, and four executioners. Most were German-born Americans—except for two Swiss and one Mohawk. Their stated mission was to "apprehend and arrest all marauders, rioters, drunkards and deserters, and all soldiers who would be found beyond the limits of their organizations without permission." A second military police force of 600 was established later that year to administer the POW compound at Charlottesville, Virginia.

THIS WAY, GEORGE, AND THANKS

At the war's end in December 1783, one of the corps' last duties was to escort General George Washington home to Mount Vernon in Virginia, after which the last remaining 12 members were discharged—making them the last soldiers discharged from the Revolutionary War. No other military police units were formally organized in the U.S. Army until the outbreak of the Civil War.

VIRGINIA ISN'T JUST FOR LOVERS

In July 1861, the Union army authorized each regiment commander to choose one officer as provost marshal who, along with a permanent guard of 10 enlisted men, had the simple duties of "preserving property" and of arresting "wrongdoers," who were sent to jail in Alexandria, Virginia. At first, commanders were particularly sensitive to the political implications of interfering with local law enforcement, so provosts weren't given authority over civilians. Things changed after the Union's defeat at Bull Run.

CRACKING DOWN

To control the ever-growing number of soldiers stationed in Washington, D.C., Major General George B. McClellan appointed a provost marshal and assigned him some 1,000 officers and men to control gambling and looting, and scoop up stragglers and deserters. A curfew was imposed, and jurisdiction was gradually extended to the local citizenry and to "places of public accommodation and amusement." Now the budding MPs had the power to legally search citizens, seize weapons and contraband, and make arrests.

Eventually, every division had a provost guard of 10 enlisted men to protect civilian property and to supervise and inspect trade between local merchants and army units and individual soldiers. For the first time, intelligence—i.e., spying—was added to the job description. And who better to create the first criminal investigation division than Major Allan Pinkerton, whose Pinkerton National Detective Agency was by then already legendary?

UNCLE SAM NEEDS YOU—OR ELSE!

As the war dragged on, Congress passed the Enrollment Act, designed to provide fresh draftees and which was so unpopular that it caused riots in the streets. As a result, Secretary of War Edwin Stanton decided that a police force was needed to oversee the draft law and to arrest deserters.

The problem was that men who could afford to hire a substitute or pay the government $300 could avoid enlistment. And blacks, who were not official citizens, were exempt from the draft. The general feeling of unfairness prompted a mob of mostly Irish immigrant protesters to riot across New York City in July 1863. An estimated 100 people, mostly black, were killed; churches were burned down, as was an orphan asylum housing more than 200 black children—most of whom escaped unharmed.

The provost troops were vastly outnumbered, as were the local police, but they did what they could to contain the violence. The riots continued until President Lincoln, on the fourth day, sent in 4,000 combat troops from Gettysburg. It had been the deadliest civil disturbance in America's history.

SOUTH OF THE BORDER

Like its Union counterpart, the Confederate States Army Provost Guard was created to maintain military discipline over vast numbers of soldiers. Their responsibilities expanded to include guarding captured Union soldiers (eventually numbering about 200,000). The guard gradually assumed control over civilians as well, mostly in the suppression of disloyalty and subversion to the cause, which naturally entailed more stringent controls over civilian activities.

The provost guard walked a thin line: marshalling the Confederacy's available resources for war while also making allowances for the South's long-standing inclination against anything resembling a strong central government. The guard was fairly unsuccessful in picking up stragglers and deserters—a fact that historians say was a major factor in the Confederate defeat. Some 15,000 troops who should have been at General Robert E. Lee's battle line at Antietam—the bloodiest single-day battle in American history, with about 23,000 casualties—were in fact AWOL, leaving Lee's 45,000 men to face McClellan's 87,000. By late 1864, more than 100,000 Confederate troops had gone AWOL, never to return.

DOUGHBOYS AND BAD BOYS

The Provost Marshal General's Bureau stayed pretty much the same for 50 years—until the American Expeditionary Forces (AEF) entered France in 1917. As crime rates among American troops mounted, the bureau saw the need for a detective branch. The War Department established the Criminal Investigation Division (CID) in November 1918 to detect and prevent crimes in AEF-occupied territory. The CID operated like a big-city detective squad. Most members—selected by the provost marshals—were detectives, lawyers, and journalists in civilian life. The more than 4,000 cases investigated in 1918 were everything from black-market activities to the theft and illegal sale of government supplies.

OVERDOING IT

Congress authorized the establishment of a Military Police Corps in October 1918 on a limited, nonpermanent basis. Relatively well equipped with 50 horses, six mules, one wagon, 18 motorcycles, and 105 bicycles, the corps was one of the most mobile in the entire Army. Congress's decision proved to be a smart move.

In 1940 Benjamin O. Davis Sr. became the first black general in the U.S. Army...

The hordes of American doughboys (described by an anonymous European as "over-paid, over-sexed, and over here") who took unauthorized leave to see the sights of a now-liberated Europe kept the MPs busy: detachments of military police were stationed in 476 cities in France, England, Italy, Luxembourg, and Germany.

AU REVOIR!

The number of U.S. military police peaked in March 1919 with 1,100 officers and 30,000 enlisted men. The 2nd Provost Guard Company, assigned to American military prisoners at the La Roquette Prison in Paris, were among the last MPs to leave Europe in 1922, at which point they returned control of the prison to the French. At the time of the armistice ending World War I, the entire corps stood at 463 officers and 15,912 men stationed throughout France and with the troops of the 3rd Army who would participate in the occupation of the Rhineland.

When war in Europe broke out in 1939, the possibility of subversion and invasion on U.S. soil made America nervous. Secretary of War Henry L. Stimson established the Military Police Corps as a permanent branch of the Army on September 26, 1941.

BACK TO THE FRONT

The branch performed its traditional military duties in World War II. Civilian duties included protecting designated buildings, public works, and localities of special importance; supervising the evacuation of civilians; assisting in the enforcement of blackouts; and performing security investigations. By mid-1942 the Army had 17 battalions of military police units. As the Army expanded toward full wartime strength, military police companies became increasingly specialized. The corps, which started with a paltry 2,000 men in 1941, grew to a strength of more than 200,000.

A CLOSE CALL

In 1949 the newly formed Department of Defense was in the process of reorganizing the Army and a plan was underway to disband the Military Police Corps, but it survived the 1950 Army Reorganization Act and remained a separate branch of the Army. Most MPs who arrived during the early months of the Korean War came from Japan, where they'd been serving as occupation forces

...In 1954 Benjamin O. Davis Jr. became the first black general in the U.S. Air Force.

following World War II. Their duties in Korea included harbor patrol, traffic control, arresting violators, escorting POWs, guarding installations, and controlling guerrilla activities. Today, the U.S. military police still serve in Korea alongside Republic of Korea (ROK) military police, Korean National Police (KNP), and other police organizations there.

A DIFFERENT KIND OF WAR

America's next war would be the most intense and dangerous to date for its military police. This time, aside from their usual duties, MPs took part in combat operations, patrolling jungles and villages throughout Vietnam. They provided support for large-scale combat operations, constantly contending with ambushes, mines, and snipers. One platoon spent 20 days on patrol with the infantry.

MPs also worked as "tunnel rats," locating and destroying enemy tunnels, and aiding in the capture of suspected enemy soldiers. They supplied security and route reconnaissance, escorted convoys, and performed sweeps, patrols, and search operations. Saigon assignments were no less treacherous. In a one-week period, the total losses for one battalion were 27 killed and 45 wounded. More than one MP lost his life on duty calls to break up bar fights.

EVEN MORE DIFFERENT

MPs were also kept busy guarding the U.S. military prisoner population, which peaked at 10,450 in 1970. By the end of that year there were 117 arrests for refusals to obey orders and 239 incidents of "fragging" (the killing of an American by another American, usually a superior officer or a noncommissioned officer). Another 333 fragging incidents were reported in 1971. In September 1971, U.S. military police had to conduct a siege at Cam Ranh Bay—not against the Vietcong but against 14 soldiers of the 35th Engineer Group who refused to come out of their bunkers.

At height of the war, there were more than 30,000 military police in the U.S. Army, the largest and only combat-tested military police brigade in the history of the Military Police Corps. Today, each branch maintains its own military police force. In addition to the U.S. Army Military Police Corps there are the Provost Marshal's Office (Marine Corps), Master-at-Arms aided by the Shore Patrol (Navy), and the Air Force Security Forces.

"Heaven, Hell, or Hoboken by Christmas." —attributed to Gen. John Pershing, 1918

HIGH FLIERS

Life could be exciting—and short—aboard the Flying Fortresses.

FLYING TO VICTORY

Crippling Hitler's manufacturing and transportation capabilities was crucial to America's victory in World War II. To achieve that goal, the United States relied on squads of heavy bombers stationed in England, the most famous aircraft used being the B-17 Flying Fortress. Crews gave their planes names like *Memphis Belle*, *Shoo Shoo Baby*, and *Hit and Run* and painted their nosecones with everything from Donald Duck in aviator gear to pinups of long-legged girls in bathing suits. During World War II, Flying Fortresses and their crews became American icons.

BOEING BUILDS A BOMBER

In 1934 the country was still suffering through the woes of the Great Depression. Boeing, a struggling seaplane company, built a prototype of a four-engine bomber for the U.S. Army. Officially called the B-17, it was so well armed for its time, with five 30-caliber machine guns, that a reporter dubbed it "the Flying Fortress," and the nickname stuck.

The first mass-produced Fortresses (model B-17E) flew into combat carrying 4,200 pounds of bombs and nine machine guns. But they were vulnerable to head-on attacks from German fighter planes because most of their firepower was on the sides of the planes, so new B-17Gs were introduced. These had a "chin turret" that carried a machine gun just below the nose of the plane. B-17Gs, which helped tip the war in favor of the Allies, carried 13 machine guns and 8,000 pounds of bombs.

Flying Fortresses used a Norden bombsight, a device with both a telescopic sight and a calculator that computed bomb trajectories. Linked to the autopilot, the Norden could essentially fly the Fortress to an exact spot for a bomb drop; it was claimed that B-17s could drop bombs into a pickle barrel from 25,000 feet. Though that was more than a slight exaggeration, heavy firepower combined with bombsight accuracy made B-17s one of World War II's most deadly weapons.

More than 14,000 helicopters (from all services) saw action in Vietnam.

MAGNIFICENT MEN IN THEIR FLYING MACHINES

B-17s carried a flight crew of 10; the pilot and copilot were the only crew members who didn't also man machine guns. The navigator directed the flight path. The flight engineer was in charge of the plane's mechanical condition. Behind the bomb bay (where bombs were stored in racks) was a radio station where the radio operator sent and received coded messages. Central to the mission was the bombardier, who took control when the plane neared its bombing target. The rest of the crew defended the plane. A ball-turret gunner crouched in a small enclosure protruding from the plane's belly. In the plane's central section, two waist gunners manned each side of the plane, and a tail gunner knelt in a two-gun turret at the rear. Bomber crews were heroes at home and were glorified in films, but life in the B-17 wasn't glamorous.

A DAY IN THE LIFE

On days that a mission was planned, airmen were awakened before dawn. They were given a hearty (some called it greasy) breakfast, which was followed by a briefing. The fliers viewed a map with the twisting route to their target; routes were never straight because of a need to confuse the enemy. And they also received weather information and intelligence on anticipated enemy actions.

Bombers taxied down runways in assigned order. On some missions, hundreds of bombers took off while "lead planes" guided them into battle formation at about 6,000 feet. To protect one another, B-17s flew in packs of about 36, in rows, forming a three-dimensional box formation that let them fire in all directions. Although they flew at altitudes of up to 30,000 feet, where the air was thin and temperatures could plunge to 60 below zero, B-17 cabins weren't pressurized or heated. As the planes reached 10,000 feet, the crew donned oxygen masks and electrically heated flight suits, boots, and heavy gloves. Oxygen deprivation and frostbite from malfunctioning equipment in B-17s could be a problem. Airmen performed the mentally and physically demanding jobs that the mission required under freezing, uncomfortable conditions.

As the plane approached the bombing target, the men put on flak suits and steel helmets and a harness for a parachute. Bombing was the most vulnerable aspect of the mission because a plane had to be kept on a precise and level course even if they were flying through heavy antiaircraft fire or being attacked by the German Luftwaffe. The crew had a healthy respect for the death-dealing capacity of the German fighter planes, and for most, terror was an unavoidable part of the job. A mission deep into Germany could last over eight hours before the planes returned to base. The B-17s would often limp home badly shot up. Crews sometimes returned to base with only one out of four engines still working, or made a successful "belly landing" if the landing gear had been shot away.

A HISTORY OF HIT-AND-RUN

The first American-manned B-17 bomber raid occurred on August 17, 1942. From a base in southern England, 8th Air Force pilots launched a daylight attack on a railway yard at Rouen, France. At least half the bombs hit a precise target area and all the B-17s returned safely. Nearly two years before the Allies had ground troops in Europe, the B-17s began an attack on German-occupied territory. B-17s had a range so great that Allied fighter planes, which had less fuel capacity, couldn't accompany them. In 1943 that lack of fighter escorts—and a vulnerability to being attacked head-on—led to high casualties. It was estimated that a B-17 crewman had a one in four chance of completing 25 missions. Army Air Force strategists were on the verge of giving up daytime precision bombing, which would be a huge blow to the Allies.

Failure turned to success in 1944 when the new B-17Gs arrived in England with their chin turrets and an ability to counter head-on attacks. That year also saw the addition of Mustang fighter planes that carried extra fuel tanks and could escort B-17s to targets in Germany. The combination of better-armed Fortresses and far-flying Mustangs gave the Allies a weapon that not even Germany's skilled fighter pilots could overcome.

During World War II, 12,000 B-17s dropped 640,036 tons of bombs on European targets in daylight raids. They helped to devastate the German capital of Berlin and destroy transportation sites. They also destroyed manufacturing sites and fuel locations, and by December 1944, the German tanks trying to beat back the Allied invasion were stranded due to lack of fuel. War in the air had definitely affected the war on the ground. Flying Fortress bombing raids were such a deadly success that they did more than help win World War II. They put modern warfare into the skies.

...to receive prize money for taking a German blockade runner, on November 6, 1941.

THE STORMY DAYS OF BULL HALSEY

How a couple of typhoons nearly sank the reputation of one of America's most admirable admirals.

AND THAT'S NO BULL

Admiral William F. "Bull" Halsey Jr., one of the great personalities of World War II, didn't answer to his nickname, which he said came "from some drunken newspaper correspondent who punched the letter 'u' instead of 'i' in writing Bill." But the nickname fit his pugnacious personality. Naval operations off the Philippines in October 1944, and again off Okinawa in May 1945, showcased his aggressive and risk-taking tendencies.

MAN OF ACTION

Halsey had already seen a lot of action before World War II. He'd spent 44 years in the Navy establishing an unblemished record as a commander. After graduating from Annapolis in 1904, he rose through the ranks of a growing Navy that was short on officers. He commanded a destroyer in World War I and was a captain when he decided, in May 1935, at the age of 52, to complete flight training so that he could qualify as a Navy pilot. This enabled him, two months later, to take command of the USS *Saratoga*, America's third aircraft carrier. He predicted aircraft carriers would displace battleships as the fleet's strongest ships, and he planned to prove it.

His efforts early in the war marked him as a top carrier commander when, in April 1942, he carried Lieutenant Colonel James H. "Jimmy" Doolittle's B-25 bombers across the Pacific for their raids on Japan. In command of the South Pacific forces, with the only three carriers available at the time, Halsey checked Isoroku Yamamoto's powerful Japanese navy at the Battle of the Santa Cruz Islands, an action that paved the way for extensive amphibious operations in the Solomons. As the war began to move in another direction, so too did Halsey; he arrived in the Philippines in October 1944. That's where the trouble started.

"Nobody ever drowned in sweat." —Marine Corps slogan

THE PHILIPPINES SETUP

Admiral Chester W. Nimitz was commander in chief of the Pacific Fleet, and operated with two alternating fleet commanders: the Third Fleet under Halsey and the Fifth Fleet under Admiral Raymond A. Spruance. If Nimitz wanted the fleet used conservatively, he put Spruance in charge; if he wanted the fleet used aggressively, Halsey was his man. When General MacArthur requested heavy air support for the October 1944 invasion of Leyte—the largest Allied amphibious campaign to date—the job went to Halsey.

The Japanese had anticipated the assault and sent their entire fleet to stop it. They used three groups: the Southern and Center forces were to strike MacArthur from different directions and ward off the landing, and the Northern Force—a suicide fleet of carriers, with a few planes and old combat ships—was to decoy Halsey away from Leyte so the other forces could defeat MacArthur.

HALSEY AND THE DECOYS

Once Halsey set his mind to a task, the "bull" sometimes took over. The Center Force arrived on the night of October 23, too late to stop the landings. After an attack by Halsey's carrier planes in the morning, the Japanese withdrew with heavy damage. Halsey, thinking he'd repulsed the Center Force in San Bernardino Strait, took the bait and steamed from Leyte to intercept the decoy force, which had stopped a few hundred miles to the north, off Luzon. The Center Force returned during the night. In the morning, it threatened MacArthur's beachhead from the north while Halsey's aircraft converged on the decoys. The Southern Force arrived in Surigao Strait and threatened Leyte from the south.

LIVING UP TO HIS NAME

Halsey had been ordered by Nimitz to protect MacArthur's beachhead, and his reckless abandonment of his position left the Allied landing fleet unprotected and unopposed by the Japanese fleets. The Seventh Fleet signaled for help; Halsey didn't respond until he received a message from Nimitz: "Turkey trots to water. Where is repeat where is Task Force 34? The world wonders."

Nimitz regarded Halsey's aggressiveness an ostensible breach of orders and a grievous mistake, and ordered the Third Fleet back to Leyte. What Halsey never learned until later was that the clerk

In 1945 Eddie Slovik was the first U.S. soldier to be executed for desertion since 1865.

sending the message had added "The world wonders"—not Nimitz.

Halsey, who still wanted time to destroy the enemy, left enough ships off the northern Philippines to rid the seas of the last carriers in the Japanese fleet. But by the time he returned to Leyte, the Seventh Fleet, commanded by Vice Admiral Thomas C. Kinkaid, comprised of old battleships and cruisers that had been lent by Nimitz to MacArthur, had destroyed the Japanese Southern Force and repulsed the Center Force.

Despite warnings from some of his officers that the Japanese carriers of the Northern Force were decoys, Halsey would not be restrained. His nature was to fight, to push anything out of his way, and to destroy every vestige of the Japanese navy regardless of the consequences. Skylarking to the north left a small blemish on his record. Regardless of the criticism, he believed in using his fleet to remove any obstacle standing in his way.

THE BIG BLOW

Halsey felt the same way three weeks later when, on December 17, the Third Fleet staff aerologist reported a strong tropical disturbance 500 miles to the east, moving northwest at 12 to 15 knots. The storm appeared to be heading for the Philippines. The Third Fleet, having consumed much of its fuel on the 900-mile round-trip to and from Cape Engaño, now had to steam another 800 miles to reach the supply base on Ulithi Atoll in the Carolines.

Nimitz wanted the fleet off Luzon to strike enemy airfields in support of MacArthur's invasion of Mindoro on December 19. Halsey wanted to get out of Nimitz's doghouse, so he didn't want to bungle another mission. Although storm warnings posed an element of risk, his ships had ridden out tropical storms before.

HEADING BACK TO THE DOGHOUSE

While plowing westward under mounting seas on the evening of December 17, Halsey shifted course from west to south to avoid what he thought to be a tropical storm and instead moved directly into the path of a powerful typhoon. His ships, riding high in the waves with empty fuel tanks, became unseaworthy. He tried refueling more than a hundred ships at sea, but the task proved impossible, so he canceled the fueling operation and radioed MacArthur that he wouldn't be able to support the Mindoro operation.

Mitsubishi was the manufacturer of the famous World War II Zero fighter plane.

On December 18, Halsey received reports from his destroyers of men being washed overboard. Other ships lost steering control. Planes were swept off the decks of light carriers and broke loose on the hangar decks, slamming into bulkheads and catching fire.

FROM BAD TO WORSE

At 10:00 p.m., staff aerologists reported the wind at 73 knots (84 mph) and rapidly increasing. Destroyers began to heel over with their stacks almost horizontal with the sea. Ventilators and intakes were flooded, knocking out power and shorting circuits to the pumps, steering, lights, and communication equipment. Halsey rode out the storm on the battleship *New Jersey*, writing: "Our chairs, tables, and all loose gear had to be double-lashed; we ourselves were buffeted from one bulkhead to another; we could not hear our own voices above the uproar." He didn't have it as bad as some of the rest. Riding out a typhoon on a 45,000-ton battleship was a lot easier than doing so on a 1,400-ton destroyer.

At noon on December 19 the winds slowed, but visibility remained poor. At dusk, the search for survivors began. Halsey called the three-day rescue effort the most exhaustive in Navy history. Of 839 missing sailors, only 74 were rescued. Three destroyers sank because their skippers failed to ballast the fuel tanks with seawater. No ship survived undamaged, including eight carriers. The typhoon destroyed 186 planes, which were blown overboard, jettisoned, or collided on deck and burned.

RAMIFICATIONS

A court of inquiry found Halsey principally responsible for an error in judgment, but he didn't suffer any official sanctions. The problem actually stemmed from the inability of aerologists to accurately track and predict the path and velocity of storms.

Nimitz relieved Halsey of duty on January 26, 1945, and turned the Third Fleet, which then became the Fifth Fleet, over to Admiral Spruance. Halsey did nothing for four months while Japanese planes hammered the Fifth Fleet off Okinawa. Annoyed by the losses, Nimitz relieved Spruance and on May 27 sent Halsey, once more in charge of the Third Fleet, to Okinawa to rid the sea of kamikazes. In his characteristic bull-like manner, Halsey set about the task by bombing Japanese airfields with carrier planes.

The U.S. Navy currently uses Trident, Poseidon, Tomahawk, and Polaris missiles.

THE DOUBLE-HEADER

On June 3, another tropical storm was boiling up from the south. Aerologists informed Halsey the fleet would be safe where it was. Halsey said, "I can't take a chance. If I should be forced to go westward, I would be in shallow waters with no room to maneuver." Instead, he considered going south. Aerologists suggested first sending some of the heavier ships south to report on weather conditions. Two carrier groups moved southeast about the same time another ship to the south reported the storm at typhoon intensity. Unfortunately, Halsey did not receive the report until the morning of June 5 because it lay in a tray waiting to be decoded.

When the typhoon hit with 127-knot (146-mph) winds later in the day, it brought 75-foot waves. It damaged 36 ships, including four carriers and the cruiser *Pittsburgh*, which had 104 feet of its bow ripped off. Fortunately, its watertight bulkheads had been closed and the crew had been sent to battle stations, so no lives were lost. Despite being better prepared to deal with typhoons after the previous disaster, 76 planes were lost or damaged.

Halsey said, "No one who has not been through a typhoon can conceive its fury. The seventy-foot seas smash you from all sides. The rain and the scud (spray) are blinding; they drive you flat out, until you can't tell the ocean from the air."

A SLAP ON THE OTHER WRIST

A court of inquiry once again found Halsey guilty of bad judgment. Nimitz understood the situation better than Secretary of the Navy James V. Forrestal, who wanted to relieve Halsey of command. Nimitz didn't want to lose his top commander and managed to change Forrestal's mind. Halsey then went about his business, patched up his ships, and ended Japanese air and naval power by pulverizing their air bases and crippling ships in Japan's seaports.

WHERE THE BUCK STOPS

In December 1945, Congress provided legislation for four admirals, including Halsey, to be promoted to five-star rank. Forrestal would not award a fifth star to Halsey without awarding one to Spruance. But there was only one award left, so he let Truman make the call; it went to Halsey—the admiral who, if not for two typhoons, might be known as the greatest commander in the Navy's history.

The Korean War was the first conflict to initiate widespread use of jet aircraft in combat.

WE BUILD, WE FIGHT!

That's the proud motto of the U.S. Navy Seabees, a.k.a. the Naval Construction Force.

SOMEBODY'S GOT TO DO IT

The Naval Construction Force was the brainchild of Rear Admiral Ben Moreell, who was enough of a visionary to realize that the Navy and the Marines would need massive military construction support in the remote locations where they would be posted after the attack on Pearl Harbor.

Moreell made his request on December 28, 1941, and had his answer—a resounding yes—within a week. He immediately started putting together the First Construction Detachment, which consisted of 296 electricians, carpenters, plumbers, and equipment operators. Two weeks later, the detachment was deployed to Bora Bora in the South Pacific, where the first "Seabees" started construction of a fuel tank "farm"—a fueling station for ships at sea.

By July the Seabees landed on Midway Island to begin work on a new airstrip and to start the massive cleanup of damage caused by Japanese bombing. But that was only the beginning. The Seabees would participate in every major amphibious assault in World War II, including the Normandy invasion.

ACTION IN THE PACIFIC

The Seabees' first foray into a combat zone was at Guadalcanal. Using mostly captured Japanese equipment, they built the strategically crucial Henderson Field, the airfield that would be used by United States Navy, Marine, and Army forces in the war in the South Pacific. While they were building the base and airstrip in addition to fighting the elements, the Seabees were subjected to sniper fire, artillery, and bombing from the enemy. As soon as a bomb crater was made, the Seabees made a (ahem) beeline for it, and filled it in.

After Guadalcanal, Seabees took part in every island invasion in the Pacific, building airstrips, roads, and camps, usually—as they had at Guadalcanal—working while under fire.

THEIR NOT-SO-SECRET WEAPON

The Seabees—and the rest of the armed forces—owe much of their success in World War II to Commodore John W. Laycock and the buoyant steel box he invented. Laycock had been working on the idea as early as 1935, but he'd been unable to interest any company in producing it. Early in 1941, he came up with a model built from cigar boxes, based on the idea of pontoon boats and bridges. The full-size version would be built of sheet steel, seven feet long, five feet wide, and five feet deep. Each pontoon weighed about 2,600 pounds. Held together with self-tightening interlocking bolts and straps, Laycock's pontoons could be reconfigured into nearly unsinkable docks and piers. Strung together as causeways (usually two by 30), they were first used in the invasion of Sicily and later in the Pacific.

MOVABLE FEATS

Huge outboard motors turned the pontoons (six of them by 30) into self-propelled landing barges that became known as "Rhino" ferries (presumably because they were big and gray like a rhinoceros). First used at the Normandy invasion, the Rhinos transported trucks, tanks, and artillery from an LST (Landing Ship, Tank) to the beach, carrying about 40 vehicles, thus unloading one LST in just two trips. The ferries had one downside and that was their speed, which was only about three knots. Other than that, they did the trick.

A SEABEE'S WORK IS NEVER DONE

The Seabees manned the Rhino ferries, put up pontoon causeways on the beach for troops and armor to travel over, and worked alongside U.S. Army engineers in demolition units to clear the beach of steel and concrete obstacles and plant explosive charges to breach the German defenses. Immediately after the invasion, they were put to work again, this time on their biggest project in Europe: building an artificial harbor at Normandy.

Over the course of World War II, the Construction Battalions participated in every theater of operation, building 111 major airstrips, 700 square blocks of warehouses, hospitals for 70,000 patients, storage tanks for 100 million gallons of gasoline, and housing for 1.5 million men.

WE DON'T NEED NO STINKIN' BRIDGES

On March 22, 1945, General George S. Patton moved his forces across the Rhine at Oppenheim in a frontal assault that swept away the German defense. The Seabees built pontoon ferries similar to the Rhinos of D-day fame and used them to transport Patton's tanks across the river. The Seabees operated more than 300 craft that shuttled thousands of troops into the heart of Germany. One Seabee crew even had the honor of ferrying Winston Churchill across the Rhine on an inspection tour.

POST-POSTWAR

Demobilization after World War II reduced the Seabees' ranks to a few thousand men, but their effectiveness earned them a permanent place in the Navy. They continued to serve in Korea, Vietnam, the first Gulf War, Somalia, and Bosnia—and more currently in Afghanistan and Iraq, where they've built and repaired everything from schools, hospitals, and roads to power and water supply systems. They also work in areas hit by natural disasters like Hurricane Katrina, which devastated New Orleans, near the home base of their own Naval Mobile Construction Battalion 133 in Gulfport, Mississippi.

WHICH CAME FIRST, THE SEABEE OR THE C.B.?

The Seabees' insignia, the "Fighting Bee," is a cartoon bee in a sailor's cap, flying through the air holding a variety of hand tools and a tommy gun. According to the Bee's creator, Frank Iafrate, the idea of a "seabee" was based on his drawing and didn't originate as a play on the "C" and "B" in "Construction Battalion." Iafrate was working as a civilian file clerk in at the Naval Air Station in Quonset Point, Rhode Island, in January 1942 when the officer in charge of the new Naval Construction Battalions heard about his talents as an amateur caricaturist and asked him to design a "Disney-type" insignia. Iafrate used the image of a bee to convey industriousness; the bee as a symbol for men who worked industriously at sea led naturally to the name "Seabees." Later in 1942, Iafrate became a Seabee himself and served as a chief carpenter's mate. He made it through the war safely, and when he got home he began his lifelong career in graphic design.

THE U.S. COAST GUARD IN WWII: EUROPE

Pearl Harbor wasn't the first military action of the U.S. armed forces during World War II. America's first and second wartime captures were carried out by a few humble Coast Guard cutter crews.

YOU'RE IN THE NAVY NOW

The Coast Guard had served under the Navy before, dating back to the War of 1812 and in every major conflict since then. Not until World War II, however, would the Coast Guard see combat in so many parts of the globe.

After Germany conquered Denmark on April 9, 1940, Danes in Greenland appealed to the United States for assistance, and the State Department sent the Coast Guard. The Battle of the Atlantic between German U-boats and Britain's Royal Navy convoys was just switching into high gear when Admiral Russell R. Waesche organized the Northeast Greenland Patrol under Captain Edward H. "Iceberg" Smith and detailed the cutters *Northland*, *North Star*, and *Bear* for operations in the Denmark Strait. Long years of Arctic service made the ships perfect for the task. The *Northland* was refitted with depth charges and carried a Curtiss SOC-4 single-float seaplane for reconnaissance.

On September 11, 1941, after the German submarine *U-652* attacked the Navy destroyer USS *Greer* on patrol off Greenland, President Roosevelt issued this directive: "The Coast Guard . . . shall, during the period of the present unlimited emergency, operate as a part of the Navy, subject to the orders of the Secretary of the Navy." The order included a "shoot on sight" mandate. Admiral Waesche issued instructions to all cutters on the Atlantic and Gulf coasts: "Reduce use of radio to minimum: paint all vessels war color; destroy any German or Italian submarine or aircraft sighted: take such action against hostile surface craft as may be deemed practicable and circumstances warrant."

TWO FOR THE RECORD BOOKS

On September 12, Captain Smith, acting on a tip from a dogsled patrol, sent the *Northland* to investigate a suspicious Norwegian fishing trawler named the *Buskoe*. A boarding team found a German radio transmitter and receiver on the ship. The next day, a search party from the *Northland* found the radio base, surrounded it, and took the men into custody—America's first military action of World War II.

The capture took place before the United States declared war on Germany and provided a sample of the role the Coast Guard would play in the war to follow. Admiral Waesche, the longest-serving commandant of the Coast Guard, oversaw the transformation of the small peacetime Coast Guard fleet into a force of 160,000 men and women manning 30 destroyer escorts, 75 frigates, 750 cutters, 290 Navy ships, 255 Army vessels, and scores of smaller craft.

BEACH PATROL

Within weeks after the United States went to war against Germany, U-boats began depositing English-speaking saboteurs along the American coast. The Navy turned beach patrols over to the Coast Guard, which added stations, lookout towers, and an elaborate communication system covering 3,700 miles of Atlantic, Gulf, and Pacific coastline. Some 24,000 coastguardsmen served on beach patrols, which typically consisted of rotating two-man teams armed with rifles or sidearms covering two miles or less of coastline. Horse-mounted patrols began on the East and Gulf coasts in November 1942, and more than 2,000 dogs became part of the organization. Although less than a hundred saboteurs were ever caught, beach patrols saved uncountable numbers of flyers and sailors by reporting downed airplanes and ships in distress.

U-BOAT? NOT IF WE CAN HELP IT

Meanwhile, coastguardsmen assigned to patrols and as convoy escorts between America's mid-Atlantic coast and Europe were kept plenty busy in skirmishes with U-boats. In January 1942 the 2,750-ton cutter *Campbell* encountered a German sub on the surface. The *Campbell* closed as the enemy submerged, then reappeared some distance away. The *Campbell* fired, but missed. Closing on the site where the submarine submerged, the cutter dropped two spreads of depth charges, causing the U-boat to surface. Instead of waiting to confirm the kill, the *Campbell* pulled

Gyrenes: This jocular reference to Marines was first used in England as early as 1894.

away to rescue survivors of a torpedoed tanker. What may have been the Coast Guard's first sinking of a U-boat didn't make it into the record books.

In November 1942, during the peak of the Battle of the Atlantic, U-boats sank 700,000 tons of Allied shipping. The cutter *Ingham*, escorting a convoy on December 15, made sonar contacts for three days in a row and dropped depth charges on each occasion. Commander George E. McCabe didn't know until after the war that the *Ingham* had sunk the *U-626*.

WOLVES AT THE DOOR

Whenever a German "wolf pack" (a concentration of submarines working together) struck a convoy, Coast Guard cutters and escort destroyers chose to save lives rather than pursue the subs. When convoy SC-118 got clobbered by U-boats on February 5, 1943, the cutter *Bibb* picked up 202 survivors and the *Ingham* picked up dozens more. Three U-boats went to the bottom before British air support arrived and the wolf pack withdrew. During four days of wolf pack raids, the *Bibb* and *Ingham* saved more than a thousand lives.

After the remnants of convoy SC-118 unloaded cargo in the British Isles, the empty ships began the voyage back to the United States. The cutter *Campbell* and five Navy corvettes (small patrol boats) escorted the ships. Because of strong gales, the convoy limped along at four knots, and U-boats began picking off the stragglers. One night the cutter *Spencer* spotted the conning tower of a submarine on the surface and fired several 5-inch shells. When the U-boat crash-dived, Commander Harold S. Berdine located the U-boat on the *Campbell*'s sonar, dropped a nine-charge pattern of depth charges, and sank the *U-225*.

Coast Guard ships accounted for the sinking of 18 submarines in the European theater and one in the Pacific. Most of the U-boats were sunk when Coast Guard sailors were occupied in rescue tasks rather than search-and-destroy missions. The outcomes did not always favor the Coast Guard. Two cutters, the *Escanaba* and the *Alexander Hamilton*, were both sunk by torpedoes.

THE NEW GANG IN TOWN

Destroyer escorts (DEs) went into mass production in 1943.

During World War II, Japanese submarines fired at both Fort Stevens in Oregon...

Weighing up to 1,450 tons, a DE could generate 24 knots (27.6 mph), and carried enough 3- or 5-inch guns, torpedo tubes, depth charges, and antiaircraft weapons to sink and destroy any German or Italian sub or plane. As they became available, the Navy formed five escort divisions of 30 ships each with 216-man crews. The Coast Guard manned and operated one of them.

DEs became immediate targets in war zones. Crews spent day and night searching the seas for submarines and the skies for bombers and torpedo planes. On the night of March 9, 1944, an acoustic torpedo fired from the *U-255* struck the *Leopold* 400 miles south of Iceland. Forced to abandon ship, men spilled into the icy water. A sister ship, *Joyce*, closed on the sinking *Leopold* but had to interrupt rescue efforts to avoid torpedoes. Only 28 men were rescued alive. The *Joyce* took revenge on April 16; aided by the *Peterson* and the Navy-manned *Gandy*, she forced the crew of the *U-550* to scuttle their U-boat.

In the Mediterranean on April 20, 1944, German torpedo planes struck a convoy at nightfall. The *Menges* and the *Newell* helped beat off the attack with antiaircraft fire and spent the next four hours rescuing 137 survivors from the torpedoed destroyer *Lansdale*, and two of the German air crews. A few days later the *U-371* closed on the same convoy and the *Menges* went in chase, only to have her stern blown off by an acoustic torpedo, killing 31 sailors and wounding 25. Her skipper refused to abandon the ship, which was patched up and helped back to New York for repair. The Coast Guard DEs continued convoy work, but by the end of 1944 most German submarines had been sent to the bottom or were safeguarded in protected pens until the war's end.

In October 1944, the 6,515-ton Coast Guard weather ships *Eastwind* and *Southwind*, commanded by Captain Charles W. Thomas, spotted a suspicious vessel breaking through the ice in an effort to reach open water. Both ships slit paths through the ice and converged on the unidentified ship. The *Southwind* trained a searchlight on her, and the *Eastwind* bracketed her with two 5-inch forward guns. The German crew of the *Externsteine* surrendered but made no effort to scuttle the ship because they thought it couldn't be freed from the ice. The *Eastwind* broke the ship free the next day. Captain Thomas put a crew on her, rechristened her *Eastbreeze*, and added her to his squadron.

...and oil production facilities near Santa Barbara.

D-DAY AND BEYOND THE CALL OF DUTY

The first Coast Guard-manned LSTs (Landing Ship, Tank) and LCI(L)s (Landing Craft Infantry, Large) made their debut in Europe in 1943 during the Sicily and Salerno landings—without a loss. The two landings served as on-the-job training for the first group of Coast Guard LST and LCI(L) crews designated for Normandy. Dozens of ships were destroyed or damaged by assault mines on D-day, during which the men of Rescue Flotilla 1 distinguished themselves by lifting 1,438 persons from the sea, even going over the side to pull them out of fields of blazing fuel.

As Admiral Richard S. Evans, deputy chief of Naval Operations, acknowledged to Admiral Waesche at the end of the war, "No one knows better than I do how much the Navy owes to the Coast Guard . . . not only for the outstanding achievements in the war but also for the painstaking preparation in the years leading up to the war . . . Well done." Waesche had earned that praise, and so had the men and women of the service he headed.

For more about the Coast Guard in WWII, turn to page 377.

* * *

YOU'RE PROBABLY A MILITARY BRAT IF YOU . . .

- Answer the question "Where are you from?" with "All over the place."
- Still make your bed with hospital corners.
- Graduated from 12th grade and it was your 13th school.
- Have been asked "Where did you learn to speak English?"
- Know how to ask for a beer in most European languages.
- Don't remember the names of your childhood friends.
- Had a supply of K-rations that you traded with friends when you were a kid.
- Remember having Thanksgiving and Christmas dinners in a mess hall.
- Meet another military brat and instantly bond.
- Thought that a firing range made a great playground.
- Went to school in a converted POW camp.
- Get all warm and fuzzy when you see battleship gray.

KEEP ON TRUNKIN'

A short history of the military storage locker that got its name because it was typically found at the foot of the bed—the very necessary "footlocker."

FANCY THAT

When detail-oriented, workaholic Napoléon Bonaparte first headed into war in 1799, he insisted on maintaining order in the field. One of his tools? The "campaign chest," a fancy piece of furniture with multiple drawers and a lift-top writing surface—the precursor to today's military footlocker. Only officers would have had personal trunks then, and some may have been as detailed as Napoléon's, but most were more likely simple boxes or old ammunition containers and packing crates. A foot soldier could make do with a rucksack.

A PLACE FOR EVERYTHING

By the Civil War, many soldiers had their own crude version of a campaign chest: a simple wooden box, often weighing 30 to 40 pounds *before* it was packed with personal items like pocketknives and clothes. At first, most trunks didn't have locks. Wooden or metal handles on the side made for easier carrying. In the 1900s, plywood versions with metal strapping or metal-capped corners (for added stability) made for less strenuous hauling.

These trunks were formerly used to store extra bedding, clothes, and toiletries. A World War II footlocker typically held handkerchiefs, a shaving brush, a button polishing kit, shoe polish and brush, toilet kit, field manual, Bible, socks, spare shoelaces, toothbrush, comb, belt and buckle, sewing kit, safety razor, cigarettes, condoms, a paperback book and notebook, medicine tins, personal pictures, and more. Unlike with a child's toy chest, though, a soldier of yore couldn't just toss in his paraphernalia. Most items had an assigned spot, and tidiness was mandatory (socks and clothes had to be folded and stored just so). Nowadays, more personal items (MP3 players, laptops, and even body armor and extra gear) may be tucked inside—neatly, of course. Today's footlockers are pretty much ice chests on steroids, constructed of high-tech, airtight, waterproof materials, with stainless-steel ball-

GI slang: "Groundhog Day" refers to every day of your tour in Iraq.

bearing wheels and extendable handles; they're lighter, sturdier, and easier to move. And military regulations require that all footlockers be locked.

STAY-AT-HOMES

Footlockers don't travel with soldiers when they're on the move—that's what rucksacks and duffel bags are for. Instead, they stay at the base camp as a sturdy symbol of a soldier's home away from home. Even then, today's soldiers have to be deployed for 12 months or more to bring a footlocker along.

Neither sentimental memories nor footlockers are just for soldiers. Once the military created bases around the globe, the families who accompanied the servicemen often brought footlockers, too. Childhood remembrances uncovered in a footlocker led two grown military "brats" (as the children of servicemen are known) to help other brats find each other, since many moves in a lifetime made it too easy to lose touch. In 1996 Mary Edwards Wertsch and Reta Jones Nicholson decided to use a footlocker to track down fellow military brats they'd grown up with. They started gathering memories in a single old-fashioned footlocker and asked nearby military brats to add to it. So began Operation Footlocker—a.k.a. "OpFoot."

Soon, the footlocker was being sent all over (the program is free; recipients only need pay shipping), as participants in military brat reunions and other groups keep asking to see it. OpFoot's Web site (www.operationfootlocker.com) says: "This is how we brats connect to our lost childhoods, and celebrate the unusual way we grew up."

STILL TRUNKIN'

Today, the trunk has crisscrossed the country, going from reunion to parade to air show and more, and brats far and wide have added more and more of their memorabilia. Despite shipshape packing, the first footlocker turned out to be too small to satisfy demand, thus spawning OpFoot Jr., a second trunk that makes the rounds, too. These oversize memory boxes help military families get in touch with old friends and bring a sense of pride to spouses and children, proving that you don't have to be a soldier to serve your country.

Germans first used poison gas in World War I in April 1915 against the British at Ypres.

A WOMAN'S PLACE

World War II changed the rules for everything in the United States, including the military. It marked the founding of the Women's Army Auxiliary Corps (WAACs), the Navy's Women Accepted for Volunteer Emergency Service (WAVES), and saw the acceptance of other official roles for women in the armed forces.

A FEW GOOD WOMEN

Women had long played an important role in the military during wartime, most visibly as nurses. There's a record of General George Washington asking the Second Continental Congress to authorize female nurses to care for soldiers during the Revolutionary War. (They were paid $2 a month, plus one meal a day!) Clara Barton, who founded the American Red Cross, was a battlefield nurse during the Civil War, and Florence Nightingale, a matriarch of modern nursing, was famous for the care she provided soldiers during the Crimean War. Even at the start of the 20th century, when Army nurses were a commonly accepted presence during war and peace, they did not hold military rank and did not receive military-scale pay, pensions, or veterans' benefits.

A shortage of manpower—in the truest sense of the word—prompted U.S. Army officers to request the help of women to fill jobs during wartime and free up men for fighting duty. During World War I, General John J. Pershing hired 100 women who could speak French to serve as telephone operators for the American Expeditionary Force in France; although they were classified as civilian contractors, they wore Army uniforms. Other women were conscripted to serve in clerical and other noncombat positions, but when a request was made for 5,000 women to replace the enlisted men who were doing clerical jobs, the Army balked and sent raw male recruits instead.

The concern, it seems, was that only "women of doubtful character" were interested in working for any length of time in an Army camp. It was considered too complicated and time-consuming to recruit women for employment in the military, and in 1917, when Congress proposed a plan to enlist women for service to the military, the secretary of war responded with a terse memo stating:

In 1969 Ross Perot spent $1.5 million on supplies for American POWs in North Vietnam.

"The enlistment of women in the military forces of the United States . . . is considered unwise and highly undesirable."

Despite bureaucratic opposition, however, plans for some sort of women's auxiliary, similar to the one instituted by the British during World War I, were steadily developed. They were finally put into action when the United States entered World War II.

YOU'RE IN THE ARMY NOW

Sponsored by Massachusetts congresswoman Edith Nourse Rogers and endorsed by First Lady Eleanor Roosevelt, a bill to establish the Women's Army Auxiliary Corps (WAAC) was proposed in May 1941, but it wasn't approved until nearly a full year later—after the attack on Pearl Harbor and when it was clear that the United States would require all the reinforcements it could get.

Women were officially in the Army—sort of. For even though the women of the WAAC would be trained in military skills and protocol, such as drilling, driving, supply and mess management, and company administration—and even though they were given ranks and uniforms and many were shipped overseas—they were not considered active military. They did not receive overseas pay as soldiers did, they were not guaranteed protection if captured, and if they were killed in the line of duty, their parents did not receive military death benefits. Nevertheless, women signed on by the thousands—more than 35,000 responded to the initial call for WAAC officer training in May 1942 for 1,000 available positions.

Oveta Culp Hobby, a well-connected Texan with a background in newspapers and public relations, was tapped to head the WAAC. Those who knew her say she would not have considered herself a feminist, and as the wife of a former Texas governor, she certainly did not come from a hardscrabble background. Yet Hobby was a relentless advocate for the women under her command. "You will find a lot of people with a bureaucratic frame of mind that would kill anything new unless you fought for it. It is my job to fight for it," she told some male colonels when the Army dragged its feet in supplying WAAC training schools with uniforms and equipment.

Without official status in the Army, the WAAC had to battle for everything: appropriate uniforms, construction of barracks, even permission to attend movie nights. Hobby fought and prevailed; and once the WAAC had demonstrated its tremendous value to the Army, she spearheaded a campaign to change the name of the Women's Army Auxiliary Corps to the Women's Army Corps (WAC), officially a part of the Army although with numerous restrictions.

In May 1945, Hobby retired from the U.S. Army as a colonel—the highest rank permitted to a woman in the WAC—and she received the Distinguished Service Medal. What she had done to aid the war effort, and to alter the history of the Army, was immeasurable—and just in time, too, because the U.S. Navy had introduced a successful women's program of its own.

GIVE US A WAVE

When the Army discovered how valuable women could be to its wartime efforts, the top brass became overly enthusiastic about recruiting women for the WAAC—at one point, they talked about bringing in a million women for the corps. Oveta Culp Hobby used this as a bargaining chip to get her women better status within the Army, pointing out that the WAAC would be recruiting head-to-head with the U.S. Navy's Women Accepted for Volunteer Emergency Service—and the WAVES gave women a much better deal.

The WAVES were signed into being by President Franklin D. Roosevelt in July 1942, a little more than two months after the WAAC; but unlike the WAAC, the WAVES started out as part of the Navy (technically the Naval Reserve). WAVES held the same ranks as men—including the rank of seaman—and they received the same pay, although they did not serve aboard warships. Mildred McAfee, then the president of Wellesley College, took a leave of absence from her job to be sworn in as a lieutenant commander, the first female commissioned officer in the U.S. Navy and the first director of the WAVES.

The way for the WAVES had been paved during World War I when the Navy, in need of clerical support, recruited women as yeomen—classified as yeomen (F), for female. Most of the more than 11,000 yeomen (F) were stationed stateside, performing clerical duties and working as translators, drafters, fingerprint experts, camouflage designers, and recruiters. (During the same period, the Marine Corps included a group of about 300 female enlisted per-

...the military also used Agents Blue, Green, White, Pink, and Purple.

sonnel known as "marinettes.") All women who served as yeomen (F) were released from active duty in July 1919.

Like yeomen (F), WAVES were enlisted purely as a wartime measure—thus the E for "Emergency" in their name—but during World War II the WAVES numbered more than 80,000 and accounted for 2.5 percent of the Navy's personnel. Yes, they did clerical work, but they also worked as machinists, drill press operators, hospital staff, radio operators, cartographers, and camouflage artists, among other occupations. One of the fields with the most opportunity for women in the Army and the Navy was aviation.

FLY GIRLS

WAVES were a critical part of Navy flight operations, where they worked as machinists and mechanics repairing aircraft, operated air station control towers, and, most importantly, served as parachute riggers, inspecting, mending, and packing parachutes.

In the Army, about 40 percent of the WAC—40,000 women—worked in the Army Air Forces, and unlike at some Army bases, where the WAC force was confined to barracks surrounded by a fence (whether to keep the women in or the men out was unclear), the Army Air Forces appreciated them from the start. Virtually any job was open to women, even the job of pilot. Just months after the WAC and the WAVES had come into existence, there already were women in the air for the Army Air Forces.

The Women's Auxiliary Ferrying Squadron (WAFS) was a group of 28 female civilian pilots who worked shuttling new aircraft from factories to Army bases where they were put into action. Headed by 28-year-old Nancy Harkness Love, the WAFS was initially restricted to flying trainers and light aircraft, but soon proved their mettle and shuttled bombers, cargo planes, and other heavy aircraft. There were plans to roll the WAFS into a proposed group within the WAC to be called Women Air Service Pilots (WASP), and women were being trained for air duty, when infighting at the supervisory level drew unwanted attention to the group and it was disbanded.

It would take a few generations and a few more wars before women had parity with men in the military, but the seeds of change were sown by the women of World War II on land, at sea, and in the air. (The U.S. Navy didn't assign women to ships until 1978.)

John Paul Jones was a rear admiral in the Russian navy in 1788.

HEALER OF HEARTS

Treating wounded soldiers during World War II gave Army physicians an opportunity to make amazing medical breakthroughs to save lives—as in the case of Dr. Dwight Harken, the first person to repeatedly operate successfully on the human heart.

STANDARD NONOPERATING PROCEDURE

For centuries, the human heart was considered too complex and too vital for surgical intervention. Even as recently as the 20th century, heart surgery was rare—usually limited to attempts to treat stab wounds to the heart—and, in most cases, fatal.

During World War II, a young U.S. Army surgeon, Dr. Dwight Harken (1910–93), was stationed in Britain, where wounded soldiers from the European front would be transported for treatment. Many of the men had shell fragments and bullets lodged in their hearts and surrounding organs, but physicians refused to operate on them. It was widely thought that to operate on a human heart was as good as a death sentence, whereas leaving the material in place at least gave the patient a chance at survival. Harken called the material an "unwelcome visitor."

GETTING RID OF UNWELCOME VISITORS

Frustrated by his inability to help these wounded men, Harken began a series of experimental surgeries on animals. In his first round of tests, all of his subjects died, but with each round, Harken improved his methods to locate, dislodge, and finally remove any foreign objects. His first human patient was a volunteer and the operation was a success. Harken went on to operate—without a single fatality—on more than 130 wounded soldiers with bullets and shrapnel embedded in their hearts, becoming the first surgeon with repeated success in operating on the heart and establishing ground rules for cardiac surgery that helped develop techniques that are commonplace today.

HARKEN'S HEART IN PEACETIME

For the rest of his career, Harken focused on different aspects of heart surgery: treatment of narrowing valves, the first implantation of artificial mitral and aortic valves, the development and implantation of the first device to assist the heart's pumping, and the first internal pacemaker in the 1960s.

Harken was a pioneer in acknowledging patients' emotional needs, too. He developed a support group for four of his cardiac patients, which grew into the international organization Mended Hearts.

Dr. Dwight Harken's work fundamentally changed how we think about the heart. As he later said, "We discovered that the heart wasn't such a mysterious and untouchable thing after all."

* * *

JAPAN'S SECRET WEAPON: BALLOONS

On May 5, 1945, a group of picnickers in Oregon fell victim to one of the oddest weapons used in World War II. The party found a 32-foot balloon in the woods. When they tried to move it, it exploded, killing six of them—the only fatalities of World War II to occur on American soil.

In 1944, feeling intense pressure from American air raids, Japan came up with a seemingly brilliant way of striking back. Their planes couldn't fly all the way to the United States mainland, so they started sending balloons made of rubberized silk, each carrying an explosive device. The balloons were supposed to ride high-altitude winds across the Pacific and come down to wreak havoc in the American heartland.

The U.S. Air Force estimates that Japan launched 9,000 balloon bombs between November 1944 and April 1945. About 1,000 of those actually made it to the United States, but they inflicted only minor damage. Designed to be a weapon of mass terror, Japan's balloon bomb campaign was a total . . . uh . . . bomb.

But it could have been much worse: Japan conducted extensive biological warfare research during the war. Had the Japanese added "germ bombs" to their balloons, casualties might have been immense. It's likely that they balked at such a step for fear the United States would retaliate with their own germ weapons.

Soldiers in WWII cooked with solid fuel tablets of hexamine that did not require kindling.

SAVING SERGEANT NILAND

"The boy's alive and we're going to send someone to save him . . . and we are going to get him the hell out of there." —from Saving Private Ryan

FACT OR FICTION?

In 1998 *Saving Private Ryan* gave moviegoers an infantryman's view of the 1944 invasion of Normandy on D-day. The film follows Captain John Miller (Tom Hanks) and the survivors of his unit as they battle their way onto Omaha Beach. Then, instead of getting a hoped-for rest, they get another dangerous assignment—to go behind enemy lines and find a missing soldier, Private James Ryan (Matt Damon). Private Ryan's three brothers have all recently died in combat and, in accordance with War Office policy, the last living son must return home alive to his family. Private Ryan must be "saved."

Directed by Steven Spielberg, *Saving Private Ryan* won five Academy Awards and the admiration of Word War II veterans who said the movie faithfully depicted their experiences. The film renewed interest in the men who fought at Normandy, but filmgoers also wanted to know if there was a real-life Private Ryan.

THE REAL PRIVATE RYAN

The fictional Private Ryan was inspired by Sergeant Frederick "Fritz" Niland—a paratrooper in the 101st Airborne Division and 501st Parachute Infantry Regiment. Just after midnight on D-day, June 6, 1944, a plane dropped Sergeant Niland into France. He was supposed to land near the city of Carentan, but—like Private Ryan—got "lost" when his plane was hit by enemy fire and he had to jump miles away from his target.

Fritz, 24, was born in Tonawanda, New York, the youngest of four brothers, from oldest to youngest, Edward, Preston, Robert, and Fritz. Their mother, Augusta "Gussie" Niland, later recalled that the brothers had always been the best of friends. They graduated from Tonawanda High and attended local colleges, but they were all attracted to military service. Their father had been a Rough Rider with Teddy Roosevelt during the Spanish-American War, and they grew up listening to his war tales. By spring 1944, they were all overseas: Robert was a mortar sergeant in the 82nd Airborne, Preston was a lieutenant in the 4th Infantry Division, and Edward was flying B-25s for the Army Air Force in the Pacific. Robert, Preston, and Fritz were all stationed in England, waiting for the invasion of Europe.

But 1944 didn't go well for them. On May 20, Edward's plane was shot down over the jungles of Burma. On June 6, Robert parachuted into France and was killed in heavy fighting at the village of Neuville-au-Plain. The following day, Preston, who'd landed at Utah Beach, died while defending the wounded. And Fritz, of course, was "lost" somewhere behind enemy lines.

THE TELEGRAMS ARRIVE

In *Saving Private Ryan*, one of the women in the military's secretary pool is typing condolence letters to parents of dead soldiers when she notices that three letters are all going to the same name and address. She brings the matter to the attention of her commanding officer, and the order goes out to search for Private Ryan.

On D-day, Gussie later said, she was thinking how glad she was that Edward was far from Normandy's fierce fighting; then the telegram came with the news about his plane crash stating that he was presumed dead. On June 21, another War Office telegram arrived, this one about Preston's death, followed two days later by one about Robert. The courier who'd delivered the telegrams begged not to be sent back to deliver the second and third telegrams. Within the space of a few weeks, the Nilands were grieving for three sons lost to the war.

In Spielberg's film, Private Ryan knows nothing of his brothers' fates until Captain Miller finds him. Fritz, separated from his unit, also knew nothing of his family's pain. When he regrouped with Company H, he got the news about Edward's plane being shot down. Then Robert's company commander found the grieving sergeant and told him that his brother Robert had been killed and was buried at a cemetery in the French village of Sainte-Mère-Église. Stunned by the loss of two brothers, Fritz sought out the company chaplain, Father Sampson, and asked for a ride to

Robert's grave. New cemeteries had been hastily created for the Allied dead. Fritz and Father Sampson searched the village but were unable to find Robert's grave. They tried another cemetery, and when Father Sampson saw Preston Niland's grave, he thought that the wrong name had been recorded in error and showed it to Fritz. The distraught young man said, "Father Sampson, Preston is my brother, too." Eventually they found Robert's grave, and Fritz realized that he'd lost all three brothers.

LOST BANDS OF BROTHERS

What about the film's premise that the War Department would send a soldier home after his siblings had died in battle? Many people believed that the United States had a law forbidding families to serve on the same ship or in the same military unit—a myth repeated in the movie. In fact, no such law existed. Instead, the War Department adopted the "sole survivor policy." If a soldier's or sailor's siblings were killed, he was not allowed to serve in combat zones. After Father Sampson brought Fritz back from the cemetery, he filled out paperwork to notify the Army that Fritz was the Niland family's sole survivor and had to be sent home.

THE ONLY BROTHERS I HAVE LEFT

When Captain Miller finally finds Private Ryan, the young man is defending a bridge from the Nazis and refuses to leave his post. He explains that he's with "the only brothers I have left . . . I wouldn't desert them." Private Ryan could have been speaking for Fritz Niland, who refused to leave his fellow soldiers, insisting, "I'm staying here with my boys." Determined to avenge his brothers' deaths, Fritz managed to remain on the front lines until August, when he was finally ordered to return stateside. He served out the rest of the war as an MP, always longing to get back to Company H. He would later say that it took an edict from President Roosevelt to get him to leave the front.

In a miraculous turn of events, Edward, presumed dead, came home in May 1945 after nearly a year in a Japanese prison camp. Though happy to have Edward back, Fritz never fully got over the deaths of Robert and Preston. Fritz's daughters were invited to the premiere of *Saving Private Ryan*, but their father never got to see it; Fritz Niland died of a heart attack in 1983.

HORSE HEROES SOLDIER ON

Only a few of the great U.S. military horses have made it into the history books. These are stories of our most famous military horses—with a mention of their people, too.

WAS OLD NELSON CHEATED?

General George Washington was such a renowned rider that Thomas Jefferson called him "the best horseman of his age." Most portraits of General Washington showed him mounted on a snow-white, spirited charger. The problem is that the charger never existed. Apparently, the artists weren't interested in showing Washington's true, brave warhorse—a calm, sturdy chestnut named Nelson.

Washington bred horses for pleasure and profit, but none of his horses had the steady nerves or stamina necessary to take on the Redcoats. His spirited hunter Blueskin cowered under cannon fire, and another of his mounts died from exhaustion underneath Washington during the Battle of Trenton. Brigadier General Thomas Nelson came to his commander's rescue with the gift of a chestnut hunter. Washington gratefully accepted the well-conformed, big-boned animal with the speed, temperament, and endurance he required.

Washington named the horse Nelson in honor of its first owner and made him his favorite mount during the war. Some historians say the chestnut carried his hefty commander—six foot two and about 200 pounds—on long marches from Boston to South Carolina. Old Nelson, as he came to be known, withstood the British fire with a placid calm. And it's believed that he carried George Washington to the American victory at Yorktown in 1781.

The chestnut remained Washington's favored mount as president, and both retired to Mount Vernon, where Old Nelson lived out his days neither knowing nor caring that all those fanciful portrait artists would cheat him out of his true place in history.

MRE? That means "Meal Rejected by the Enemy," say our fighting funnymen.

THE GREAT CONFEDERATE GRAY

Traveller, one of America's most admired warhorses, belonged to Confederate General Robert E. Lee. Born in 1857 in Greenbrier, Virginia, Traveller was the foal of Grey Eagle, a famous racehorse. By either coincidence or fate, the valuable colt was originally named Jeff Davis after the Mississippi senator and future president of the Confederacy.

Traveller was a beautiful light-gray mount with a black mane and tail. Captain Joseph Broun, a quartermaster in the Confederate cause, sold the horse to General Robert E. Lee in 1861. Lee renamed him Traveller for his quick, miles-eating walk.

Traveller became more than Lee's favorite mount; the two shared a bond that was never broken, not even after the Second Battle of Bull Run when the spirited horse took fright, plunged, and threw Lee to the ground. But after Bull Run, Traveller became an ideal warhorse, tame enough to come at a whistle, spirited enough to charge in battle, strong enough to carry Lee for hours on end. In 1864, during the Battle of the Wilderness, when Lee had been in the saddle so long that his legs went out from under him after he dismounted, he held onto Traveller's neck and the horse stayed still until his master could stand.

The general's devotion was expressed in a letter to an artist who wanted to paint Traveller:

> If I were an artist like you I would draw a true picture of Traveller . . . Such a picture would inspire a poet, whose genius could then depict his worth and describe his endurance of toil, hunger, thirst, heat, and cold, and the dangers and sufferings through which he passed. He could dilate upon his sagacity and affection and his invariable response to every wish of his rider . . . But I am no artist . . . I can therefore only say he is a Confederate grey.

After the war, Traveller grazed on the campus of Washington College in Lexington, Virginia, where Lee was president. His beautiful mane and tail grew thin because his many fans plucked them for souvenirs. When the great general died in 1870, Traveller followed the hearse at his funeral, and he died only a year later.

THE UNDEFEATED COMANCHE

In 1868 Comanche, a buckskin gelding, was purchased for the U.S. Army in St. Louis and sent to Fort Leavenworth, Kansas, where he caught the eye of Captain Myles Keogh of the 7th Cavalry. Keogh bought the horse for use as his personal mount during battle. According to legend, Comanche got his name during a skirmish with Plains Indians on the Cimarron River. The horse was wounded by an arrow and "screamed like a Comanche."

Captain Keogh was a handsome Civil War veteran known for his bravery. Even when wounded, the horse carried the captain, going forward despite his pain. In 1870 the horse was wounded in the leg; in 1871 he was wounded in the shoulder. Both times Comanche recovered and returned to service.

When Sitting Bull led an uprising of Plains Indians in May 1876, the 7th Cavalry traveled from Fort Lincoln in the Dakota Territory to Montana. Keogh and Comanche made the trip under the authority of Lieutenant Colonel George Armstrong Custer, who took them on marches that lasted late into the night and resumed before dawn. Comanche was gaunt and exhausted by the time they arrived at the Little Bighorn River on June 25. Despite the scouts' warnings of the immense strength of his enemy, Custer led his detachment of weary soldiers into a ravine where an overwhelming force of Indian warriors ambushed them. The battle lasted only an hour, and Custer and everyone under his command were killed. After the battle, Sitting Bull's warriors took the surviving cavalry horses and left the wounded ones to die. Among those left behind was Comanche.

More American cavalrymen arrived two days later at the Little Bighorn to find no human survivors. Most of the horses and Indian ponies were past saving and were put out of their misery. Comanche came toward them, bloody but still on his feet. He was given water, his bullet wounds were tended to, and he was taken in a steamboat to Fort Lincoln, where he slowly recovered. The Army and the public respected Comanche as a heroic survivor. He was officially retired with honors. With no one allowed to ride him, the survivor of Custer's Last Stand roamed at will, lining up for parade drills on his own, begging beer at the local canteen, and trampling through the officers' wives' gardens in search of tasty sunflowers. In 1891, at the age of 29, Comanche died. His body was preserved and he's often visited at his exhibit at the Natural History Museum at the University of Kentucky.

ON GUARD: THE QUIZ

Answer true or false to these statements about the sentinels who guard the Tomb of the Unknown Soldier.
(Answers are on page 485.)

1. Sentinels guard the Tomb of the Unknown Soldier 24 hours a day, seven days a week.

2. The changing of the guard takes place every four hours.

3. The sentinels of the Tomb Guard are a special detail of Marines.

4. Tomb Guards never speak when on duty.

5. Members of the Tomb Guard have to be at least 5' 10" tall.

6. Women are not permitted to serve as Tomb Guards because the unknowns are all male.

7. Tomb Guards don't carry real weapons.

8. Tomb Guards spend five hours a day preparing their uniforms for duty.

9. When they become Tomb Guards, members take a lifetime pledge not to swear or drink alcohol.

10. Members of the Tomb Guard live in an underground barracks in Arlington Cemetery.

11. Only 20 percent of the soldiers who volunteer to be Tomb Guard sentinels actually become full-fledged guards.

12. In 2003 the members of the Tomb Guard continued to guard the Unknown Soldier during Hurricane Isabella, despite orders to suspend their duty until after the hurricane had passed.

13. The sentinels once protected the tomb from an armed assailant.

The American Civil War took more than 620,000 lives.

WORLD WAR II MUSEUM

Despite the invasion of vandals following Hurricane Katrina, the National World War II Museum in New Orleans is up and running, offering pretty much everything you ever wanted to know about World War II.

D-DAY

The National D-day Museum, as it was originally designated, opened on the anniversary of its namesake day in 2000, the culmination of the dreams of the late Stephen E. Ambrose, who wrote *Band of Brothers*, biographies of Eisenhower and Nixon, and other works. Ambrose, who died in 2002, wanted a museum to commemorate the sacrifices and victories of the military, focusing on the invasion of Normandy on June 6, 1944.

A year later, on December 7, 2001, the museum opened an additional wing of galleries honoring the D-days of the Pacific War. (Yes, there were D-days in the Pacific; according to the Department of Defense, a D-day is the unnamed day on which a particular operation commences or is to commence.)

BIGGER AND BETTER

In September 2003, the United States Congress recognized the museum's mission by designating it the National World War II Museum. With the honor came a new mandate: to tell the complete story of the Allied victory in World War II, including every theater and every campaign.

K-DAY

A different sort of invasion took place on August 29, 2005, when Hurricane Katrina slammed into New Orleans. Winds tore into homes and businesses, levees collapsed, and neighborhoods were flooded. Tens of thousands of residents fled the city.

The storm spared the museum significant direct damage; located in the historic Warehouse District, it sits above the floodplain. But looters broke into the ground-floor coffee shop and gift shop, taking or destroying what they found. What was worse, the museum's audience disappeared. New Orleans residents were evacuated and tourism came to a standstill.

In 1910 the Wright brothers established the first U.S. civilian flying school in Montgomery, AL.

The museum reopened three months later, but the logistics of operating a multimillion-dollar museum with few potential visitors and barely any staff or volunteers created a challenge no board of directors could have envisioned. Average attendance in pre-Katrina days was 900 visitors a day. Numbers for 2008 dropped to about 400.

A NEW V-DAY

An appeal for emergency fund-raising went out to the museum's members, many of whom are World War II veterans. More than 10,000 responded, and on June 2, 2006, the museum rebranded itself. A 10,000-square-foot piece of fabric was unfurled to reveal the museum's new name as howitzers boomed in celebration.

Just two months earlier, the museum had launched another ambitious expansion, opening the first phase of "The Road to Victory" in the E. J. Ourso Discovery Hall, a state-of-the-art education center that operates the museum's distance learning program. The program is designed to allow teachers in the United States and elsewhere to use the museum's expansive collections and archives to teach World War II history.

A major $300 million expansion is well underway. The museum's footprint will triple as it spreads outward into new buildings and a nearby vacant lot. After that is the $50 million Victory Theater, scheduled to open in summer 2009.

WHY NEW ORLEANS?

There are two reasons the museum was built in New Orleans. For one thing, the museum's founder, Stephen Ambrose, was a professor at the University of New Orleans. As he began researching and writing about World War II history, he came into contact with many veterans who donated artifacts in hopes that someday there would be an official World War II museum.

Second, a New Orleans resident, Andrew Jackson Higgins, was the designer and builder of Higgins boats—landing craft used in the Normandy invasion and in other landings in the European and Pacific theaters. Two assembly lines in New Orleans produced the Higgins craft (LCM) and two more made the Higgins PT boat.

In his biography of Dwight D. Eisenhower, supreme commander of the Allied forces in Europe, Ambrose quoted Eisenhower as say-

Baseball Hall of Famer Tom Seaver joined the Marine Corps Reserves in 1962...

ing about Higgins, "He's the guy who won the war." In fact, Ike is quoted as saying there were four vehicles that won the war for the Allies: the Higgins boat, the Sherman tank, the C-47 transport, and the jeep. All four are on display in the museum's main building, the Louisiana Memorial Pavilion.

HEADS UP!

The skies inside the entrance of the museum are filled with combat aircraft, the most prominent of which is a still-flyable C-47, a nine-ton aircraft that was bought on eBay for $150,000 and flown to New Orleans for the display. During the war, the C-47 ferried troops and supplies in all theaters, making it the most-used air transport of its day. It flew the 82nd Airborne Division into the night skies over Normandy, ahead of the parachute drops that heralded the beginning of D-day. It also dropped a team of Pathfinders from the 101st Airborne into Holland later in 1944 as part of Operation Market Garden. (The aircraft even played itself in the film about that campaign, *A Bridge Too Far*.) Later, it dropped supplies during the Battle of the Bulge and took part in the largest paratroop drop of the war, Operation Varsity, an allied assault over Germany.

THE OTHER SIDE

Also hanging from the ceiling in mock flight is a German Messerschmitt (Bf-109). Germany produced an estimated 300,000, but only a handful survived. There's a British Spitfire, too. And the fourth plane overhead is a SBD dive-bomber used by the U.S. Navy in the battles of Midway and the Coral Sea; this one is on loan from the U.S. Naval Air Museum in Pensacola, Florida.

SOLDIERLY STUFF

The museum's extensive collection of memorabilia and artifacts come from all sides of the conflict. Many are donations from veterans; others were part of Ambrose's collection. After he wrote *Band of Brothers*, readers began to send him their World War II artifacts, filling first a closet, then a storage room, then a warehouse. The collection covers just about every aspect of the war.

- From the U.S. Navy's Silent Service, submarine artifacts include keys and a qualification notebook.

...He was stationed at the Marine Corps base at Twentynine Palms, California.

- Pathfinder artifacts include a parachute, signal lamp, telephone, radio, and some items on loan from the Airborne Museum in Sainte-Mère-Église, France.
- Surgical notes from a neurosurgeon in the Italian campaign, including information on future U.S. senator Robert Doyle, who served as a lieutenant in the 10th Mountain Division and was severely wounded.
- A Norden bombsight, famous for being a secret weapon in the bombing campaigns by B-17s, B-24s, and B-29s.
- A POW dog tag worn by a GI captured in Italy.
- A concentration camp jacket worn by a Polish prisoner.

NOISEMAKERS, ETC.

Most of the museum's impressive collection of artillery is on display on the ground floor. One of the key pieces is a M2 A1 105-mm howitzer, the artillery workhorse of the war. There is also a German FLaK 37 88-mm dual-purpose gun, the infamous "88" that the Germans used not only for antiaircraft fire but also as field artillery, an M3 105-mm light howitzer and a M1 57-mm antitank gun (both American), a German 1G 18-mm infantry support gun, and an American 57-mm recoilless rifle.

The artillery collection is rotated, but more permanently displayed are a Sherman tank and a jeep. Plus, there are two versions of the Higgins boat—a "rounded bow" LCP (Landing Craft, Personnel) from which troops had to disembark over the side, and the LCVP (Landing Craft, Vehicle, Personnel), with a front ramp that lowers, similar to the type used in the Normandy invasion.

VETERANS HONORED

When visitors come to the museum, volunteers are on duty to greet them, answer questions, hand out literature—and talk about the war. Approximately 30 of the museum's volunteers are World War II veterans, who encourage their fellow veterans to talk about their war memories.

The museum also collects oral histories, many of which, combined with still and film images from the war, are on display on the upper floors. These powerful narratives are much sought after; volunteers are crisscrossing the country hoping to capture oral

"Doughboy" was the slang term for an American infantryman in World War I.

histories as the pool of World War II veterans dwindles at an estimated pace of 1,000 to 1,200 a day.

About 3,000 oral histories have been collected so far, beginning with Ambrose's own research. Veterans can go to the museum's Web site (www.nationalww2museum.org) and answer a series of questions to help record their memories.

THE HAT THAT STARTED IT ALL

Ambrose was interviewing for a book on D-day when veterans started sending him artifacts. The first one was a red beret sent by Wally Parr, a soldier in the British Airborne—the company that began the D-day action at 17 minutes after midnight on June 6. The beret had a rip caused by shrapnel that cost Parr 18 stitches in his head. Other artifacts started coming in: knives and crickets (signaling devices) and even cigarettes that GIs had actually carried and saved as souvenirs. Finally, Ambrose said to Nick Mueller, his friend and fellow history professor, "Nick, we've got to build a museum to show these things off." Mueller agreed, and the two committed themselves to the task.

In a 2002 interview, Ambrose was asked where the museum ranked among his accomplishments. He replied, "First. Absolutely." Because "what we demonstrate in this museum is how it happened that the Boy Scouts from America beat the Nazi youth. Because they would take initiative. They would accept responsibility. They could make up their own minds. They knew what they were fighting for and they went out and they did it . . . you've always got to be ready to fight for democracy."

* * *

Oscar-winning actor Tom Hanks was inducted into the United States Army's Ranger Hall of Fame. The actor was nominated for an Academy Award for his portrayal of Army Ranger company commander John H. Miller in the 1999 World War II movie *Saving Private Ryan*. The Rangers recognized Hanks because of his services to World War II veterans; Hanks was the national spokesman for the World War II Memorial Campaign and the honorary chairman of the D-day Museum Capital Campaign.

5-STAR WISDOM

When General of the Army Omar N. Bradley died in 1981, the five-star ranking was consigned to history. Here are words of wisdom from America's nine five-star generals.

ARMY's FOUR 5-STAR GENERALS

General George C. Marshall (1880–1959)

- "When a thing is done, it's done. Don't look back. Look forward to your next objective."
- "If man does not find the solution for world peace it will be the most revolutionary reversal of his record we have ever known."

General Douglas MacArthur (1845–1912)

- "No man is entitled to the blessings of freedom unless he be vigilant in its preservation."
- "I know war as few other men now living know it, and nothing to me is more revolting. I have long advocated its complete abolition, as its very destructiveness on both friend and few has rendered it useless as a means of settling international disputes. . . . In war there is no substitute for victory."

General Dwight D. Eisenhower (1890–1969)

- "Bravery is the capacity to perform properly even when scared half to death."
- "What counts is not necessarily the size of the dog in the fight, it's the size of the fight in the dog."
- "There is not greater pacifist than the regular officer. Any man who is force to turn his attention to the horror of the battlefield, to the grotesque shapes that are left there for the burying squads he doesn't want war!"
- "When you appeal to force, there's one thing you must never do—lose.

World War II's B-17 crew D-1 leather flying jacket saw service up until the Korean War.

General Omar N. Bradley (1893–1991)

- "I am convinced that the best service a retired general can perform is to turn in his tongue along with his suit, and to mothball his opinions."

AIR FORCE'S ONE 5-STAR GENERAL

General Henry H. "Hap" Arnold (1886–1950)

- "Offense is the essence of air power."
- "It's got to be done and done quickly, so let's get it done."

NAVY'S FOUR 5-STAR FLEET ADMIRALS

Admiral William Daniel Leahy (1875–1959)

- "You may be the boss, but you're only as good as the people who work for you."

Admiral William Frederick "Bull" Halsey (1882–1959)

- "There are no extraordinary men . . . just extraordinary circumstances that ordinary men are forced to deal with."

Admiral Ernest Joseph King (1878–1956)

- "If a ship has been sunk, I can't bring it up. If it is going to be sunk, I can't stop it. I can use my time much better working on tomorrow's problem than by fretting about yesterday's. Besides, if I let those things get me, I wouldn't last long."
- "A ship is always referred to as 'she' because it costs so much to keep one in paint and powder."
- "God grant me the courage not to give up what I think is right even though I think it is hopeless."

Admiral Chester William Nimitz (1885–1966)

- "That is not to say that we can relax our readiness to defend ourselves. Our armament must be adequate to the needs, but our faith is not primarily in these machines of defense but in ourselves."

During the Korean War, the U.S. dropped approximately 250,000 pounds of napalm per day.

THE GOLD STANDARD

Need a synonym for the ultimate in security? Try Knox. Fort Knox.

SAFE AND SOUND?

The country's valuable gold reserves—hundreds of heavy bars of pure gold weighing more than 4,600 tons—are tucked away safely in the U.S. Department of Treasury's Kentucky Bullion Depository at Fort Knox. Or are they?

CONSPIRACIES ABOUND

In the early 1970s, Peter Beter, the former general counsel of the Export-Import Bank of the United States, insisted that the vaunted vault at Fort Knox was empty. He claimed that President Lyndon B. Johnson moved the bulk of the gold to London in the 1960s but tried to convince everyone the gold was still right at home in the heart of Kentucky. The conspiracy theory was so loud and convincing that on September 23, 1974, a contingent of members of Congress and the news media descended upon Fort Knox to get a glimpse of the gold. But a glimpse is all they got: they were only allowed to peek at the dusty lumps of gold through a window. Their conclusion? It "looked" like it had been there quite a while. Nevertheless, that view was enough to tarnish the theory of the long-lost gold.

THAT'S A RELIEF!

Assuming the bullion wasn't fake—and that the periodic audits of the gold by the General Accounting Office between 1975 and 1981 are trustworthy—then it's safe to say that the safest place in the United States still is.

Not even James Bond's famous nemesis Auric von Goldfinger was able to do his worst at Fort Knox, where he tried (in the 1964 movie) to render the gold radioactive, thus lessening its value and increasing the value of his *own* stash of gold. (Thanks, 007, for lending us a hand in protecting our monetary system.)

NOT THAT IT MATTERS

Our monetary system didn't need protecting for much longer after that, though. In the beginning, gold *was* the actual standard, because he who had the gold ruled the world. In 1944, when the Bretton Woods Agreement (an international pact among 44 nations) made the U.S. dollar the dominant monetary unit, replacing the British pound, it was because America had vast gold reserves and the world was willing to place its trust in the Yanks. To be specific, all the countries agreed that each U.S. dollar was worth 1/35th of an ounce of gold—a concept that worked really well for at least a few minutes. In no time at all, America was printing more and more money that *wasn't* backed by the gold reserves.

In the late 1960s, the French and others decided to make the United States walk the walk; they wanted to be paid in gold for their exports. The drain on U.S. gold became acute and the gold standard went downhill fast. On August 15, 1971, President Richard M. Nixon unilaterally decided to close the "gold window." The dollar was no longer tied to gold. It marked the first time that the world's currencies weren't tied to a specific commodity.

WHAT'S GOING ON HERE?

Our monetary system may no longer be tied to the stores of gold at Fort Knox, but we're still closely guarding all that glitters there. Thirty-five miles south of Louisville, Fort Knox is its own city as well as an Army base, composed of 109,000 acres spread across three counties, and home to more than 23,000 soldiers, family members, and civilians. The Bullion Depository (also called the Gold Vault)—the structure most people think of when you say "Fort Knox"— isn't even the main function of the base, nor is it actually *on* the base but, rather, is adjacent to it.

Fort Knox is the site of the Armor Center and School, which provides personnel, equipment, and guidance for the training of the Armor Force. Spread throughout the hilly, forested terrain are 18 different training areas for vehicle-based and on-foot exercises. Almost half the area is an impact zone for ordnance (weapons, ammunition, combat vehicles, and so on). It houses the U.S. Army Recruiting Command, the Eastern Region of ROTC, and Army Accessions Command, as well as the Patton Museum of Armor and Cavalry. Built in 1949, the museum features equipment, vehicles, and other artifacts of the United States and its

Pucker factor: in military slang, a measure of how scary a situation is.

allies and foes from decades' worth of warfare. An original section of the Berlin Wall is also on display.

MY NEW KENTUCKY HOME

Soldiers have staked out spots around Fort Knox since the Civil War, but it wasn't official military property until 1918, when it was established as a field artillery training center. It was named Camp Henry Knox National Forest in honor of Major General Henry Knox, chief of artillery for the Continental Army during the American Revolution and later the United States' first secretary of war. In 1928, when infantry companies were assigned to the post, its name was changed to Fort Knox.

In 1936 the U.S. Treasury Department started building the Bullion Depository (on land deeded to it by the military). It opened in 1937 to begin receiving its first shipment of gold via railway.

SAFE AND SOUND

Constructed of granite, steel, and concrete, it was built to be impermeable. The two-level vault is divided into two compartments, and the vault door weighs more than 20 tons. In fact, there might be more steel than gold here: the vault itself is made of steel plates, steel beams, and steel cylinders. Steel bands wrap around everything, then concrete encases it all. Don't plan on schmoozing the guy in charge to get him to open the vault and give you a look-see. Even the president of the United States doesn't have the combination to the vault. To open the door, several staffers at the depository must each dial separate combinations known only to them.

The outer wall of the building is used for offices and storerooms. Each corner of the building has its own exterior guard box, and another sentry is posted at the entrance gate. A steel fence encompasses the whole property. We'd tell you all about the high-tech protective devices in the building, but then we'd have to kill you.

WHAT'S INSIDE STAYS INSIDE

The gold bullion never sees the light of day. Each bar is a little smaller than your average building brick, measuring about 7 by 3⅝ by 1¾ inches. Each weighs about 27½ pounds and contains approximately 400 troy ounces of gold. At that original price of $35 per ounce, each bar was worth about $14,000. But when gold hovers around $900 per ounce, as it does today, each bar is worth about $360,000. Some of the bars are "standard," made of almost pure gold. Others are "coin bars," made from melted gold coins that are mixed with other metals for strength. No one is saying exactly how many bars are kept at Fort Knox, though. Additional gold reserves reside at the Philadelphia Mint, the Denver Mint, the West Point Bullion Depository, the San Francisco Assay Office, and other facilities of the United States Mint.

WORTH MORE THAN GOLD

The Gold Vault has also been used to safeguard a host of other important items over the years, including the gold reserves of several other countries, the English crown jewels, the Magna Carta, and the Gutenberg Bible. On December 26, 1941, Fort Knox was the protector of the original U.S. Constitution, the Bill of Rights, and the Declaration of Independence—all of which stayed on the property until October 1, 1944, when they headed back to Washington, D.C., for permanent display.

A MIGHTY FORTRESS

Contrary to popular belief (and cinematic imaginings), no one has ever tried to rob Fort Knox, probably because the gold simply weighs too much to make a quick getaway. Still guarded heavily today—thanks in large part to that Armor Center and School next door—Fort Knox's Bullion Depository allows no visitors and conducts no tours. Its uninspired concrete exterior has no markings or "The Gold Is Here!" signs posted nearby. You'd think that such a famous stash deserves a little more excitement—instead of just sitting there gathering dust.

* * *

A PRIVATE JOKE

A group of soldiers were standing in formation at an Army base. The drill sergeant said, "All right! All you idiots fall out."

The squad wandered away, but one soldier remained at attention.

The drill sergeant walked over to him and raised an eyebrow. The soldier said, "Sure was a lot of 'em, huh, sergeant?"

WILLY AND APHRODITE

It sounded like a good idea at the time: remote-controlled weapons that would keep American airmen out of danger over heavily defended targets. It was called Operation Aphrodite, after the goddess of love and beauty.

BRASS MEETS SCIENCE

The U.S. Army Air Forces entered World War II convinced that high-altitude, daylight precision bombing was the way to win the war. They had a point: piloted bombers were so accurate they could drop a bomb, as some proponents liked to say, from a high altitude "into a pickle barrel." But meanwhile, Army scientists were at work on top-secret projects that would allow for kamikaze-style bombing missions—*sans* pilot. Two different types of weapons were developed for the experiment, code-named Operation Aphrodite: one was a series of "glide bombs," the forerunners of guided "smart" bombs. The other was a remote-controlled bomber filled with TNT.

WATCHING TV

The 8th Air Force, based in England, was given the job of making it happen. The first glide bombs, capable of gliding one mile for every thousand feet of altitude, were initially unguided and not very accurate. Early tests had impact errors of up to one mile from the intended target. Later models were slightly more accurate because bombardiers used radio-controlled steering to aim the glide bomb via a bomb-mounted television camera. For many soldiers, it was their first exposure to television, which was a secret and classified technical system at the time. The downside to glide bombs was that they required clear visual conditions.

The glide bomb series (GB-1 through GB-8) consisted of standard 1,000- or 2,000-pound bombs affixed with a small set of wings that included radio-controlled steering. The 8th Air Force tried them out from mid-1943 to May 1944, but the lack of accuracy and dependency on weather drove the project into the ground.

The fact that the series was developed at all was proof that the Army Air Forces commander, General Henry H. "Hap" Arnold, was not completely sold on piloted bombers. Arnold hadn't attended the

***Memphis Belle* was the first U.S. bomber to complete 25 missions over Europe in World War II.**

Air Corps Tactical School, the place where young officers were taught about precision bombing. In fact, he'd supported unpiloted bombs since World War I, when he advocated launching hundreds of small "flying bombs" against enemy positions beyond the trenches.

MAKING BOMBERS INTO BOMBS

Immediately after the glide bombs were shelved, they were replaced by surplus B-17 and PB4Y bombers that were taking up valuable space and maintenance time. The old bombers were called "Weary Willies," one of several nicknames for aircraft that had been removed from service. Once they were loaded with explosives, they could be flown by remote control against enemy targets.

By late 1943, General Arnold had directed Florida's Eglin Field engineers to outfit the drone bombers with automatic pilots so that the planes could be used against German submarine pens and missile sites in general—and heavily guarded U-boat construction facilities on the French coast in particular.

Each Aphrodite aircraft was packed with about 20,000 pounds of TNT. Then two pilots (who would receive credit for five missions and the Distinguished Flying Cross if they volunteered for one mission) would fly the plane to an altitude of approximately 10,000 feet, manually arm the explosives, and parachute out of a hole cut in the bomber's fuselage. After that, the flying bomb would be piloted by another aircraft, the "mother ship," which flew a few miles behind.

About a dozen drones were guided across the English Channel and detonated near targets in France, but all they managed to do was leave huge holes in the ground, inflicting very little damage.

FRAUGHT WITH DANGER

A few unlucky pilots blew themselves out of the sky when the explosives went off prematurely. In fact, this was how John F. Kennedy's older brother, Joseph Kennedy Jr., was killed. Previous to Kennedy's flight, pilots had to manually arm the bomb before parachuting to safety, but in this case the plane was equipped with a new electronic arming switch. On a mission to northern France, Kennedy's plane, filled with 21,700 pounds of explosives, blew up before he and his crewmate could evacuate. Speculation is that the tragedy was due to a short-circuit in the electric arming switch.

"Operation Granby" was the British military's name for its Gulf War operation.

A concept that was obviously well ahead of the technology of the day, Operation Aphrodite was eventually shelved when the British began to fear reprisals in the form of V-2 rockets, powerful rocket-powered bombs launched from the Continent and aimed at targets in and around London.

HAP AND APHRODITE

The Aphrodite programs showed the Army Air Forces that precision daylight bombing wasn't the *only* way to attack enemy targets from the air. But successful, accurate dronelike weapons would have to wait for decades. At the very least, the operation demonstrated Hap Arnold's willingness to supplement the precision bombing doctrine in an effort to save the lives of American aircrews, particularly since he was feeling confident that the air war in Europe was under control by late spring 1944.

* * *

SOLDIERS OF LOVE

In 1994 scientists at Wright-Patterson Air Force Base were assigned the task of creating nonlethal weapons that would affect enemy combatants but leave civilians unharmed. Among their ideas: a "gay bomb." A strong aphrodisiac would be sprayed on the enemy, who would become so overwhelmed with desire that they would drop their weapons and start kissing each other. The project died when the scientists couldn't find any hormones or chemicals that did the trick. (They also proposed spraying the enemy with bee pheromones, then hiding beehives in combat areas, resulting in attacks from amorous bees.)

* * *

A BOUNCE FOR PILOTS

When World War II started, George Nissen, the inventor of the trampoline, convinced the Army that trampolines could train pilots to not only achieve better balance but also to be less fearful of being upside down. And jumping on a trampoline was great for physical conditioning. The military agreed; thousands of cadets learned to jump on trampolines.

Nov. 3, 1917: James B. Gresham of Indiana became the first U.S. soldier to die in World War I.

STAYING ALIVE

"I am a SERE specialist . . . an expert in Survival, Evasion, Resistance, and Escape. I can survive anywhere in the world and prepare others to do the same." (The SERE Creed)

SURVIVAL 101

Established by the Air Force at the end of the Korean War, the SERE program was expanded during the Vietnam War to include the Army, Navy, and Marine Corps. Service personnel at high risk of being captured and exploited by the enemy—such as Special Forces, Rangers, and airmen—are taught how to evade capture, survive in hostile territory, resist interrogation, and escape from the enemy. The instructor is typically someone who has lived through one or more phases of the SERE experience. The training course is rigorous. *The Unit*, starring Dennis Haysbert, provides a look at Special Forces operations using SERE training.

Every trainee goes through an intensive three-week "stress inoculation" program to learn basic wilderness survival tactics along with techniques for camouflage, signaling and rescue, escape and evasion, and POW resistance. Training is done under all major climatic conditions including arctic, desert, tropical, ocean, and temperate in remote wilderness locations in all possible weather conditions. Much of the training is directed to airmen and naval personnel, so water survival and equipment maintenance is also taught. A resistance training lab simulates conditions in a POW compound, including torture methods. Some techniques taught are still top-secret.

The Air Force has four training schools, including Arctic survival training at the Eielson base in Alaska and parachute water survival training in Pensacola, Florida. The Army runs two schools in the South. Lieutenant Commander James Rowe of the Special Forces established the first school at Camp Mackall, North Carolina, after surviving 62 months in a North Vietnamese prison camp before escaping. The Navy runs two highly specialized schools for pilots as well as sailors, both at remote training sites on the East and West coasts. The Marine Corps operates its own training centers, one in California and the other on Okinawa.

A record? Confederate General Nathan Bedford Forrest had 30 horses shot from under him.

THE HERNDON CLIMB

The official end of a midshipman's first year at the U.S. Naval Academy is marked by all 1,000 "plebes" attempting to mount a greased-down, 21-foot obelisk on the campus in Annapolis, Maryland. It's one of the Navy's most bizarre rituals and dates back 100 years.

SHIP OF GOLD

The gray granite obelisk was raised in June 1860 to honor the memory of Commander William Lewis Herndon, who fought valiantly to save his passengers before going down with his ship, the SS *Central America*, during a hurricane off the North Carolina coast in September 1857. The side-wheel steamship known as "the Ship of Gold" was carrying 477 passengers, a crew of 101, and 30,000 pounds of California gold rush coins and gold bars when it was lost in seas 8,000 feet deep.

WHAT'S LOVE GOT TO DO WITH IT?

The monument is situated in a landscaped area of the academy bisected by a walkway lined with benches informally known as "Love Lane." There, upperclassmen can stroll with their dates. But not the first-year plebes, who must concentrate on their studies and are forbidden to date. They can't set foot on the walkway until the end of the school year.

In June 1907, the plebes ran cheering from graduation at Dahlgren Hall and swarmed around the Herndon monument, cheering wildly to mark their transition to third-year "youngsters" who could now date girls and stroll down Love Lane. This "swoop out" became an annual ritual that involved the graduates wearing their uniform jackets and hats reversed as they swarmed about the monument.

THE MOUNT EVEREST OF ANNAPOLIS

The ritual continued until 1940, when the plebes of the class of 1943 thought to climb the Herndon monument. The objective was to have one of the midshipmen stand atop the obelisk with the support of others as a figurative conquest of the first year at Annapolis. By 1947, a white officer's hat was left on the summit as further evidence of a transition by the plebes to "youngsters." Even that tradition was tweaked when upperclassmen began placing a plebe "dixie cup" hat atop the monument before the climb, only to be replaced by the white officer's hat at the end of the climb.

GREASE 'ER DOWN, MATE

Because topping the granite shaft was relatively easy, upperclassmen in 1953 began laying on as much as 200 pounds of lard to slow the ascent by the human pyramid. Because of the goo, plebes had to change from their dress whites into work whites, and eventually shorts and T-shirts.

In 1962, when the academy began timing the climb, the plebes flung a cargo net over the greasy obelisk, enabling them to scale it in a mere 3 minutes. But they earned an asterisk in the record book. That kind of chicanery was disallowed in subsequent years. The official record without a net was set in 1969—1 minute and 30 seconds—but someone had forgotten to grease the shaft. The longest ascent and removal of the dixie cup hat took an astonishing 4 hours 5 minutes and 17 seconds because upperclassmen had glued and taped the dixie cup hat to the top of the monument. In most hijinx-free years, the times range between two and three hours. Naturally, the spectacle in mid-May delights the huge crowds who gather to view the sloppy ascent and to cheer on the midshipmen. Said one witness, "The scene is unforgettable as the sweating, grunting, red-faced midshipmen at the bottom, their arms linked, support a human pyramid surging to the top of the monument. The pyramid often collapses, but the plebes invariably make it to the top whether it takes them minutes or hours."

MAKE ME AN ADMIRAL

The superstition at the Naval Academy is that the first plebe to snag the hat on the top would become the first admiral in the class. So far, that has not come to pass. However, in 1973, the academy's superintendent, Vice Admiral William P. Mack, gave his shoulder boards to Midshipman Fourth Class Lawrence J. O'Donnell for topping the Herndon. That began a new shoulder-board tradition by the superintendent.

Wing weenie: U.S. Air Force pejorative slang for a nonflying staffer at wing headquarters.

THE RING DANCE

Born out of tragedy in the 1920s, the Ring Dance at the U.S. Naval Academy has become one of the most romantic rites of passage at the Annapolis campus.

THE TRADITION

Gold class rings, for which the Ring Dance came into being, have been a fixture at the academy since 1869. By 1906, they became standardized with the Naval Academy coat of arms on one side of a stone setting, and the other side showing a crest designed by the fourth class in its initial "plebe" year. The rings were coveted. But members of the second class couldn't put them on until after their final exam in navigation at the end of their third year. The tradition then was for graduating members of the first class, who were about to get their commissions, to drag those of the second class to the seawall overlooking the Severn River. There, they pushed or threw their younger counterparts into the river as a de facto baptism of the rings.

TRAGEDY ON THE SEAWALL

In late May 1924, Midshipman Leicester R. Smith, on receiving his ring, hit his head on a rock after being thrown from the seawall. He drowned. The resulting scandal resulted in the birth of the "Ring Dance" to replace throwing classmates into the Severn. The ceremony began with a formal dance at the academy, at which the midshipmen's dates wore the rings around their necks on ribbons. At a certain point in the dance, each couple passed through the center of a 10-foot-tall replica of an academy ring. There the date would slip the ring onto the midshipman's finger after dipping it in a binnacle, a waist-high metal housing for a ship's compass. The binnacle contained water collected from the Atlantic Ocean, Caribbean Sea, Pacific Ocean, and a few drops from the Severn.

That tradition has continued to this very day, only now the water in the binnacle is drawn each year from the "Seven Seas"—the North Pacific, South Pacific, North Atlantic, South Atlantic, Indian Ocean, and the Antarctic and Arctic oceans.

Oliver Wendell Holmes Jr., future chief justice, was wounded three times during the Civil War.

CROSSING THE LINE

For more than 400 years, the world's navies have observed a sometimes funny, sometimes brutal initiation rite when newbies cross the equator for the first time.

KING NEPTUNE'S COURT

When a ship approaches the equator, crewmen who have never crossed are summoned to appear before the vessel's "shellbacks," veterans dressed up as Neptunus Rex and members of his court: typically consisting of the Royal Doctor, the Royal Navigator, and the Royal Scribe—none other than Davy Jones—who carries out the rules set down by Neptune. No one knows the exact origin of the ceremony, but this version has its roots in the Royal Navy of Great Britain.

The "slimy" pollywogs are accused of offenses against the gods of the seas for daring to cross the equator and have to prove to the court that they deserve the privilege of becoming experienced seafaring sea turtles, that is, shellbacks. Tests and punishments are extracted by the court, from being forced to dance, sing, recite nonsensical rhymes, and answer ridiculous questions to running a gauntlet of paddles, crawling through garbage-filled canvas tubes, or other unappetizing and/or dangerous forms of hazing. Sessions normally end with a dunking to certify the 'wogs are worthy to join the brotherhood of shellbacks, including golden shellbacks—sailors who have crossed the equator at the 180th meridian.

DON'T DROWN ME, BRO

The tradition of "crossing the line" has been documented as early as the 1400s on French ships when they rounded a major cape. Ceremonial hazing became associated with crossing the equator in subsequent years aboard the British tall ships. It was plenty dangerous in those early days. A pollywog was tethered to a rope, thrown overboard, dragged from the stern—and sometimes drowned.

Captain James Cook, the famed English explorer, described his ship heaving to at the equator and all pollywogs being hoisted out over the ocean from the mainmast and dunked in the ocean some 40 feet below. If the pollywog was an officer, no dunking was allowed; however, he had to pay for the privilege of becoming a shellback by providing bottles of rum for the after-the-dunking party for all hands. In the 19th century, crossing-the-line rituals became more involved, sans the dunking. A major dousing with seawater and rough treatment continued into the 20th century.

HIJINKS ON THE HIGH SEAS

A typical ceremony took place aboard the American destroyer USS *Rowe* in 1954. With 90 percent of the officers and crew pollywogs, the shellbacks constructed what they called "the Royal Bath," a pool about four feet deep and seven feet square containing seawater mixed with diesel oil. Pollywog Carl Cramer explained, "Word was passed that Davy Jones was to come aboard that evening and we were to entertain him . . . Some had to dance for him, others told stories or recited poetry. I was lucky in being in a singing group."

After the performances, the pollywogs were summoned to appear before a seaweed-draped King Neptune and his court. By morning, the destroyer remained at a dead halt on the equator as the ship's ensign was lowered and the Jolly Roger pennant hoisted to denote that the hazing was underway.

Various "charges" and punishments were levied against the initiates. No one was spared. A lieutenant accused of painting the town in New York had to climb the rigging with a bucket of paint. Another officer had to stand lookout with two soda bottles as binoculars. Cramer, the enlisted man, was accused of impersonating an Irishman and forced to eat a raw onion (the so-called Irish apple).

KISS THE BABY

The hazing aboard the *Rowe* continued with the pollywogs kneeling before King Neptune, who ordered each to kiss the Royal Baby—the ugliest of the shellbacks. "A bucket of mustard was behind him and when you went to kiss him he reached back to the bucket and hit you with a handful of mustard," recalled Cramer. The Royal Barber was next in line, crisscrossing each 'wog's head haphazardly with electric clippers.

Next was the ceremonial dunking in the Royal Bath. Each pollywog had to say "shellback" three times between each dunk.

...Its purpose was to lure submarines to the surface, where they could be attacked.

Running the gauntlet on the destroyer *Rowe* was the last item of business. A tarp had been spread out on the deck and greased with graphite. Hanging over the tarp about a foot high was a cargo net. Each pollywog had to crawl about 30 feet across the tarp under the net. Shellbacks paddled the 'wogs at one end while others drove them back with a fire hose when they got close to the other end. As Cramer put it, "When it was all over you could take a deep breath and with great pride say: Now I am a shellback."

VARIATIONS ON A THEME

Ceremonies in 20th-century navies varied widely. Flogging a pollywog's behind with canvas or rubber fire hoses was common. On the U.S. Coast Guard cutter *Chautauqua*, the ship's garbage was saved for a few weeks and put into a large canvas bag and well stirred. Each pollywog climbed into the bag, which was shaken until garbage completely covered him. The Royal Doctor then forced garbage into the man's mouth and smeared it over his head.

LET'S GET CIVILIZED

Reports of severe hazings in other navies have resulted in modern reforms to control the degree of harassment. The inclusion of women in crews has also toned things down.

But the rite of passage continues, on merchant ships and even on equatorial cruise ships where an appearance by King Neptune serves as entertainment. "Crossing the Line" certificates are passed out, making passengers honorary shellbacks.

OTHER LINES CROSSED

Crossing the equator isn't the only milestone in a sailor's life; there are plenty of other "fraternities" he or she can join, including:

- The Order of the Blue Nose—crossed the Arctic Circle
- The Order of the Red Nose—crossed the Antarctic Circle
- The Order of the Golden Dragon—crossed the International Date Line
- The Order of the Ditch—passed through the Panama Canal
- Royal Diamond Shellback—crossed the equator at the prime meridian (at 0 degrees longitude off the coast of West Africa)

Since their inception in 1946, the Blue Angels have flown for more than 393 million fans.

THE U.S. COAST GUARD IN WWII: THE PACIFIC

During World War II, the Coast Guard had an especially challenging time in the Pacific.

READY FOR ANYTHING

The first wave of the attack on Pearl Harbor began at 7:51 a.m. on December 7, 1941. Docked alongside a pier at Honolulu, the Coast Guard cutter USCGC *Taney*'s antiaircraft batteries opened fire on formations of Japanese aircraft shortly after 8:00. The Japanese pilots were after battleships, not Coast Guard cutters. The men of the *Taney* spent the rest of the day pulling survivors from burning ships and fuel fires blazing on the waters of the harbor. Months passed before the Coast Guard faced the enemy again at Guadalcanal in the Solomon Islands.

THE BATTLE BEGINS

The assault on Guadalcanal and Tulagi in the southern Solomon Islands on August 7, 1942, was the first major Allied amphibious landing of the war. Among Rear Admiral Richmond Kelly Turner's South Pacific Amphibious Force were 23 naval troop transports, 19 of which were entirely or partly manned by Coast Guard sailors. Their role, as in every campaign to follow, involved the landing of troops and supplies and the removal of the wounded.

During the afternoon of August 8, Lieutenant Commander Dwight H. Dexter and 25 other coastguardsmen went ashore from the attack transport *Hunter Liggett* to establish a supply base on Lunga Point, a few miles from the unfinished Japanese air base that later became Henderson Field. Dexter assumed the task of beach master, directing the movement of men from the 1st Marine Corps and their supplies to shore. Japanese planes appeared the following day, and Coast Guard gunners claimed several kills.

On the night of August 9, the Japanese navy struck Rear Admiral Turner's flotilla and sank four heavy cruisers; the *Hunter Liggett* picked up survivors and transferred them to a hospital ship. The battle for Guadalcanal went on for six months, with

Overlord: Code name of the final plan for the Normandy (D-day) landings in 1944.

coastguardsmen in the thick of the fighting. Signalman First Class Douglas Munro led an evacuation of Marines, becoming the first and only coastguardsman to receive the Medal of Honor. (See page 240 for the whole story.)

THE SUMMER OF '43

From June to July 1943, the Marines and Coast Guard moved up the Solomons. On August 15, Coast Guard crews drove two LSTs (Landing Ship, Tank) ashore at Vella Lavella and for weeks provided troops with reinforcements and supplies. On September 25, Japanese bombers struck the *LST 167*, knocking it out of commission. When the Marines moved on to Bougainville—their final objective—nine of the 11 transports attached to the assault contained coastguardsmen. By the end of 1943, most of the Japanese had been driven from the Solomons.

ISLAND-HOPPING

In November 1943, Admiral Chester W. Nimitz, commander of the naval forces in the Pacific, ordered the first assaults in the Gilbert Islands: the objectives were Tarawa Atoll and the Japanese-occupied islands of Betio and Makin. Nimitz assembled 200 vessels, some of which were Coast Guard–manned, to put ashore 27,600 Marines, 7,600 garrison troops, 6,000 vehicles, and 117,000 tons of cargo. The beaches were narrow, well defended, and without natural cover. Unlike Guadalcanal, there would be no surprise landings.

On November 20, the invasion force hove to three miles offshore. Five Coast Guard–manned LSTs chugged toward Betio, followed by dozens of Coast Guard–manned 36-foot Higgins boats (landing crafts with a low bow) carrying 36 troops and a crew of three each. The first problem was the coral reef around Tarawa Atoll; the invasion force had to disembark from LSTs outside the atoll and enter the lagoon in Higgins boats. A miscalculation of the lagoon's depth forced the troops to wade ashore in waist-deep water under heavy machine-gun fire. Some Coast Guard smallboat crews grounded on reefs; the rest came under fire from snipers and mortar batteries. Coxswains and their crews worked around the clock rescuing wounded Marines, delivering supplies, and directing shore operations. Only 19 Japanese surrendered on Betio. The other 4,817 fought to the death.

The War of 1812 was spurred by a small group in Congress known as the War Hawks...

NO PROBLEM A-TOLL

The Navy learned some lessons from Tarawa. In the assault on Majuro, Kwajalein, and Eniwetok atolls in the Marshall Islands, the Joint Expeditionary Force consisted of 300 ships and more than 84,000 men divided into three assault groups. On February 1, 1944, the Coast Guard–manned transport *Cambria*—flagship for the Majuro assault force—sent troops ashore. When they found the atoll evacuated, the Marines garrisoned the island and used it as a staging area for operations in the Pacific.

The Northern Attack Force attacked Roi and Namur islands on Kwajalein Atoll simultaneously. Six transports with full or partial Coast Guard crews put Marines ashore and set up beach positions for transporting the wounded to hospital ships standing offshore. After securing Kwajalein, the task force moved 330 miles to the northwest to assault Eniwetok.

Once again, the *Cambria* served as the flagship for a force that included attack transports all manned or partially manned by the Coast Guard. The island was only lightly defended, but the Japanese soldiers held strong positions. The island was secured on February 23. Now the United States controlled the entire Marshalls, and the Seabees (Naval Construction Battalion) were already building airstrips to support a strike on the Mariana Islands.

THIS IS A TEST

The Mariana Islands lay 1,300 miles east of the Philippines, 1,300 miles due south of Tokyo, and 1,200 miles west of the closest U.S. base on Eniwetok. The attack on three of the Marianas' 15 islands—Saipan, Tinian, and Guam—by an invasion force of 535 ships carrying 127,000 troops would be a test of the Navy's amphibious assault doctrine in anticipation of invading Japan at a later date.

The Northern Attack Force tasked with landing troops on Saipan and Tinian consisted of 37 transports and four LSTs operated by the Coast Guard. Seven other transports had partial Coast Guard crews. At dawn on June 15, 1944, 8,000 Marines streamed toward the beach along a four-mile front in 600 landing craft, many of which were operated by Coast Guard crews. Some Coast Guard boats had to skim along the reef under fire before finding water deep enough to cross. While Marines drove the enemy

...That's the origin of the term "hawk" for one who advocates waging war.

inland, the Coast Guard came ashore and began managing the beachhead. Twenty-five days passed before American troops secured Saipan.

The Navy waited until July 21 to attack Guam, the largest and most important island in the Marianas. Assault ships began arriving on July 20, including Coast Guard transports, the 180-foot buoy tender *Tupelo*, four LSTs, and seven other Navy ships with partial Coast Guard crews.

The USS *Arthur Middleton* had been in on all the action. On July 24, it performed a diversion on the north coast of Tinian by sending a wave of amphibious LVTs (Landing Vehicle, Tracked) ashore with no troops, which opened the way for the principal landings to the south. The Coast Guard's *Cambria* landed troops on central Tinian and spent most of the day removing more than 290 wounded from the beaches. Resistance on Tinian ended on August 1, but the Japanese on Guam took refuge in the jungle and continued fighting until August 10.

D FOR DISASTER

Admiral Nimitz set February 19 as D-day on Iwo Jima. The small volcanic island, some four miles long and two miles wide, lay squarely between Saipan and Tokyo. Major General Curtis E. LeMay of the Army Air Forces wanted the island occupied and converted into an emergency air base for crippled B-29s returning from strikes on Japan. Admiral Raymond A. Spruance assembled 900 ships, 70,000 Marines, and 36,000 garrison troops to assault the eight-square-mile island defended by 21,000 Japanese.

The assault forces arrived at seven predetermined beaches spanning no more than 3,500 yards total. The transports *Bayfield* and *Callaway*, 14 LSTs, and the submarine chaser *PC-469* were all manned by the Coast Guard. The assault force arrived before daylight and began disembarking troops. With no reefs to hurdle, the coastguardsmen expected good beach conditions, which unfortunately did not exist. The surf broke directly on the beach, carrying their small landing craft sideways onto shore. Ten minutes later, the beach was littered with them. Beach masters tried to clear away damaged vessels, but intense enemy fire forced every fresh wave of men coming ashore to take cover. The beach had to be closed until tugs and Coast Guard salvage crews cleared the mess

The Persian Gulf War was a conflict between Iraq and a 34-nation coalition led by the U.S.

so landing operations could resume. Wounded Marines were beginning to pile up on the beaches, and for the next several days coastguardsmen worked to keep the beaches open, supplies unloaded, and the wounded removed to hospital ships. As one coxswain recalled, "Iwo Jima was sheer hell, and many of us never expected to come through it alive."

ONE MORE ISLAND

There were plenty of other landings in the Pacific, but the final amphibious action took place at Okinawa, just a doorstep away from Kyushu, Japan. On March 26, 1945, 1,400 ships carrying 548,000 soldiers converged on the island. The Coast Guard commanded and provided crews for 53 ships, including 40 landing craft; six more ships carried partial Coast Guard crews. The landings began on April 1, Easter Sunday. Soon after, a kamikaze crashed into the *LST-884* and struck the ammunition cargo. Twenty-four coastguardsmen died in the fiery explosion, and the commanding officer ordered the ship abandoned.

Coral reefs put the Coast Guard ships on a tight schedule: they could only reach or depart from the island six hours a day during high tide. Sailors piled supplies on the beach at high tide and then moved them inland at low tide. Transports waiting outside the reef at anchor were easy targets for Japanese kamikazes and torpedo-bombers. One sailor who'd been in several landings said no assault ever went smoothly, but that the Coast Guard had "learned to improvise and complete their task regardless of the impediments."

MAGIC CARPET RIDE

When the Japanese surrendered on August 15, 1945, the same coastguardsmen who had manned the transports and the LSTs finished their work in the Pacific by transporting thousands of troops home in what was called Operation Magic Carpet. Not until 1946 did the Coast Guard sailors themselves go home.

Of the 241,093 men and women who served in the Coast Guard in World War II, 574 died in action and 1,343 died from crashes, accidents, disease, or drowning. The number of wounded has never been tallied. There are no records of how many soldiers, sailors, and civilians the Coast Guard saved during World War II, but the number could easily exceed 100,000.

Dixie cup: The round white canvas hat that sailors wear with their dress uniforms.

TOYS FOR TOTS

It all started with a homemade Raggedy Ann doll in 1947 Los Angeles.

A CHARITABLE IMPULSE

Diane Hendricks handcrafted the doll and asked her husband Bill to give it to an organization delivering Christmas toys to needy children. To their surprise, there was no such group, so Diane informed Bill that he needed to start one. A Marine knows how to follow orders, so Major Bill Hendricks, a member of the U.S. Marine Corps Reserves, duly enlisted his fellow reservists and collected and distributed 5,000 toys that year. They called their toy drive Toys for Tots.

Toys for Tots was so successful that the Marine Corps promptly adopted it as an official Marine charity; in 1948 they made it a national program. Every American city with a Marine Reserve Center sponsored campaigns with the announced goal to "bring the joy of Christmas to America's needy children."

Major Hendricks was a Marine Reservist on weekends, but his day job was as director of public relations for Warner Brothers Studio, and he used his expertise and connections to advance the Toys for Tots program. In 1948 Walt Disney designed the logo still in use today. Nat King Cole, Peggy Lee, and Vic Damone recorded the Toys for Tots theme. Hollywood continued to help through the years as John Wayne, Bob Hope, Frank Sinatra, Tim Allen, Kenny Rogers, Clint Eastwood, and Billy Ray Cyrus are on a long list of celebrities who've donated their time and talent to the program. First Lady Nancy Reagan served as the national spokesperson in 1983, as did First Lady Barbara Bush in 1992.

A TOY UNDER EVERY TREE

As Marine Reservists were being mobilized in 1990 for Operation Desert Shield, Hollywood and corporate America stepped in help ensure that the Toys for Tots campaign was carried out. Merv Griffin's popular *Wheel of Fortune* TV show teamed with Pizza Hut for a three-week promotion of Toys for Tots that raised in excess of $3 million and, while in the midst of deploying, the reservists still managed to distribute 7.9 million toys.

Bedpan commando: World War II slang for a U.S. Navy pharmacist's mate.

In 1991 the Marine Corps established the Toys for Tots Foundation as a tax-deductable public charity, which enabled individuals and American corporations to donate even more money, toys, and time. In 2003 *Reader's Digest* named the Toys for Tots Foundation "America's Best Children's Charity." *Forbes* magazine also named the foundation one of the top 10 charities on its "Gold Star" list.

Since Diane Hendricks crafted that first doll, the Marine Corps Reservists have built a program that has procured more than 100 million toys for more than 70 million children and has distributed toys in 558 communities in all 50 states, Puerto Rico, Guam, the Virgin Islands, and American Samoa, as well as Japan.

To help what is arguably one of the most worthwhile charities in the United States, look to donate a toy at the Toys for Tots barrel in your local shopping mall during the holiday season. During the rest of the year, donations can be made through their Web site, www.toysfortots.com. As former U.S. Marine Wilford Brimley said, "It's the right thing to do."

* * *

THAT "WASCALLY WABBIT"

First appearing in "A Wild Hare" in 1940, Bugs Bunny quickly became a favorite with audiences because of his carefree attitude. Defeating bullies and enemies with a calm wit, Bugs always came out on top. By 1942 Bugs, the creation of Leon Schlesinger Productions (now Warner Bros. Cartoons), was the main celebrity of the company's Merrie Melodies series. During many of the series' cartoon shorts, his primary rival, Elmer Fudd, challenged Bugs. During wartime, audiences enjoyed his rivalry with notable enemies such as Adolf Hitler, Hermann Goering, and the Japanese.

MASTER SERGEANT BUGS BUNNY

Is it possible that a cartoon character can join the Marines? Apparently so! During the cartoon "Super-Rabbit" (1943), Bugs sports a United States Marine Corps dress uniform. Flattered that Bugs wanted to become a Marine in the cartoon, the U.S. Marine Corps officially inducted the character into the force as a private. They even assigned him dog tags! The character was regularly promoted until Bugs was officially "discharged" at the end of World War II as a master sergeant.

Two-thirds of the men who served in Vietnam were draftees.

THE ROAD TO JAPAN

One important stepping stone on the World War II road to Tokyo was the Tarawa Atoll's island of Betio and the bloody battle that was fought there.

BETTING ON BETIO

Rear Admiral Keijo Shibasaki, commander of the Japanese defense at Betio, said, "A million men fighting for a thousand years cannot take Tarawa." To hold the narrow two-mile long island, Shibasaki had 4,836 men, including 2,619 elite Naval Marines known as "Rikusentai." His plan was to "destroy the enemy at the waters' edge" and then have his troops build blockhouses, pillboxes (concrete bunkers), and more than 500 heavy machine gun emplacements.

Shibasaki had assumed that a reef 600 yards out in the water would halt the Marine invasion. But he and his men stared in disbelief as the landing vehicles struck the reef, slowing down as they crawled over the sharp coral, and then relaunched themselves toward the beach with machine guns firing at the Japanese defenders. In response, the Rikusentai's heavy machine guns tore into the landing craft as they struggled to clear the reef and advance.

THE LONG WALK TO THE BEACH

The Marines had to wade to the beach, holding their rifles over their heads in a fruitless attempt to keep them dry. Many stepped into holes in the coral and drowned. Bullets and artillery shells rained into them, and soon the water turned a foamy crimson. Marines in the landing craft were disintegrated as Japanese artillery targeted the small boats. Hundreds bobbed dead in the lagoon, or hung up on the barbed wire or other obstacles that Shibasaki had planted in the water. The few remaining landing craft burst into flames under the shellfire, and burning Marines leapt into the water as they died. But the advance to the beach continued.

It took Colonel David Shoup, who'd been put in charge of the assault, some four hours to make it to shore, during which 75 percent of his troops were killed. But he set up a command post in the

Daisy cutter: A 15,000-pound conventional bomb with a huge lethal, destructive radius...

sand, and began to take charge of the disorganized battle. The carnage was so bad that Smith sent a message requesting immediate usage of the Marines held in reserve.

BRINGING IN THE BIG GUNS

Lieutenant Colonel Presley Rixey, 1st Battalion, 10th Marines knew that the Marines ashore desperately needed the small 75-mm pack howitzers he commanded, but his guns were hung up on the reef in their Higgins boats. So he and his Marines dismantled the howitzers and, over the next 15 hours, brought them on shore piece by piece (many of which weighed more than 200 pounds). As one Marine was killed by the Japanese or dropped of exhaustion, another one took his place. By daybreak of Day 2, Rixey had 12 guns on the beach firing point-blank against Japanese bunkers only hundreds of yards away.

DEATH OF A HERO

The surviving Marines spent the first night crouched behind the low seawall as naval guns fired through the night to keep the Japanese pinned down; a concerted banzai attack could have thrown the Marines back into the water, the assault on Tarawa was that close to disaster. The second day began as a replay of the first. Exhausted and seasick from spending all night in their Higgins boats, the 1st Battalion, 8th Marines tried to wade ashore from the reef and were slaughtered.

The sight of this infuriated Lieutenant William Deane Hawkins, a decorated veteran of Guadalcanal. Armed only with hand grenades and a terrible rage, Hawkins attacked bunker after bunker, stuffing grenades in the firing slits and down vent tubes. The Japanese gunners shot at him, and he was hit multiple times before he died—surrounded by his Marines. "Boys," he said, "I sure hate to leave you like this." But his sacrifice was significant; with so much Japanese fire directed at him, hundreds of Marines had leapt up from behind the seawall and raced across the island, cutting off the Japanese forces from each other. "Casualties many," Shoup reported, "percent dead unknown. Combat efficiency: we are winning." Shoup later credited Hawkins's actions as the turning point in winning the battle.

...It was originally designed to create instant clearings in the jungles of Vietnam.

THE MARINES WIN THE BET

One last huge battle remained, though, triggered by 1st Lieutenant Alexander Bonneyman. With his Marines pinned down near a large bunker, Bonneyman assembled a rag-tag team with flamethrowers and demolition gear, and charged up the 25-foot-high sand bunker. The defenders reacted quickly, killing half of Bonneyman's little force. But as the flamethrowers torched the topside Japanese machine gunners, other Marines dropped grenades down the air vents. Hundreds of Japanese burst out of the bunker, only to be killed by Marines who were finally seeing their targets in the open. Bonneyman was killed during the assault.

Organized resistance ended, although the Japanese made a final banzai attack that night. Fighting hand-to-hand with knives and fists and using rifles as clubs, the Marines stopped it. The final toll of three days fighting was 984 dead Marines. Only 17 Japanese prisoners—all wounded—were taken; none had surrendered.

LIFE OF A HERO

He'd already appeared in 10 or more movies as Eddie Albert—and would later go on to star in TV's *Green Acres*—but Navy Lieutenant Albert Heimberger had the role of a lifetime as skipper of a Higgins boat parked outside the reef at Tarawa during the famous battle. When the Japanese Rikusentai (elite Marines) swam out to sweep the reef and approaching Higgins boats with machine gun fire, Albert maneuvered his boat between the wounded Marines and the Japanese, then hauled Marines on board and brought them to a nearby hospital ship. When his own boat began to sink from gunfire holes, he switched to another craft. When his new boat caught fire, Albert and his crew stomped out the flames, continued to shoot at the Japanese, and went back to rescuing more Marines.

* * *

PRESIDENTIAL PRISONER OF WAR

Andrew Jackson was the only president who was a prisoner of war. While serving as a 14-year-old messenger during the American Revolution, Jackson and his brother were taken prisoner by the British. While in captivity, Jackson refused to shine a British officer's boots and received a beating that left permanent scars on his face and body.

Iraq's Scuds were ballistic missiles developed by the Soviet Union during the Cold War.

SINCE YOU ASKED

The National World War II Memorial started with a question, and proceeded with a little help from Hollywood.

ASK AND YOU SHALL RECEIVE (EVENTUALLY)

World War II veterans—the people we now call the "Greatest Generation"—are not known for tooting their own horns. They went to war because it was their duty; then they came home and brought the United States to a new level of prosperity. They never really asked for applause, let alone for a national tribute to their service.

"They're the most unselfish generation America has ever known," Ohio representative Marcy Kaptur told the *Washington Times* in 2004. "That's why there was no World War II memorial before; because they never asked for it themselves." Instead, Kaptur asked for them. And when she was turned down, she asked again. And again.

Kaptur's interest in a memorial began when she met a World War II vet named Roger Durbin in 1986, after the Vietnam Veterans Memorial had been dedicated in Washington, D.C., and plans for the Korean War Veterans Memorial had been given a green light. Durbin pointed out to the congresswoman that there was no memorial for all of those who served and died in World War II. The Iwo Jima statue was a fine tribute to the Marines, he said, but it left out the other branches of the armed forces. Kaptur did a little research and discovered Durbin was right, and she began asking questions.

From 1987 to 1993, Kaptur kept asking, and finally, just a few days before Memorial Day 1993, President Bill Clinton signed a law authorizing the construction of a national World War II memorial.

A QUESTION OF FUNDING

Once the question of whether there would be a memorial was answered, the next question was how to pay for it. The plan was to cover the costs with private donations.

By 1995 about $7 million had been raised, and by 1997 the

total was up to about $10 million—not bad, but nowhere near the estimated $182 million it would eventually take to build the memorial. To enhance the fund-raising profile, former senator Bob Dole, himself a World War II vet, was named the national chairman of the campaign and a scheme was put into place to have each state donate one dollar on behalf of every one of its residents who served in the war. Ohio alone pledged $500,000 toward the construction (the state sent an estimated 893,000 Buckeyes to fight in the war), and Pennsylvania gave more than $2 million. In the end, all 50 states and Puerto Rico contributed to the project, and they were joined by dozens of veterans' groups, corporate donors, organizations, schools, and individuals.

A site for the memorial was chosen in 1995. Friedrich St. Florian, an architect from Providence, Rhode Island, won a national design competition that drew 400 submissions. Progress was slow and steady, but by 1998, five years after the memorial project had received approval, the funding still wasn't approaching the totals necessary for work to start.

Then, like a scene from a Hollywood movie—complete with an A-list star—something utterly unexpected, and utterly wonderful, rallied the troops.

HOORAY FOR HOLLYWOOD

In 1998, five years into the fund-raising campaign, Tom Hanks starred in the World War II film *Saving Private Ryan*. The fact that the film, directed by Steven Spielberg, was a big success didn't surprise anyone. The fact that Hanks won a People's Choice Award for his role probably didn't surprise anyone, either. But what Hanks did at the January 1999 awards ceremony left everyone floored—especially those involved with the memorial. The two-time Oscar winner used his award acceptance speech to call attention to the fund-raising campaign for a World War II memorial and he even read the toll-free phone number for donations on air.

Calls came flooding in: more than 19,000 on the night of the awards show and another 11,000 the next day. And with the calls came the money. Hanks then volunteered his time to do public service ads for radio, television, and print. By June 2000, the toll-free hotline had received more than 230,000 calls, and by the time the memorial was finished in 2004, a total of $197 million had been raised—enough to pay for the construction and to create a fund for the monument's maintenance and upkeep.

A FITTING TRIBUTE

Unlike the Vietnam Veterans Memorial and the Korean War Veterans Memorial, both of which were plagued by controversy over their unconventional designs, the World War II Memorial design process flowed fairly smoothly. Friedrich St. Florian, a longtime professor at the Rhode Island School of Design, created a stately, classically influenced monument of granite pillars encircling an existing water feature known as the Rainbow Pool. Each of the 56 pillars is dedicated to the U.S. states, territories, and the District of Columbia, whose native sons and daughters fought in the war. Bas-relief sculptures lining the entrance to the memorial depict scenes from the war at home and abroad. On the far side of the monument is the Freedom Wall, a tribute to the more than 400,000 Americans who died in the war. It is covered with 4,048 gold stars, each meant to represent 100 Americans who died in the war.

Fittingly, the official groundbreaking for construction was on Veterans Day, November 11, 2000. The project was completed in 2004 and the dedication took place on Memorial Day weekend of that year. Yet by April 2004, the National Park Service decided that the vets had waited for this tribute long enough, so it took down the construction fences and let them in to see it nearly a month before the official opening. Thousands of veterans and civilians visited the memorial before its dedication. Sadly, one who didn't live to witness the memorial's completion was a veteran of the 10th Armored Division: Roger Durbin, the man whose question had started it all. Durbin had died in February 2000, knowing that the monument he championed would be built—an honor the Greatest Generation rarely asked for, but so richly deserved.

* * *

THANKS, MOM!

According to William Manchester's book *American Caesar*, Colonel Douglas MacArthur's mother wrote a letter on behalf of her son to General Pershing, suggesting that it was time for MacArthur to be promoted to general.

CHRISTMAS AT ARLINGTON

Every year, visitors lay 5,000 wreaths at headstones in Arlington National Cemetery. It all started when a paperboy won a trip to Washington, D.C.

READ ALL ABOUT IT!

As a kid, Morrill Worcester worked as a paperboy for Maine's *Bangor Daily News*. He won a contest there, and the prize was a five-day trip to Washington, D.C. When he grew up, Worcester operated a wreath company. In 1992, when his company had a surplus of wreaths, he remembered his boyhood visit to Arlington Cemetery and the rows of white grave markers on the green lawns. That gave him an idea: he'd lay those extra wreaths on graves that didn't get many visitors.

As word of the plan spread, others joined in—another businessman provided free transportation; the American Legion and VFW Posts made hand-tied red bows to decorate each wreath. Then Worcester personally accompanied the wreaths to Arlington and laid many of them himself.

DON'T MONKEY WITH TRADITION

What started as one random act blossomed into a tradition. Today, it's an entire campaign called Wreaths Across America, which places holiday wreaths at cemeteries across the United States.

Worcester also continues to provide 5,000 wreaths every Christmas to Arlington Cemetery, and dozens of volunteers help him distribute them. Over the years, the group has been escorted on the drive from Maine to Virginia by the Patriot Guard Riders, a national motorcycle group dedicated to patriotic events. The cemetery's director now selects the location for the wreath-laying each year and plans to cover all areas over the years.

Worcester's motto: "Our Mission: Remember—Honor—and Teach. To Remember the fallen; Honor those who serve; and Teach our children the value of freedom."

What the heck is a *frizzen*? In a flintlock musket, it's the piece of steel that the flint strikes.

THE REAL M*A*S*H

You've seen the antics and heroics of the 4077th on the big screen and TV. But do you know about the real Mobile Army Surgical Hospital and its history of heroism?

After World War II, the Army Nurse Corps was in bad shape. In the 1950s, the United States was all about prosperity and personal achievement. Medical students wanted to land jobs where they could specialize—and bring home the big bucks. Nobody wanted to be stuck in a noble-but-nowhere role of keeping soldiers alive. And then along came the Korean War. The U.S. government passed the Doctors Draft Act, calling in the markers of the many who'd taken Uncle Sam up on a free education in exchange for potential military service.

MEDS ON THE MOVE

Korea ushered in a whole new way of mending soldiers. In World War I, most of the fighting was done from the trenches, so hospitals were set up in the rear, far from the action. Teams of ambulances would haul the wounded from the front lines. In World War II, the fighting moved around a lot more, so a group of vehicles was set up closer to the front lines to handle emergencies and prep soldiers for the ride back to the rear hospital.

When Korea rolled around, the Army came up with an improved version of their frontline aid trucks: a complete mobile hospital. Composed entirely of tents, the Mobile Army Surgical Hospital (MASH) was a fully functional surgical facility right there at the front lines, a whole hospital that could pack itself into its own trucks and move with just six hours' notice. Soldiers could get immediate care early—in the vital stages of an injury—and then be shipped back to the rear for longer-term care. When the fighting moved, the MASH moved with it.

HOSTILE WORKING CONDITIONS

With their whole hospital right at the front lines, medical teams could hear the explosions and gunfire, see the smoke, and watch the enemy planes approach. Doctors migrated from place to place,

Peanut: American code name (semiofficial) for General Chiang Kai-shek.

serving an endless stream of patients. And every part of the hospital was a tent: living quarters, operating room, X-ray room, offices, nurses' station, scrubbing room. The odd tin building popped up here and there, but the whole MASH unit was pretty much a tent city.

Drafted MASH doctors weren't trained soldiers or military medics. They had no combat experience and weren't really versed in military culture and customs. And none of them were experienced in the types of trauma that they would encounter during their tour of duty. The longest tour possible for a MASH doc was only a year or so, but in that year, they'd perform more emergency surgeries than in a whole lifetime of civilian service. The painfully understaffed crew snatched an hour of sleep here or there, but their operating hours included "whenever there was fighting." And there was nonstop fighting between 1950 and 1953.

NONE OF THE COMFORTS OF HOME

Even experienced military medics had never been in a hospital like the Korean MASH unit. At any given time, all of their patients might have to be loaded up and moved. The Korean climate ranged from zero to 100°F, and the tents provided no warmth in the cold and no relief from the heat. The bathroom was basically a simple trench. Flies the size of pennies swarmed in the summer; rats overran the perimeters. Add that to the constant smells and sounds of gun battles, often just a few miles away, and you had a whole new level of stress for docs and nurses.

GRACE UNDER FIRE

The working conditions forced MASH doctors to be creative, and they made some serious innovations along the way. For example, in the old days patients would be moved from a stretcher to an ambulance to a surgical table to a bed—lots of moving around of some very sick folks. But MASH units, pressed for time and equipment, performed surgery and let patients rest on the same stretchers they'd come in on. The need for mobility led to the practice of early ambulatory—making recovering patients move around as soon as possible to promote blood circulation. Doctors also made big strides in blood-loss shock and vascular surgery.

The words "In God We Trust" first appeared on a U.S. coin in 1864, during the Civil War.

MASH VS. M*A*S*H

So was life in the real MASH anything like the TV show? Well, yes and no.

The characters in the fictional 4077th *M*A*S*H* we all know and love first popped up in 1968 with the Richard Hooker novel *MASH: A Novel About Three Army Doctors*. The movie and the TV show followed. And while the 4077th was based on a real MASH unit—the 8076th—Dr. Otto Apel (an 8076th veteran, and author of a memoir of his experience) notes that like any work of fiction, it was a little removed from the truth. While the social lives of the TV show's characters took center stage, almost everyone in the real MASH unit worked nonstop. Such intensity bred a deep and lifelong camaraderie, but not a lot of conversation—much less riotous sexual antics. Turnover in the units was fast-paced, so doctors and nurses would come and go before ever being formally introduced. Nobody ate meals at the same time, thanks to their work schedules. And while there were good times, the horrors of war were always minutes away.

But the television version was still pretty realistic. Apel was a consultant for the show, and many episodes were based on actual people and events. There was one other difference: the Korean War had no laugh track. *M*A*S*H* wouldn't have had one either, if the producers had gotten their way, but CBS insisted. As a compromise, only scenes in the operating room were shown without a laugh track—but thanks to DVDs, the entire laugh tracks can now be "surgically removed."

*　　*　　*

BOMBS AWAY

In June 1944, the U.S. Army rolled into Rome as the Germans were retreating northward. In his book *The Battle for Rome*, historian Robert Katz recounts the story of one American GI, Thomas Garcia, who, on seeing the Roman Coliseum for the first time, said, "My God, they bombed that, too!"

Scullery slut: Royal Canadian Navy slang for a mess hand, dishwasher, server, etc.

CHOSIN RESERVOIR

The odds: 20,000 to 200,000.

FLASHBACK

Hill 698, November 4, 1950, late afternoon: First Lieutenant John Yancey studied the hill through his binoculars. It was the key position in the Chinese lines, all rock and steep slopes—and aggressively defended by a Chinese battalion. There was just one route for attack, and both the Marines and Chinese knew it; the Marines had already attacked the hill twice that day, and very few had returned alive.

But the hill had to be taken. "Fix bayonets!" Yancey yelled to his Marines, "Take the hill!" Shooting as they ran, his platoon surged towards the hill as Chinese mortars and machine gun fire rained down on them. But halting meant certain death. Yancey yelled, "Run through it!" and they did, leaving a trail of Marines behind them, dying in the snow. When they reached the top, the Chinese charged them; Yancey's Marines shot them down. They'd taken the hill, but were too few to keep it.

STAND FAST!

On Yancey's left, only three Marines survived, and he had only one Marine on his right; two wounded Marines crawled around bringing ammunition to the five Marines still fighting. The Chinese buglers sounded a new attack and Yancey yelled, "Here they come, boys—stand fast and die like Marines!"

Private First Class James Gallagher burst through the frozen scrub, carrying a machine gun and two cans of ammunition. He finished loading the gun just as the Chinese attacked across the crest of the hill; he and Yancey's few Marines drove them back. The Chinese Communist Army had met the U.S. Marines for the first time, and the Marines had prevailed. Hill 698 was just one of many in the Marines 38-day fight out of Chosin Reservoir.

FLASH FORWARD

Ignoring China's repeated threats about entering the war if American forces crossed the 38th Parallel—the boundary between North and South Korea—General Douglas MacArthur ordered Marine and Army units north toward the Chinese border.

The Marine advance was led by Major General Oliver Smith, 1st Marine Division, who had three infantry regiments commanded by Colonel Lewis "Chesty" Puller, Lieutenant Colonel Ray Murray, and Colonel Homer Litzenberg, and an artillery regiment, for a total of 12,000 Marines. Unknown to the Marines, the Chinese had 300,000 soldiers waiting in reserve, with almost 140,000 already waiting for them at the Chosin Reservoir.

The first Chinese units slammed into Litzenberg's Marines at midnight, whistles screeching, bugles blowing, and green flares bursting. After counting enemy dead in the morning (662 in front of one Marine position alone), they discovered that they'd defeated three Chinese regiments that night.

THE FROZEN CHOSIN

When the weather changed and winter winds swept through the mountainous countryside, the water in the reservoir froze, as did the blood on the gloves of the surgeons and corpsmen treating the wounded. Smith's Marines marched forward in the -20°F cold, fighting off attacks up and down the 14-mile stretch of road. Chesty Puller was overjoyed. "We've been looking for the enemy for some time," he said, "We've finally found him. We're surrounded. That simplifies things."

Smith ordered his Marines to break out of the trap. That meant that Toktong Pass, seven miles to the south, had to be secured so that the 8.000 Marines north of it could get out. The night temps there in the high mountains dropped to -25° as more than 1,000 Chinese attacked Toktong. Many of the Marines were forced to fire their half-frozen automatic weapons one round at a time, and had trouble pulling the "spoons" off their ice-covered hand grenades. By daybreak they'd killed some 450 Chinese.

With the pass still tenuously open, the Marines fought their way south toward its relative safety. It took three days of hard fighting for them to reach it, with one unit making a desperate night march. As Marine mortar fire and air strikes cleared the way into Toktong, Marines stumbled across the frozen hilltops . . . in one company, only 82 of 240 Marines could still walk . . . but they carried or dragged their brother Marines with them.

In the Persian Gulf War, Operation Desert Storm launched more than 1,000 sorties per day.

A DIFFERENT DIRECTION

Outnumbered as they were, the Marines couldn't shoot the Chinese fast enough. They were low on ammunition and the extreme cold was freezing the powder. By now, many of the Marines were using weapons and ammunition taken from dead Chinese to supplement their own M-1s and BARs. At one point the Chinese were so close that they were lobbing grenades into the trucks and jeeps passing by; there were almost too many targets for the Marine infantrymen and their brothers flying close air support in World War II Corsairs to shoot. The word came down from Smith to make a run for Hagaru-ri, just south of the reservoir.

The fighting was virtually nonstop for 79 hours. A fresh Chinese division hurled themselves against the Marines, who used mortars, artillery and point-blank fighting to defend themselves. The following night was even more brutal; when 800 Chinese attacked the artillerymen, the cannoneers lowered their tubes, cut the powder charges, and cut down the massed attackers at less than 50 yards. When the weak December dawn came, the Marines still owned Hagaru-ri. "Retreat, hell," Smith snarled at a British journalist, "we're just attacking in a different direction."

THE CHOSIN FEW

The Marines trudged south to the Funchillon Bridge, the last place where the Chinese could trap the Marines. When they got there, they discovered the Chinese had blown the narrow bridge. Unless the Marines could reconstruct it, they were trapped. But by air-dropping four bridging sections, they could bridge the 25-foot gap blown in the bridge and keep moving.

Two sections were lost in the airdrop, but as the engineers muscled the two remaining sections into position, they filled the gap, but with only inches to spare. With bodies tied to the hoods, bumpers, and rooftops of trucks and jeeps, and with wounded Marines lying in between the corpses, a three-mile-plus line of Marines crossed the bridge. Within hours the entire 1st Marine Division cleared the pass and were safe. One of the last Marines out was Colonel Puller, whose jeep had one dead Marine tied to the bumper and two others lashed to the hood, honoring the Marines motto: "Leave no man behind." As General Smith said "We're coming out as Marines."

Behind his back, the 290-lb German Gen. Hermann Goering was known as *der Dicke* ("Fatty").

FROCKING

Being "frocked" sounds like some sort of insult or hazing, but that's hardly the case. In the U.S. military, being frocked is quite an honor in most cases.

IS THAT A FROCK OR FROG COAT?

Most historians trace "frocking" to a type of 15th-century garb worn by monks. The drab, loose garments were similar to a cape and were known as "frocks." By the early 19th century, the "frock coat" was popular with men. The military adopted a similar look for officers' uniforms. The record is unclear, however, whether it was the monk's frock or a type of ornamental button known as a "frog" that gave the military frock uniform its name. (The "frog" was a spindle-shaped closure that passed through a loop of material.) So, was it a frock coat or a frog coat? No one knows for sure.

GETTING FROCKED

In Old English, the verb "to frock" made reference to a monk's frock investing him with "priestly office or privilege." In military history, "frocking" came to mean a lower-ranked officer adopting the uniform or insignia of the next-highest rank. At the Naval Academy in the early days, a midshipman's undress uniform was a short coat. A lieutenant outranked him and wore a frock coat to symbolize that. Whenever a midshipman was appointed to act in the role of lieutenant, he wore the uniform of a lieutenant—thus, he was "frocked."

Navy regulations as early as 1802 allowed for frocking prior to the actual promotion, but sometimes without the pay normally accorded the higher rank. This was more frequent during wars, especially the Civil War, when new leadership was needed quickly and there wasn't enough time to go through the Department of the Navy's normal approval process. In modern times, frocking without the authority of the U.S. Senate has resulted in repercussions for those involved, including censure. A set of criteria has to be met before a promotion to the next rank among officers. Among the key measures: The officer must be nominated by the U.S. president and confirmed by the Senate, and the frocking must be essential for the officer to effectively perform the duties of the higher rank.

Duckpin: An Allied code name for General of the Army Dwight D. Eisenhower.

WHERE CAN I SEE...?

The National World War II Museum (see page 356) has plenty of interesting stuff, but there are other fascinating artifacts spread all over the country. Here are some that are worth checking out.

Messenger Pigeon Carrier: U.S. Army World War I messenger pigeon carrier, a two-wheel cart pulled behind a 1917 Harley Davidson 1000cc motorcycle that still runs. *Wheels Through Time Museum, Maggie Valley, NC, www.wheelsthroughtime.com.*

1917 Renault Tank: Recovered during a scrap metal drive during World War II, this tank is the only one of its model whose turret was not reconfigured from the Martin machine gun to the Browning machine gun. *Pennsylvania Military Museum, Boalsburg, PA, www.pamilitarymuseum.org.*

Davy Crockett Bomb: Considered the smallest bomb, the Davy Crockett was a bazooka-type missile with a W54 nuclear warhead. It could be mounted on a jeep, or a three-man team could carry it—only 30 inches long and 76 pounds. *National Atomic Museum, Albuquerque, NM, www.atomicmuseum.org.*

Mobile Field Kitchen: This World War I Trailmobile field kitchen was capable of baking bread and brewing soups and coffee. With a canvas canopy over the work area, It resembles an Old West chuck wagon. *Anderson County Museum, Anderson, SC, www.andersoncountysc.com/museum.*

Curtiss P-40C Tomahawk: Made in the United States, this P-40—the only one in the world still in flying condition—was sold to the British, who then gave it to the Russians in September 1941, where it saw combat for nine months defending Murmask from German forces. *Flying Heritage Collection at Paine Field, Everett, WA, www.flyingheritage.com.*

U.S. Destroyer Escort: The only destroyer escort fully restored to its World War II configuration, the USS *Slater* (DE-776) and its

216-man crew saw combat duty escorting convoys from the United States to England in the North Atlantic. She was also used in a recent film, *Orion in Midsummer. USS* Slater, *Albany, NY, www.ussslater.org.*

Enigma Code Machine: This code machine, along with the transcription machine, was recovered from the wreck of the German submarine *U-85*. The *U-85* was the first German sub sunk by the United States in World War II on April 14, 1942. *Graveyard of the Atlantic Museum, Hatteras, NC, www.graveyardoftheatlantic.com.*

World War II Torpedo: A 1943 U.S. Navy Flash MK 14, Model 5 torpedo with a cross-cut opening to show part of its warhead. It is 21 feet long and 3,000 pounds. An estimated 14,748 were fired in World War II, sinking more than 1,100 ships. *Armed Forces Military Museum, Largo, FL, www.armedforcesmuseum.com.*

Aldbourne, England, Stables/Barracks: Anyone who has seen the HBO series *Band of Brothers* will recognize the 70-foot-long stables from Aldbourne, England, that served as barracks for Easy and Able Companies of the 506th Parachute Regiment. *Curahee Military Museum, Toccoa, GA, www.toccoahistory.com.*

D-day Life Belt: Washed up on Omaha Beach in Normandy, France, more than 55 years after the D-day invasion, this inflatable canvas belt with two rubber tubes and a CO_2 canister to inflate it was discovered in 2000. *National D-day Memorial Foundation, Bedford, VA, www.dday.org.*

Remagen Bridge Tank: A 42-ton Pershing tank, part of the country's largest collection of fully operational vintage military vehicles. This tank is the only known survivor of the U.S. crossing of the Rhine River into Germany via the Remagen Bridge in World War II. *Wring Museum, Wolfenboro, NH, www.wrightmuseum.org.*

Mighty Midget: The last surviving LCS gunboat from World War II was known as "the Mighty Midget" for the firepower of its mounted machine guns and six rocket launchers. *Mare*

...He ended his governor's inaugural address with the SEAL war cry "Hoo-yah!"

Island Historic Park Foundation, Mare Island, Vallejo, CA, *www.mareislandhpf.org.*

Troop Glider: Fully restored Waco CG-4A glider, of the type used for landings during World War II. *The Airborne and Special Operations Museum, Fayetteville,* NC, *www.asomf.org.*

***Enola Gay*:** The B-29 Stratofortress bomber that dropped the atomic bomb on Hiroshima, Japan, in August 1945. The plane's name—painted on its silver side—was that of the pilot's mother. *Smithsonian National Air and Space Museum, Washington, D.C., www.nasm.si.edu.*

A-Bomb Debris: Two stones taken from ground zero in Hiroshima, Japan, the first city to be attacked by an atomic bomb in August 1945. The museum is on the parade grounds of the Virginia Military Institute. *George* C. *Marshall Museum, Lexington,* VA, *www.marshallfoundation.org.*

U.S. Missile Set: One of only two known "sets" of U.S. missiles that include the Titan ICBM, the AIM4 Falcon, AIM7 Sparrow, AIM9 Sidewinder, AIM54 Phoenix, and the AIM120 Abraham. *Estella Warbird Museum, Paso Robles,* CA, *www.ewarbirds.org.*

Huey Helicopter: The workhorse of the Vietnam War. While not the only place in the United States to see a full-sized example, this one is located in the basement of the Indiana War Memorial. *Indiana War Memorial, Indianapolis, IN, www.in.gov/wm.*

Saddam Hussein Uniform: A complete dress uniform worn by former Iraqi president Saddam Hussein is one of scores of uniforms from several armies and wars. This uniform was found in one of his many palaces during the current Iraqi war. *Armed Forces Military Museum, Largo, FL, www.armedforcesmuseum.com.*

AH-64 Apache Helicopter: One of more than 45 aircraft on display. This model is still used by the U.S. Army in Iraq, Afghanistan, and elsewhere. *U.S. Army Aviation Museum, Fort Rucker, AL, www.armyavnmuseum.org.*

The typical German U-boat of World War I had a crew of 30 and could dive to 300 feet.

FIGHTIN' WORDS: KOREA

A groundbreaking conflict (remember, we can't call it a "war") that brought us a lot of now-familiar phrases.

The Korean War was the first conflict for which an international organization recommended the use of force; the first war that couldn't be called a war because Congress never declared it to be one; and the first war in which jet fighters and helicopters were widely used.

BAMBOO CURTAIN

Coined by *Time* magazine in 1949, it refers to the barrier of mistrust between China and its allies on the one hand and the non-Communist nations of Asia and the West on the other. The *bamboo curtain* was a counterpart to the "Iron Curtain" between the Soviets and the West.

POLICE ACTION

When Communist North Korea attacked Haesong, South Korea, in June 1950, the United Nations demanded the attackers withdraw completely. When that demand was ignored, the Security Council decided to send in troops. The UN didn't have a police force, but recommended that member nations take action, and 30 of them agreed to do so. President Harry Truman called out U.S. air and sea forces. He was acting without a vote of Congress because he was responding to a security measure recommended by the UN. At a press conference, a reporter asked him if the war could be called a *police action* under the UN's supervision, and Truman agreed that it could.

CHOPPER

Helicopters saw a lot of action, too, and were nicknamed *choppers*, probably from the "chop-chop" noise made by helicopter rotors.

AIRSTRIKE

The widespread use of jet fighters was new in this war, giving rise to the term *airstrike*, for attacks on enemy positions.

Rita Hayworth's pinup photo adorned the test bomb dropped on Bikini Atoll in July 1946.

BUG OUT

The term originated during World War II, but in Korea it acquired enormous currency. To *bug out* didn't just mean a retreat or withdrawal, but a fast pulling out, to avoid being killed or captured.

BUY THE FARM

An air war called for training flights, generally carried out in American rural areas. When an Air Force training flight crashed on a farm, the farmer could sue the government for damages sufficient to pay off his mortgage and thus *buy the farm* outright. Since the pilot in such a crash usually died, he "bought the farm" with his life.

EYEBALL TO EYEBALL

Korea was primarily a ground war. When MacArthur's headquarters sent a dispatch to the 24th Regiment to ask if they had contact with the enemy, they replied, "We is *eyeball to eyeball.*" It was widely quoted, and later was used with reference to the Cuban Missile Crisis, when the Cold War threatened to become hot.

HOOCH

As in all wars, there was fraternization with the local populace. From it came the use of *hooch* for a peasant shack, hut, or any place a serviceman might set up housekeeping with a Korean woman. From the Japanese *uchi*, for "house," it was used to mean a bunker or other frontline living quarter. Later, it was widely used during the Vietnam War.

BRAINWASHING

The sick and wounded who were taken prisoner by the Chinese were subjected to *brainwashing* to indoctrinate them with Communist beliefs. The technique used physical and mental torture to break down a soldier's loyalties and family ties. The word itself is a translation from a Chinese term for "thought reform," and the effectiveness of the technique was shockingly demonstrated during POW exchanges when a number of American soldiers said they did not wish to be repatriated. Since then, the term is used to mean changing someone's outlook or opinions, usually by underhanded means.

The Civil War was the first war in which soldiers wore machine-made uniforms.

HEAT STROKE OF GENIUS

The British army's fancy scarlet tunic looked sharp, but was agonizingly uncomfortable in the heat. The soldier's warm-weather option was a dazzling white uniform—spiffy but impractical for daily use. How to solve the problem?

JUST WILD ABOUT HARRY

Legend has it that a British colonial officer dabbled with the idea of creating his own lightweight, light-colored clothing to wear while he was stationed in India. What began as an off-duty ensemble evolved into military attire when it proved to be more comfortable and sensible than the existing uniform.

That officer was Lieutenant Harry Lumsden, the son of a British colonel. After schooling in England and Scotland, by age 17 Lumsden was serving in the infantry in India. In 1846, when he was just 25, he was tapped for the duty that would lead to his greatest claim to fame.

Serving in Peshawar in what was then northwestern India (now Pakistan on the Afghanistan border), Lumsden was given the task of forming the Corps of Guides, a new regiment of infantry and cavalry soldiers. The 300 handpicked men were to serve as guides and scouts as well as fighting forces. Irregular cavalry regiments such as the Corps of Guides were allowed to wear what they wanted, within reason. Lumsden had an idea about what that should be. He'd been experimenting with loose-fitting cotton garments patterned after the local men's attire and dyed a muddy tan color, which hid the dirt and made the wearer less conspicuous in the dusty landscape of the battlefield. Locals dubbed the duds *khaki*, from the Hindi and Urdu word *khak*, meaning dust. Fellow British soldiers started calling the Corps of Guides the "mudlarks" because of the muddy color of their uniforms.

DUSTING OFF SOME FACTS ABOUT KHAKIS

Lumsden achieved that characteristic mud color by dunking the fabric in mud. In another version of the tale, he took his clothes to the local bazaar and had them colored with a dye made from the local mazari palm. When khaki caught on, Lumsden tried unsuccessfully to obtain drab uniform fabric from England. So he had the dyeing done locally, either by the soldiers themselves or by civilians. While other regiments scoffed at the mudlarks initially, they soon adopted khaki as well, especially during the Indian Rebellion of 1857, which took place primarily during the summer months. Even then, the troops were left to color their own garments using mazari, coffee, tea, or even tobacco juice.

Fortunately, the rise of khaki uniforms coincided with the growth of the textile industry and the use of synthetic dyes. Khaki wasn't the first synthetic dye color developed in England—that distinction goes to aniline purple, better known as mauve, which was patented in 1856—but a patent for khaki dye was registered in England in 1884. It wasn't long before the British discovered it made more economic sense to import dye from Germany (which was leapfrogging ahead of other nations in the synthetic dye game). And that's where things became awkward: By World War I, the British army was importing all the khaki dye for its uniforms from Germany, whom it happened to be fighting in the Great War. Color them embarrassed. (Before Americans start feeling smug, consider this: about 90 percent of the khaki dye used for U.S. uniforms in World War II was produced by the General Aniline and Film Corporation—better known as GAF—a German-owned company until the U.S. government seized it in 1942.)

DRESS FOR SUCCESS

The U.S. military began wearing khaki during the Spanish-American War of 1898, but it didn't work for all purposes. In Guadalcanal's tropical jungles during World War II, khaki was deemed too conspicuous, so Army and Marine combat troops were issued green twill fatigues that blended better with their surroundings. The same was true for ground troops in the Vietnam War.

Of all the branches of the U.S. military, the Navy may have the closest association with khaki. It was first worn by Navy aviators in 1912, and a short time later, regulations required that ships carry enough khaki dye for "two suits of clothing for each man of the landing force," so the men could dye their "undress" white uniforms "when, in the opinion of the commanding officer, it is advisable to do so." (Generally, that would be when white uniforms would be dangerously obvious to the enemy, or when they became unduly soiled.) Khaki uniforms became standard issue for submariners in 1931, but khaki is best known as naval officers' attire, so much so that the word "khaki" became a euphemism for "officer."

KHAKI COMES HOME

It didn't take long for military-style khaki to become a fashion statement on the home front. After the Second Boer War in South Africa, which ended in 1902, shops in England began showing khaki clothing and accessories for dapper Victorian gents, who liked its sportsmanlike, heroic connotations. In America, the hard-wearing khaki that served U.S. soldiers so well in World War I was adapted for Depression-era civilian work clothing. In the 1940s, movie stars like Katharine Hepburn and John Wayne wore khakis on-screen and off; in the 1950s, khakis were standard issue for young American males, from the *Leave It to Beaver* boys to James Dean.

In spite of changing fashion trends, khakis hung on in civilian life, with a reputation that ranged from conservative or square in the late 1960s and early 1970s, to preppy in the late 1970s and early 1980s, to fashionable in the mid-1980s, when the Levi's Dockers brand was introduced and the rise of casual Friday for office workers made khaki sales skyrocket.

Meanwhile, the military's endorsement of khaki continues. In July 2008, the U.S. Navy introduced a new dress khaki uniform inspired by the dress khakis worn from World War II through the Vietnam War, which officers may wear in place of formal dress blues, dress whites, or service khakis. And a new service uniform was introduced for enlisted personnel, with a khaki shirt and black trousers. The idea, Navy spokespeople explain, is to reduce the number of uniforms a sailor has to carry when deployed. Whites are fine for the tropics, and dress blues work well for cooler climates, but khaki goes with everything, everywhere—and that's the point.

...was expected to fire off a shot every 20 seconds.

THE BLUE ZOO

Also known as "The Hill," "Wild Blue U," and the United States Air Force Academy.

ROCKY MOUNTAIN HIGH

One of the final transitions the newly independent U.S. Air Force made during its separation from the Army was the establishment of an academy on par with the Military Academy at West Point and the Naval Academy in Annapolis. President Dwight D. Eisenhower made it official in 1954.

The U.S. Air Force Academy class of 1959 began its training at Lowry Air Force Base in Denver, Colorado, where it remained for three years. Construction of the ultramodern, aluminum-and-glass-adorned cadet area near Colorado Springs was finished in 1958, which permitted the first graduating class to actually live on the academy grounds for their final year. On June 3, 1959, the first diplomas were awarded and commissions bestowed upon the 207 graduates. Since then all graduation week activities have been called "June Week"—even when the graduation is in May.

A TOUR OF THE CAMPUS

Nestled in the foothills of the Rampart Range of the Rockies on a somewhat remote parcel of land about 12 miles north of Colorado Springs, the academy is a fully autonomous community consisting of the academy grounds, an airfield, a preparatory school, a massive sports complex, a housing area for the faculty and administrative staff, a commissary, base exchange (retail store), service station, and hobby shop complex.

The superstar of the cadet area is the spectacular all-faiths Cadet Chapel, a modernist take on chapels in France and Italy, where weekly services for the Protestant, Catholic, Jewish, Buddhist, and Muslim faiths are held. Its A-frame design consists of 17 spires that soar 150 feet skyward; between each spire, tall Frank Lloyd Wright–style stained-glass windows filter the sun in ever-changing colors. The details in the Protestant Chapel on the topmost floor are variations on a theme: the pews were designed with propeller-like end pieces and aluminum prayer rails with the aerodynamic lines of modern jet fighter planes.

BACK TO BASICS

Academy cadets are enrolled in a four-year officer-training program. Graduates earn a bachelor of science degree and receive a commission as a second lieutenant in the Air Force. A cadet's education begins with basic military training. This includes a crash course in basic soldiering—marching, the rifle manual of arms, memorization of military and cadet knowledge from the little cadet book known as *Contrails* (including famous quotes, history, and military stuff), and demanding physical training. During this six-week program, students are introduced to the concept of teamwork, selfless service, duty, and—perhaps the most important concept—the cadet honor code.

The code states that no cadet will "lie, steal, cheat, nor tolerate among us anyone who does." It's the foundation of the cadet experience and the pillar upon which the Air Force officer corps is built. New cadets are called "doolies" (from the ancient Greek word for "slave") or SMACKs (Soldier Minus Ability, Courage, and Knowledge)—the more popular term among cadets.

JUST LIKE ANY COLLEGE, ONLY DIFFERENT

After mastering that host of military skills, the cadets take on an intense academic course load. Freshmen endure such traditions as having to greet all upper-class cadets, running on thin strips of white tiles while outdoors at all times, eating "square" meals (moving utensils to and from the mouth at right angles) while under close scrutiny, and restricted off-base privileges. Rigorous studies are complemented by participation in a wide variety of extracurricular activities—either NCAA athletics, intramural sports, or other typical collegiate activities like choir or the Cadet Drum and Bugle Corps, a brass and percussion extravaganza also known as "the Flight of Sound."

Near the end of the freshman year, the newest class is "recognized" after a short period of intense retraining that includes physical challenges, team-building exercises, and regurgitation of cadet knowledge—historically known as "Hell Week." After Hell Week, the SMACKs receive the coveted prop-and-wings emblem that is

...World War II and Vietnam, and was a UN "police action" rather than a declared war.

worn proudly on each upper-class cadet's flight cap, which marks a major milestone in a cadet's life and signals the end of the first difficult year.

KNOWING YOUR PLACE

Members of the three lower classes are also referred to as "four degrees" or "fourth classmen" (freshmen), "third degrees" (sophomores), or "two degrees" (juniors). First-class cadets, referred to as "firsties," act as the cadet officers, second-class cadets act as the cadet noncommissioned officers, and third-class cadets (sophomores) act as junior noncommissioned officers or senior airmen.

"NO TRASH IN THE TRASH CAN . . .

. . . No water in the sink, no dust in the dustpan." Academy cadets are constantly scrutinized and tested. On most weekends, parades (which are graded, just like tests) and uniform and room inspections are the usual activity. During these meticulous examinations, cadets stand at rigid attention while upperclassmen give their room and personal appearance the white-glove treatment. Points are deducted for dusty dustpans, wet sinks, and anything less than a spotless and trash-free trash can.

Cadet officers and sergeants are responsible for each cadet's compliance with room regulations and personal appearance. Every score is tallied and recorded throughout the year, and one squadron earns the coveted "Right of Line" award as the overall top squadron of the year. (A squadron consists of about 35 members of each class who live in the same "quad" of a dorm building.)

"FLY YOU FALCONS DOWN THE FIELD"

Seventeen men's and 10 women's teams are part of the NCAA program. But one of the highlights of every cadet's fall Saturday is cheering the "Fighting Falcons" on the gridiron. Victory on the field often means rewards for cadets in the form of additional off-base privileges or the cancellation of military formations. Like any team, the Falcons have enjoyed the thrill of victory and the agony of defeat on the field, but the rivalry among the service academies is as strong as any that exist in college football. The Air Force Academy team has played in more than 15 bowl games, which has brought additional prestige to the school.

Toenails: World War II code name for an operation to capture New Georgia (Solomon Islands).

GUERRILLA WARFARE, PART V

Delta Force is located in a remote area of Fort Bragg, North Carolina. The Pentagon maintains tight control over information about this unit that is rumored to number around 2,500 personnel. *(Part IV is on page 212).*

Delta Force was formed in 1977 by Special Forces commando Colonel Charles "Chargin' Charlie" Beckwith, in response to terrorist activities in the 1970s. The unit was modeled after the British Special Air Service, one of the most elite special forces units in the world. Delta Force is a counterterrorist unit specializing in hostage rescue and reconnaissance, equipped with the most advanced weaponry and technology available in the U.S. special ops arsenal.

Delta Force "operators" are recruited from the U.S. Army, mainly from the Green Berets and Rangers. The exact composition and strength of Delta Force is a closely guarded secret. For years, the Army denied the existence of Delta Force—though it was known that the unit took part in the failed attempt to rescue American hostages in Iran in 1980.

The unit conducted successful hostage rescue operations during the invasions of Grenada (1983) and Panama (1989–90), and participated in the first Iraq war (1991), although the full extent of what they did there has not been revealed. What is known is that Delta operators provided security for senior U.S. officers and government officials, including General Norman Schwarzkopf, and took part in the hunt for SCUD missile launchers in Iraq.

BLACK HAWK DOWN

In 1993 UN relief efforts in Somalia were being hampered by local warlords. UN troops were sent to protect the humanitarian workers, among them a group of Pakistani troops who were ambushed and killed. So Army Rangers and Delta Force launched a mission to capture the most powerful warlord—General Mohamed Farrah Adid—and several of his lieutenants. But during the mission two

In the Civil War, more than 2,000 boys in the Union ranks were 14 years old or younger.

Black Hawk helicopters were shot down. The mission then changed to rescuing the crews from the downed choppers.

Two Delta snipers circling above in a helicopter volunteered to defend one of the crash sites that was about to be overrun by Somali gunmen. They knew it was probably a suicide mission, but they agreed to be dropped off at the crash site because they could see that at least one of the American soldiers there was still alive. They held off hundreds of Somali gunmen until they were overrun and killed. They saved the life of the chopper pilot, Michael Durant, who was captured by the gunmen and later released. The snipers, Master Sergeant Gary Ivan Gordon and Sergeant First Class Randall D. Shughart, were each awarded the Medal of Honor posthumously for their extraordinary heroism.

By the time the Rangers and Delta Force operators arrived at the crash areas and set up defensive perimeters, they were surrounded by hostile natives and under near-constant attack. They were trapped in the city overnight and suffered heavy casualties. But the next morning, a relief force arrived, led by the 10th Infantry Division, and they managed to fight their way out along what became known as the "Mogadishu Mile."

AFGHANISTAN AND THE INVASION OF IRAQ

Before the war in Afghanistan began in 2001, Delta operators were sent to the major cities and contested areas in the north to do reconnaissance. During and after the war, Delta Force searched for the leaders of the Taliban and al Qaeda, including Mullah Omar and Osama bin Laden.

Just before the second Iraq war in early 2003, Delta Force operators entered Baghdad and established a network of informants, while also eavesdropping on and sabotaging Iraqi communications lines. During the invasion, they searched for senior Iraqi officials and weapons of mass destruction. After the capture of Saddam International Airport (now Baghdad International Airport), Delta Force set up a secret "battlefield interrogation facility" for insurgents and suspected terrorists; it went under investigation by the Pentagon inspector general's office for allegations of torture and other prisoner abuses.

Turn to page 424 for Part VI (Navy SEALs).

V-E (Victory in Europe) was May 8, 1945; V-J (Victory over Japan) was September 2, 1945.

THE FLYING WHITE HOUSE

You've heard of Air Force One, *but what do you really know about it? Here's a short history of what's now considered the "Flying White House."*

HOMEBOUND

For the first 130 years of the republic, not a single American president left the United States while in office, not even once. (Well, okay, once. Grover Cleveland briefly sailed across the U.S.–Canada border in the 1890s.) In January 1943, when Franklin D. Roosevelt flew to North Africa to meet with Winston Churchill and plan the Allied invasion of southern Europe, he became only the third president to go overseas (the others: cousin Teddy Roosevelt inspected the Panama Canal in 1906 and Woodrow Wilson attended the Paris Peace Conference at the end of World War I).

SMALL WORLD

FDR hated airplanes, but German submarines were patrolling the Atlantic and sinking American ships, so the Secret Service forbade him from traveling by sea. He flew in a chartered PanAm Flying Boat seaplane called the *Dixie Clipper*. That changed everything.

Within weeks of Roosevelt's historic journey, the U.S. Army Air Corps (precursor to the Air Force) began making plans to provide a custom-made plane for the president's exclusive use. Since then, each president has had an official plane, and today the president's airplane is considered an extension of the White House. On September 11, 2001, when all ground positions seemed vulnerable to attack, *Air Force One* served as a mobile bunker.

THE NAME

Technically speaking, although there is a special presidential airplane, it doesn't have the radio call sign *Air Force One*. The call sign is attached to the president himself; it is given to whatever

Air Force plane in which he happens to be flying. Likewise, any plane in which the vice president flies is known as *Air Force Two*. If the president flies on an Army aircraft, that aircraft is called *Army One*.

Before JFK, each presidential aircraft had its own name: Roosevelt's plane was nicknamed the "Sacred Cow" by the White House Press Corps; Truman's plane was the *Independence* (Truman named it himself, out of fear that it might otherwise become the "Sacred Cow II"); and Eisenhower's was the *Columbine*.

Then, in 1962, Kennedy took delivery of a Boeing 707, the first presidential jet airplane . . . and never bothered to name it. With no other name to go by, the media began referring to the plane by its call sign. The term *Air Force One* has been used for presidential aircraft ever since. In 1971 Richard Nixon renamed his plane *The Spirit of '76* in advance of the U.S. bicentennial, but the name never took hold.

MADE TO ORDER

One of the perks of being president is that you get to have *Air Force One* remodeled to suit your own tastes. Truman had his plane painted to look like a giant eagle, with stylized blue feathers, cockpit windows that looked like eyes, and a nose painted to look like a big brown beak. (The nose was later repainted yellow, out of fear the White House Press Corps might nickname the plane "Brown Nose.")

Lyndon B. Johnson had all of the passenger seats unbolted and turned around so that they faced the rear of the plane—toward his compartment. He also ripped out the cherry wood divider separating his compartment from the rest of the plane and replaced it with clear Plexiglas, Jerry terHorst writes in *The Flying White House*, "so that he could keep an eye on everybody—and they on him." LBJ also installed a secret taping system, which, ironically, President Nixon ordered removed after he took office.

Air Force One has three levels and 4,000 square feet of interior floor space. Master carpenters fashioned most of the furniture on board. The president has his own bedroom, bathroom, office space, and workout room. A comfortable capacity for the plane is 26 crew members and 70 passengers. According to the Air Force, there is no escape pod as shown in the 1997 movie *Air Force One*.

EXTRAORDINARY SOLDIERS

Every war has its heroes—and here are two from the Korean and Vietnam wars.

TOP-SECRET HERO

Hiroshi "Hershey" Miyamura: The son of a coal mine worker, Hershey was a Nisei, a first-generation Japanese-American born in Gallup, New Mexico, in 1925. In 1944, when many Japanese-Americans were still being held in internment camps, Hershey entered the U.S. Army to serve with the famous 442nd Infantry Regiment—a group that was highly decorated for their brave service in World War II. However, the war was over soon after he enlisted.

Miyamura returned home, worked as an auto mechanic, and married his sweetheart, Terry Tsuchimori, who had returned from an internment camp. Later, as a member of the Army Reserves, Miyamura was sent to Korea as a machine-gun squad leader in Company H, 7th Infantry Regiment, 3rd Infantry Division.

Above and Beyond: On April 22, 1951, UN forces in Korea were overwhelmed by waves of Chinese communist soldiers and began retreating. Colonel Miyamura's squad of machine-gunners and riflemen defended a hill near Taejon-ni, Korea, to slow the Chinese advance. On the rainy night of the 24th, the communist Chinese attacked Taejon-ni in such huge numbers that their grenades and rifle fire decimated the defense on the hill. Miyamura did everything he could to defend his men. He fought off the Chinese with his bayonet in hand-to-hand combat. He killed at least 10 of the enemy, and when he had a few moments of quiet, he tried to give first aid to his men and help them evacuate from the hill. When the next attack came, Miyamura held off the enemy with machine-gun fire and grenades. Fighting until his ammunition was gone, Miyamura destroyed his machine gun so it couldn't be captured by the enemy, and then made his way to another gun emplacement, where he ordered the last of the defenders to evacuate while he provided covering fire—possibly

In 1996 the Pentagon spent $7 million to add a third golf course to Andrews Air Force Base.

being the last American on a hill swarming with enemy troops.

Before Miyamura (who was wounded) retreated, he'd killed more than 50 Chinese. He collapsed from exhaustion. The next morning, he was captured and marched to a North Korean prison camp, where he as a prisoner for 28 months. He lost 50 pounds suffering from starvation and dysentery. During most of that time, his family didn't know if he was still alive.

Recognition: On August 20, 1953, Miyamura was released along with a group of other prisoners. They arrived in Freedom Village, South Korea, and after medical examinations and ice cream, Miyamura was led out to meet reporters. Brigadier General Ralph M. Osborne made an announcement that stunned an already disoriented POW: "It is my pleasure to inform you that you have been awarded the Medal of Honor."

The prestigious medal had actually been awarded on December 21, 1951, but it was kept secret because the Army didn't want Miyamura to be tortured by his captors as punishment for his heroic actions. On October 27, 1953, at a White House ceremony, President Dwight D. Eisenhower presented Miyamura with the Medal of Honor and he became the second Japanese-American to earn the award.

Today, when he speaks at memorial services, Miyamura urges Americans to appreciate the efforts of veterans who served in the Korean War.

ORDERS OF THE HEART

Ed "Too Tall" Freeman: Ed was born in Neely, Mississippi, in 1927. When he saw a troop of soldiers doing maneuvers in his hometown, he knew he wanted to join the military. At 17, he joined the Army and served through the Korean War as an infantryman. During the war, he found a new goal: becoming an airman. But in 1953 he was turned down for flight school because, at six foot six, he was two inches taller than regulations allowed—a dilemma that gave him his nickname, "Too Tall." The height restriction was eased in 1955, allowing him to become an Army aircraft pilot.

Above and Beyond: On November 14, 1965, helicopters dropped about 450 American troops off in a clearing in the Ia Drang Valley, a remote area of Vietnam. The troops were of the 1st Battalion,

7th Cavalry, led by Lieutenant Colonel Harold Moore, and the clearing was code-named Landing Zone (LZ) X-Ray. LZ X-Ray turned out to be a sanctuary for the North Vietnamese Army (NVA), and Moore's battalion was surrounded by over 2,000 NVA troops. They were attacked with machine-gun fire and rocket-propelled grenades. Joseph Galloway, a reporter at Ia Drang, later compared the dire predicament of Moore's troops to a modern version of Custer's Last Stand.

At that time, Captain Freeman was flying an unarmed Huey helicopter with Company A, 229th Assault Helicopter Battalion. Company A's Hueys were a lifeline to American soldiers in Ia Drang, but after the NVA shot up two helicopters so badly that they couldn't fly, Lieutenant Moore ordered the LZ closed.

No helicopters were supposed to fly into the combat zone after the closure because it was too dangerous, but Major Bruce Crandall decided to fly in anyway. He asked for any volunteers and only one pilot stepped forward—Captain Freeman. At the risk of his own life, Freeman flew into combat fire to transport ammunition, water, and medical supplies. The gunfire was so intense that medical evacuation helicopters wouldn't fly into the LZ, so Freeman took over their job evacuating over 30 severely wounded men—in some instances saving their lives. Though enemy fighters were sometimes as close as 30 yards away, Freeman kept returning to help the battalion. He did it not once or twice, but 14 times.

Thanks in large part to Freeman and his commander Crandall, (who flew in needed ammunition), the Americans staved off the initial attack and by the end of the fighting at Ia Drang, American troops overcame the North Vietnamese.

Recognition: Freeman initially won the Distinguished Flying Cross for his actions, but Major Crandall and other witnesses believed he deserved an even higher honor. Crandall, with the help of another decorated Vietnam veteran, Arizona senator John McCain, persuaded Congress to award the highest medal to Freeman, and on July 16, 2001, he received the Medal of Honor. (Major Crandall received a Medal of Honor in 2007.)

We Were Soldiers Once . . . and Young, by Lieutenant General Hal Moore and reporter Joseph Galloway, tells Freeman's story. The book was made into a film starring Mel Gibson. In the movie, Too Tall Freeman is portrayed by Mark McCracken.

...stayed free of communism. (Indonesia expelled the Soviets in 1966.)

FLYING HIGH

The development of precision targeting weaponry, military demand for stealth characteristics, improvements in avionics, smaller-quantity orders, and inflation drove aircraft prices higher. Today's huge infrastructure costs are spread across a smaller number of units. Secrecy measures surrounding the manufacture of some aircraft add to the bill.

The United States builds the best combat and auxiliary planes in the world, but excellence comes with a price. Here are stats on some of the most expensive planes in the world.

1. NORTHROP GRUMMAN B-2 SPIRIT

First deployed in 1993.

When flying low at night, the aircraft's triangular-shaped configuration resembles people's descriptions of an unidentified flying object.

Cost and Justification: At a project cost of $875 million and an actual cost of $1.157 billion, the B-2 multirole bomber represents a radical leap in technology for the intercontinental delivery of conventional and nuclear munitions. It has stealth characteristics and can bring massive firepower to bear in a short time anywhere in the world by operating undetected through previously impenetrable defenses.

- **Crew:** Two
- **Dimensions:** Wingspan 172 feet, length 69 feet, height 17 feet
- **Power Plant:** Four General Electric F118-100 engines
- **Weight:** 167,000 lb. empty, 336,500 lb. fueled and armed (takeoff weight)
- **Speed:** 604 mph
- **Ceiling:** Above 50,000 feet
- **Range:** Intercontinental
- **Payload:** 40,000 lb. of conventional and nuclear weapons, which is four times greater than the B-17s of World War II.

Inventory and Deployment: There are 20 B-2s in the Air Force's current inventory. All B-2 Spirits are based at Whiteman Air Force Base in Missouri and have flown nonstop combat missions to Iraq and Afghanistan.

General John J. Pershing was given number 0-1 when the military first issued dog tags.

2. BOEING NORTH AMERICA B-1B LANCER

The first B-1B was delivered to the Air Force in October 1985.

Cost and Justification: More cost efficient at $283 million, the multimission B-1B long-range intercontinental bomber carries the largest payload of guided and unguided weapons in the Air Force. The aircraft is designed to replace the B-52 for heavy bombing missions.

- **Crew:** Pilot, copilot, and two weapons systems officers
- **Special Configuration:** The aircraft has multiple wing settings ranging from 137 feet for takeoff, landing, and air refueling, to 79 feet when swept aft for combat and high-speed subsonic flying.
- **Dimensions:** Wingspan 137 feet, length 146 feet, height 34 feet
- **Power Plant:** Four General Electric F101 turbofan engines with afterburners
- **Weight:** 190,000 lb. empty, 477,000 lb. fueled and armed
- **Speed:** 900+ mph at sea level
- **Ceiling:** 30,000 feet
- **Range:** Intercontinental
- **Payload:** 75,000 lb. of conventional and nuclear ordnance

Inventory and Deployment: Of the 65 B-1s in the Air Force's inventory, only eight planes were used during the first six months of Operation Enduring Freedom, but those eight Lancers dropped 40 percent of the total tonnage deployed against Iraqi targets.

3. BOEING AEROSPACE E-3 SENTRY (AWACS)

The Air Force received the first E-3 Sentry in March 1977.

Cost and Justification: The $270 million aircraft is not a conventional combat plane but a modified Boeing 707/320 commercial airframe with an airborne warning and control system (AWACS) mounted on the fuselage. The 30-foot diameter dome of the AWACS, mounted 11 feet above the fuselage, monitors and delivers real-time battle space management, which includes surveillance, target detection, and a tracking system capable of distinguishing between friendly, neutral, and hostile activity. Each aircraft covers command and control of a designated sector, provides all-altitude and all-weather surveillance, and communicates early warning of enemy actions during joint operations among all branches of the armed forces.

In the Revolutionary War, Continental Army soldiers had a daily hard liquor ration of 4 oz.

- **Crew:** Flight crew of four, with 13 to 19 electronic mission specialists
- **Dimensions:** Wingspan 146 feet, length 153 feet, height 42 feet
- **Power Plant:** Four Pratt & Whitney TF33-100A turbofan engines
- **Weight:** 335,000 lb.
- **Speed:** 360 mph
- **Range:** More than 5,000 nautical miles

Inventory and Deployment: There are 33 E-3s in the Air Force's inventory, and some are currently deployed in Iraq and Afghanistan. AWACS are not armed, but are packed with electronic equipment for battlefield control.

4. BOEING C-17 GLOBEMASTER III

First deployed in 1993.

Cost and Justification: At a current cost of $241 million, the Globemaster is the newest, most flexible cargo military aircraft in the world.

- **Crew:** Two pilots and one loadmaster
- **Dimensions:** Wingspan 170 feet, length 174 feet, height 55 feet
- **Power Plant:** Four Pratt & Whitney F117-100 turbofan engines
- **Weight:** 585,000 lb. maximum when loaded
- **Cargo Load:** 170,900 lb.
- **Optional Load:** 102 troops/paratroops or 36 litter and 54 ambulatory patients and attendants
- **Speed:** 518 mph
- **Ceiling:** 45,000 feet
- **Range:** Global with in-flight refueling

Inventory and Deployment: There are 158 C-17s on active duty around the world, eight with the National Guard and eight with the Air Force Reserve.

5. LOCKHEED-GEORGIA C-5A/B GALAXY

First deployed C-5A in 1969; its current cost is $158.2 million.

First deployed C-5B in 1980; its current cost is $179 million.

Cost and Justification: The gigantic C-5s, with their tremendous payload capacity, provide the Air Force with mobility for transporting either vast amounts of cargo or fully equipped combat-ready military units to any point around the world.

- **Crew:** Pilot, copilot, two flight engineers, and three loadmasters
- **Dimensions:** Wingspan 223 feet, length 247 feet, height 65 feet
- **Power Plant:** Four General Electric TF-39 engines
- **Weight:** 769,000 lb. peacetime, 840,000 lb. wartime maximum when loaded
- **Cargo Load:** 270,000 lb.
- **Speed:** 518 mph
- **Range:** 6,320 nautical miles; unlimited with in-flight refueling

Inventory and Deployment: The Air Force operates 111 C-15s around the world. They are unarmed, among the largest airlifters in the world, and transport more cargo than any other aircraft, including the more expensive Globemaster. Older C-5As are being continuously refurbished and upgraded.

6. LOCKHEED MARTIN F-22 RAPTOR

First deployed in December 2005.

Cost and Justification: The F-22 Raptor is the Air Force's fighter aircraft of the future. The initial $90 million cost estimate is now $142 million—and growing. In terms of stealth, supercruise capability, maneuverability, and integrated avionics, there is no other aircraft like it anywhere.

- **Crew:** One
- **Dimensions:** Wingspan 44½ feet, length 62 feet, height 16½ feet
- **Power Plant:** Two Pratt & Whitney F119-100 turbofan engines with afterburners and two-dimensional thrust vectoring nozzles
- **Weight:** 43,340 lb. empty, 83,500 lb. armed and fueled
- **Speed:** 1,500 mph with supercruise ability
- **Ceiling:** 50,000+ feet
- **Range:** 1,850 miles
- **Payload/Armament:** One 20mm cannon, two AIM-9 infrared air-to-air missiles, six AIM radar-guided air-to-air missiles, with options for two 1,000-pound GBU precision-guided bombs

Inventory and Deployment: There are 91 Raptors in the Air Force's inventory. The F-22A is a critical component of the Air Force's Global Strike Task Force because it can shoot and kill air-to-air threats before being detected.

7. LOCKHEED MC-130H COMBAT TALON II

First deployed in 1992; the current cost is $155 million.

Cost and Justification: The original Lockheed C-130 Hercules filled a variety of applications, dating back to the gunships of Vietnam, which then were armored and carried massive firepower. The most recent versions, the Combat Talons, were designed for Special Forces missions involving infiltration, extraction, and resupply of troops in hostile or denied territory.

The MC-130H can carry 77 troops, 52 paratroopers, or 57 litter patients.

- **Crew:** Seven, with two pilots, a navigator, an electronic warfare officer, a flight engineer, and two loadmasters
- **Dimensions:** Wingspan 133 feet, length 100 feet, height 38½ feet
- **Power Plant:** Four Allison T56-A-15 turboprop engines
- **Weight:** 155,000 lb. loaded
- **Speed:** 300 mph
- **Ceiling:** 33,000 feet
- **Range:** 2,700 miles; unlimited with in-flight refueling

Inventory and Deployment: There are 20 MC-130H Combat Talons in the Air Force's inventory. They have participated in every conflict from Desert Storm to Iraqi Freedom, including current operations in Afghanistan.

PROJECT TEAMWORK

Today the Air Force, Navy, and Marine Corps are working together to produce a basic F-35 Joint Strike Fighter II (JSF), which will be a fighter designed for all the services instead of having several expensive special-purpose aircraft for each service. Because the Air Force has different requirements than the Navy and the Marine Corps, there will be differences in armament, avionics, and usage. The starting price will be lower for the Air Force version at $28 million, while the Navy version will cost $38 million and the Marine Corps version $35 million. How long these estimates hold depend on rising costs, new technology developments, and the accelerated wear on existing aircraft caused by war.

The Marine Corps deployed the first JSF in 2008. In all, the Air Force is asking for 2,036 aircraft, the Marine Corps 642, the Navy 300, and the United Kingdom 60. Boeing and Lockheed Martin have each produced their versions of the JSF and are currently waiting for orders.

In March 1945, 724 crewmen on the USS *Franklin* died when it was hit by a kamikaze pilot.

ARMY VS. NAVY

The Army and Navy are always in competition.
Here they go again . . . in quotes.

ARMY

"Take time to deliberate; but when the time for action arrives, stop thinking and go in."

—Andrew Jackson

"The only terms I can accept are immediate and unconditional surrender."

—Ulysses S. Grant

"It doesn't take a hero to order men into battle. It takes a hero to be one of those men who goes into battle."

—Norman Schwarzkopf

"There are no secrets to success. It is the result of preparation, hard work, learning from failure."

—Colin Powell

"No bastard ever won a war by dying for his country. He won it by making the other poor dumb bastard die for his country."

—George S. Patton

"Americans never quit."

—Douglas MacArthur

NAVY

"The Navy has both a tradition and a future—and we look with pride and confidence in both directions."

—Theodore Roosevelt

"I wish to have no connection with any ship that does not sail fast, for I intend to go in harm's way."

—John Paul Jones

"You're only as good as the people who work for you."

—William D. Leahy

"There are no extraordinary men . . . just extraordinary circumstances that ordinary men are forced to deal with."

—William F. "Bull" Halsey

"A ship is always referred to as 'she' because it costs so much to keep one in paint and powder."

—Chester W. Nimitz

"No matter what happens, the U.S. Navy won't be caught napping."

—William Franklin Knox

Bloodiest single day of the Civil War: the Battle of Antietam, with 22,726 casualties.

THE BRIDGE AT DONG HA

John Ripley had always wanted to blow up a bridge—now he had his chance. But would he survive it?

THE BUCK STOPS AT THE BRIDGE

On Easter Sunday 1972, Captain John Ripley thought he'd received an order to die. The lone Marine advisor to the 3rd Vietnam Marine Corps Battalion had received word that the South Vietnamese regiment to his north had collapsed. Several dozen North Vietnamese Army (NVA) tanks, followed by their soldiers, were barreling south to Dong Ha. If they crossed the bridge over the Bo Dieu River, there would be no Vietnamese or American force standing between them and Hue City to the south; the NVA could then make its way unopposed to the huge air base at Da Nang. They had to be stopped at Dong Ha.

GOOD NEWS, BAD NEWS

As the tanks approached his position that morning, Ripley called in gunfire from four U.S. Navy destroyers patrolling offshore. They responded with an incredibly accurate barrage of 5-inch shells that destroyed the NVA tanks approaching Ripley and his outnumbered South Vietnamese marines. Throughout the day, Ripley continued to call in fire missions from the destroyers, as well as from South Vietnamese air force jets. The North Vietnamese also understood the strategic importance of moving their tanks and troops across the river, and despite these losses, managed to dispatch a new column of some 200 NVA tanks south. On hearing this news, Ripley quickly realized that the bridge had to be destroyed.

RIPLEY'S BELIEVE IT OR NOT

Using TNT and C-4 explosives supplied by the Army of the Republic of Vietnam (ARVN) engineers, Ripley decided the best and quickest method of blowing up the bridge was to place each box of explosives under the bridge's main girders. While under constant fire from the North Vietnamese, he ran onto the bridge over and over again carrying each 50-pound box, which he then pushed into position as he hung from the bridge's I-beams. Exhausted from manhandling each box into its proper spot, Ripley finally had enough explosives in position to blow the bridge, but he needed to stay alive long enough to build and light the fuse.

A DO-IT-YOURSELF JOB

Running back to the South Vietnamese side of the bridge, Ripley discovered that the ARVN engineers and their U.S. Army advisor were nowhere to be found. Exhausted but seeing that he was running out of time as the NVA tanks were approaching, he quickly built two fuses—one electric and the other burnable—and ran out yet again to place the blasting caps, and fired the electrical fuse. Nothing. He then lit his burnable fuse, which finally blew. The center span of the bridge collapsed with a huge roar into the river, halting the NVA's advancing tanks. The bridge's timbers burned for a week.

GOOD NEWS/GOOD NEWS

For this act of incredible bravery, Captain John Ripley earned the Navy Cross. The NVA tank column eventually crossed the river seven days later, but was quickly decimated by an American Army tank unit led by another Marine advisor.

* * *

VIETNAM HERO NEMO

Robert A. Throneberg and his German shepherd, Nemo, were patrolling the perimeter of Tan Son Nhut Air Base December 4, 1966, when Nemo detected and attacked a group of Vietcong infiltrators. Even though he was shot in the eye, Nemo crawled over and saved his handler's life by covering Throneberg's wounded body with his own until help arrived. Thanks to alert canine heroes like Nemo, not a single Vietcong sapper team penetrated an air base guarded by sentry dogs between July 1965 and December 1966.

The U.S. Department of Veterans Affairs is the nation's largest employer of social workers.

GUERRILLA WARFARE, PART VI

One motto of the Navy SEALs is "The only easy day was yesterday." *(Part V is on page 409.)*

The SEALs—whose name is an acronym for **SE**a, **A**ir, **L**and—conduct special operations alone or in small groups; they're experts in weapons, tactics, demolition, martial arts, and hand-to-hand combat. The first SEAL units were authorized by President Kennedy in 1962, as the Navy's counterpart to the Army's Green Berets. But Navy SEALs trace their heritage back to the elite frogmen of World War II, who were called Amphibious Scouts and Raiders and Underwater Demolition Teams (UDTs).

During World War II, the Navy needed personnel to perform reconnaissance on areas where amphibious assaults were planned, so they recruited divers from Naval Construction Battalions (the Seabees) and gave them advanced training in reconnaissance and demolition. The frogmen scouted beaches and cleared the approaches of mines and obstacles prior to the amphibious landings in Africa and Europe and during the island-hopping campaigns in the Pacific theater. During the Korean War, the frogmen attacked railroad bridges and tunnels along the Korean coastline, and cleared mines and obstacles before the amphibious assault at Inchon, Korea's second-largest port.

VIETNAM

Once the first SEAL teams were created, they were sent to Vietnam as advisors, instructing the South Vietnamese navy in underwater demolitions and maritime special operations. Later, the Navy maintained eight platoons of SEALs that patrolled rivers, destroyed obstacles and bunkers, snatched enemy personnel, and eliminated low-ranking Vietcong officers and Communist cadre leaders. With a kill ratio of 200 to 1 in Vietnam, the enemy was justly afraid of the SEALs and put a bounty on their heads, calling them "men with green faces" because of their camouflage makeup.

The first U.S. Navy hospital ship, USS *Red Rover*, was used at the 1861 Vicksburg campaign.

GRENADA

SEAL teams provided beach reconnaissance for the invasion of Grenada in 1983. During the invasion, they assaulted the airfield and set up radar beacons to guide the aircraft carrying airborne Ranger battalions. They also captured the Radio Free Grenada transmitting station so that the enemy (the Grenadan army and a few Cuban soldiers) couldn't use it to rally their forces. SEALs also carried out an assault on the governor general's mansion and rescued Governor General Paul Scoon, who was being held there under house arrest.

PANAMA

In the invasion of Panama in 1989, SEAL teams were assigned two small, but important, missions designed to prevent the escape of the dictator Manuel Noriega by disabling his boat and Lear jet. The mission to disable the boat went as planned, but the assault on Patilla Airfield to disable the plane ran into fierce resistance. Four SEALs were killed and eight were wounded during the mission.

IRAQ

During both Iraq wars, the SEALs carried out a number of missions, most of which are still classified. It is known that SEALs were involved in the rescue of Navy pilots, in mine-clearing operations, and in the capture of ships and oil platforms.

SOMALIA

In 1994 SEAL teams provided beach reconnaissance for the marine landing in Somalia during the UN peacekeeping mission. And at least one SEAL member participated in the failed attempt to capture the warlord General Mohammed Farrah Adid.

AFGHANISTAN

During the war in Afghanistan in 2002, SEAL teams discovered an extensive network of tunnels in eastern Afghanistan that contained nearly a million pounds of ammunition and equipment. Today, SEAL teams are still involved in the hunt for members of the Taliban government and the al Qaeda leadership.

Bloodiest battle of the Civil War: In two days at Shiloh in Tennessee, more Americans fell...

SEAL TRAINING

SEAL training is conducted at the Naval Amphibious Base located in Coronado, California. The six-month basic training course is mentally and physically demanding and is designed to test the individual's stamina, leadership, and ability to work as part of a team. During the 18-week advanced training period, SEALs are instructed in airborne assaults, counterterrorism, small-unit tactics, long-distance reconnaissance, supply interdiction, and raids.

FAMOUS SEALS

• Rudy Boesch became famous after his appearance on TV's first *Survivor* series; he subsequently appeared on *Survivor All-Stars.* He joined the Navy in 1945 and volunteered for the Amphibious Scouts and Raiders. Later he completed Underwater Demolition Team training in 1951. In 1962 he was one of the first men selected to join the original SEAL team. Rudy retired from the Navy in 1990, after 45 years of distinguished service.

• Jessie "the Body" Ventura, a former professional wrestler, actor, and governor of Minnesota, served as a Navy SEAL in Vietnam.

• Former Nebraska senator Bob Kerrey lead a SEAL team in Vietnam that was nicknamed "Kerrey's Raiders." He was awarded the Medal of Honor "for conspicuous gallantry and intrepidity at the risk of his life above and beyond the call of duty." Kerrey led an assault on an enemy headquarters and was severely injured when a grenade landed at his feet. Though bleeding profusely and suffering great pain, he led his men in the assault, called in fire support on the radio, and directed the evacuation of captured prisoners.

* * *

TARGET PRACTICE

The general had just arrived at the front lines when a sniper's bullet whizzed past his ear. He threw himself to the ground. When the rest of the men stood around doing nothing, the general yelled, "Isn't somebody going to kill that sniper?"

The sergeant looked over and said, "No way, general. If we shoot him, they'll replace him with someone who's a better shot."

MAN WITH A CAMERA

Bringing a war to the folks back home isn't without its risks.

HAVE CAMERA, WILL TRAVEL

English photographer Tim Page spent his 21st birthday dodging bullets and mortar fire to chronicle the war in Vietnam. By that time, Page had been bumming around Europe, the Middle East, and southern Asia for four years.

Although a novice with a camera, Page arrived in Vietnam as an accredited UPI freelance photographer. More vagabond hippie adventurer, occasional smuggler, and black marketeer than photographer, he'd been offered the job based on photos he'd shot for UPI of an attempted Laotian coup. At the time, the Vietnam conflict was ramping up and UPI was short-staffed in Saigon. It was 1965, and by year's end, 200,000 American troops would be fighting there. During that year, working primarily out of Saigon, Da Nang, and Hue, Page built a reputation for getting the best shots of the worst events.

SUCCESS OUTSIDE THE BOX

Daily situation briefings (known as the "five o'clock follies") and the structured photo opportunities laid on by military information officers were not for him. Instead, he went where the action was—flying in-country on Hueys, patrolling on swift boats and cutters, and hunkering with Special Forces in remote jungle base camps.

By the time he was repatriated from Vietnam, Page's photos had appeared in hundreds of newspapers and magazines, including *Time*, *Life*, *Paris-Match*, the *Daily Telegraph*, and *Der Spiegel*. But fame came with a cost. Drugs, death, and rock 'n' roll were the meat of his diet, and none were particularly nutritious. Each would continue to affect his life long after he returned to peace. In addition, in pursuit of that ultimate "shot" during his first 18 months in Vietnam, Page was wounded three times and more than once had to put aside his camera and pick up a rifle.

BATTLE SCARS

During 1969's Operation Starlite—the first major battle between

1834: Congress places the Marine Corps under the Navy Department.

U.S. and veteran North Vietnamese regulars—Page suffered minor shrapnel wounds. Despite the wounds, some of which were in his right hip and buttock, he persevered. His Starlite photos earned him a six-page spread in *Life* magazine. Later that year, in Da Nang, he was wounded again, this time by shrapnel when a grenade exploded a few feet from him.

The third incident was the result of friendly fire from the USAF. Operating from Da Nang in the predawn hours of August 11, 1966, the Coast Guard cutter *Point Welcome*, on patrol near the mouth of the Ben Hai River, drew friendly fire from a B-57 returning from a bombing run. The plane made two runs, wiping out the cutter's bridge, killing two guardsmen—the first deaths of U.S. Coast Guard personnel in Vietnam—and wounding several others. Two F-4s then made several strafing runs. Abandoning the ship and trying for shore in life rafts, the survivors came under small-arms and mortar fire from enemy junks and shore positions. They were later picked up by the cutter *Point Caution*, and the wounded, including Page, who'd received multiple shrapnel wounds were transferred to a hospital.

BACK FOR MORE

After his recovery, Page was assigned by Time-Life to cover the Six-Day War from Beirut, but in early 1968, he was back in Vietnam. By then, the war had changed. The battle for Khe Sanh was raging, and in March of that year, the Vietcong brought the conflict to Saigon in a prolonged battle that came to be known as Mini-Tet. Page roamed the streets with his cameras throughout.

In 1969, in the Parrot's Beak area, a land mine blew shrapnel into Page's head moments after he jumped from a Huey into a firefight. He was briefly pronounced dead during his evacuation, but medics revived him. Later, while on the operating table, he flatlined three more times. He lived, but his war was over. The injury not only left Page with a permanent plate in his head, but also partially paralyzed. He moved to the United States for long-term rehabilitation.

ONE MORE JOB

The war would eventually end for other Vietnam photojournalists, though differently than for Page. Between 1962 and 1975, more than 300 photojournalists from both sides were killed. Page's best friend from the earliest Saigon days, Sean Flynn (son of film star Errol Flynn), was among them. In 1970 Flynn was captured in Cambodia, then held prisoner for more than a year. Page helped spearhead a 20-year search for Flynn to determine the circumstances of his death, but his eventual fate remains a mystery.

BACK TO THE REAL WORLD

As the war entered its final stages, Page became active in the antiwar movement in the United States. After the war, he continued to work as a photojournalist, still traveling extensively throughout Southeast Asia. He authored several books, many as platforms for the 250,000 photographs in his portfolio. He is currently an adjunct professor of photojournalism at Griffith University in Brisbane, Australia. Along with several other Vietnam photojournalists, Page became part of the amalgam that shaped Dennis Hopper's memorable character in the movie *Apocalypse Now*. He has also become a prominent anti–land mine activist.

Years later, Page said, "Vietnam was the first war in color, the first war for freelancers, the first war for photo agencies, the first war for television." He called it "an incredible small period of time when we could capture anything we wanted to." By comparison, he said, "Today the inhumanity and horror of conflict are never more than a station break away—Iraq is almost conducted like an American football game. Never drawn. Only won."

* * *

ACES HIGH

- In 1972 Captain Richard S. "Steve" Ritchie becomes the first ace of the Vietnam War when he, along with his weapons system officer, Captain Charles DeBellevue, shoots down his fifth MiG-21.
- Later, DeBellevue shoots down his fifth and sixth enemy aircraft to become the leading ace of the Vietnam War.
- Captain Jeffrey S. Feinstein, an F-4 weapons system officer, shoots down five MiGs and becomes the third and final Air Force ace of the war.

From 1965 to 1968, the U.S. dropped about a million tons of bombs on North Vietnam.

FLATTOPS

The traditional first order as an active unit of the Navy is: "Man the ship and bring her to life." The crews on the ships profiled in this story certainly took that to heart.

The first aircraft carrier to be named after a living president was christened on March 4, 2001, by First Lady Nancy Reagan, and commissioned on July 12, 2003. The USS *Ronald Reagan* is the newest aircraft carrier in the world. Built at a cost of $4.5 billion, the carrier displaces 97,000 tons of water and features a 4.5-acre flight deck. The superstructure (the structure above the flight deck) towers 20 stories over the sea. At 1,096 feet long, the flight deck is nearly as long as the Empire State Building is tall.

MODEL OF SELF-SUFFICIENCY

Distillation plants provide 400,000 gallons of fresh water every day, enough to supply 2,000 homes. The *Reagan*'s sophisticated nuclear power plant generates enough electricity to supply a small city, powering—among everything else—the carrier's nearly 30,000 light fixtures and 1,400 telephones.

Supply officers order, organize, store, and retrieve enough food and related supplies for 90 days at sea. That means 14,000 pillowcases, 28,000 sheets, and food for the more than 18,000 meals that are served every day, including 205 loaves of bread, 100 dozen fresh eggs, and 250 gallons of milk.

Talking care of 6,000 sailors are five doctors, five dentists, and an oral surgeon. There's a 63-bed hospital facility for the sick and five fitness centers for the healthy. To keep its sailors in touch with home, the *Reagan*'s post office processes more than one million pounds of mail per year. There's a radio station, television station, newspaper, library, and Internet café on board as well.

There are more than 2,000 rooms inside the hull, many below the waterline. Each sailor has a bed that is only 6.5 feet long and 2 feet wide. Total private storage space per sailor is just 5 cubic feet (a box 20 inches wide, 20 inches deep, and 20 inches tall). In some places more than 100 sailors sleep in one compartment.

Ulysses S. Grant, not fond of military music or ceremonies, said he could only recognize...

MIDWAY MAGIC

In 1945 the world had never seen a ship like the USS *Midway*. At 968 feet long, the aircraft carrier dwarfed every ship afloat and remained the largest ship in the world until 1955. She was the first U.S. Navy ship too large to fit into the Panama Canal. The *Midway* displaced 45,000 tons when commissioned, and the 212,000 horses generated by her massive turbines enabled her to sail so fast that a sailor could have water-skied behind her.

The *Midway*'s crew numbered 4,500. Imagine the city limits being 1,000 feet long, 258 feet wide, and 18 decks high. Then imagine 4,500 young men living for months at a time inside. Everything a small town could ask for was aboard the *Midway*: radio and television stations, 6 galleys serving 10 tons of food a day, laundry, post office, power plant, chapel, metal shops, carpentry shop, barber shops, tailor's shop, and even an ice cream and convenience store. Only about 200 of the 4,500-man crew were pilots. Everyone else performed jobs that enabled the ship to stay at sea and conduct flight operations when necessary.

PIONEER OF THE SEA

The USS *Midway* continually set new naval aviation standards. In 1946 she was the first carrier to operate extensively in the subarctic during the winter on a mission appropriately named Operation Frostbite. In 1947 the *Midway* became the only ship to ever launch a V-2 rocket captured from the Germans in the waning days of World War II, ushering in the dawn of naval missile warfare. About 20 years later, she helped prove the viability of autopilot technology that was later used in the space shuttle program.

The *Midway*'s crew was perhaps more famous for its humanitarian missions. In 1975 more than 3,000 refugees were rescued in 24 hours during the fall of Saigon during Operation Frequent Wind. The carrier's final mission came in 1991, when she rescued nearly 2,000 Americans fleeing the eruption of Mt. Pinatubo in the Philippines.

More than 225,000 young men served aboard the *Midway*, especially remarkable since their average age was only 19. The *Midway*'s accomplishment became known as "*Midway* Magic" throughout the Navy—and persists today. The retired carrier is now a naval aviation museum open to the public in San Diego.

...two tunes. "One was 'Yankee Doodle,' " he said. "The other one wasn't."

THE GIRL BEHIND THE WALL

How a 21-year-old daughter of immigrants won a contest and became part of American history.

THE MEN BEHIND THE WALL

The idea for a memorial to honor Vietnam veterans originated with Jan Scruggs, who'd been an infantry corporal in Vietnam from 1969 to 1970. Scruggs established the Vietnam Veterans Memorial Fund (VVMF) with some fellow vets and, while trying to raise money, lobbied Congress for a plot of land in an area of the Washington Mall known as the Constitution Gardens adjacent to the Washington Monument.

In July 1980, Congress authorized three acres as the future site of a memorial and announced a design competition, open to the public. One of the conditions was that the names of the 57,661 casualties known at that time had to be included in the design.

MORE MEN BEHIND THE WALL

By December, more than 2,500 hopefuls had registered, and by the end of March of the next year, 1,421 designs were submitted. The anonymous entries were displayed in an airport hangar at Andrews Air Force Base, each with an envelope on the back that contained the designer's name. The vets in charge of the project considered using all vets for the panel, or a mix of vets, Gold Star mothers (American women who had lost a child in a war), and designers, but in the end decided on a jury of professionals: two architects, two landscape architects, three sculptors, an urban analyst/author, and one architect who served as an adviser—all men. They narrowed down the possibilities and in the end unanimously chose a design. It took a little convincing, but eventually they persuaded the vets that the winning design had the potential of being one of the finest and most famous structures in the world.

The media went wild when the designer turned out to be a 21-year-old architecture major at Yale, Maya Ying Lin. The choice set off a controversy that would take years to die down.

Actress Hedy Lamarr coinvented a radar system to help direct torpedoes at moving ships.

BEHIND THE GIRL

Maya Lin's parents had immigrated to the United States just before the 1949 Communist takeover of China. Maya was born ten years later and raised in Athens, Ohio, where her parents were faculty members at Ohio University: her father was the dean of the Ohio University College of Fine Arts, and her mother was a professor of literature. Lin and her brother had a typical—if intellectual—American upbringing. She read a lot as a child, and liked to build miniature towns. Math came easy; in high school, she took college-level courses and worked after school at McDonald's. She didn't date, didn't wear makeup, and admits to being a little "nerdy." She says she grew up with little sense of ethnic identity; she considered herself a typical Midwesterner. After high school, she went to Yale to study architecture. She was part of a student group studying funereal design when someone told her about the contest.

THE WALL

Lin's concept was to create an opening, or a "wound," in the earth to symbolize the gravity of the loss of the soldiers. The back of the Wall is dug into the earth, signifying death and mourning, the front is open in a wide V. The highly polished black granite surface is like a mirror that reflects the surrounding trees, lawns, monuments, and visitors, and is inscribed with the names of the fallen Americans—in chronological order of their deaths or the date they went missing.

How confident did Lin feel about her design? She said she was sure that "it wouldn't be chosen because it wasn't a politically glorified statement about war, that it focused only on the individual, and the losses, and the sacrifices."

Lin's design was as controversial as the war had been. Because the design was modern, some people just didn't get it. Some thought that the dark stone made it look like a gravestone—"a black gash of shame and sorrow." Others believed that the part of it that was "buried" was a reminder of the way many vets thought of themselves in relation to their homecoming. Some were upset that the granite was from the East Indies instead of America, or that more money was being invested in the memorial than in the care of the vets themselves. The controversy grew, and things got

American troops in the Mexican-American War: 78,790. Mexicans: 25,000 to 40,000.

ugly. Scruggs and the rest of the VVMF members stood behind the design, but a group of vets mounted a negative campaign that they took all the way to Congress. Some thought a Vietnam vet should have been the designer, some that a panel of vets should have been the judges. Some were affronted because the winner was female—and Asian. At a media event, one vet called it "insulting and demeaning." Lin was called derogatory names in public. The project came close to being scuttled. Secretary of the Interior James Watt put the project on hold while a vocal group of vets, senators, and media types argued for a more conventional design.

THE OPENING OF THE WALL

The Vietnam Veterans Memorial was officially opened to the public on Veterans Day 1982.

Traditionalists who wanted a statue of a soldier eventually got their wish. A bronze statue of three soldiers, sculpted by the third-place winner of the original competition, was added in 1984—but not as close to the Wall as at first was intended, due to Lin's objections to its addition. One more statue was added in 1993: the Vietnam Women's Memorial, honoring the women—mostly nurses—who served in Vietnam.

AS THEY STAND NOW

Maya Lin earned her master's degree in architecture in 1986 and still designs memorials and landscape sculptures on a grand scale out of her studio in New York City.

Her controversial Wall is now much acclaimed, and is considered—as was predicted by the judges—a world-class piece of art, visited by hundreds of thousands every year. The names on it now number 58,260 (approximately 1,200 of whom are listed as missing or who later died as a result of injuries incurred in the war). It's a pilgrimage site for relatives of casualties, who can literally touch the names of their fallen sons, daughters, husbands, and fathers. And for the now-aging combatants who survived, and who visit and revisit to pay homage to their comrades, it's a place that bears witness to the once-unappreciated sacrifices they made for their country.

Musketeer was the name of the operation to liberate the Philippines in World War II.

DETAILS, DETAILS

• The Wall is 40 inches thick; each section of the V is 246.75 feet long, composed of 70 separate inscribed granite panels, plus four at the end without names; it runs from ankle-high to just over 10 feet high where the V meets.

• It was built with more than $8 million in contributions from 275,000 individuals.

• The first known casualty on the Wall was Richard B. Fitzgibbon of North Weymouth, Massachusetts, who died on June 8, 1956. His son's name is also on there: Marine Corps Lance Corporal Richard B. Fitzgibbon III died on September 7, 1965.

• Telephone book–sized directories stand at each side of the entrances, filled with the names listed and where to find them on the Wall. When alphabetizing the names on the memorial was suggested to Lin, she nixed the idea: She didn't want the friends and relatives of Charles Smith to have to find his name among the many other Charles Smiths. She wanted *their* Charles Smith to be with the men who died with him.

• There are eight women's names on the Wall. Seven were Army nurses, the eighth was a USAF flight nurse whose plane crashed outside Saigon during an airlift of Vietnamese orphans.

WHAT'S LEFT

Visitors have been leaving mementos at the Wall since 1982—the first while it was still under construction: a Purple Heart laid in the foundation by the brother of a dead soldier. Since then, tens of thousands of items have been left, including some unusual—but surely meaningful—items, including a pair of lace panties, a basket of Easter eggs, an electric guitar, a 1940s vintage southpaw baseball glove, a fishing pole, a Christmas tree angel, and a full-size Harley-Davidson motorcycle honoring Wisconsin's 37 dead.

Every night, the Park Service collects the nonperishable items and adds them to the more than 100,000 objects now in storage at the Museum Resource Center in Landover, Maryland. Some of the mementos are on exhibit at the Smithsonian's National Museum of American History. The collection will find a permanent home when a planned Vietnam Veterans Memorial Center is completed on the Mall, across the street from the Wall.

Actor Charlton Heston was a B-25 radio operator and gunner in the U.S. Army (1944–46).

WAR (TV) IS HELL

In the last two decades or so, military television has turned away from sitcoms like Hogan's Heroes *and action shows like* Combat! *in favor of gritty, realistic, mature, and historically accurate war dramas. Here are a few.*

GENERATION KILL (2008)

On this seven-part HBO miniseries, a *Rolling Stone* reporter (Lee Tergesen) is embedded with the 1st Reconnaissance Marine squad as it travels across Iraq and eventually into Baghdad during the early days of the March 2003 American invasion. *Generation Kill* is based on the book of the same name by *Rolling Stone* writer Evan Wright, who really was embedded with the group and who really faced enemy fire. Shot in the deserts of Namibia and South Africa, the realism of the series was enhanced with handheld cameras and a cast of mostly young, unknown actors. In fact, two of the actors are real-life Marines: Rudy Reyes plays himself and Eric Kocher plays a gunnery sergeant. For its frequent scenes of combat, enemy ambushes, and a constant aura of terror and machismo, *Generation Kill* is regarded as one of the most accurate depictions of war life ever made.

OVER THERE (2005)

Debuting on the FX Network, *Over There* was the first series set in a war that was still ongoing. It detailed the daily lives of a unit of young, frightened soldiers in the Army's 3rd Infantry Division on a tour of duty in Iraq. The show was also notable for its graphic violence; in the first episode, a main character loses his legs in a landmine explosion. Perhaps *Over There* was made too soon: it lasted just one season.

BAND OF BROTHERS (2001)

Produced by Tom Hanks and Steven Spielberg, it was one of the largest-scale TV projects ever undertaken. *Band of Brothers,* a 10-episode miniseries, had a budget of $140 million and included more than 500 speaking roles. Based on the book of the same name by historian Stephen Ambrose, the plot followed the complete World War II experience of Easy Company, the 506th

Top sniper? U.S. Marine Carlos Hathcock, 93 confirmed kills and 300 probable kills.

Parachute Infantry Regiment of the 101st Airborne Division. Viewers see the squad training in Georgia in 1942, parachuting into Normandy before dawn on D-day, fighting in the Battle of Bastogne, and liberating a concentration camp. Actors (including Donnie Wahlberg and Ron Livingston) were cast for their resemblance to the real members of Easy Company. They were also subjected to a 16-hour-per-day, 10-day boot camp session for which they were required to remain in character. *Band of Brothers* premiered in June 2001 at a special screening at Utah Beach in Normandy. More than 40 surviving Easy Company veterans were flown in. Airing on HBO in September 2001, it became one of the most acclaimed miniseries ever produced; it was nominated for 19 Emmy Awards and won six.

TOUR OF DUTY (1987–90)

Less than two decades after its end, *Tour of Duty* became the first TV show about the Vietnam War. The series followed Bravo Company, a light infantry platoon, in 1967 Vietnam. The first season of the show was filmed in Hawaii, whose jungles stood in for Vietnam's hellish jungles as the soldiers stalked around—deeply terrified. In the second season, the action shifted to the outskirts of Saigon, which allowed for the addition of women cast members (to compete with the female-centric Vietnam War series *China Beach*). The production moved to California to save money—*Tour of Duty* filmed on *M*A*S*H*'s old sets. *Tour of Duty* lasted three years, but faltered for two reasons: It was a grim show, with plenty of violence and episodes about accidental civilian deaths, soldier drug abuse, and mental illness. Reason #2: it got crushed in the ratings by *The Golden Girls*.

CHINA BEACH (1988–91)

Not just a war show, *China Beach* was a medical show, a soap opera, and a pensive character study. Going against the grain of nearly every other military TV series in history, *China Beach* detailed what life was like for women in wartime, specifically the Vietnam War. The show took place at a U.S. Army hospital and recreational area in Da Bang. Characters included a nurse (Dana Delany), an Armed Forces radio DJ (Nancy Giles), a Red Cross volunteer (Ricki Lake), and a prostitute (Marg Helgenberger).

In 1798 Paul Revere cast a bell weighing 242 pounds for the frigate *Constitution*.

THE BLUE ANGELS

About 15 million spectators come out each year to watch the Naval Flight Demonstration Squadron, the brainstorm of Chief of Naval Operations Adm. Chester W. Nimitz to encourage recruitment.

YES, THEIR PLANES ARE BLUE BUT . . .

Their nickname doesn't come from their heavenly flights. The team's members noticed an ad for the Blue Angel, a New York City nightclub, in the *New Yorker* magazine and thought it would be the perfect nickname for the team.

Since 1946, approximately 225 Navy and Marine Corps pilots have served with the Blue Angels squadron of 16 officers. The Blue Angles have always flown the most advanced planes, beginning with the Grumman F6F Hellcat and flying the $18 million F/A-18 Hornet today. The Hornet can climb 30,000 feet per minute at speeds of up to 1,400 mph. During shows the Blue Angels speeds range from 120 to 700 mph. In 2009 the blue jets with gold stripes and wing tips will participate in 67 shows at 34 locations.

FAT ALBERT AIRLINES

Without Fat Albert there would be no angels. Fat Albert Airlines is the nickname for the Lockheed-Martin C-130T Hercules that carries 40 maintenance personnel, spare parts, and communication equipment to Blue Angels shows. The Fat Albert is staffed by an all-Marine crew of three officers and five enlisted men.

The Hercules cargo plane is a far cry from the sleek Hornets, but has its own characteristics that make it an asset in combat. Although it only flies at speeds of up to 360 mph, it can take off using runways as short as 2,500 feet. It can also perform a jet-assisted takeoff (JATO) by using eight solid fuel rocket bottles to thrust the Hercules into the air. With JATO the huge aircraft can take off within 1,500 feet by climbing at a 45-degree angle and rising 1,000 feet in 15 seconds.

An estimated 25 Cobra attack helicopters are privately owned by Americans.

FAMILY SECRETS

If John Walker Jr. had been nicer to his ex-wife, the U.S. Navy might never have learned that it was the victim of the KGB's most successful spy ring.

A WOMAN SCORNED

On November 17, 1984, a furious and intoxicated Barbara Walker contacted the Boston office of the FBI. She claimed that her former husband owed her $10,000 in alimony even though he spent a fortune on his young girlfriend and his spying activities allowed him to buy a big home and expensive toys like a houseboat and a small plane. At first the FBI wrote off Barbara's complaints as those of a bitter and inebriated ex-wife. But when she passed a polygraph, the agents realized that she was telling them the truth about her ex, John Walker Jr., who for the past 17 years had been selling U.S. Navy secrets to the KGB.

A LARCENOUS BENT

Born in Washington, D.C., in 1937, John Anthony Walker Jr. was a troubled kid whose abusive and alcoholic father had abandoned the family when John Jr. was a teenager. John dropped out of school and, when he was 17, was arrested for robbing a gas station.

At John's trial, his older brother Arthur, a Navy man, argued that the Navy would "straighten him out." The judge gave John a choice: go to prison or join the Navy. John signed up in 1955, and for a time seemed like a different person. He studied and worked hard. By 1957 John was married to Barbara and they were expecting what would be the first of four children. And he was working toward his goal of serving on submarines, like Arthur.

In 1965, after five promotions, John was assigned to run the radio room on a nuclear-powered submarine, the USS *Simon Bolivar*. He had access to top-secret communications including, at one point, a list of the nuclear targets that the United States would hit if the country were plunged into World War III.

Walker was tempted to steal secrets and sell them, but he claims he didn't give in—at least not at first. Instead, he borrowed money from Arthur to buy a property in Landon, South Carolina, near a Navy port and opened the Bamboo Snack Bar, confident that the bar would be a cash machine. Instead, John and Barbara plunged deeper into debt. While John was at sea, Barbara had to manage the bar and raise four children. She resented the extra work coupled with the constant lack of money. John wouldn't give up on the business, and the couple argued constantly.

John's naval career was still going well. In 1967 he worked at the Navy's Atlantic Submarine Attack Headquarters in Norfolk, Virginia, where he supervised the communications center for an entire fleet of nuclear subs. At that time, 99 percent of U.S. naval radio communications were machine-encrypted. The encryption settings were changed daily so that the codes for radio messages would constantly change. Walker had access to key lists, and with these anyone could easily read America's top-secret messages. Later, Walker would cite Barbara's nagging about money as the reason for his decision to sell information to the Soviets.

DEAD DROPS AND LIFE IN THE FAST LANE

In December 1967, Walker brought a copy of a key list into the Soviet embassy in Washington, D.C. He told a KGB officer that he wanted to trade classified information for money. A deal was made; Walker became the KGB's man for $4,000 a month.

Dead drops were arranged for Walker to leave information at secluded, prearranged spots. Although no one he worked with suspected anything, Barbara watched John spend money on good times, fast cars, and faster women. One day she pried open a metal box in his office and found photographic equipment along with KGB instructions on dead-drop locations. When she confronted John, he admitted that he was a spy.

Barbara was the first to be pulled into John's ring. She began to go along on dead drops. The KGB often paid John with bills rolled up in soda cans, and Barbara ironed the spy cash to flatten it and make it less suspicious. As the years passed, Walker grew paranoid. He was a trusted warrant officer, but to retain his clearance to handle naval secrets, he had to undergo background checks. By now his party-hearty lifestyle had made his neglected wife bitter, and he worried that she might turn him in. John needed to get out of the Navy, but he also wanted that KGB income. He used his best friend to solve the problem.

WITH A LITTLE HELP FROM HIS FRIENDS

Jerry Whitworth, a radioman trained in satellite communications, looked up to Walker, so he was easily manipulated. At first, Jerry didn't know that the data he provided went straight to America's enemy. In 1973 Whitworth provided information on the Navy's sophisticated satellite communications. Soon the Soviets were making remarkable progress in naval satellite communications, and they considered Whitworth their most valuable spy.

John and Barbara divorced in 1976, the same year that he quit the Navy. There were no more background checks to trip him up, but now John worried about Jerry and the Russians working together without him. John needed spies who would be loyal—like family. When his brother Arthur got into financial difficulties, John eased him into the spy business, and soon Arthur was providing classified material. John took his mother along when he did dead drops in Europe, so that she could unknowingly transport his cash payments through customs. After years of neglect, he took an interest in his kids and tried to recruit them. Only John's son Michael, who'd always adored his father, agreed to help. Michael was a U.S. Navy seaman assigned to clerk duties where he could sometimes get to the "burn bag" of discarded classified documents. Under his father's tutelage, he learned to steal and copy information. John thought Michael's involvement would keep Barbara from blowing the whistle on the spy ring, but Michael had kept his espionage a secret from his mother. When she went to the FBI, Barbara had no idea that her son was involved.

THE LAST DEAD DROP

On May 19, 1985, hoping to catch Walker in the act, the FBI tailed him as he drove through rural Maryland. Walker left a paper bag of what seemed to be garbage beside a utility pole. Agents grabbed the bag after he drove away. Inside were classified documents and a letter incriminating the other members of his spy ring. Late that night, Walker was arrested. John, Jerry, and Arthur were all sent to prison for life. Michael got a 25-year sentence but was paroled after serving 15 years. Since it was peacetime, everyone avoided execution. The U.S. government spent more than $1 billion changing compromised codes and equipment. They also changed their communications procedures.

"The end of the Cold War is our common victory." —Mikhail Gorbachev, January 1992

A MONUMENTAL PHOTO

Formally known as the Marine Corps War Memorial, the monument is a replica of Associated Press photographer Joe Rosenthal's famous picture.

LAST STOP, IWO JIMA

By February 1945, U.S. troops had recovered most of the territory taken by the Japanese in 1941–42 except for the small island of Iwo Jima, 660 miles from Tokyo. Recapturing Iwo Jima would bring America's Pacific campaign to a successful conclusion.

The Marines landed on Iwo Jima on February 19 and made their way toward Mount Suribachi, the island's highest point. They reached and surrounded their destination on the 21st, but it took them until the afternoon of the 23rd to capture the summit. When five Marines and a Navy corpsman raised the American flag at the summit of Mount Suribachi, Joe Rosenthal was lucky and quick-witted enough to capture an iconic image. Rosenthal's photograph was splashed onto the front pages of newspapers everywhere. By the end of March 1945, *Time* magazine had called it "the most widely printed photograph of World War II," it was the centerpiece of the seventh war bond drive, and it had earned Rosenthal a Pulitzer Prize.

BRINGING A PICTURE TO LIFE

The Iwo Jima monument was the brainchild of Felix de Weldon, an Austrian immigrant who came to America in 1937. An internationally known sculptor and artist, Weldon had joined the Navy and been assigned to the Construction Corps. Like most Americans, he was enthralled by Rosenthal's photograph, and submitted a small wax model of the photograph to his superiors. The Navy Department immediately ordered him to make a life-size plaster cast. The first likeness was presented to President Harry S. Truman on the 170th birthday of the Marine Corps, November 10, 1945; its duplicate was sent on a national tour as part of the Victory Bond Drive.

The two statues were immediately popular, and soon the Marine Corps was talking with Weldon about using his design for

Clint Eastwood was drafted into the U.S. Army during the Korean War. An expert swimmer...

a permanent memorial to all Marines. In July 1947, Congress authorized that the monument be built in the nation's capital, and the Marine Corps established the Marine Corps War Memorial Foundation to raise the necessary funds. By 1950 the Fine Arts Commission, the executive branch, and the Marine Corps' friends in Congress ensured that the War Memorial Foundation was awarded a choice piece of property adjacent to Arlington National Cemetery. From there, one can look across the Potomac River and see the Lincoln Memorial, the Washington Monument, and the Capitol, all in a line.

Weldon was hired to build a bronze casting of Rosenthal's photograph at four times life size. With Marines now fighting in the snow and bitter cold of Korea, Marine commandant General Clifton Cates made the ceremonial first donation, then appealed to his fellow Marines for contributions to build their monument.

CASTING CALL

Weldon's plan was to cast the entire monument in plaster, cut it into sections, cast it in bronze, and then reassemble the monument on-site. The estimated cost was $350,000. First he cast the heads, which were five feet tall from the neck to the tops of their helmets. He sculpted the likenesses of the three surviving flag raisers in clay prior to casting them in plaster. The survivors were Private First Class Ira Hayes, Private First Class Rene Gagnon, and U.S. Navy Pharmacist's Mate Second Class John Bradley. Sergeant Michael Strank, Corporal Harlon Block, and Private First Class Franklin Sousley all died on Iwo Jima—killed in later phases of the battle within days after the Mount Suribachi flag raising. In order to model their faces accurately, Weldon used physical statistics and photographs of the three Marines who gave their lives.

Next, he modeled the six bodies in the nude so he could realistically depict their straining muscles as they lifted the flagpole. He studied combat fatigues under a microscope in order to capture any details and re-create the effects of wind and combat wear. De Weldon used exacting methods to cast their equipment and weapons in order to ensure that his depiction was completely accurate.

When the full-size plaster monument was finished, Weldon cut it into 108 parts, which he shipped to a New York foundry that created huge molds from the plaster pieces. Molten bronze was

...he once swam three miles back to shore after a plane crash into the Pacific Ocean.

poured into the molds to make the castings, which took nearly three years, after which a dozen pieces—the largest weighing 20 tons—were shipped to Washington for assembly.

FINISHING TOUCHES

As the statue was being cast, the Arlington site was being prepared. The base was poured and the Marine Corps placed a time capsule inside with two vials of Iwo Jima's coarse sand, the Rosenthal photograph, the "Marine's Hymn," and other memorabilia.

General Lemuel Shepherd, then the commandant, approved a list of battles to be carved into the polished Swedish granite used to face the concrete base. Every substantial battle in which the Marine Corps has fought in has been engraved in four-inch gold letters around the base, which also bears the inscriptions "In honor and in memory of the men of the United States Marine Corps who have given their lives to their country since November 10, 1775," and "Uncommon valor was a common virtue," Admiral Chester W. Nimitz's tribute to the Iwo Jima soldiers.

The completed memorial stands 78 feet high, and the bronze statue weighs 200,000 pounds. The final cost of $850,000 was paid entirely by donations. By order of a 1961 presidential proclamation, a flag flies 24 hours a day from a 60-foot bronze flagpole that the 32-foot-high figures are shown erecting. The actual flag from Mount Suribachi is on display at the National Museum of the Marine Corps, located in Quantico, Virginia.

The Marine Corps War Memorial was dedicated on November 10, 1954, the 179th anniversary of the Marine Corps. President Dwight D. Eisenhower gave the keynote address to a crowd that included the three surviving Marines in the photograph—Hayes, Bradley, and Gagnon—along with photographer Joe Rosenthal.

The memorial is a living heritage. Fresh inscriptions for Marine battles in Korea, Vietnam, Lebanon, and the Persian Gulf have been added. Frequent Marine-related events, such as veterans' reenlistment or retirement ceremonies, take place there. The annual Marine Corps Marathon begins and ends in its shadow. The largest number of visitors are Marine Corps veterans who come and stand in front of the memorial to the battles in which they fought, bow their heads, and silently remember the Marines with whom they served.

Deeply religious, General Stonewall Jackson was a deacon in the Presbyterian Church.

THE BONEYARD

Just like the scads of Americans who've retired to Arizona, America's military aircraft head there, too, when they're ready for some well-deserved rest and relaxation.

RETIRING TO THE DESERT

The Army established a base for out-of-commission B-29 and C-47 aircraft after World War II. Often referred to as the "Boneyard," the 309th Aerospace Maintenance and Regeneration Group (AMARG), is an Air Force aircraft and maintenance facility that houses aircraft, aerospace vehicles, and other military equipment from all branches of the armed forces and from several federal agencies, including NASA.

Davis-Monthan Air Force Base, in the Sonoran Desert at Tucson, Arizona, is an ideal location to store retired aircraft because of its sparse rainfall, low humidity, and smog-free climate, all of which make it possible to store aircraft indefinitely with minimum deterioration and corrosion. An added benefit is that aircraft can park on the hard alkaline soil instead of on hot, sticky pavement.

On its more than 2,600 acres, it continues to store and preserve aircraft, but it also specializes in aircraft regeneration that restores aircraft to flying status. AMARG's 600 or so employees provide tender loving care to more than 4,200 aircraft, aerospace vehicles, and other military equipment worth approximately $27 billion.

TAKING INVENTORY

On arrival, each aircraft gets a unique inventory number stenciled into the airframe that might look something like this: AAFV2345. Here's a handy decoding chart.

• The first character stands for the type of equipment (attack, bomber, cargo, fighter, helicopter, patrol, or trainer).

• The second for the branch of military to which the aircraft is assigned (Air Force, Coast Guard, Army, Navy, other U.S. agencies, or foreign).

• The third and fourth characters designate the aircraft type (Navy and Marines have number/alpha designators: 1K, 3A, 6A;

Air Force and Army have alpha/alpha designators: TF, FE, HV).
• The fifth to eighth are four-digit numbers that sequentially designate each new arrival of that aircraft type.

MOTHBALLING

When aircraft are removed from duty—even temporarily—they're prepared for exposure to the hot desert environment in a process called "mothballing." After the aircraft is delivered to AMARG, the aircraft is tied down and engine oil, hydraulic fluid, and landing gear fluid samples are taken and analyzed by a laboratory. Dangerous and/or hazardous materials are removed. Next, an aircraft's weapons, classified items, and items subject to deterioration are removed for safe storage, after which a complete inventory is performed to document any missing items. Fuel tanks are drained and replaced with preservation oil that's pumped through the fuel system to coat the tanks, pipes, and pumps.

After cleaning and inspection for corrosion, most aircraft are double-coated by a vinyl compound called Spraylat. The first coat seals the aircraft, protecting it from dust, moisture, animals, and insects. The second coat protects the aircraft from sunlight and heat, reflecting solar heat so that the aircraft's interior remains within 10 to 15 degrees of the temperature outside. (Without it, the interior could heat up to 200°F during the summer months.) Finally, doors and small openings are sealed with tape and the aircraft is towed to its designated storage plot.

Aircraft are categorized, too, according to the shape they're in:

• Category 1000: Preserved as though it may fly again.
• Category 2000: Maintained for spare parts.
• Category 3000: Kept in near ready-to-fly condition with a likely deployment.
• Category 4000: Displayed at museums, base entrances, or in towns; most are made into scrap metal and sold whole or in parts.

If your curiosity has been piqued, you can tour the Boneyard as part of Tucson's Pima Air and Space Museum. While you're there, you can get a look at John F. Kennedy's *Air Force One*, grab a gourmet sandwich at the Thunderbird's Grill, and buy a model plane and/or flight jacket for your little future aviator at the museum store.

...That's a sample question from the Armed Services Vocational Aptitude Battery.

NMUSAF

What does that spell? Nothing, but it stands for the National Museum of the United States Air Force—the world's largest and oldest military aviation museum.

FLIGHT TOWN, U.S.A.

Everyone should at some point in their lives take a trip to Dayton, Ohio. In their hometown bicycle shop, Wilbur and Orville Wright conceived and built the world's first power-driven, heavier-than-air machine capable of free, controlled, and sustained flight. And it was at the nearby Huffman Prairie Flying Field that the Wrights perfected their invention in the early 1900s. Thus, it is fitting that this is also the location of the world's largest and most complete collection of U.S. Air Force aircraft and artifacts.

Since the 1920s, artifacts related to Army aviation had been collected and displayed in a variety of locations, usually on air bases. In order to preserve and protect these priceless and important pieces of American service history for future generations, the National Museum of the U.S. Air Force was established in 1922 and opened in 1923.

Located adjacent to Wright-Patterson Air Force Base in a complex of hangarlike buildings are housed more than 75,000 small items, including flight suits, G-suits, and space suits; trophies and memorabilia; technical equipment; and more than 300 aircraft and missiles. On display are balloons and aircraft dating from the early 1900s made of wire, wood, and fabric. Nearby are many of today's most modern aircraft, molded of composite materials formed to reflect radar energy—some piloted, some not. Creative displays invite visitors to imagine the challenges faced by pilots and support troops throughout the Air Force's history. A whimsical yet familiar life-size exhibit of an early military training aircraft transports anyone who has ever flown or maintained training aircraft back to a moment immediately following a minor "ground looping" accident. Mannequins represent the angry instructor pilot, the dejected student, the irritated maintenance chief, and the dumbfounded apprentice—all reacting to the nosed-over propeller-driven plane.

The U.S. Army Intelligence School was based at Fort Holabird, MD, from the 1940s until 1971.

Every piece of hardware in the museum is accompanied by stories about its creation, construction, and utilization. Visitors can wander through acres of some of the most rare and iconic aircraft ever flown by America's air arm. The museum is the world's largest and oldest military aviation museum and today is charged with portraying the heritage and traditions of the Air Force. It is a treasure trove of Air Force history for those seeking to understand the evolution of American military airpower.

STEWARDSHIP FOR FUTURE GENERATIONS

But the NMUSAF is far more than just a museum. As a large part of the Office of Air Force History, the museum staff provides technical and professional guidance to the U.S. Air Force Heritage Program. This extensive program includes 12 field museums and 260 domestic and international heritage sites. In addition, the staff is accountable for more than 6,000 historical artifacts and aircraft and spacecraft on loan to 450 civilian museums, cities, municipalities, and veterans' organizations throughout the world.

* * *

THUNDERBIRDS

When the United States Air Force Demonstration Squadron was formed at Luke Air Force Base in 1947, they knew they needed a memorable nickname. After all the Navy had the Blue Angels. The Arizona-based squadron turned toward their Native American neighbors and their rich folklore for a name. Indian legends describe the Thunderbird, a bird (perhaps an eagle or hawk?) that received great respect as a protector of all good men. Oral legends say that when the Thunderbird flew "the earth trembled...his eyes shot balls of lightning." Twelve officers and 120 enlisted support staff make up the Air Force's Thunderbirds Squadron that flies the F-16C Fighting Falcon

THE GREAT CARRIER REEF

The aircraft carrier USS Oriskany *saw combat in both Korea and the Vietnam War, but then it got a new job . . . as the world's largest artificial reef.*

IN ITS YOUTHFUL DAYS

To commemorate the 1777 Battle of Oriskany, the bloodiest fight of the Revolutionary War, Congress decided to build an Essex-class attack aircraft carrier—the USS *Oriskany*. The ship was finished on September 25, 1950.

In 1952 the *Oriskany* headed for Korea to serve with the U.S. Seventh Fleet. Planes from its flight deck dropped 4,600 tons of bombs and exhausted more than one million rounds of ammunition. But its most important achievement came in November 1952 when *Oriskany* Panther jets engaged in the first multi-jet aerial dogfight in naval history. Four Panthers battled seven MIG-15s—two MIGs were destroyed, and a third was damaged, but the Panther pilots all returned safely to their carrier.

Next, the *Oriskany* headed to the western Pacific and then to Vietnam, eventually carrying out 16 missions. In 1976 the ship docked in California for the last time, and in 1994, she was sold for scrap. But this wouldn't be a regular retirement. The Navy had big plans for the *Oriskany*: it was going to become the world's largest artificial reef.

JOURNEY TO THE BOTTOM OF THE SEA

Decommissioned naval vessels take up a lot of room in shipyards, so the Navy was looking for a new way to use (or dispose) of them. In the early 2000s, the Navy decided to try to use them to create artificial reefs in the oceans off the coasts of the United States.

The *Oriskany* would be the test ship, but finding a place to sink it required some research. The Navy had five criteria:

1. The ship had to improve its marine habitat and provide recreational opportunities.

2. The state government would have to agree to manage the reef.

3. The public in the area had to support the project.

4. The state government had to share the cost of the project.

5. The site had to hold some significance for the Navy.

After much investigation, the Navy chose a spot off the coast of Pensacola, Florida. Not only was the state willing to meet all the criteria, but most of the fighter pilots who served on the *Oriskany* had been trained at the Pensacola Naval Air Station.

Next, the ship needed an environmental cleanup. That job took almost a year (from January to December 2004) and cost $20 million. Crews removed fuels, oils, asbestos, capacitors, transformers or other liquid polychlorinated biphenyls (PCBs), batteries, mercury, antifreeze, coolants, and fire extinguishers. High concentrations of PCB were found on the wooden flight deck, so it was also removed. And to ensure diver safety, protrusions on the bulkhead and window glass had to go.

IT'S YOUR FUNERAL

Finally, the *Oriskany* was ready to travel to Florida. The Navy hoped to sink it during the summer of 2005, but bad weather and political wrangling made that impossible. It wasn't until March 2006 that tugboats guided the 56-year-old ship to the dock at Allegheny Pier at Pensacola Naval Air Station. It got a last clean-up and once-over, and then on May 17, 2006, Navy crews set off 22 explosives at various spots inside the ship. In just 37 minutes, the *Oriskany* sank to the bottom of the Gulf of Mexico—stern first—and landed in an upright position. Once it reached the bottom of the ocean, the State of Florida took ownership of the vessel.

Today, the 888-foot *Oriskany* is an international diving attraction that rests in 212 feet of water, just 22.5 miles off the coast of Pensacola. The top portion of the ship—the control tower—is only 80 feet below the ocean's surface, so even recreational divers can explore it. And more experienced divers (who can go below 135 feet) can penetrate the innermost crevices, including the control room and engine room. Divers also plant and maintain U.S. and POW flags on the ship and have the opportunity to swim with Goliath grouper, ocean sunfish, eagle rays, and the other ocean animals that now make their homes on the *Oriskany*. The 44,000-

The official colors of the U.S. Army are black and gold. Its motto is "This We'll Defend."

ton carrier is just the first ship-reef. The Navy anticipates 20 more projects like it within the next decade.

JUST IN CASE YOU'RE WONDERING . . .

Why was this particular ship selected? In addition to having seen combat in two of America's most crucial wars, the *Oriskany* has a storied history:

• The *Oriskany* was the first aircraft carrier to sail around South America's Cape Horn on June 29, 1952.

• On October 26, 1967, future senator John McCain took off from the flight deck of the *Oriskany*. A few hours later, his plane was shot down; he became a POW in North Vietnam for more than five years.

• Stars William Holden and Mickey Rooney lived aboard the *Oriskany* during the filming of *The Bridges of Toko Ri* (1955). The ship also appeared in *The Men of the Fighting Lady* (1954), *The Right Stuff* (1983), and as "Hell" in the Robin Williams film *What Dreams May Come* (1998).

* * *

MOTHBALL FLEET

The Navy maintains several decommissioned vessels in a reserve called the "mothball fleet." The ships are kept afloat and in working order in case they need to be reactivated in an emergency. But while they're waiting, the ships' weapons and parts sometimes decompose or become obsolete. When the Iowa-class battleships—taken out of commission in the 1960s—were recommissioned in the 1980s, the Navy struggled to find specialty items needed to make the ships operational. They even had to salvage parts from earlier battleships that had already been sent to museums.

HOTBUNKING

Mention hotbunking to any submariner or someone who's served on any other cramped naval vessel, and they'll know exactly what you mean. You're also apt to get a smile—or a look of disdain.

WAY OF LIFE IN A SUB

Hotbunking—the practice of sharing racks (bunks) on a ship—is one of the least talked about Navy traditions, but it has been around for as long as there have been ships at sea. It was in the early 20th century, with the birth of the first iron submarines, that hotbunking became a way of life on the so-called pig boat navies. There was only so much room for beds in the foul-smelling, cramped confines of the early submersibles, and there were more men needed to control the complicated vessels than there were racks on which they could sleep. So crewmen had to double up, so to speak.

The crews of 30, 40, 50, or more were divided into three groups known as "watches." The first watch would be a third of the crew on duty monitoring all systems and propelling the vessel for eight hours in a 24-hour cycle. The second watch would be off-duty. And the third watch would be in their bunks for eight hours of shuteye. At the end of each shift, the watches would switch roles. Thus, all the bunks were occupied at all times. One man would get out and another would take his place. The beds never got cold . . . thus, they were hot bunks.

TENSION, HEAT, AND COLD

During World War II, one of the most harrowing duties in the U.S. Navy was serving in the Silent Service in the Pacific on diesel-driven submarines far behind enemy lines, where danger from aircraft and surface ships lurked constantly. The subs patrolled in the stifling heat of the tropics and in the icy cold of the Arctic in search of Japanese targets. Hotbunking often made sleep difficult on dirty, smelly sheets, but doing laundry was out of the question. Also, at the beginning of a war patrol, the sub was crowded with food provisions and torpedoes. Don Miller was a torpedo man in the after room of the World War II submarine

USS *Barb*. He remembers how crowded conditions were and how crewmen couldn't wait to fire torpedoes, if only to give them more room to stretch out.

HOTBUNKING ON THE NUKES

Hotbunking has continued in the nuclear underseas Navy. One 12-year veteran described sleeping conditions on the 314-foot-long attack submarine *Narwhal*, commissioned in 1969 with a crew of 141. Sheets and laundry were cleaned once a week on a typical 45-day cruise. "One of my hotbunk mates sweated profusely, so much so that there was a yellow outline of his body on the sheets, reminding me of one of those crime scene diagrams when a dead body has its layout being marked on the street. Even though I was quite the hardy soul and sailor, I rejected such sleeping conditions and instead learned to wad up some blankets and sleep between two torpedoes that were racked together."

*　　*　　*

GI JOE FACTS

• One of GI Joe's distinguishing features started out as a goof: the sculptor who designed the prototype worked so fast that he accidentally transposed GI Joe's right thumbnail so it ended up where the thumbprint should be. Levine told him to leave it. "That thumbnail would act as our identifying mark," Levine says. "A mapmaker will sometimes add a nonexistent street with his name attached; if another map comes out with that same street on it, he knows he's been copied. Now we had a scar to protect the face and an error on the hand to individualize our body."

• As GI Joe was about to go to market, Hasbro and Stan Weston negotiated a royalty arrangement. Hasbro offered one half of 1 percent of sales as royalty; Weston wanted 5 percent. He eventually lowered his asking price to 3 percent, but Hasbro refused to go above 1 percent. Eventually, Hasbro offered Weston a choice between $100,000 up front or $50,000 up front, with a 1 percent royalty once sales passed $7 million. "I made my own personal decision, nobody counseled me," Weston says. "I said, 'I'll take the $100,000.'" That decision cost Weston millions of dollars in lost royalties over the next 30 years.

...in Florida, making him the first prisoner of war in the American Civil War.

TOP AIR FORCE FLICKS

From dogfighting in the skies over Europe to exploring the depths of space, flying films are a staple of American cinema. Here are some classics to enjoy from your couch cockpit.

WINGS (1927)

The only silent film to ever win an Academy Award for Best Picture, *Wings* is the story of two fighter pilots who are in love with the same woman during World War I. The movie stars Clara Bow, Charles Rogers, and Richard Arlen, and features an appearance by rising star Gary Cooper, long before he won an Oscar for his performance in *Sergeant York* (1941). Despite its historical significance, the movie is not readily available on DVD in the United States, but it has been shown on television.

AIR FORCE (1943)

Directed by Howard Hawks, who served with the Army Air Corps during World War I, *Air Force* tells the story of the crew of the *Mary Ann*, a B-17 Flying Fortress sent to Hawaii on a routine training flight. When they arrive, they find the aftermath of the Japanese bombing of Pearl Harbor. Released just 15 months after the actual attack, the film's patriotic tone often leads today's critics to call it a "propaganda movie." But *Air Force* managed to garner four Academy Award nominations, and won for Best Film Editing.

TWELVE O'CLOCK HIGH (1949)

"A story of twelve men as their women never knew them," according to the movie posters, *Twelve O'Clock High* stars Gregory Peck as Brigadier General Frank Savage, who must whip the men of his new bomber unit into shape for combat operations during World War II. One of a spate of war films that focused on the exploits of U.S. aircrews, the film made use of actual combat video to add to the intensity of the story. It was nominated for four Academy Awards, and won for Best Supporting Actor and Best Sound.

STRATEGIC AIR COMMAND (1955)

James Stewart stars as Lieutenant Colonel Robert "Dutch" Holland of the U.S. Air Force Reserve, and June Allyson plays his wife, Sally. The film begins in 1951 when Dutch, who had served with the U.S. Army Air Forces in World War II, is now a star baseball player for the St. Louis Cardinals. However, Dutch's athletic career is put on hold when he is recalled for active duty with the Air Force, which is now a separate branch of the U.S. armed forces. As Dutch and Sally adjust to their new life in the military, which has changed considerably since the end of World War II, Dutch's love of flying is rekindled and his life plans are transformed. *Strategic Air Command* has been praised for its realistic portrayal of the SAC, which can be attributed to Stewart's own experience as a combat pilot in World War II. The film was nominated for an Academy Award for Best Writing.

NO TIME FOR SERGEANTS (1958)

In one of his earliest films, Andy Griffith stars as Private Will Stockdale, a country bumpkin who is drafted into the U.S. Air Force and goes on to have one comedic misadventure after another as he tries to adjust to the military life. Originally written as a book and set in World War II with the U.S. Army Air Forces, the movie was updated to reflect the peacetime status of the U.S. military in the late 1950s and the Air Force as a separate branch. Don Knotts had a small role in the movie, which was the beginning of a long professional relationship with Griffith.

A GATHERING OF EAGLES (1963)

U.S. Air Force Colonel Jim Caldwell (Rock Hudson) is given the assignment of improving the performance of a B-52 bomber wing that has fallen into a state of disarray. With a newfound sternness that soon alienates those who are under his command—including his wife and best friend—Caldwell shapes the bomber wing into the unit he envisioned when he accepted the assignment. The timing of the film's release, when the military was falling out of favor with the public, may have influenced its less-than-stellar showing at the box office, but it has since come to be noted for its authentic depiction of the Strategic Air Command. General Curtis LeMay of the U.S. Air Force provided full cooperation to the film's producers in the hopes that it would rekindle the public's confidence in the SAC's ability to effectively manage the country's

In 2005 the Civil Air Patrol flew more than 3,000 search-and-rescue missions...

nuclear stockpiles. A *Gathering of Eagles* was nominated for an Academy Award for Best Sound Effects.

DR. STRANGELOVE (1964)

In director Stanley Kubrick's satirical comedy of the Cold War, delusional Air Force Brigadier General Jack D. Ripper (Sterling Hayden) is intent on attacking the Soviet Union by ordering B-52 bombers to drop their nuclear weapons in retaliation for an attack on the United States. The story of the attack, however, was completely fabricated by Ripper, and the people around him soon realize they've been duped—and they need to get the B-52s to abort their mission. Also starring Peter Sellers (in three separate roles) and George C. Scott, *Dr. Strangelove* is widely regarded as one of the best comedies in film history. It was nominated for four Academy Awards, including Best Picture, but didn't take home any Oscars.

THE RIGHT STUFF (1983)

Based on the book by Tom Wolfe, *The Right Stuff* contrasts the efforts of military test pilots working to field cutting-edge jets with the work of those selected to launch the United States' early efforts at space exploration. While Air Force hero Chuck Yeager—played by Sam Shepard—breaks the sound barrier and sets new altitude records and yet is excluded from NASA's program because he has no college degree, the "Mercury Seven" progress through their grueling, competitive, and often dangerous training as they prepare for the space race. The film was nominated for eight Academy Awards, winning in four of the six technical categories for which it was nominated.

THE TUSKEGEE AIRMEN (1995)

Who says a made-for-television movie can't go on the must-see list? The ensemble cast and superb production of HBO's *The Tuskegee Airmen* is better than many Hollywood films with twice the budget. The story follows the first African American combat pilots as they train and deploy for World War II, eventually earning the respect of their white peers. The cast includes stars such as Laurence Fishburne, Cuba Gooding Jr., and Andre Braugher. The film was nominated for 10 Emmy Awards, and took home three.

...and was credited with saving 73 lives.

THE MEDAL OF HONOR

Often called—in error—the Congressional Medal of Honor, it isn't granted by Congress. The awards are made by the Department of Defense. Congress merely passes the legislation. And sometimes only after a lot of debate.

GO NAVY! NAVY 1, ARMY 0

Early in the Civil War, the idea of a medal for valor was proposed to General-in-Chief of the Army Winfield Scott, but the general shot it down because he thought medals were a European affectation. The U.S. Navy had no such objections—and neither did Congress. So when Iowa senator James W. Grimes, chairman of the Naval Committee, introduced a bill on December 9, 1861, to "promote the efficiency of the Navy" by distributing "medals of honor," Congress passed it, authorizing 200 medals "which shall be bestowed upon such petty officers, seamen, landsmen and marines as shall distinguish themselves in by their gallantry in action and other seamanlike qualities during the present war." President Lincoln signed the bill and the Navy Medal of Honor was born.

AND ARMY TIES THE SCORE

Eventually, of course, the Army decided it wanted in on the act. Massachusetts senator Henry Wilson introduced a bill the following February authorizing "the president to distribute medals to privates in the Army of the United States who shall distinguish themselves in battle." This time Congress debated the resolution for several months, but on July 12, 1862, passed legislation for the Army Medal of Honor. The act authorized the president to award 2,000 medals of honor in the name of Congress to noncommissioned officers and privates who distinguished themselves in action, and for "other soldier-like qualities, during the present insurrection." The Navy medals could be awarded for either combat or noncombat heroism, but Army medals were restricted to combat heroism. With these two acts, Congress created an award that grew in prominence in American history.

World War II Underwater Demolition Teams were a precursor to the U.S. Navy SEALs.

In March 1863, Congress amended the Army act to make Army officers eligible for the medal, but not officers of the Navy or Marine Corps. The odd arrangement continued until March 3, 1915, when Congress expanded the decoration to include Navy, Marine Corps, and Coast Guard officers.

Since then, there have been three more amendments. The amendment of July 9, 1918, provided for military service abroad, and the amendment of July 25, 1963, provided for the inclusion of women. The following is the criteria for awarding the Medal of Honor as of February 25, 1995:

> The Medal of Honor is awarded by the President in the name of Congress to a person who, while a member of Armed Services, distinguishes himself [or herself] conspicuously by gallantry and intrepidity at the risk of his life [or her life] above and beyond the call of duty while engaged in an action against an enemy of the United States . . . The deed performed must have been one of personal bravery or self-sacrifice so conspicuous as to clearly distinguish the individual above his comrades and must have involved risk of life. Incontestable proof of the performance of the service will be exacted and each recommendation for the award of this decoration will be considered on the standard of extraordinary merit.

CONGRESS DEMANDS A RECOUNT

But back in 1916, Congress began questioning if the 2,635 awards that had been made by that point met with statutory requirements; a board of five officers was created to review the records. Civil War awards raised the most questions because of the huge number. Researchers discovered that the first Civil War medal awarded actually went retroactively to Assistant Surgeon Bernard J. D. Irwin for heroic action at Apache Pass, Arizona, on February 13–14, 1861, two months before the Civil War began and 16 months before legislation for the Army medal had passed. Irwin kept his medal, and so did Private Francis E. Brownell of the 11th New York Fire Zouaves, whose action on May 24, 1861, actually made him the Civil War's first Army recipient.

After completion of its review, the board recommended rescinding 911 medals. This included 864 medals issued to all the men of the 27th Maine Infantry, which the board ruled a clerical error; 29 who served as Lincoln's funeral guard; 12 that appeared to be frivolous; five because they were civilians; and one because

German U-boats sank 5,554 Allied and neutral merchant ships during World War I.

of gender. Acting Assistant Surgeon Dr. Mary E. Walker served in battles from First Bull Run in 1861 to Atlanta in 1864. The Army board rescinded her award in 1917 because she was not a man, though she served near the front lines and was held for four months in a Confederate prison camp. President Jimmy Carter restored Walker's award in 1977. William F. "Buffalo Bill" Cody lost his medal by being a civilian scout and not a soldier, but in 1989 President George H. W. Bush reinstated the award.

HONORABLE MEN AND 11-YEAR-OLDS

One Medal of Honor went to drummer boy William "Willie" Johnston of Company D, 3rd Vermont Infantry, who received the honor on September 16, 1863, at the age of 13 for acts of heroism during the June 1862 Seven Days' Battles. Born on July 1, 1850, Willie was 11 at the time and the youngest person ever to receive the award.

The Army granted 424 awards between 1861 and 1898, when soldiers were fighting American Indians on the frontier. The medal was still being liberally granted during the Spanish-American War. Because much of the action occurred at sea, sailors collected 64 awards, the Marine Corps 15, and the Army 31. The most distinguished personality of the war, Lieutenant Colonel Teddy Roosevelt, never knew he earned the medal because his was awarded posthumously on January 16, 2001. After reexamining the process in 1917, Congress began providing different decorations for lesser acts of heroism. Only 124 Medal of Honor awards were granted during World War I: 95 to the Army, 21 to the Navy, and 8 to the Marine Corps. For extreme valor during the 1918 war-ending offensives in France, five Marines received Medals of Honor from both the Army and the Navy.

THE WORLD WARS AND BEYOND

During World War I, another group of men served their country in a whole new way, by flying rickety biplanes made of wood, wire, and canvas. They were part of the Army Air Services and in 1917 were not fully appreciated by ground commanders. Still, four flyers received Army Medals of Honor—three of them posthumously. Sole survivor Eddie Rickenbacker had scored 26 victories and became America's top ace.

Compared with the 1,198 awards granted during the Civil War, only 464 were authorized during World War II. Among the recipients were First Lieutenant Vernon Baker, whose regiment was the first African American unit to go into combat in World War II, and Second Lieutenant Van T. Barfoot, a Choctaw Indian from Mississippi who showed "extraordinary heroism, demonstration of magnificent valor, and aggressive determination in the face of point-blank fire" to inspire his fellow soldiers in the capture of a new position near Carano, Italy, in 1944.

The Korean War produced 133 recipients and the Vietnam War 246, but then the flow of Medal of Honor awards drastically decreased. Congress authorized only two medals during Somalia, one during Afghanistan, and four during Iraq, all posthumously. To date, 3,467 medals have been awarded to 3,448 individuals, including one for each of the nine unknown soldiers.

SOME OF THE PERKS

Congress granted a special bonus to all Medal of Honor recipients on April 27, 1916: a $10 monthly lifetime pension at age 65, providing the recipient was honorably discharged. In 1961 Congress reviewed the 1916 law and increased the pension to $100 a month beginning at age 50. It is now $1,000 a month with no age limitation. Medalists can fly worldwide on government aircraft and are entitled, along with their families, to be buried in Arlington National Cemetery.

THE GODDESS AND THE LADY

The 1862 medals for the Army and the Navy were minted as an inverted gold star with the image of Minerva, the Roman goddess of war, surrounded by the 34 tiny stars representing the states of the Union. The traditional Army emblem of an eagle held the medal, while the flukes of an anchor held the Navy medal. Both were connected to a ribbon of 13 vertical red and white stripes below a plain blue field. The medals remained exactly as they were first designed until the beginning of the 20th century. Today there are separate Medals of Honor authorized for the Army, Navy, Air Force, and Coast Guard.

The present Army medal consists of a gold star inset with the head of Minerva, surrounded by a wreath, topped by an eagle on a bar inscribed with the word "Valor." The medal is attached by a hook to a light blue moiré silk neck band stitched with 13 embossed stars. Congress expected many of the medals to be awarded posthumously, and the count has lately reached 618.

The Navy medal is the least changed. The original design has been reengraved and is no longer flat. It's still held by the flukes of an anchor but the ribbon has been changed to the light blue moiré silk neck band like the Army medal. A Coast Guard medal has been authorized but has yet to be designed. A Navy Medal of Honor was given posthumously to the sole Coast Guard recipient, Signalman First Class Douglas A. Munro, for heroism during the Battle of Guadalcanal.

It wasn't until July 6, 1960, that legislation was passed to create a Medal of Honor for the U.S. Air Force, which Congress separated from the Army and made an independent entity in 1947. Instead of Minerva, the Air Force medal displays the head of the Statue of Liberty. The medal is more ornate than the Army or Navy versions; the star is surrounded by a large green wreath and hangs from an adaptation of the thunderbolt from the Air Force coat of arms.

AWARDS MADE TO DATE

By conflict

Civil War	1,522
Indian Wars	426
Korean Expedition	15
Spanish-American War	110
Samoan Civil War	4
Philippine-American War	86
Boxer Rebellion	59
Mexican Expedition	56
Haiti (1915–1934)	8
Dominican Republic Occupation	3
World War I	124
Occupation of Nicaragua	2
World War II	464
Korean War	133
Vietnam War	246
Battle of Mogadishu	2
Operation Iraqi Freedom	4
Operation Enduring Freedom	1
Peacetime	193
Unknowns	9

By branch of service

Service	Awards
Army	2,404
Navy	746
Marine Corps	297
Air Force	17
Coast Guard	1

POSTSCRIPT: THE BAREFOOT GENERAL

In January 2002, retired General Joe Foss, 86, a former Marine fighter pilot and one of the most highly decorated U.S. war veterans, was detained at a security checkpoint at the Phoenix, Arizona, airport because he was carrying an item with sharp edges. The sharp object turned out to be the Medal of Honor he had received in 1943 from President Franklin D. Roosevelt. The general was on his way to West Point to speak to the sophomore class there—and to show them his medal. After the general had to remove his shoes, tie, and belt three times in three different areas of the airport, he was allowed to board his plane.

* * *

The longest-delayed award to a medal of honor recipient went to Army Corporal Andrew Jackson Smith of the 55th Massachusetts Volunteer Infantry, one of the Union's all-black regiments in the Civil War. On November 30, 1864, during a bloody charge on Honey Hill, South Carolina, Smith retrieved the fallen regimental colors and carried them under extreme enemy fire throughout the battle. The Medal of Honor was granted on January 18, 2001, more than 136 years after the action.

General Douglas MacArthur was the oldest Medal of Honor recipient at age 62. The citation was awarded on April 1, 1942, for his heroic defense of the Philippines and his offensive efforts on the Bataan peninsula. His father, Lieutenant General Arthur MacArthur, had earned the Medal of Honor during the Civil War, making them the only father and son to have received the award.

The first use of a Coast Guard aircraft to chase rumrunners occurred on June 20, 1925.

REMEMBERING THE "FORGOTTEN WAR"

The battle over the Korean War Veterans Memorial in Washington, D.C., lasted longer—and at times seemed more contentious—than the war itself.

THE FORGOTTEN WAR

In June 1950, President Harry S. Truman agreed to send U.S. troops to Korea to fight the North Korean army. Three years later, a truce was signed between North and South Korea—a truce that remains uneasy to this day—the fighting stopped, and the U.S. troops went home.

Compared to what the United States had experienced during World War II, the Korean War seemed like a mere dalliance. Some insisted on deeming it a "conflict" and even Truman called it a "police action." More than one soldier has told the story of how, on returning home, old friends would say, "Where have you been? Haven't seen you around lately." When the soldier explained that he'd been in Korea, his pals responded with blank looks. Many folks stateside had never heard of the place, let alone that a war had been raging there for three solid years.

Yet in those three years, American casualties in Korea numbered more than 54,000 dead, 8,000 missing in action, 7,000 prisoners of war, and 100,000 wounded. Hundreds of thousands of American men and women served and fought in the Korean War. Something needed to be done to commemorate their bravery, to honor their service. America needed to build a Korean War memorial in Washington, D.C.

HERE'S AN IDEA—OR TWO

By 1984, more than 30 years after the war's end, at least two veterans' groups had formed to seek government support for a Korean War memorial in Washington, D.C. The highly publicized Vietnam Veterans Memorial had been dedicated two years earlier, and the time seemed right to put plans for the Korean War Veterans Memorial into action.

In 1986 both the House and Senate approved a plan to build a memorial. In 1987 President Ronald Reagan appointed 12 Korean War veterans to serve on the Korean War Veterans Memorial Advisory Board; they included the CEO of Mack Trucks, a smattering of colonels and generals, and representatives from several veterans' organizations. Things seemed to be moving forward.

AND THEN . . .

The Pennsylvania firm hired to design the memorial submitted its design and the advisory board rejected it, reportedly claiming that it was not heroic enough. When the advisory board brought in another architectural firm to adapt the original design, the Pennsylvania firm sued the advisory board, the new architects, the U.S. Army Corps of Engineers, and the American Battle Monuments Commission for breach of contract and for tampering with the original design work. By this time it was 1991: a full five years since the plan to build the memorial was approved, seven years since it was first proposed, and 36 years since the Korean War ended—and the fighting wasn't over yet!

The new architects weren't having any more luck than the original firm in receiving approval for their design. This time, resistance came from the Commission of Fine Arts, one of three reviewing bodies that had to sign off on the design before construction could commence. The CFA rejected at least four designs, calling them "unfocused" and "overwhelming."

A year later, in 1992, a design was approved and ground was broken for the memorial, southwest of the Lincoln Memorial and not far from the Vietnam Veterans Memorial. Construction was completed in three years; on July 27, 1995, the 42nd anniversary of the Korean War armistice, the memorial was dedicated in a ceremony led by U.S. president Bill Clinton and South Korean president Kim Young Sam.

Yet even then the troubles persisted. A year after the memorial was dedicated, its paving stones began sinking into the ground, the 40 trees surrounding the reflecting pool died and were removed, and the pool itself became clogged with leaves and had to be drained. Repairs cost several million dollars, on top of the $18 million in private donations that had been spent on construction. Once again, the Korean War vets seemed in danger of being forgotten—or at least of being given short shrift by American history.

...resistance groups and conducted sabotage and guerrilla warfare against the Germans.

YOU MUST REMEMBER THIS

By the time of the armistice's 50th anniversary in 2003 (nearly 20 years since the committees started forming to propose the memorial), the Korean War Veterans Memorial had been repaired and restored.

The memorial comprises three distinct elements. First are the 19 statues of soldiers on patrol—15 Army, two Marines, and one each of the Navy and Air Force. They stand more than seven feet tall and were sculpted by Vermont artist Frank Gaylord, a World War II veteran. Their faces, which show the exhaustion and determination of a tested combat patrol, are reflected in the granite mural wall.

Etched into the surface of the wall, the second principal element of the memorial, is a mural of some 2,400 images taken from photographs and representing all branches of the service and variety of jobs and assignments—pilots, corpsmen, combat troops, medical personnel, chaplains, landing forces, and even the canine corps. From a distance, the etchings are thought to resemble the mountainous landscape of Korea, and the reflected faces of the statues brings the total of soldiers represented "on patrol" to 38—symbolic of the 38th parallel, where most of the fighting in Korea took place. Beside the wall are plantings of hibiscus, Korea's national flower.

The third element of the memorial is a reflecting pool engraved with the words "Freedom is not free." And nearby, an even more apt inscription: "Our nation honors her sons and daughters who answered the call to defend a country they never knew and a people they never met."

An honor roll of the names of all military personnel who were killed during the Korean War is kept in a nearby kiosk, where visitors can search for the names of family members, friends, and loved ones.

At long last, there is a fitting tribute to those who fought and died in Korea, and who, as Korea vet Angus Deming wrote in *Newsweek* at the time of the memorial's dedication, "never understood how the Korean War could have been 'forgotten' in the first place."

The first use of telegraph lines in warfare came during the Civil War.

USO

"All the guys everywhere who sail from Tedium to Apathy and back again, with an occasional side trip to Monotony."
—Lieutenant Doug Roberts in Mister Roberts

LENDING A HELPING HAND

Mister Roberts knew that boredom was the unseen enemy of war. At the outset of World War II, it soon became obvious to newly drafted GIs in hastily built camps in rural areas that they would spend most of their off-duty hours bored and homesick. The USO, originally created as temporary diversion for World War II military personnel, has endured to this day and has been transformed into an organization that touches almost every aspect of military life.

BIRTH OF THE USO

It all started at a meeting in New York City in October 1940. Encouraged by President Franklin D. Roosevelt, the six charitable groups that attended the first meeting—the Young Women's Christian Association, the Young Men's Christian Association, the National Catholic Community Service, the National Jewish Welfare Board, the Traveler's Aid Association, and the Salvation Army—formed the United Service Organizations for National Defense (shortened to USO) on February 4, 1941. And a week before the United States was attacked at Pearl Harbor and entered the war, the first permanent USO club was built in Fayetteville, North Carolina, for Fort Bragg's soldiers. Today there are approximately 130 sites worldwide.

ON WITH THE SHOW

When the USO is mentioned, most people think of Bob Hope, who for decades was the most visible and best-known performer for the USO. But there was more to the USO than Bob Hope. During World War II, the USO had 7,000 "Soldiers in Greasepaint" performing on four circuits—three of them stateside: the Victory Circuit for Broadway shows, the Blue Circuit for smaller vaudeville shows, and the Hospital Circuit for entertaining in

Actor Harvey Keitel joined the Marines at age 16 and served in Lebanon.

military hospitals. Those performers who went overseas were on the Foxhole Circuit.

During World War II, the USO staged more than 428,000 live shows for an audience of almost 213 million. Not all of those shows had stages with microphones and spotlights. Often a mobile USO took a few entertainers close to the front lines to perform some songs for a small military unit. After V-E Day, when troops made the slow transit through the Panama Canal in anticipation of an invasion of Japan, USO entertainers performed on both sides of the narrow canal for the troops who, not authorized to go ashore, crowded the decks of their ships to watch.

With the war's end, the USO was suspended by the end of 1947, but it was quickly revived to meet the needs of the Korean War in 1950. The USO sponsored 5,400 shows during the three-year conflict, including Bob Hope's first televised USO show from Thule Air Force Base in Greenland.

NO APPLAUSE NECESSARY

But not all of the 1.5 million volunteers during World War II were entertainers. USO centers also offered libraries, inexpensive lodging, movies, sports equipment, and refreshments. Programs like the Star-Spangled Network helped soldiers record messages on records and send them home to their families. By mid-1942 the USO was reaching out to defense plant workers as well with programs such as child care for the children of all those Rosie the Riveters.

With the U.S. military establishing permanent bases around the world, the USO recognized they would be needed, even in peacetime. The first foreign USO centers were started in the early 1950s in France, Italy, North Africa, the Philippines, and Japan. By 2008 they had added centers in Afghanistan, Germany, Guam, Korea, Kuwait, Qatar, and the United Arab Emirates—bringing the number of overseas centers to 51. In addition to the traditional services that their World War II counterparts had offered, today's USO centers also provide classes on cultural awareness, local tours, and Internet and e-mail access.

With the switch to an all-voluntary military in the 1970s (with about half of the service personnel married with children), the USO recognized its responsibility to military families. They opened family and community centers to help with issues such as parent-

The Continental Army was formed on June 14, 1775, before there was a United States.

ing, budgeting, finding off-base housing, relocating, understanding foreign cultures, and even making the transition to civilian life.

The USO continued to move with the times by starting programs such as:

- Better Than a Letter in 1990, which provided camcorders, VCRs, and TVs for troops and families to exchange videotaped greetings.
- United Through Reading for soldiers to videotape themselves reading bedtime stories to their children.
- Operation Phone Home, which provides phone cards for soldiers overseas.

THE NEW USO

By the end of the Vietnam War, the pool of famous entertainers had shrunk, but in the 1980s several individuals contributed their time and talents to USO performances again: Lou Rawls; Phil Ehart, drummer for the rock band Kansas, who recruited fellow musicians; and the cast of *Happy Days*, encouraged by Anson Williams (Potsie), who was the son-in-law of General Fred Mahaffey. The most faithful performers were the Dallas Cowboys Cheerleaders, who first appeared in Korea in 1979. In 2008 they celebrated their 65th appearance with the USO, making more tours than any other entertainment group.

When soldiers deployed to Afghanistan and Iraq, a new generation of performers stepped up. Athletic celebrities have made frequent appearances. Comics such as Drew Carey and Jay Leno, and musicians such as Toby Keith and Kid Rock have taken the stage. And, in the tradition of the *Happy Days* cast, actors from TV series such as *The Unit* and movies such as *Tropic Thunder* have visited military bases. Gary Sinise tours overseas as front man for the Lt. Dan Band; "Lt. Dan" refers to the Vietnam vet he portrayed in *Forrest Gump*.

Some companies have also become USO sponsors. The NFL donated hundreds of footballs to the USO, the Lance Armstrong Foundation donated T-shirts, Electric Arts donated video games, and several production companies donated DVDs and CDs. Although Bob Hope, the most famous "Soldier in Greasepaint," died in 2003, the USO continues to serve.

The U.S. Navy operates 283 ships in active service and more than 3,700 aircraft.

What does the USO do today?

- Arranges camel rides for sailors on leave in Dubai.
- Makes hotel arrangements in South Korea for a visiting spouse.
- Makes DVDs of deploying soldiers reading children's books for their young children.
- Sends boxes of snacks to an Afghanistan outpost.
- Helps a Marine in Kosovo order his mom a birthday card online.
- Finds a team for a Little Leaguer who just moved to Germany when his mom was transferred.
- Welcomes Miss USA to Fort Leavenworth, Kansas.

* * *

BOB HOPE AND THE USO

- He went to Vietnam nine times.
- He did 24 consecutive Christmas tours, starting in 1948.
- He entertained for the USO every year from 1942 to 1990.
- He headlined approximately 60 tours.
- The first Bob Hope Christmas Tour was in 1943; he visited military bases each December for the next 34 years.
- He started carrying his trademark golf club during his 1969 USO tour.
- He became an honorary veteran by a 1997 act of Congress signed by President Bill Clinton.

* * *

MILITARY CUT

The new enlistee sat down in the barber's chair and was shocked when the barber asked him if he'd like to keep his sideburns. "I sure would!" he said as he sat back and got comfortable. With a flourish, the barber cut off the sideburns and said, "Here—catch!"

Gen. Henry H. "Hap" Arnold was the first and only aviator to attain five-star rank.

WILD BLUE YONDER

More than 54,000 airmen have died in combat while serving in the Air Force and its predecessor organizations. In 2006 a new monument was dedicated to honor their service and sacrifices.

THE AIR FORCE MEMORIAL

Under development for nearly 15 years, the memorial was funded almost entirely from private donations. Located on a promontory in Arlington, Virginia, it overlooks the Pentagon and is adjacent to Arlington National Cemetery. It was dedicated on October 14, 2006, the 60th anniversary of the birth of the U.S. Air Force, by President George W. Bush, the first president who'd served in the Air Force, as a member of the Texas Air National Guard. As part of the ceremony, the U.S. Air Force Thunderbird Demonstration Team performed their signature aerial maneuver directly overhead. The memorial has a breathtaking impact resembling the famous and often showstopping "bomb burst" maneuver that concludes every Thunderbird aerial performance. Architect James Ingo Freed designed the 270-foot-tall array of three skyward-reaching stainless-steel arcs to evoke images of soaring aircraft climbing ever higher away from the bounds of the earth below.

SYMBOLS OF THE AIR FORCE

The spires also represent the three components of today's Air Force—active duty, reserve, and National Guard—and its three core values: "Integrity first, service before self, and excellence in all we do." Embedded beneath the spires is the Air Force star, which is emblazoned on all aircraft and is also the rank insignia worn by all members of the Air Force. Around the base are black granite panels inscribed with the sage words of Air Force pioneers.

A bluestone path connects two features positioned at opposite ends of the memorial. At the memorial's western entrance, four eight-foot-tall bronze statues of the Air Force Honor Guard stand at attention on vigilant watch over the American flag. At the other end is the Glass Contemplation Wall with meditative inscriptions. This unique glass panel affords visitors a vision of a soaring "missing man" fighter formation that is superimposed over the skies of Washington when the viewer is positioned at just the right angle.

Francis Scott Key was a distant cousin and the namesake of author F. Scott Fitzgerald.

FIGHTING COMMUNISM IN THE CLOUDS

During the Cold War, the United States was determined to prove to the world that democracy was better than communism. They used a variety of stages ranging from the space program to the chess board to . . . the clouds.

PARACHUTING FOR GOLD

The Strategic Army Corps Sports Parachute Team, made up of 13 men, was formed by Brigadier General Joseph W. Stilwell in 1959 to compete in international skydiving competitions that were, at the time, being dominated by the communists. But communist domination didn't last for long after the Americans arrived. In 1962 the American group adopted the nickname Golden Knights: golden because of how many gold medals they won and knights because they conquered the skies.

Headquartered at Fort Bragg, North Carolina, the team now consists of 90 soldiers and six teams. There are two demonstration teams that perform throughout the country to encourage morale and recruitment. The Black and Gold Teams are named after the Army colors, as well as the colors of their parachutes. Two competitive teams are 'Style and Accuracy" and "Formation Skydiving."

Team Six is the all-important transportation team made up of 6 fixed wing aircraft, the F27 Fokker and UV-18 Twin Otter, their pilots and crewmembers. Headquarters team is the administrative branch in charge of scheduling and publicity.

SKY KINGS

In order to apply for the Golden Knights, soldiers must have a minimum of 150 freefall parachute jumps, a class C international skydiving license, and an excellent military and civilian record. The soldiers average 600 jumps per year during their three years with the Golden Knights. Those with the group now range from 250 to 11,000 jumps each. Eleven thousand jumps. If you jumped once a day it would take you over 30 years to top that number.

Golden Knights jump from aircraft flying at 12,500 feet and reach a speed of over 120 mph during freefall. Some flights are

The Army is the oldest U.S. military service, established on June 14, 1775.

mass exit, when a large number of soldiers exit the plane at the same time, while others involve smaller groups doing special formations such as the baton pass, cutaway, diamond track, and diamond formation. The parachutists add to the drama of their jumps by releasing smoke from canisters attached to their legs and taking both still and video images using cameras attached to their helmets.

A similar group of Navy jumpers made up of SEAL and SWCC commandos was formed in 1969. In 1974 they were christened the Leapfrogs. During their three-year tours they also perform throughout the country.

*　　*　　*

THE "F" WORD

A grandfather who'd been a pilot in World War II was telling his adolescent grandkids about his adventures in the war. "German pilots were a force to be reckoned with. One day, I was on a strafing mission when these Fokkers appeared out of nowhere." The kids looked at each other and giggled. Granddad went on, "I shot down one of them, but then I saw another Fokker coming at me." More giggles. Their mother, who'd been listening in, said, "You silly kids, 'Fokker' was the name of the German-Dutch aircraft company." "Right," said Granddad, "but these Fokkers were flying Messerschmitts."

*　　*　　*

"Previous to this time I had never even seen a balloon except from a distance. Being interested in their construction, I was about to institute a thorough examination of all its parts, when the aeronaut announced that all was ready. He inquired whether I desired to go up alone, or he should accompany me. My desire, if frankly expressed, would have been not to go up at all; but if I was to go, company was certainly desirable."

—*George Armstrong Custer, while a cavalry captain, commenting on an order to go aloft in one of Thaddeus Lowe's balloons to observe the movements of the Confederate forces. Quoted from* Son of the Morning Star, *1862*

SEVEN THINGS YOU DIDN'T KNOW ABOUT THE WAR IN IRAQ

Have you been paying attention?

1. THE EMBEDDED REPORTER PROGRAM

Secretary of Defense Donald Rumsfeld began the program in 2002 as an effort to get the message out. He believed that, with technology providing instant access to news; if he placed reporters (print, TV, and radio) with the troops, they would be more believable than the typical military public relations press releases. "We need to tell the factual story—good or bad," he said, "before others seed the media with disinformation." The program was a resounding success; over 770 journalists were embedded with coalition troops during March-April's Operation Iraqi Freedom, 550 of them traveled with Marine, Army, and British ground forces. During the height of the fighting, they were generating some 6,000 stories weekly. Being on the frontlines is just as dangerous for the media; since the war began on March 19, 2003, more than 100 reporters have been killed in Iraq.

2. WOMEN COMBATANTS KILLED

More than 70 women have been killed on the battlefield; more than Korea, Vietnam, and Desert Storm combined, and more than 450 have been wounded. Army Sergeant Leigh Ann Hester became the first woman since World War II to be awarded the Silver Star with Combat "V" for leading her team of MPs in a counterattack against more than 50 insurgents who ambushed their convoy. Specialist Ashley Pullen received a Bronze Star with Combat "V" for laying down fire to suppress an insurgent attack and then exposed herself to enemy fire while assisting her critically wounded comrades. Marine Major Megan McClung was killed in an IED blast in Ramadi, becoming the first female graduate of the Naval Academy killed since Annapolis was founded in 1845.

Sioux chief Sitting Bull's name in his own language: Tatanka Yotanka.

3. AL-JAZEERA NEWS

Based in Doha, Qatar, Al-Jazeera is a privately owned global television network with offices in Washington, D.C., and London and has correspondents stationed around the world. Like its Western counterparts, it focuses on politics, economics, and sports with reporters drawn from the ranks of the BBC, ABC, and other Western networks. It might be the only global network criticized in Washington for being pro-Arab while simultaneously being banned in Saudi Arabia for being pro-West.

4. MARINE RECRUITING

Even as the casualty count from Iraq rose, and the economy boomed (until mid-2008), the Marine Corps continued to attract qualified recruits in record numbers. When all four branches of the service were ordered in 2005 to increase their size within five years, the Marine Corps met the new goal within three years.

5. SKILLED INTERPRETERS

With few soldiers and Marines fluent in Arabic, communications and relations between Iraqi citizens and our "boots on the ground" were often reduced to childlike pantomimes, with frustrating results for both. A good interpreter was an integral part of every line company (three or four platoons), and on more than one occasion fought side-by-side with the Marines and soldiers. Most of the first interpreters were local Iraqis who had to wear scarves, masks, and other disguises to protect themselves and their families from reprisals. With more "terps" needed as the American troops spent more time in the towns and villages, the military began to bring them in from Egypt, Somalia, Yemen, and Turkey. Others came from the Iraqi-heavy populations of Detroit, Los Angeles, and New York-New Jersey.

6. CHOW IN IRAQ

The Army and Marines lived on MREs (Meals Ready to Eat) and bottled water in 2003–04, but after the Pentagon hired Halliburton's KBR to operate the chow halls, the food choices on the big bases escalated astronomically. Run cafeteria-style, the halls offered hot meals, sandwich bars, omelet stations, desserts, and multiple beverage choices. Open for four meals daily—breakfast, lunch, dinner, and "mid rats" (midnight rations)—the Friday night dinner on base was steak and crab legs. Some chow halls offered ethnic food selections like Mexican, Indian, and Asian. Of course, Marines and soldiers living out in the field with the Iraqi Army and police were still eating MREs as late as spring 2008. And plenty of them returned home with an appreciation of the communal meals their Iraqi Army counterparts had shared with them: roasted chicken, basmati rice, tomatoes, and a naan-like bread.

7. SUPPORT GROUPS

Within months of the invasion in March 2003, dozens of groups sprang up to donate goods to the fighting troops fighting or to provide emotional and financial assistance to the families back home: Soldiers' Angels, Marine Parents United, Spirit of America, and Wounded Warriors, to name a few. Others collected and mailed books, magazines, food, powdered drinks, beef jerky, disposable razors, and other items to the troops overseas. The old standbys like the American Red Cross and the U.S.O. continued their history of support; the Red Cross even provided financial assistance to families of fighting troops.

* * *

IRAQYWOOD

The most successful stories coming out of Iraq have been the television specials oriented toward the "boots on the ground" who did the fighting. HBO produced two: the highly-rated *Generation Kill*, which covered a 1st Marine Division Reconnaissance Company in the opening days of the March 2003 invasion, and the award-winning *Taking Chance*, the heartbreaking story of a Marine bringing the coffin of Lance Corporal Chance Phelps home for burial. Other respected television specials included *Baghdad ER*, *Combat Diary—The Marines of Lima Company*, *Gunner Palace*, *Off to War—From Rural Arkansas to Iraq*, *Home of the Brave*, and *American Soldiers: A Day in Iraq*.

DAY IS DONE

For more than a century, "Taps" has been the bugle call to mark the day's end and evening rest in the U.S. military. Its soothing 24 notes have comforted many when played as a final farewell to a former soldier laid to rest. Given its long history, it's not surprising that it is the subject of many legends.

BIRTH OF "TAPS"

By the Civil War, bugle calls existed for all types of commands—from "Time to get up!" to "Wear your overcoat today!" or "If you're sick, now's the time for sick call!" But it was during the Civil War's Peninsula Campaign in July 1862 that "Taps" became the bugle call command to extinguish all lights and fires and to prepare for sleep. Historians agree on when and where "Taps" was first played, but there's more than one version of the story surrounding its origin and composer.

BELIEVE IT OR NOT

One popular story says that the man who first ordered "Taps" played was Union Captain Robert Ellicombe. While encamped with the Army of the Potomac at Harrison's Landing, Virginia, Ellicombe risked enemy fire to rescue a wounded soldier. When the captain lit a lantern, he realized that the young man was dead, and a Confederate soldier, but even more shocking—the young man was his own son. Inside the soldier's pocket was a musical score. Ellicombe requested that a bugler play his son's composition at the burial, and that was when the Army of the Potomac first heard the somber music of "Taps."

The country's foremost authority on the tune as well as the former curator of Arlington National Cemetery's "Taps" Bugle Exhibit, Jari A. Villanueva, researched the story and found no record of any Captain Ellicombe in the Union army or at Harrison's Landing. What Villanueva did find was an episode of *Ripley's Believe It Or Not* television show where the tragic tale of a Union father and a Confederate son first aired.

BUTTERFIELD'S LULLABY

The true history of the birth of "Taps" was told by bugler Oliver

Only Confederate soldier executed for war crimes: Henry Wirz.

Norton in an 1898 letter he wrote in response to a *Century Magazine* article that claimed the origin of the tune was unknown. Norton explained that he knew how "Taps" originated because he'd been the first to play it.

According to Norton, one July evening he was called to the tent of Major General Daniel Adam Butterfield, the chief of staff for the Army of the Potomac. Encamped at Harrison's Landing, recovering from a defeat at the hands of General Robert E. Lee's army, Butterfield's exhausted and wounded soldiers suffered from heat, mosquitoes, dysentery, and typhoid. The standard bugle call for lights-out had a harsh military cadence, and Butterfield thought a more soothing bugle call might help his men rest.

The general handed Norton an envelope with musical notes written on the back and asked the bugler to play them. The bugler lengthened some notes and shortened others until the sound was melodious and slow enough to suit Butterfield, who ordered the melody played every evening as the final bugle call. *Century*'s editors wrote to Butterfield, who confirmed the incident.

LAST CALL, BOYS!

General Butterfield didn't actually compose the tune, sometimes called "Butterfield's Lullaby," but had simply revised an early French version of the "Scott Tattoo." (A tattoo was a bugle call used to order soldiers to leave a tavern and return to their quarters for the night.) The name "Taps" probably came from an obsolete drum roll command called "Taptoe" that ordered tavern keepers to turn off their keg spigots at the end of an evening.

A SMASH HIT

From the night he first played it, Norton knew that "Taps" would be a hit. In his letter to the magazine he wrote, "The music was beautiful on that still summer night, and was heard far beyond the limits of our Brigade. The next day I was visited by several buglers from neighboring Brigades, asking for copies of the music which I gladly furnished."

"Taps" wasn't just a Union favorite. Confederates heard the tune in their nearby camps and liked it so much that by 1863 the Confederate army's mounted artillery drill manual contained the order that "'Taps' will be blown at 9:00 at which time all officers will be in quarters."

"Artillery" is the term for large-caliber weapons such as cannons, howitzers, and mortars.

THE LAST GOODBYE

"Taps" was first used for military funeral services out of necessity. In 1862 Captain John Tidball presided over the burial of one of his fallen men. Tradition ordered that three rifle volleys would be fired at the ceremony, but Tidball's troops were hidden in the woods, and he feared that any nearby enemy would hear the gunshots, figure out their location, and then attack them in the belief that there was a resumption of hostilities. To substitute for the rifle volley, the captain ordered the bugler to sound "Taps."

Playing "Taps" became an unofficial custom at Union army funerals. The rebels also played the call to honor fallen soldiers—most notably at the 1863 funeral of General Thomas "Stonewall" Jackson after his death by friendly fire in the Battle of Chancellorsville.

After the Civil War, "Taps" became an official bugle call of the U.S. Army, and by 1891 an official order in the *U.S. Army Infantry Drill Regulations* made the bugle call mandatory at formal military funerals and memorial ceremonies.

A FALLEN PRESIDENT

Possibly the most memorable rendition of "Taps" was played on November 25, 1963, at the funeral of President John F. Kennedy. A World War II veteran, Kennedy was buried with full military honors at Arlington National Cemetery. At the ceremony, the command for present arms was given, and the traditional three volleys were fired. Then Sergeant Keith Clark of the U.S. Army Band played "Taps"—not on a bugle but on a B-flat trumpet.

Clark had played the call perfectly hundreds of times at hundreds of ceremonies. In fact, he'd played it in President Kennedy's presence only two weeks earlier at the Tomb of the Unknowns on Veterans Day. But this time, as he played, he "cracked" the sixth note so that it sounded shortened and off-key. Clark admitted that nervousness was the cause, but the media immediately assumed that the cracked note was intentional, and they found it especially poignant.

Newsweek described the broken note as "a tear." William Manchester, author of *Death of a President*, described it as a "catch in your voice or a swiftly stifled sob." For about two weeks following the presidential burial, other Arlington buglers missed that same sixth note.

In 1917 the average life expectancy of a pilot on the western front was three weeks.

ARLINGTON CEMETERY BY THE NUMBERS

Of the 3.8 million square miles in the United States of America, none is more sacred than Arlington Cemetery's land, which holds dead veterans from every American war since the Revolution.

0—Cost to families for burial of a veteran and veteran's spouse.

1—Number of people buried at Arlington Cemetery who were born there: James Parks, a former Arlington House slave, helped bury the first soldiers and is laid to rest there himself.

2—U.S. presidents buried there: William H. Taft and John F. Kennedy.

3—Enemy soldiers from nearby POW camps buried at Arlington Cemetery in accord with the Geneva conventions during World War II: Italian soldiers Arcangelo Prudenza and Marlo Batist, and German soldier Anton Hilderath.

3—Iwo Jima flag-raisers buried at Arlington: Privates Michael Strank, Ira Hayes, and Rene Gagnon.

3—Hours it takes soldiers to place a flag before each soldier's gravestone and niche in preparation for Memorial Day.

13—Number of times the funeral flag is folded, into a triangle, stars out, in one minute and 54 seconds, while the hymn is played.

4:00—Time that the caisson team reports to stables each morning.

28—Average number of funerals held each day there.

30—Years Mary Curtis Lee, great-granddaughter of George Washington, lived at Arlington House with her husband, Confederate General Robert E. Lee.

The Pentagon contains no marble because it was built during World War II...

47—Most burials in one day—during the Vietnam War.

60—Section where most of the soldiers who died in Afghanistan and Iraq are buried.

$92.07—Unpaid property tax that allowed tax officers to seize Arlington House and grounds in 1862.

409—Confederate soldiers buried at Arlington Cemetery.

624—Acres of ground that constitute Arlington Cemetery.

2025—Estimated year when Arlington will run out of burial space.

3,800—Former slaves buried in section 27 who lived in Freedman's Village on the Arlington grounds between the Civil War and the 1890s.

4,735—Unknowns buried in Arlington Cemetery, mostly from the Civil War era.

16,000—Soldiers already buried on Arlington House grounds when the U.S. Supreme Court awarded the right to return to Arlington House to George Washington Custis Lee, Robert E. Lee's eldest son, in 1882.

$26,800—Amount the U.S government paid for Arlington House and grounds at a government tax auction in 1862.

$150,000—Amount the U.S. government paid George Washington Custis Lee for the deed to Arlington House in 1882 so they wouldn't have to disturb those already laid to rest there.

300,000—Approximate number of people buried at Arlington Cemetery.

4,000,000—Annual visitors to Arlington Cemetery.

...when Italy, the source of marble, was an enemy country.

GOT WHAT IT TAKES?

To be eligible for an elite unit in the armed forces, there are minimum fitness standards. Most candidates are better off exceeding the standards in order to pass muster with the recruiters.

U.S. ARMY SPECIAL FORCES

The U.S. Army Special Forces, better known as the Green Berets, have five key responsibilities: unconventional warfare, foreign internal defense, special reconnaissance, direct action, and counterterrorism. Many activities emphasize cultural skills when working with another country's troops and maintaining a peacekeeping or humanitarian presence on foreign soil.

To qualify for the Special Forces Assessment and Selection Course (SFAS), you'll want to achieve close to a perfect 300 score on the Army Physical Fitness Test (PFT), which entails:

- 71 push-ups in 2 minutes (100 to be competitive)
- 78 sit-ups in 2 minutes (100 to be competitive)
- 2-mile run in under 13:00 (under 12:00 to be competitive)

If you get in, you'll be subjected to two weeks of tough physical training: endless push-ups, sit-ups, and pull-ups; running; swimming; marching with heavy packs; obstacle courses; and orienteering. At the end of two weeks, the instructors decide who moves on to the Special Forces Qualification Course, or "Q Course."

The Q Course lasts from six months to a year, and training for some specialties can last longer. In the Q Course, candidates undergo more physical training, and instruction in direct action (e.g., raids and patrols), survival techniques, and foreign languages. The course also includes instruction in an individual's specialty, lasting up to 48 weeks. Once the course is completed, the soldier is given his green beret and is eligible to be deployed. Of course, the training never ends for a Special Forces soldier, as there are many advanced courses that can be completed to further hone his skills.

U.S. ARMY RANGERS

The 75th Ranger Regiment is made up of light infantry forces that can deploy anywhere in the world within 18 hours. Rangers utilize their skills in many ways: airborne assault, direct action, and infiltration by land, sea, or air, and also support regular Army forces.

To qualify for the Ranger School, you must be able to do:

- 49 push-ups in 2 minutes (80 to be competitive)
- 59 sit-ups in 2 minutes (80 to be competitive)
- 6 pull-ups, no time limit (12 to be competitive)
- 2-mile run in 15:12 (under 13:00 to be competitive)
- 5-mile run in 40:00 (under 35:00 to be competitive)
- 16-mile hike carrying a 65-pound pack in 5 hours 20 minutes (under 5 hours to be competitive)
- 15-meter swim with full gear

And if you get in, training at the Ranger School will consist of:

Camp Benning Phase: 20 days of intense physical training, including marches in full gear, obstacle courses, night and day patrols, reconnaissance, demolitions courses, airborne operations, and close-quarters combat tactics.

Mountain Phase: 20 days in rugged terrain with a small unit, dealing with severe weather, hunger, sleep deprivation, stress, and fatigue while leading a platoon through an exercise designed to simulate what a Ranger would expect to find on a real battlefield.

Florida Phase: 16 days in a marine/swamp environment, learning how to best utilize one's skills and equipment in a combat situation and survive in a harsh climate.

Upon successful completion of the course, a soldier has earned the right to wear the Ranger tab. It is not unusual for a candidate to lose up to 30 pounds in body weight during Ranger School.

U.S. NAVY SEALS

The Navy SEALs (Sea, Air, and Land Forces) work in small units, deploying from the sea to conduct a variety of clandestine missions: unconventional warfare, direct action, counterterrorism, foreign internal defense, and personnel recovery. They comprise less than 1 percent of U.S. Navy personnel. Highly qualified U.S. Coast Guard personnel are sometimes accepted into the SEALs.

To qualify for the training program, you must be able to do:

- 500-yard swim using breast- or sidestroke in 12:30 (under 10:00 to be competitive)
- 42 push-ups in 2 minutes (100 to be competitive)

Marine Captain A. N. Parker was the first person to fly over unexplored Antarctica (1929).

- 52 sit-ups in 2 minutes (100 to be competitive)
- 8 pull ups, no time limit (15 to be competitive)
- 1½-mile run in boots and trousers in 11:30 (under 10:20 to be competitive)

And if you get in, training will consist of:

- 8 weeks at the Special Warfare Preparatory School.
- 3 weeks at the Indoctrination Course.
- 24 weeks of Basic Underwater Demolition/SEAL training (physical conditioning, diving, and land warfare), including "Hell Week," 132 hours of continuous physical activity; a typical class loses 70–80 percent of its trainees in this phase.
- 15 weeks of SEAL Qualification Training (learning special skills and tactics, as well as developing the ability to lead men), including 4 weeks of cold-weather training in Kodiak, Alaska; those left standing are awarded the SEAL trident and assigned to a team—but the training isn't over yet!

Prior to deployment, a SEAL goes through 18 months of individual and team training to develop specialized skills (such as sniping, surveillance, advanced driving, and foreign languages) and the ability to function within a cohesive unit.

U.S. AIR FORCE SPECIAL TACTICS

There are two specialties. Combat controllers are sent on advance deployments to establish battlefield parameters. Pararescuemen are trained to recover personnel in hostile territory and provide medical treatment.

To qualify for the training, you must be able to do:

- 20-meter underwater swim, done twice (pass/fail)
- 500-meter swim using freestyle, breaststroke, or sidestroke in 14:00 (under 9:00 to be competitive)
- 1½-mile run in 10:45 (under 9:00 to be competitive)
- 6 pull-ups in 1 minute (13 to be competitive)
- 45 sit-ups in 2 minutes (100 to be competitive)
- 45 push-ups in 2 minutes (100 to be competitive)
- 45 flutter-kicks in 2 minutes (100 to be competitive)

Combat controllers will undergo a 35-week training program that covers a wide range of skills, including air-traffic control,

On average, the Coast Guard engages in 109 Search and Rescue missions each day.

parachuting, survival, and combat tactics. Once this has been completed successfully, a combat controller will spend the next 12 months in an advanced program that includes free-fall parachuting, combat diving, and further mental and physical training.

Pararescuemen spend 14 months in a training program to learn emergency medical techniques, mountaineering, recovery, and how to escape from an aircraft that has been ditched into the water. Pararescuemen also go through some of the same training as combat controllers, such as free-fall parachuting, combat diving, and survival. Both specialties attend the U.S. Army Airborne School at Fort Benning, Georgia, to learn basic parachuting skills.

U.S. MARINES SPECIAL OPERATIONS COMMAND

MARSOC is the newest component of the U.S. Special Operations Command, having been activated in 2006. These Marines are responsible for conducting direct action, foreign internal defense, special reconnaissance, unconventional warfare, and counterterrorism in other nations. MARSOC emphasizes the ability to work seamlessly in a foreign environment by learning new languages and understanding different cultures.

To qualify for the MARSOC training, you'll need a score of 225 on the U.S. Marines physical fitness test, which entails:

- 15 pull-ups, no time limit (20 to be competitive)
- 75 sit-ups in 2 minutes (100 to be competitive)
- 3-mile run in 22:10 (under 18:00 to be competitive)
- In addition, candidates must pass a swimming test that involves a 25-meter underwater swim, rifle retrieval, tower jump, 30-minute water tread, 5-minute flotation with trousers, and a timed 500-meter swim. An aptitude test and psychological evaluation are also conducted.

Candidates who pass the initial screening are then subjected to an assessment course, a two-week program to determine whether the soldier has the maturity, intelligence, determination, and physical attributes necessary to be a member of MARSOC. From there, the selected Marines spend the next six months in courses to acquire new language, cultural, tactical, and technical skills. When they are assigned to their 14-man units, they will receive even more specialized training based on their upcoming assignments.

The U.S. Naval Academy covers 338 acres, with 4,400 midshipmen enrolled annually.

ANSWER PAGES

ON GUARD: THE QUIZ

(Answers for page 355)

(Answers for page 355)

1. True. The tomb has had a military guard 24/7 since July 1, 1937. When the tomb was dedicated on November 11, 1921, there was no guard. But because the tomb had a beautiful view of Washington, it became a favorite resting spot (and often a table) for picnickers who were escaping the bustling city for the quiet beauty of Arlington. That led to a guard during cemetery hours—a civilian job that was started in 1925 and handed over to the military in 1926. The sentinels' distinctive march, as well as the changing of the guard, continues through the night.

2. False. The guards walk back and forth (21 steps each way), so they're changed every hour during daylight in the winter (from October 1 to March 14) and, due to the sweltering heat of Washington summers, every 30 minutes from March 15 to September 30. When the cemetery is closed to the public, the guards "walk the mat," as it's called, for two hours at a time.

3. False. Maybe it's the super-short haircuts that cause tourists to mistake the sentinels of the tomb for United States Marines. Actually, they are members of the Third U.S. Infantry Regiment of the Army and are nicknamed "the Old Guard."

4. False. At the changing of the guard, the relief commander inspects the rifle of the relieving sentinel, and then tells the active sentinel, "Pass on your orders." The active sentinel replies, "Post and orders, remain as directed." The relieving sentinel says, "Orders acknowledged." Experienced sentinels will sometimes honor the unknowns by doing the changing of the guard in "silent mode." There are no verbal orders. Instead orders and replies are given with clicks of the soldiers' heels. During the time on duty, a soldier can call out a challenge—"Step behind the ropes"—to an ornery child or an overenthusiastic amateur photographer who has disregarded the velvet ropes surrounding the tomb.

5. True. There are three relief rotations every 24 hours. Members of the first relief are 6' 2" to 6' 4", members of the second are 6' to

6' 2", and members of the third are 5' 10" to 6'. Guards also have to have a waist measurement of no more than 30".

6. False. The unknowns *are* all male, but the lack of female guards was due to other factors. First, not many women meet the height requirements. Second, until 1994, when women were first allowed in combat, the sentinels came from the Old Guard infantry regiment, a combat unit. When a military police unit was attached to the Old Guard in 1994, with it came female soldiers and the first woman to apply for sentinel duty, Sergeant Heather Lynn Johnsen. Since then, two other female soldiers have become Tomb Guards.

7. False. Today's sentinel guards carry an M14 with a bayonet; the noncommissioned officer who inspects the guard carries an M9 pistol. Although they are not loaded, the weapons are very real.

8. True. If they're lucky! Sentinels can spend up to eight hours readying their uniforms. Sentinels report for duty in their civilian clothes—you can spot them walking through the cemetery from Fort Myer if you watch for the super-short haircuts. When not standing guard, they spend their time ironing their uniforms, shining their shoes, shaving, getting their hair trimmed (twice a week!), and being inspected before they're allowed to stand guard.

9. False. The Army has no control of the legal consumption of alcohol by off-duty soldiers over the age of 21—let alone a 60-ish vet who retired decades ago. After nine months as a sentinel, soldiers are awarded a Tomb Guard Identification Badge that can be revoked for offenses that discredit the tomb, but we're talking big things like abandoning your post or committing a crime—not having a beer.

10. False. The sentinels live nearby at Fort Myer in Virginia or off-base. There are quarters under the nearby amphitheater, but this is because a group of relief guards are on duty for 24 hours. Those not standing guard are in the Tomb Guard Quarters (the basement, known as the "catacombs"), preparing for their turn.

11. True. Becoming a sentinel is challenging in many ways. "Walking the mat" or standing watch on the darkest, coldest nights and the most blindingly hot and sweltering summer days is a mental and physical challenge. During an eight-month training period, soldiers have to master the changing of the guard perfectly, become accustomed to being alone in a vast cemetery at night,

Don Adams (*Get Smart*) was a U.S. Marine drill instructor.

and memorize information about the Tomb of the Unknown Soldier, Arlington Cemetery, the location of grave sites of notable veterans, and a dozen poems, including "The Vigil," written by the cousin of a Special Forces soldier who was killed in Vietnam.

12. False. No order was given. Although their duty is to guard the tomb, the Tomb Guard always puts the safety of the soldier first. That's why they have contingency plans for extreme weather, first guarding the tomb from the protection of a small green tent called "the Box" near the tomb and then from the protection of the cemetery's amphitheater. If it had been necessary to give the order to stand down, no sentinel would disobey this direct order from a superior.

13. True. On the afternoon of March 23, 1984, a lone man carrying a small gun approached the Tomb of the Unknown Soldier and stepped over the rope. The guard on duty, Corporal Michael Kirby, challenged the man. Six sentinels, who were practicing the wreath-laying ceremony nearby, subdued the intruder while Kirby stood guard over the tomb. No one was injured in the incident.

* * *

SOLDIERS' BEST FRIENDS GET HELP FROM MILITARY MOM

When Starline Nunley offered to send her son, Major Parker Frawley, a cooling vest to help him cope with the brutal temperatures in Iraq, he told her that human soldiers received appropriate equipment, but their canine counterparts desperately needed assistance too. Starline and the Gem City Obedience Club provided cooling vests, Doggles (to protect canine eyes,) and Muttluks (to protect their feet) for the 15 dogs in Parker's unit. The club is raising funds to help other units with military dogs.

Zeke: One of the Allied code names for the Japanese Zero, a formidable fighter plane.

UNCLE JOHN'S BATHROOM *READER* CLASSIC SERIES

Find these and other great titles from the *Uncle John's Bathroom Reader* Classic Series online at **www.bathroomreader.com**. Or contact us at:

Bathroom Readers' Institute
P.O. Box 1117
Ashland, OR 97520
(888) 488-4642

Also available from *Uncle John's Bathroom Reader!*

THE LAST PAGE

FELLOW BATHROOM READERS:

The fight for good bathroom reading should never be taken loosely—we must do our duty and sit firmly for what we believe in, even while the rest of the world is taking pot shots at us.

In brief, now that we've proven we're not simply a flush-in-the-pan, we invite you to take the plunge: Sit Down and Be Counted! Become a member of the Bathroom Readers' Institute. Log on to *www.bathroomreader.com*, or send a self-addressed, stamped, business-sized envelope to: BRI, PO Box 1117, Ashland, Oregon 97520. You'll receive your free membership card, get discounts when ordering directly through the BRI, and earn a permanent spot on the BRI honor roll!

Well, we're out of space, and when you've gotta go, you've gotta go. Tanks for all your support. Hope to hear from you soon.

Keep on flushin'!